THE POLITICS OF OPERATIONS

THE
POLITICS

Excavating Contemporary Capitalism **OF**

OPERATIONS

SANDRO MEZZADRA & BRETT NEILSON

DUKE UNIVERSITY PRESS *Durham and London* 2019

Printed in the United States of America on acid-free paper ∞
Designed by Matthew Tauch
Typeset in Whitman by Westchester Publishing Services

Library of Congress Cataloging-in-Publication Data
Names: Mezzadra, Sandro, [date] author. | Neilson, Brett,
    [date] author.
Title: The politics of operations : excavating contemporary
    capitalism / Sandro Mezzadra and Brett Neilson.
Description: Durham : Duke University Press, 2019. |
    Includes bibliographical references and index.
Identifiers: LCCN 2018027900 (print)
LCCN 2018040971 (ebook)
ISBN 9781478003267 (ebook)
ISBN 9781478001751 (hardcover : alk. paper)
ISBN 9781478002833 (pbk. : alk. paper)
Subjects: LCSH: Capitalism—Political aspects. |
    Capitalism—Social aspects. | Economic development.
    | Labor. | Globalization. | Postcolonialism—Economic
    aspects.
Classification: LCC HB501 (ebook) | LCC HB501 .M626 2019
    (print) | DDC 330.12/2—dc23
LC record available at https://lccn.loc.gov/2018027900

Cover art: Mercado de Abastos, Mexico City. Photo by
    Orbon Alija / Getty.

Contents

Acknowledgments

The Politics of Operations was written within a dense fabric of complicities, sites, relations, and encounters. The principal cities in which the writing took shape are Berlin, Bologna, Buenos Aires, and Sydney. The argument and concepts emerged sometimes uneasily and sometimes rapidly from experiences and encounters in cities such as Athens, Kolkata, and Valparaíso. During the writing process, we had the privilege to discuss our main hypotheses and research findings with diverse audiences in many cities, including Chicago, Hong Kong, Jakarta, Melbourne, Mexico City, Rome, Singapore, and Taipei. We thank the organizers of these and other events.

The KOSMOS summer university grant "Investigating Logistics" (Berlin Institute for Migration Research, Humboldt University) provided us with an effective framework to meet, live, and discuss our work in Berlin, especially over the period 2015–16. We are particularly indebted to Manuela Bojadžijev for making this possible, and for her important contribution to the debates that propelled the writing of this book. Discussions prompted by seminars at the Institute for Advanced Studies (IDAES), Universidad Nacional de San Martín and the Franklin Humanities Institute, Duke University also proved helpful. These two seminars were conducted with Verónica Gago and Michael Hardt, respectively. Along with Giorgio Grappi, Maurizio Ricciardi, Ned Rossiter, and Adelino Zanini, these two friends also provided valuable feedback on the manuscript. We also thank our editor at Duke University Press, Courtney Berger, for her unwavering support and two anonymous reviewers for their critical engagement with our arguments.

Articles published in the journals *Radical Philosophy*, *South Atlantic Quarterly*, *Scienza & Politica*, and *Cultural Studies* foreshadow arguments in this book. Thanks to the editors on all occasions.

Much of the research for this book was supported by two Discovery grants awarded by the Australian Research Council: "Logistics as Global Governance: Infrastructure, Software and Labour along the New Silk Road" (DP130103720) and "Data Centres and the Governance of Labour and Territory" (DP160103307).

Finally, we thank those whose loving presence accompanied us in the writing of this book. You know who you are.

Introduction

Imagine you are traveling by bus across the Argentinean pampas. You are absent-minded, reading a book without really paying attention to it. Looking out of the window, you see a giant billboard with the words "Intacta RR2 Pro" emblazoned across it. Beneath this product name runs a slogan: "Desafiar los limites en soja" (Challenging the limits of soy). Gazing into the distance, you see only the green of soybean fields extending to the horizon. You do a quick search on your phone to discover that Intacta RR2 Pro is a product of Monsanto, part of a new generation of transgenic seeds expanding "into even more marginal areas" (Cáceres 2014). Suddenly, you feel a sense of disorientation. What can marginal mean, you ask, in such a uniform and nondescript landscape? Reading on, you realize that, of course, there are marginal areas in the pampas, as there are elsewhere in the Latin American countryside and other parts of the world. You continue to search and read and you come to learn—if you did not already know—that the extensive cultivation of soy, enabled by seeds such as Intacta RR2 Pro, has a violent and disruptive effect on established social as well as spatial arrangements, prompting dispossession and expulsion of peasant and often Indigenous populations. You recall the passage from the *Grundrisse* in which Marx (1973, 408) discusses capital's "tendency to create the world market" by making "every limit" appear "as a barrier to be overcome." And as your

thoughts roll on, you contemplate the multifarious operations needed before a capitalist actor such as Monsanto can extract value and foster its
accumulation process in an area like the pampas: genetic manipulation,
testing, prospecting, advertising, selling, relying on the police or goons to
do the dirty job of expulsion and dispossession, and so on. You think of the
living labor involved in and disrupted by these operations, and perhaps you
resolve to engage and learn more about people's resistance to their deployment. Finally, you ponder how the concatenation of these operations links
with mutations of the world market—with China's rise as an economic
power, for instance.

    This banal story provides a point of entry into several of the topics that
we discuss in the following chapters. Crucial to our engagement here are
the notions of *operation* and *politics of operations*. But what is an operation?
And do operations have politics? If so, what are the implications of these
politics for the continued entrenchment of capitalism across diverse scales
and spaces, for existing institutional and political architectures, and for
struggles that contest and seek to reverse these same processes of entrenchment? These are among the primary questions we take up in *The Politics of
Operations*, a book that picks up on, but by no means confines its attention
to, the infectious rhetoric of big data and algorithms that has gripped capitalist discourses and practices over the past half-decade. Expanding our
understanding of operations beyond this field to encompass a wide variety
of processes both historical and contemporary, we set out to investigate the
operative dimensions of capital and capitalism, charting their political significance and examining their relevance for a politics that seeks to operate
within, against, and beyond capital.

    The Politics of Operations examines how particular operations of capital
"hit the ground" not simply to furnish an analysis of their local or wider
effects but also to supply an analytical prism through which to investigate
how their meshing, and conflicting, with other operations of capital remake
the world. We imagine this as a means of *excavating* contemporary capitalism, which means surveying and tracing the history and present expansion
of capital's operations to unearth and expose some of the most important
tendencies shaping current processes of capitalist transition and upheaval.
The book is deliberately global in scope, dealing with examples from a range
of planetary settings and exploring resonances between them to work constantly between theoretical and empirical perspectives. Although we draw
on our own research experiences, we do not imagine the book as a report
on these engagements. Rather, we let these experiences give impetus to our

inquiry even beyond the explicit discussion of some of them we offer in the following chapters. Our case studies are more wide-ranging than these experiences have allowed and include developments in port logistics, mineral extraction, data mining, and the penetration of finance into "popular" and subaltern economies in many parts of the world. In each of these instances, our inquiry focuses not only on the underlying rationalities and operations of capital at work but also on struggles and contestations that emerge from the deep implication of these logics in specific material and social circumstances. At this juncture, some of the most important tensions between the diversifying and homogenizing aspects of contemporary capitalism become evident. By addressing our investigations to this juncture, we seek not to offer a comparative analysis of different manifestations of these tensions, identified according to the established geographies of the world map, but to discern and follow resonances among trends and processes that traverse multiple boundaries, temporalities, and scales.

The role of spatial and scalar arrangements in contributing to this variegation is far from passive. In this regard, there is a need to specify the meaning of the conceptual image we deployed earlier and will use quite a lot in the following chapters—that is, the image of capital "hitting the ground." This image might be taken to imply a kind of Promethean lightning strike that violently destroys and rearranges existing spatial and social realities. We certainly do not want to disavow the force of this basic implication of the phrase. However, a more careful unpacking of what we seek to grasp through the use and elaboration of this image reveals attentiveness to the qualities of the ground. It is important to explain that we use the word "ground" in a sense that is at once material and prospectively constructed as an operative surface on which capital intervenes. While ground is neither merely terrain nor land, it registers the specificity of spatial, social, legal, and political formations with which capital must grapple as it becomes enmeshed in dense constellations of flesh and earth. It should be very clear that we do not think such an operative surface is a smooth ground, since the registration of tensions, frictions, and differences along capital's frontiers is a constant element of our analysis. We understand space at large as a field of tensions and struggles, where established spatial formations are far from passive with respect to operations of capital, while those operations often have a disruptive effect on the production of space. Capital operates across places, territory, and scales, deploying a logic that is ultimately planetary but must continuously come to terms with resistances, frictions, and interruptions that crisscross the expansion of its frontiers and geographies.

The Politics of Operations draws its material inspiration primarily from an investigation of the entanglement of three prevalent areas of contemporary economic (and, we would hasten to add, political) activity: extraction, logistics, and finance. Although there is convenience in approaching these activities as distinct "sectors" of the global economy, this is a nomenclature we tend to avoid or undercut, as it does not sufficiently capture the ways in which each of these three areas in recent years has provided conceptual orientations and empirical grids for the analysis of contemporary capitalism. We thus steer clear of understanding extraction, logistics, and finance merely as economic sectors or taking them as paradigmatic for an analysis of capitalist operations, as tends to happen, for instance, in Latin American debates concerning extractivism (see Gago and Mezzadra 2017a; Mezzadra and Neilson 2017). Instead, we treat extraction, logistics, and finance as intersecting sets of operations and practices that provide different points of entry or relative framings for a wider analysis of the mutating fields of politics and capital. By working through and across these overlapping and mutually implicated operative domains, *The Politics of Operations* forges a framework that aims to exhibit the distinctive rationality and logics of contemporary capitalism. Departing from literal understandings of extraction as the plundering of natural resources, we work toward an expanded definition that allows us to explore how some of the most prominent and forceful operations of capital today rely on material practices of prospecting and extraction. We find this to be the case even in highly abstract fields of capitalist endeavor, such as finance, whose operations are frequently attributed an almost metaphysical quality and too often analyzed in isolation. The notion of extraction writ large thus features centrally in our efforts to discern the logics of contemporary capitalism, providing a way to describe how operations of capital interact with and draw on their multiple outsides. Such an understanding of extraction also provides a background against which we investigate transformations of the state and the composition of global struggles, particularly in the wake of the Occupy movement, the Arab rebellions, and other important contestations that flared up and seemingly dissipated in the early years of the present decade.

Although we provide a full definition and genealogy for the concept of operations in chapter 2, it is worth briefly dwelling on the notion at this stage since it provides the underpinning for our approach to capital and capitalism. Despite its etymological origins in the Latin *opus* and historical elaboration in fields as diverse as the military, mathematics, and philosophy—where it has often been associated with the category of work as opposed to labor, as, for instance, in the writings of Hannah Arendt (1998)—the concept of operations is often considered too straightforward to warrant serious investigation. To give an example, discussions of community (Nancy 1991) and politics (Agamben 2014) have been advanced on the basis of the concept of inoperativity, without deep consideration of what an operation itself might be or do (which is surely necessary if we are to ask what it means to be inoperative). Too often, the operation is reduced to a device of "techno-economical organization" (Nancy 1991, 23), as if it were a simple relation of cause and effect, or input and output. Such a perspective overlooks what the operation itself does, reducing the complex interactions of space and time that occur between its seeming moments of cause and effect, input and output, to linear processes, and leaving no scope for understanding how these interactions relate to arrangements of space and time external to the operation. For instance, if we understand the workings of a financial algorithm as an operation in this limited sense, we are likely to ask questions about its relevance for market dynamics, ignoring the complexity of its technical functioning as well as its dependence on and contribution to wider transformations of capitalism.

With regard to this last example, it is worth noting that this more restricted understanding of operation is a feature not only of philosophical theories that explore notions of community and politics but also of recent celebrations of predictive data analytics and algorithms based in electronic information processing systems. For us, the operation is never merely technical. Its workings, while providing a way to open discussion around contemporary capitalism, also offer a means of analyzing past entanglements of politics and capital, as becomes evident in our engagement with the history of the chartered company in chapter 3. The important point to grasp is that an operation can be equated neither with activity nor potentiality; however, in providing a conceptual ground that allows us to think these two dimensions together, it offers a powerful conceptual and practical way to interrogate the workings of capital. Once such a ground is in place, we can begin to ask questions about capital's interactions with different kinds of social, legal, and political institutions; its effects on natural environments; and the political possibilities for its contestation and overcoming.

This reading of operations of capital holds important implications for our attempt to pick up and reframe in the book two important Marxian concepts: *Gesamtkapital* and exploitation. Marx amply uses the notion of *Gesamtkapital* (as well as *gesellschaftliches Gesamtkapital*), particularly in volumes 2 and 3 of *Capital*, which were notably left unfinished (a fact that should invite further creative work in the critique of political economy). This concept assists Marx in grasping the general configuration and logic of movement of capital. For reasons that will become clear in chapter 2, we prefer to translate *Gesamtkapital* as "aggregate capital" rather than as "total capital," which is more common in English. While Marx never really provided a full-fledged theory of aggregate capital, we are convinced that elaborating on this concept can be particularly productive for understanding the peculiar ways in which capital constitutes itself as an actor, and even as a political actor understood as an aggregation of forces.

The investigation of the relations, tensions, and conflicts among "individual capitals" (which Marx also terms "fractions" of aggregate capital) always figured prominently in Marxist debates—in particular about the state, but also about the relation between capital and capitalism. Cutting through these debates, we attempt to map the political and spatial constitution of contemporary global capitalism, which we consider to be caught in a tumultuous and risky transition that is taking it beyond established arrangements of territorialism and capitalism. To put it succinctly, we are convinced that the crucially important historical moment of national and industrial capitalism is over. In that moment, the mediation of the nation-state (its always contradictory and never fully accomplished attempt to perform the representation of national aggregate capital) played an essential role—to put it in the words of Henri Lefebvre (2009, 226)—in attempting to "control flows and stocks by ensuring their coordination" within the world market. In the present conjuncture, extractive operations such as those we analyze in the cases of logistics and finance dominate the composition of aggregate capital and tend to command and submit other operations of capital to their logics—including industrial ones, which continue not only to exist but also to expand at the global level. Extractive operations of capital have to come to terms with nation-states, although their spatial scope and working logics are by no means contained by national borders.

While we stress the relevance of the concept of aggregate capital, we never forget—and this may be the main reason that we are cautious about translating *Gesamtkapital* as total capital—that "capital is not a thing, but a social relation between persons which is mediated through things" (Marx 1977, 932). The analysis of the current mutations of this social relation—which also means of the composition of capital's main "other," living labor, to take a category that Marx particularly develops in the *Grundrisse*—is one of the main stakes of *The Politics of Operations*. Mapping those mutations also implies for us carefully analyzing the ways in which they are inscribed in and produce space, making the geography of contemporary capitalism far more complex than suggested by such binaries as global North and global South or center and periphery. Moreover, our investigation of the expanding "frontiers of capital" leads us to return to Rosa Luxemburg's *The Accumulation of Capital* (1913 [2003]) and to propose a new reading of her emphasis on capital's structural need for an "outside" for its operations.

Once this outside is conceptually reframed in nonliteral and nonexclusively territorial terms, as we try to do in chapter 2, it becomes possible to single out a specific set of operations of capital that aim to open up and occupy new spaces and temporalities for valorization and accumulation. We thus join a debate on the relation of capital with its multiple outsides that has been particularly lively in recent years—involving, for instance, Marxist geographers such as David Harvey (2003), postcolonial critics of political economy such as Kalyan Sanyal (2007), and feminists such as Nancy Fraser (2014) and J. K. Gibson-Graham (2006). What distinguishes our approach within this important debate is our emphasis on the need to rethink the second Marxian concept we mentioned earlier: exploitation. Working through the difference but also the important relations between exploitation, on the one hand, and dispossession, power, domination, and alienation, on the other, we try to rescue this crucial notion from the "economistic" reading that has long prevailed in Marxism. As we show in chapter 5, the need to stress the political nature of exploitation becomes clear once the concept is plunged into the dense material relations that surround the production of subjectivity. Once the relation between exploitation and subjectivity comes into view, raising issues of embodiment as well as social difference, the very possibility of considering questions such as race and gender as secondary with respect to some primary contradiction of capital and labor simply vanishes. The conceptual fabric of *The Politics of Operations* is therefore crisscrossed by intense dialogues with antiracist and feminist thinkers.

We continue to struggle with the attempt (and need) to give a name to the subject that constitutes the main "other" of contemporary capitalism. We are aware that the notion of exploitation requires further conceptual elaboration and detailed empirical investigation to support such an attempt. As in previous writings, we continue to emphasize heterogeneity as a crucial feature of the composition of contemporary living labor, which is also reflected in the heterogeneity of struggles confronting the operations of capital on the global scale. We cannot but repeat—and we try to substantiate this statement in the chapters that follow—that this heterogeneity is a source of both power and vulnerability. We are still skeptical regarding attempts to identify a single figure as the strategic subject in the struggle against capitalism, whether it is the "cognitive worker" or "surplus populations," the new working class somewhere in the "global South" or the "precariat." At the same time, we are convinced that the debates about the affinities and tensions between the concepts of class and multitude offer the most fertile ground on which to discern and produce a political subject adequate to the times. We suggest the continuation of these debates and related investigations within the open field of tension that—again with a reference to Marx—can be thought of as being constituted between the two poles of the "working class" and the "proletariat" (Balibar 1994, 125–49), the former referring to the subject of an "economic" struggle internal to capitalism and the latter naming a political subject whose actions and organization contradict and go beyond this same system (Balibar 1994, 128).

What we emphasize in this book against the background of our analysis of the extractive operations of contemporary capitalism is that social cooperation—even in an "abstract" figure, particularly as far as processes of financialization are concerned—emerges as one of the main productive forces spurring the processes of capital's valorization and accumulation. The concept of exploitation must be therefore reframed in a way that takes this essential social dimension of capital's operations into account. We also attempt to shed light—particularly on the basis of an analysis of several social and political struggles in chapter 5—on the huge gaps, tensions, and conflicts between social cooperation and living labor. In so doing, we turn our attention to the multiple hierarchies, fractures, and obstacles that make difficult, to say the least, the political appropriation by living labor of the terms on which social cooperation is organized (to put in terms that evoke a quite accurate definition of communism on the basis of several texts by Marx).

Raising the question of the discord and discrepancies between social cooperation and living labor is our way to formulate a political riddle that engages a huge number of thinkers, activists, and movements in many parts of the world. In the chapters that follow, we engage in several sympathetic and, we hope, constructive conversations with such thinkers and activists. We agree with Lawrence Grossberg (2015, 261) when he writes that "the left needs new forms of cooperation and organization, conversation and dis-agreement, new ways of belonging together in intellectual, political and transformational struggle." Many parts of this book are written in the spirit of "dissensual conviviality" that Grossberg traces back to the interventions of the Women's Studies Group at the Center for Contemporary Cultural Studies in Birmingham in the late 1970s. We try to clarify and flesh out our arguments while at the same time deepening and intensifying a common search for a politics capable of effectively confronting contemporary capital's operations and opening up new vistas of liberation and life beyond the rule of capital.

We share, for instance, several analytical and conceptual points with Saskia Sassen's book *Expulsions* (2014) and more generally with her contributions to the understanding of the extractive character of finance. At the same time, we take a critical distance, on the basis of our notion of differential inclusion, from the way in which Sassen builds her analysis on the incorporation-expulsion binary. Likewise, we have learned from Maurizio Lazzarato's (2012) work on "indebted man" and acknowledge more generally the relevance of debt and indebtedness in the workings of contemporary capitalism. We caution, however, against a kind of absolutization of the logics of debt, which often leads to a downplaying or even denial of the salience of exploitation. To work toward a reframing of the notion of exploitation, which is indeed one of the main theoretical and political stakes of *The Politics of Operations*, we also critically reconsider the distinction formulated by David Harvey (2003) between "accumulation by dispossession" and "accumulation by exploitation." In many current debates and struggles—for instance, in the Latin American debates on "neo-extractivism" we analyze in chapter 4, but also in struggles against gentrification in many parts of the world—this distinction has led, even beyond Harvey's intentions, to an obfuscation of the concept and reality of exploitation.

In our attempt to come to grips with the political riddle concerning the fractious relations between living labor and social cooperation, which basically means to specify the contours and stakes of these relations and indicate possible directions for continuing to work on them, we also take into account current debates on postcapitalism (Mason 2015), including their feminist (Gibson-Graham 2006) and accelerationist (Srnicek and Williams 2015) elaborations. While we find these theoretical efforts and the concrete practices and experiences related to them important and hopeful, we also find questionable, in descriptions and theories surrounding "life after capitalism," the lack of interest in the problematic that in historical Marxist discussions has been termed the "transition." The search for noncapitalist modes of organizing life, society, and economy, whether predicated on an investigation of communitarian networks or on the potentialities of technology, cannot skip the question of how to confront capital's rule and command in the present. Picking up again the question of transition does not mean for us to rehearse the dream of a kind of irenic or paradisiac condition that follows a toppling or decline of capitalism somehow imagined as inevitable or ordained. A communist politics today cannot but take a radical distance from such millenary and chiliastic dreams, which all too often have turned into nightmares. As we explain later in this book, such a politics must radically come to terms with the lessons of history. Nevertheless, we are determined to contribute to the opening up of spaces for the political imagination of horizons of life after capitalism, at the crossroads between a reinvention of liberty and a radicalization of equality. Differently in this regard from theories of postcapitalism, we stress the relevance of this "after" to capitalism, seeking to problematize it and asking what it might mean to imagine forms of organization that can confront, negotiate, and possibly break capital's rule.

Old questions emerge again here in new clothes. Let us list some of them. What is the relation of democracy to capital and capitalism? Is democracy the exclusive horizon of politics, as post-Marxist theories of radical democracy have seemed to suggest since the 1980s? (For an analysis of this tendency, see, e.g., Mitropoulos and Neilson 2006.) What about the distinction between reform and revolution? What is the shape taken today by such important forms of organization as the party and the trade union? What roles can they play, along with social movements, in a more general anticapitalist politics? What is the position of the state in practical efforts to develop a politics of emancipation and even liberation? From Slavoj Žižek (2013) to Jodi Dean (2012), there is no shortage of political thinkers who emphasize, often employing Lacanian concepts and idioms, the need for a new vanguard party particularly in the wake of the "defeat" of the Occupy movement in the United States. (For a discussion of the topic, see "The Party We Need" 2016.) We do not dismiss the problem of the party—the politicization of "a part," to recall the phrasing of Dean (2012, 245). But we are very cautious regarding a simple rehabilitation of old party models that takes into consideration neither their historical failures nor the subjective composition of contemporary movements and struggles—which was, for instance, the essential point of departure for Lenin in *What Is to Be Done?* ([1902] 1978). We think it is more promising to interrogate both the accomplishments and limits of existing parties in countries where the "left" has been able to seize the government (as has occurred in several Latin American countries and for a very short period in Greece) or has at least realistically attempted to do so (as happened with the rise of the Podemos political party in Spain). This is a task we undertake in chapter 6, against the background of a more general analysis of the transformations of state and government in the current conjuncture of global, extractive capitalism. We repeat and substantiate here what we wrote in a previous essay: "The state is not powerful enough to confront contemporary capitalism; in order to reopen politically a perspective of radical transformation, something else, *a different source of power*, is absolutely necessary" (Mezzadra and Neilson 2014, 787).

Expanding on this statement, we foreshadow at the end of the book a theory of "dual power," which we combine with an attempt to mobilize a revolutionary geographical imagination to produce and occupy new spaces beyond the boundaries of the nation-state. In so doing, we try to develop what Luxemburg once called a "revolutionary political realism" (quoted in Haug 2009, 12, our translation). We join a number of other thinkers who are starting to reflect anew on the nexus between dual power and transition in the face of the crisis of traditional leftist theories of reform and revolution (most notably, Hardt and Negri 2017; Jameson 2016, 3–8). We stress the need, in specific conjunctures, to negotiate with the state or some of its structures and even to "seize" them. But we insist on the fact that what is needed is a politics that is not centered on the state, a politics that is capable of confronting neoliberalism and the extractive operations of capital at the level of their encroachment in the material fabrics of daily life. We thus enter a dialogue with several interpretations of neoliberalism that stress the need to go beyond its usual rendering in terms of a set of economic theories and policies that could be simply deleted by "seizing the state" (see, e.g., Dardot and Laval 2014; Gago 2017). And we emphatically contend that the alternative to neoliberalism cannot be some kind of return to a more or less mythologized "welfare state" (see also Hall, Massey, and Rustin 2015, 18–19; Walker 2016a), a figure whose conditions, material constitution, and limits we investigate in chapter 3.

We do not know whether our political search can be contained by the concept of democracy. Despite the lively critical debates surrounding "radical democracy," we have over the past couple of decades—and even more in the wake of the crisis of 2007–2008—witnessed a process of emptying and manipulation of representative democracy, as well as the ascent of new, "post-democratic" (Crouch 2004) forms and techniques of governance. At the same time, democracy maintains a mobilizing power, as became clear, for instance, through the main slogan of the powerful movement of square occupations in Spain in 2011: *Democracia real, ya!* (Real democracy, now!). This is something one cannot simply dismiss from a kind of superior intellectual point of view. Moreover, debates such as those spurred by the publication of Pierre Rosanvallon's *Counter-Democracy* (2008) nurture a notion of "conflictual democracy" (see, e.g., Balibar 2016, 186, 206–7) that is challenging from the angle of a theory of "dual power" as a stable political framework. Even Antonio Negri's *Insurgencies*, which we regard as a kind of milestone in this regard, starts with a quite apodictic sentence: "to speak of constituent power is to speak of democracy" (Negri 1999, 1). So although today we cannot easily shrug off an unease regarding the concept, we handle democracy with care. We note that the old and almost forgotten definition of democracy provided by Aristotle in his *Politics*, where he plainly and simply equates it with rule by the poor, has been taken up again in recent times by several thinkers who share with us the search for a new politics of radical transformation (see, e.g., Brown 2015, 19; Dardot and Laval 2016; Varoufakis 2015). Once this materiality and even partiality (as far as its subject is concerned) of democracy is emphasized, the vexed question of its relation to communism can be resumed under conditions that are completely new, although no less threatening than those under which the discussion of that question was violently and tragically interrupted.

Before describing our work in individual chapters, it may be helpful for readers to gain a sense of how *The Politics of Operations* relates to our earlier book, *Border as Method, or, the Multiplication of Labor* (Mezzadra and Neilson 2013a). We do not imagine the present work as a sequel to this earlier text. Notwithstanding the distinct ambitions of *The Politics of Operations*, we continue to use several of the concepts developed in *Border as Method*— from "frontiers of capital" to the "multiplication of labor," to mention just two important examples. Discussions of and engagements with the politics of migration, and the subjective stakes that crisscross it, are also present in the chapters that follow, given the extent to which migratory movements interact with operations of capital and are an increasingly sensitive flashpoint in political contestations today. But readers who approach this book with the expectation that we extend or complicate the analysis of borders and migration offered in *Border as Method* are likely to be disappointed. *The Politics of Operations* marks a new departure even as it furthers our interest in the changing spatial and temporal formations of capitalism initiated in the earlier book. There are also important continuities between the books regarding method. Both works take a deliberately wide approach, drawing examples and case studies from a variety of global sites and similarly combining discussions of our own research experiences with accounts drawn from other sources. While the inclusion of the word "method" in the title of *Border as Method* registers an attempt to take the perspective of the border as an epistemic angle through which to examine a range of issues relevant to the analysis of contemporary capitalism—and not just those relating to borders and migration—something similar can be said of our approach to operations in this work. Understanding operations as a crucial hinge between capital's workings in specific spatial and social circumstances and its articulation into wider planetary vistas of capitalism means our investigations are not limited to particular cases in which capital "hits the ground" but range across a number of relevant issues, including the historical role of capital as a political actor, the pains and joys of anticapitalist struggles, and the changing roles of the state. The following summary of our interests in each chapter gives an idea of this breadth of concerns.

▄▄▄▄▄

CHAPTER 1 PROVIDES the background of the analysis pursued in the book. We interrogate the scenarios that emerged after the global financial crisis of 2007–2008, following the multiple mutations and variegations of this crisis and stressing how it has reshaped the capitalist world system. We dwell in particular on the vexed question of the relation between capital and difference, on emerging degrees of combination between neoliberalism and nationalism that shape the current global conjuncture, as well as on the changing status of territory in contemporary economic, political, and legal arrangements. We also begin to flesh out our general argument regarding the extractive nature of contemporary operations of capital.

Chapter 2 asks crucial questions regarding the "unity" of capital and the ways in which it can be considered a political actor. To tackle these questions, we offer a new reading of the Marxian concept of aggregate capital and develop our notion of operations of capital. This notion allows us to revisit the difference between capital and capitalism by means of a discussion of capital's multiple outsides, a topic that has attracted the attention of several thinkers in recent years. We close the chapter with an analysis of the power of abstraction in contemporary capitalism, which leads us to a more general attempt to reframe the question of capital's relation to politics.

Chapter 3 continues our discussion of the relation of capital to politics by investigating the time-honored question of the role of the state with respect to capital. Starting from a short review of Marxist debates on this topic, we stress the relevance of colonialism and empire in the history of the modern state. We also suggest that there is a need to go beyond the "Weberian" baseline model against which many claims regarding the crisis and transformations of the state in the global present are assessed. To this end, we provide a historical excursus on the scattered geographies of state and empire, singling out the relevance of such formations as chartered companies, colonial factories, and concessions, whose uncanny mutations resonate in present meldings of capital and the state. The chapter continues with an attempt to develop a typology of figures of the state in the second half of the twentieth century, predicated on distinguishing among the democratic social state, the socialist state, and what we call the developmental state. We conclude the chapter with a genealogical investigation of the origins of neoliberalism and globalization from the angle of developments in Asia, Africa, and Latin America.

Chapter 4 presents our analysis of extraction, logistics, and finance. While we stress the relevance of these "sectors" for contemporary capitalist development and crisis, we also emphasize the need to carefully investigate their multiple overlapping. Inter-referencing some of the most recent trends in extraction, logistics, and finance, the chapter aims to shed light on a set of principles or logics that increasingly play an important role in driving the dynamics of global capitalism and the composition of aggregate capital as a whole. The chapter ends by proposing a widening of the concept of extraction to understand the contemporary operations of capital well beyond the "sectoral" boundaries of extraction, logistics, and finance.

Chapter 5 interrogates the relations between the extractive operations of capital discussed in the previous chapter and the characteristics of emerging social struggles in different parts of the world. We attempt to map diverse landscapes of struggle, from Latin America to Europe, from India to South Africa, from Turkey to China, and from the United States to Nigeria, to set the stage for a conceptual discussion of what seems to us a crucial theoretical and political problem today: the constitutive relation, as well as the tensions and gaps, between social cooperation and living labor. In pursuing this analysis, we discuss such questions as the new formations of labor and life looming beyond the crisis of "free" wage labor as a "standard" employment relation, the condition and struggles of surplus populations, and the enduring relevance of so-called primitive accumulation. In line with our discussion, we focus particularly on the need to reframe the concept of exploitation.

Chapter 6 brings together the multiple analytical and theoretical threads followed in the book and discusses some of their political implications. We contribute to the ongoing discussion of the crisis, transformations, and persistence of the state within capitalist globalization by shifting the ground on which these debates are usually set. Keeping in mind our criticism of the baseline model of the state in chapter 3, we review current discussions of governmentality, governance, states of exception, and sovereignty, as well as the proliferation of labels, prefixes, and adjectives that haunt efforts to describe the global landscape of states. We also try to make sense of the important tasks performed by states in the present while at the same time carefully investigating the limits and pressures exerted by extractive operations of capital on their actions. The chapter ends with a discussion of the role of the state within a politics of emancipation and liberation, taking stock of recent political experiences—most notably, the long decade of "progressive" governments in Latin America since the early 2000s. Briefly put, our conclusion is that although the state or some of its structures can be "occupied" for a politics of transformation, such a reformatted state is not powerful enough to confront contemporary capitalism. A different source of power is necessary, and we close the book by outlining a sketch of a politics that is not centered on the state but capable of combining the establishment of a system of social counter-powers with wider, transnational attempts to seize political spaces or even create new ones. Needless to say, the further development of this theoretical sketch can only be part of collective efforts, where "weapons of criticism" will have to go hand in hand with "criticism by weapons."

The Space and Time of Capitalist Crisis and Transition

At Don Mueang Airport

Put yourself in the old Bangkok airport. Handling more than thirty-eight million passengers per year at its peak, Don Mueang was Asia's second busiest airport until its closure in September 2006. This relic of twentieth-century jet travel has emerged as a hub for low-cost and charter operators. As you move through the terminal, connecting to flights bound for regional destinations such as Chennai, Kunming, and Phnom Penh, you encounter an old world map stylized in 1960s design and featuring at its base a row of clocks displaying the time in twelve cities: Dallas, San Francisco, Montreal, Sydney, Moscow, Zurich, Rome, Frankfurt, London, Amsterdam, Paris, and Copenhagen. As Max Hirsh notes in *Airport Urbanism* (2016, 119–24), no flights leave from Don Mueang these days for those destinations. If you wish to fly to those cities from Bangkok, you must pass through Suvarnabhumi International Airport, the massive glass and metal structure to the city's east that replaced Don Mueang as Thailand's major gateway in 2006. Yet despite the shopping amenities, environmental engineering, and modular design that makes Suvarnabhumi feel much like any other world airport, one experiences a more striking sense of global contemporaneity staring at the old world map at Don Mueang. The radical disjuncture marked by the mismatch between the times on the clocks and the cities to which flights depart suggests the impossibility of forcing together in a single historical moment the heterogeneous times and spaces of the present.

The dizziness and disorientation induced by moving through a space such as Don Mueang Airport provides an appropriate prelude for this book. Readers may wonder how a study that begins in the Argentinean pampas ends up taking them to a discount air hub in Bangkok, a shipping port in Athens, a national park in Bolivia, or any of the other sites and installations visited in this book. As in the case of the cities listed on the world map at Don Mueang, the lines of connection are not obvious or given. But this is precisely the point. By seeking to excavate and analytically describe the operational logics that animate and drive the making and unmaking of global arrangements of space and time, we interrogate the workings of contemporary capitalism and delineate their changing relations with political practices, subjectivities, forms, and institutions. Such an investigation requires a wide-ranging analysis that is capable of confronting the continuities and dissonances of these logics as they play out across a vast and variegated panorama. To make our analysis, we draw on an array of sources, including but not confined to academic works produced within the disciplinary limits of anthropology and geography. Occasionally, we supplement these accounts with knowledge drawn from our own research and political experiences. We are committed to the proposition that concept production is most effective when it stems from specific, concrete situations, and we try to stay true to this proposition even when we do not directly discuss the experiences and encounters that have driven our thought. Conversely, we are very much interested in the labor of translation that is always needed when such concepts are applied to concrete situations that may be significantly different from the ones in which they originate. We are convinced that the ensuing frictions and even clashes may generate resonances that are very productive in terms of knowledge production (both regarding the concrete situations at hand and the terrain of conceptual elaboration). We thus present a study that is intentionally broad and, dare we say, purposely disorienting. This choice is only partly a question of writing style. Certainly, we try to convey a sense of the turbulence of contemporary capitalism. But we also suggest that a wide-ranging analysis offers insights and conclusions unavailable to studies that restrict themselves to a single locale or a closed set of sites. While we respect the lures of ethnographic immersion, we are wary of claims that the distinct forms of engagement it offers provide an exclusive or reliable index of analytical depth. Rigorous and probing analysis, we submit, can be generated in other ways.

In moving across sites, experiences, and processes, the giddying surface of our text searches for the multiple edges and frontiers along which contemporary capital expands. We aim to specify how this expansion displays a systemic logic that both exploits discontinuities between existing social differences and produces new forms of spatial and temporal heterogeneity. Our writing seeks not simply to claim solidarity with the many populations and struggles it encounters along the way, but also to ask what form such solidarity might take and how it might be meaningfully expressed in the current conjuncture. To this extent, we are not too invested in drawing parallels between the book's wide analytical remit and the itineraries of passengers who pass through Don Mueang Airport. Many of these travelers are, as Hirsh (2016, 5) points out, "*nouveaux globalizes*—new members of Asia's flying public, such as migrant workers, students, retirees, pilgrims, tourists, and traders from the Global South." In this case as in many of the others we study in this book, the differences between the lives of these populations and our own circumstances and positionality are manifest. Nonetheless, the problem of getting from A to B remains, and the operational logics governing the making and breaking of air routes apply, regardless of who occupies the seat on the next flight.

The sensory overload experienced standing before the world map at Don Mueang is complicated by the fact that some of the clocks have stopped. Different times are displayed for cities such as Frankfurt and Rome, which are in the same time zone. It is as if time has gone awry, and the neat demarcation of the world into uniform time zones has been consigned to a past moment of history. Although clocks around the world are still set against Greenwich Mean Time, the fractured moment of the present is not easily flattened onto a single cartographic surface. It is not only that the movement of time along scales not representable on the clock face weighs so heavily on our sense of the contemporary—whether it is the millisecond differences that provide arbitrage opportunities for high frequency financial traders or the slow geological time that underscores planetary existence itself. More important, the "*disjunctive unity of present times*" (Osborne 2013, 17) that underlies the global sense of contemporaneity cannot be separated from the growing heterogeneity and interconnectedness of global space.

Not accidentally do these spatial and temporal complexities come to a head in an airport, a space deliberately made to facilitate transfers and connections. Recent critical thought has struggled to give a name to such spaces of transit and circulation, whether they are fixed locations such as airports or container terminals, distributed nexuses of exchange such as financial markets, or networked spaces produced by communication technologies or transport infrastructures. The first-wave globalization theory in the 1990s located sites of this kind within a "space of flows" (Castells 1996) or described them as "non-places" (Augé 1995), seeking to define their specificity by building a contrast with the embedded sociality and plenitude of "places." With echoes of the classical sociological distinction between *Gesellschaft* and *Gemeinschaft*, this specification provided a rough conceptual vocabulary with which to begin an analysis of global space in the making. However, the tendency, particularly marked in the writings of Manuel Castells (1996, 416), to attribute to this "space of flows" an "ahistorical" or "timeless time" obscured the way in which these spaces occupied a historical present that was part of a longer trajectory of change and development. Formulations such as David Harvey's (1989) notion of "time-space compression" came closer to describing this condition. But it was ultimately difficult to distinguish such compression from earlier rearrangements of space and time—for instance, those facilitated by technologies such as the telegraph, railway, automobile, or airplane in the late nineteenth and early twentieth centuries (Kern 1983). Harvey (2001a, 30) argued that contemporary globalization is the product of "distinctive processes of the production of space on the ground under capitalism." By contrast, many subsequent attempts to account for the current proliferation of global flows, such as the "mobilities" paradigm in sociology (Urry 2007) and arguments drawing on Foucault's (2007) concept of "governmentality," have become disconnected from accounts of the production, circulation, and exchange of capital.

This book combines the analysis of the spatial and temporal complexities of globalization with an analysis of capital's circulation and colonization of social life by exploring what we call *the politics of operations*. We focus in particular on three "sectors" that provide strategic points of entry for discerning and examining an operative logic whose effects on contemporary capitalism extend way beyond any "sectoral" boundary: extraction, logistics, and finance. In particular, we are interested in how the intersection of operations in these domains provides coordinates for an analysis of the changing circuits of contemporary capital and the dynamics of capitalism's transition, by which we mean the processes of change that carry capitalism toward an uncertain future. In the case of Don Mueang Airport, this intersection brings together the extraction of the fossil fuels that allow jet travel, the logistical organization of transport and human mobility, and the financial arrangements that underlie the "yield management" systems of low-cost air carriers. By conducting analyses that work through and across operations in these mutually implicated fields, we seek not only to investigate how capital produces its own politics but also to contribute to the imagination of a politics beyond capital.

The concept of operations is elucidated in chapter 2. At this stage, we want only to suggest that joining an analysis of the space and time of globalization to an account of capital's operations is important in a time of capitalist crisis. What we call operations of capital provide a thread that allows us to map both the mutations of the current crisis and capitalist attempts to move beyond it, often working within the space opened up by the crisis. There are two primary reasons for this. First, one of the most salient features of capitalist crisis is its geographical variegation, a factor often ignored in accounts that emphasize the financial moment of Wall Street's subprime crisis. Second, the structural features of such crisis require a rethinking of capital's circulation and its implications for political questions of space, labor, life, regulation, institutional coherence, sovereignty, and governance.

There is a growing sense that capitalism now, more than at any other time since the end of World War II, has entered a critical condition. The crisis of 2007–2008 has cemented a historic downturn that began with the end of postwar prosperity in the 1970s and, punctuated by spikes and troughs, acquired intensity as the world economy became more interconnected and globalized. Declining growth rates, deflation, rising levels of indebtedness, bailouts, labor precarity, and ever widening gaps in social and economic inequality are only the most obvious symptoms of this change. A peculiar temporal scrambling of crisis and recovery characterizes the current economic transition, such that a cyclical logic of boom and bust no longer seems to apply. Deep-lying structural factors guide the transformations at hand. Yet more is at stake than economic turmoil. A social and spatial disruption has crossed the processes of capitalist globalization, shattering geographical hierarchies. The faltering of US hegemony in the face of the rising BRICS (Brazil, Russia, India, China and South Africa) economies, "currency wars" and turmoil around the persistent global hegemony of the dollar, the reshuffling of geographies of development, novel articulations of nationalism and neoliberalism, and the emergence of new regionalisms and patterns of multilateralism are some of the features of this reorganization of the contemporary world. Within this turbulence, the need for a spatial perspective on current capitalist crisis and transition is manifest. New and emerging centers of accumulation have become sites of intense social struggle, as attested, for instance, by the insurgencies that have rocked Istanbul's Gezi Park, the streets of Rio di Janeiro, and Bangkok's Suvarnabhumi Airport. It has also become difficult to easily locate the "most advanced" tendencies of capitalist development, because systems of production and assembly have become globally dispersed and incorporated the negotiation of spatial, economic, and cultural differences as one of their most important internal features. Under these conditions, we need to go beyond the image of a smooth space of flows in the analysis of the global present. Only by identifying lines of antagonism crossing the production of global space can we begin to locate and politically analyze the cleavages and flash points around which these tensions and transitions unfold.

The identification of such lines of antagonism is no easy task. Territorial borders are no longer fully coincident with the borders of the nation-state, and the frontiers of capital expand and complicate our sense of geographical scale. We suggest that the Marxian concept of the "world market" provides an important analytical framework within which to track the changing relations between political borders and economic frontiers. This is not only because Marx's introduction of this concept posits a spatiality of capital that structurally exceeds the topographic space of the nation-state. It is also because Marx offers a critique of the capitalist mode of production that recognizes capital's need to continuously expand by constructing an abstract and global space for its movement. This extensive moment of capital's expansion is matched by an intensive reshaping of social life, which is submitted to the imperative of capitalist accumulation. With implications for the production of subjectivity and the theory of value, the concept of the world market can productively inform an analysis of the geographical disruption lying at the heart of contemporary global processes. In doing so, it can also register the ways in which capital "hits the ground" and shapes conditions of everyday life, always working in consonance or conflict with the active role of space and multifarious resistances in guiding and molding capital's operations. From this perspective, arguments about the relation between "territorialism" and capitalism, such as those articulated in world systems theory (see, e.g., Wallerstein 1974), are challenged and complicated. An emphasis on the nexus that links specific operations of capital to the wider networks of capitalism is a central feature of this book.

Our intention is not to belittle insights about uneven development, dependency, or the aftermath of colonialism derived from world systems theory. We recognize that Wallerstein (1985) and others have questioned the perspective that superimposes state borders over the spatial and temporal boundaries of economic systems. Such recognition, however, does not prevent us from finding the tendency of world systems theory to categorize economic spaces according to large abstractions such as core, periphery, and semi-periphery too rigid and insufficiently attuned to the "conflictual imaginary" sparked by "colonial difference" (Mignolo 2000, 57). Our focus in this book is on lines of antagonism that do not follow the established macro-divisions of international political economy, world systems theory, or development studies: core-periphery, North-South, or minority-majority world. We question the possibility of identifying global divisions of wealth and power according to established binaries or the scheme of three worlds: First, Second, and Third. Equally, we question models of the new international division of labor (see, e.g., Fröbel et al. 1980), which trace the shift of international production from more developed to less developed countries as a result of economic and logistical processes that allow different phases of production to be undertaken in different parts of the world. Nonetheless, we remain acutely aware of the analytical need to understand how patterns of power and hegemony cross the workings of the world market. This is a problematic raised in Robert W. Cox's (1987) writings on "world order," which identify the realm of "global civil society" as the battleground on which struggles for hegemony occur. Our approach contrasts this emphasis on global civil society, pointing instead to material practices of struggle that cross specific operations of capital. In this way, we test established nomenclatures of economic space against the background of the geographies of contemporary capitalism, investigating its development and crises with attention to the changing dynamics of politics and power.

Giovanni Arrighi's explorations of changing patterns of world power in *Adam Smith in Beijing* (2007) are relevant for the investigation of capitalist crisis and transition we propose. Arrighi offers the thesis of a decline of US American hegemony, beginning in the 1970s and resulting in "a growing dependence of Northern and especially US global financial domination on a flow of money from the very countries that are most likely to become victims of that domination" (Arrighi 2007, 191). He argues that this leads to a situation in which the United States currently exercises "dominance without hegemony" and China emerges as the next likely center of global capitalism. Although Arrighi's narrative is provocative, we emphasize how the territorial logic of capitalism is tested and altered by spatial and temporal mutations facilitated by operations of capital. Current geopolitical and economic transitions are uncertain, irregularly paced, and (as our analyses of extraction, logistics, and finance suggest) unevenly applied to different sectors of social and economic life. It is possible, for instance, for China's economic emergence not to be matched by its military strength or for the cultural influence of the United States to continue, despite its changing economic position. In our view, it is improbable that a new hegemonic system will be constituted around a single territorial or national state, even as we recognize that the increasing global extension of Chinese state enterprise and mercantilism is a crucial element to investigate in any study that grapples with changing configurations of world power. We thus seek to move beyond models of hegemony based on accounts of international relations and to fathom the more complicated and fragmented territorial arrangements of the present.

This becomes evident standing in a regional airport such as Don Mueang. A major command and logistics hub for the US Air Force during the Vietnam War, the airport is now part of a Southeast Asian transition in which the growing influence of China is registered by the number of flights departing to destinations such as Kunming, Chongqing, and Wuhan. Standing before the world map at Don Mueang, one has the sense of passing through the space of what world systems theorists call the periphery—or, perhaps, a space verging on entry to the semi-periphery. When boarding a flight at Suvarnabhumi, by contrast, a sense of transit through the core is manifest. Yet these two airports serve the same city and host borders to the same country. Global divisions of wealth and power cannot be neatly mapped over national or even urban demarcations, and this gives rise to an analytical imperative to rethink the territorial configuration of the contemporary world and the way it relates to changing patterns of capitalist crisis and transition.

Rethinking Territory

Territory names a way to organize relations between space and power. The concept has a complex genealogy and, while judgments or predictions of territory's decline tend to be overstated, its relation to political concepts such as sovereignty and jurisdiction is neither fixed nor given. Territory is a political technology that bundles together techniques of measure and control, shaping the relation of land to terrain in diverse and contested ways. The modern concept of territory, which brings together politics, space, and state, congealed in Europe toward the end of the seventeenth century, building on a tradition of legal interpretation that began with the rediscovery of Roman law in the late Middle Ages. Such an understanding of territory, which has spread globally over the past two centuries, remains by and large extant. We argue that this state-centered view of territory is slowly being undone. As capital emerges in novel and unprecedented ways as a political actor, it acquires the power to produce territory of its own accord. In reality, capital always possessed this capacity, although it was eclipsed during the nineteenth century when the state acquired a monopoly over the making of territory, a process inherent in the legal and geographical evolution of empire. Tracing these changes, both historically and in the present, is important for an analysis that asks how the operations of capital cross the spatial and temporal configuration of the world. Today territories generated by capital take forms such as the special economic zone, the logistical corridor, the financial district, or the extraction enclave. None of these could likely exist without the involvement of states. Yet given the historical variations in the production of territory, we should not assume this is a stable scenario. The nexus of capital and territory is changing before our eyes.

The story of how states acquired a monopoly on the making of territory has been told many times. In his genealogy of the concept of territory, Stuart Elden (2013, 322) traces the historical production of the "idea of territory as a bounded space under the control of a group of people, usually a state." Territory, understood in this sense, is the political correlate of a notion of space "defined by *extension*," and can thus be defined as "*the extension of the state's power*" (322). Elden's account of how this "mainstream view of territory" spreads around the world is quite familiar: the "state in this modern form extends across Europe and from there across the globe" (322). Although there is undeniably truth to this claim, there is also a need to recognize the contentions involved, not least on the part of colonized people who resisted the spread of European imperialism. Lauren Benton (2010, 16) emphasizes the extent to which modern imperial expansion involved the creation of territories that were "differentiated, fragmented, and uneven." She demonstrates how the making of European imperial space was shaped by uncertainties in establishing boundaries, influenced by Indigenous conventions of mapping, and frequently driven more by a will to present evidence of rights to possession superior to those of other contenders than a need to establish absolute title to territory. Drawing attention to these anomalies in the spatial and legal making of empires provides a basis for identifying precedents to the current vacillations of territory, in which the centrality of state sovereignty and the coincidence of jurisdiction with state boundaries can no longer be taken for granted.

History also sheds light on the role of capital in the making of territory. The territorial claims made by chartered companies are relevant in this regard, since these entities were not only political bodies sanctioned by sovereign prerogative but also commercial organizations, many of which took the form of the joint stock company. Precisely because the territorial claims made by chartered companies pertain to a moment in which the world did not yet consist of territorial states, they exhibit the complex combination of powers that enabled the territorialization of the globe. Consider the case of Rupert's Land, the vast stretch of contemporary Canada and parts of the current United States nominally granted by the British Crown to the Hudson's Bay Company in 1670. Across this territory, the company acted as a sovereign entity in its own right, establishing a legal regime, exercising military power, engaging in diplomacy, and establishing a system of welfare provision. As Edward Cavanagh writes, the Crown, "beyond granting and extending the Company's charter at home, had barely a part to play in the operation" (Cavanagh 2011, 28). A similar situation applied to the British East India Company, which formally acquired territory only in 1765 with the grant by the Mughal emperor of the *diwani*, or right to collect revenue in Bengal, Bihar, and Orissa. Philip Stern (2011, 5) describes the British East India Company as a "company-state" that "had actually been a form of government, state, and sovereign in Asia for some time" before it became a "territorial power" in the mid-eighteenth century. The important point is that both the Hudson's Bay Company and the British East India Company were joint stock companies to which investors contributed capital to fund expeditions, military ventures, and other activities, expecting a dividend in return. That these chartered companies acquired and controlled large territories is a gauge of the role played by capital in the making of modern territories, a factor often overlooked in accounts that emphasize the global spread of the state from Europe to the rest of the world.

Investigating these historical precedents is not merely a scholarly task, as we share Michel Foucault's view that, in the "battle around the history of capitalism, around the history of the role of the institution of law, of the rule in capitalism, we are actually dealing with a whole political stake"

(Foucault 2008, 165). While we return to discuss these early modern forms of territory in chapters 3 and 6, our focus is on territory's current mutations, which articulate the history of capitalism to the fractured space and time of the present. Discussions of contemporary changes to territory often refer to one or the other of two influential maxims: John Agnew's injunction to avoid the "territorial trap" (Agnew 1994) and Alfred Korzybski's 1933 dictum "the map is not the territory" (Korzybski [1933] 1994). Agnew's warning about the territorial trap attempts to unsettle widespread assumptions about political space rooted in understandings of the modern nation-state. Korzybski's dictum is, rather, a statement about representation, making a point about the dangers of confusing a sign for its referent. We seek to join insights derived from these maxims to an interrogation of the role of law in the battle around the history of capitalism by inquiring into the relation between territory and territoriality.

Territory, as discussed earlier, is a political technology that organizes the relation of space to power; "territoriality," by contrast, is usually taken as a more open term, understood variously as biological instinct or a human "strategy to establish different degrees of access to people, things, and relationships" (Sack 1986, 20). Such an understanding of territoriality as a matter of instinct or access both posits it as a prior condition for territory and glosses over the question of operations that we highlight. We emphasize, by contrast, the conceptual priority of territory to territoriality, suggesting that the historical mutations of the former give rise to particular understandings of the latter. For this reason, we prefer Saskia Sassen's narrower definition of territoriality as "the legal construct encasing the sovereign authority of the state over its territory" (Sassen 2013, 21). It is in this sense that territoriality has become the dominant way to understand territory. The inability or refusal to understand territory outside this frame—or the mistaking of territory for the map of territoriality, to recall Korzybski's terms—produces "the conceptual invisibility of territories that exit the state's territorial authority" (Korzybski [1933] 1994, 23). While Agnew (2005) highlights the transformations of crucial aspects of state sovereignty that have become "non-territorial" in nature, Sassen (2013, 23) points to processes of unpacking national territories and to the emergence of a new assemblage of territory understood as "a capability with embedded logics of power and claim-making." Both processes are relevant not only from a political and legal point of view but also for an analysis of how operations of capital shape contemporary capitalism and its heterogeneous geographies.

Within these heterogeneous geographies, it is possible to identify forms of territory that cut across state borders or create nonnational jurisdictions within them. The proliferation of special economic zones—in both number and type—is only one index of this phenomenon (Easterling 2014, 25–69; Neilson 2014). Sassen (2013, 36) discusses instances such as the closed financial exchanges known as "dark pools," which provide a "bordered space of private financial transactions that is increasingly free from national and international regulatory authorities." To this she adds new jurisdictional territories such as those associated with the International Criminal Court or provisions of the World Trade Organization's General Agreement on Trade of Services (GATS). The new spatiality of logistics and infrastructure development, which often exists in tension with the established borders and partitions of the "international" world, is another important instance of such forms of territory (Cowen 2014; Grappi 2016). A host of more informal arrangements can also be mentioned, including those involving the mobility of forced migrants, the transnational and cross-border spaces opened by migration writ large, the formation of cross-border jurisdictions for political action, and the emergence of a "global operational space" for firms (Sassen 2013, 36–38). The question to ask of such emergent territorial formations is not simply about how they unbundle the unitary spatiotemporal domain of state territoriality, making the Earth itself "mobile" (Perulli 2014), but how, in so doing, they mobilize governmental and commercial powers that are increasingly meshed with forms of sovereign rule that are not exclusively invested in the state. Such a mobilization is not a historical novelty specific to the heterogeneous space and time of the present. Instead, as we have already noted, it has historical precedents in political forms that have long existed in alliance and tension with the nation-state and in early modern assemblages of power that the modern state needed to absorb, coopt, or undermine to spread globally.

In confronting these mutations of territory, we wish less to participate in the current refocusing of critical attention on territory pursued by authors such as James D. Sidaway (2007) and Andrea Mubi Brighenti (2010) than to ask of what this refocusing is symptomatic. Our contention is that current transformations of the relation of state to territory are driven by the operations of capital and by the changing spatial and temporal configurations of political power and economic association that accompany, spur, and complicate the crisis and transition of contemporary capitalism.

As the story is usually told, the current capitalist crisis finds its beginnings in the workings of finance, particularly the partitioning and bundling of US subprime debt. One culmination of this crisis is the convulsion of the Eurozone and the ravages of austerity visited on populations in Greece, Italy, and other countries that have experienced the institution of commissary forms of power (*troikas* and technical governments) amenable to the dictates of finance. As Ranabir Samaddar (2016, 1), among many others, has pointed out, "Europe's periphery is now playing out a script of debt, bondage, and neoliberal reforms, already performed many times in the post-colony." Much research on the origins of the current crisis claims—as, indeed, we do later in this chapter—that the buildup of household debt and subsequent wave of mortgage foreclosures associated with speculation on subprime debt amounts to a form of extraction (or so-called primitive accumulation) by which finance capital draws a quota of value from social relations external to it. The danger of this approach is that such extraction is understood as a one-off act of expropriation to which the ensuing crisis is a reaction or readjustment. This is not a vision of crisis we share. Rather, we point to a longer-term process with ongoing historical momentum that relies not only on debt relations and whose opening cannot be correlated with the subprime crisis alone.

The spatial and temporal heterogeneity of crisis is for us the key to understanding the peculiar rhythms and patterns of dispersion that not only characterize its unfolding but also transform the institutional and territorial environments in which this unfolding occurs. Rather than approaching financialization as an "external force" that transforms otherwise sound economies, we investigate "the historically and geographically variegated grounded operations of finance" (Ouma 2016, 83) while also asking how these operations are shaped "by more general principles of abstraction circulating in global financial markets" (Ouma 2016, 89). In so doing, it becomes clear that flattening the politics of the crisis onto the map of national territories means ignoring some of its most salient features. Phenomena such as dark pools, global cities, regional central banks, and offshore banking centers play a role in establishing circuits of finance capital that do not simply mimic or parallel the aggregate operations of national economies. Furthermore, the dynamics of financialization mean that differences in national models of economic governance can create tight relationships between economies that are supposedly territorially discrete. Kean Fan Lim (2010, 680) discusses how China and the United States "share an intricate, symbiotic economic relationship because of their different macroeconomic governance models. Any consideration of 'unique' Chinese economic growth models must thereby also include the impacts of corresponding US macroeconomic and fiscal policies." The same argument can be made in reverse. The geographical question of territory thus crosses the operations of capital and the transitions of capitalism in ways that exceed, as well as register, the ongoing importance of state territoriality.

One arena in which the tense relation between capital and territory comes plainly into view is the operations of currency. At once a restless token of exchange and a form of legal tender rooted in territoriality, currency is usually understood as the material representation of abstract money. Since the fall of the gold standard in 1914 and the end of the Bretton Woods system in 1971, the value of currency increasingly has been defined relationally—that is, in relation to the value of other currencies—as opposed to representationally. The foreign exchange market is now the world's largest financial market, operating twenty-four hours a day, seven days a week, and, due to the way in which currencies relate to patterns of sovereignty, it has no central governing body, clearinghouses, or arbitration panels to settle disputes. It is also a purely speculative market in that no physical exchange of currencies ever occurs. All trades exist as computer entries and are netted out depending on market prices. Yet currency does not roam completely free of territory. As Adrian Blackwell and Chris Lee (2013, iii–v) explain, it is at once "land that has become mobile" and "a system of information that circulates through the social body." The entanglement of currency and territory is evident, for instance, in the pegging of the Chinese renminbi to the US dollar, which, along with China's holding of US treasury bonds, is responsible for the "symbiotic economic relationship" described earlier. The persistent global hegemony of the dollar is at the root of manifold tensions within the world system while the dollar continues to grant the United States specific "drawing rights" at the global level (see, e.g., Xulin 2011). "The United States is the only country where demand for its currency does not just reflect an increase in the demand for the goods and services it produces," Yanis Varoufakis explains. Simply because "primary commodities are denominated in dollars," even without the involvement of American companies, "whenever a Nigerian driver puts petrol in her car, or a Chinese factory purchases Australian coal, the demand for US dollars rises" (Varoufakis 2011, 102). Currency therefore also plays a role in militarized episodes of territorialism, at least if one accepts Michael Hudson's (2003) explanation of the US-led invasion of Iraq as an attempt to stave off efforts to establish the euro as the preferred currency for oil trade. In these instances, the tension between currency's circulation and its relation to territory becomes evident. However, we want to draw attention to something more fundamental: the ways in which current mutations in territory and currency demand a rethinking of financial operations.

The growth and increasing complexity of the foreign exchange market is evident in its opening to the full panoply of contemporary financial operations and instruments, including swaps, derivatives, and options. The recent proliferation of high-frequency trading (HFT) in the foreign exchange market has increased as equity trading by these same algorithmic methods has come under scrutiny (Detrixhe et al. 2014). While the jury is still out about whether HFT will distribute liquidity across the foreign exchange market or increase its volatility, the territorial implications of this practice are manifest. As authors as diverse as Michael Lewis (2014) and Donald MacKenzie (2014) explain, HFT exhibits the spatial dimensions of finance not in the aspect of state territoriality but with regard to its infrastructural and logistical operations. The "gaming of the plumbing" (Toscano 2013) that occurs through the laying of cable, the co-location of matching engines with data center servers, and the acquisition of super-fast equipment is crucial to the reduction of latency necessary to get ahead of the game in HFT. This gives a very different territorial configuration, since what matters is not the physical location in financial hubs highlighted in the vastly influential global cities thesis (Sassen 1990) but proximity to data centers or server farms that, because of their energy and cooling needs, as well as the prohibitive costs of urban real estate, often can be feasibly located only in the logistical hinterland of these cities (Carruth 2014). As Matthew Tiessen (2012, 108) explains, today's algorithmic trading creates "a potentially more geographically distributed network of (financial) centers that derive their potency not so much from their being at the intersection of trade routes or from their being located where capital and commerce is concentrated, but by being geospatially located according to a sort of mathematics-of-in-between-ness—that is, by being optimally located in geographical space in a way that minimizes the impediments of time." Tiessen refers to the necessity to locate the hardware associated with algorithmic trading, such as server farms, in sites where the time for electronic information to travel across networked fibers is minimized. Such a calculative and optimizing approach to geographical distribution creates a territorial diagram that is very different from that drawn by the state and its borders. It is within such a territorial complex that the value of currency is increasingly determined today. Even central banks, which clearly remain important actors in this landscape, are compelled to negotiate their regulating activity within such arrangements.

The operations of finance are thus crucial to the ways in which territory is being reshaped and reconceptualized. At the same time, such a reconfiguration and rethinking of territory shifts our understanding of finance, in this case drawing attention to the logistical and infrastructural factors that shape its workings. This is but one instance of the intertwining of finance and logistics that we investigate in this book, adding, importantly, an analysis of extraction and its intersection with these influential "sectors" or fractions of capital. While we examine these intersections in depth in chapter 4, our emphasis at this point is on the spatial and temporal logics of their operations. Insofar as these logics are implicated in the circulation of capital, they are inseparable from the current transformations of territory and territoriality. But this raises a deeper and thornier issue which we now confront: the problem of capital and difference.

Capital and Difference

Bringing together the concepts of capital and difference is tricky. The unity and supposed universality of the concept of capital implies for many, at least since the influential interventions of Georg Lukács ([1923] 1971), a commitment to totality that sweeps all difference in its wake. Most prominently in contemporary Marxian thought, Fredric Jameson has critically extended such an understanding of capital's totality. Drawing on Jean-Paul Sartre's concept of totalization, he repudiates a "bird's-eye view of the whole" and affirms a project that "takes as its premise the impossibility for biological or individual human subjects to conceive of such a position, let alone to adopt or achieve it" (Jameson 1991, 332). By this argument, largely directed against poststructuralist positions popular at the time of its elaboration, we can only ever partially perceive or represent the totality of capitalist relations, and thus there is need for "cognitive mapping" to analytically delineate the contours of the world system. The question remains open as to whether such totality provides a background against which visions and experiences of difference can thrive or whether it is asserted in the face of a proliferation of differences that threatens to tear it apart. Feminist and postcolonial arguments that position the concept of capital as inimical to the politics of difference (see, e.g., Bhabha 1994, 303–38; Gibson-Graham 1996, 1–24) have been no less rife than those that seek to intertwine or reconcile these theoretical strands (see, e.g., Chakrabarty 2000, 47–72; Spivak 1985). More recently, this standoff has been replayed between Marxian thinkers who are partial to the concept of totality (see, e.g., Toscano and Kinkle 2015, 33–77) and assemblage or actor-network theorists who argue that social processes cannot be explained by concepts such as capital since these concepts themselves are precisely what need to be explained (see, e.g., Latour 2014). The argument rolls on with plenty of political innuendo but no apparent resolution.

We seek to avert the rhetorical flourish and amplified tensions of this debate by recognizing at once the moment of unity that pertains to the concept of capital and the heterogeneity of capital's operations in space and time. This means understanding the laws of capital as tendential, as opposed to totalizing or deterministic—an important point that allows us to take stock of the problems implied by the postcolonial notion of difference for the understanding of capital without affirming simplistic critiques of postcolonialism such as the one recently articulated by Vivek Chibber (2013; see Mezzadra 2018). A central tenet of our approach derives from strains of feminist and queer thought, as well as postcolonial and critical race studies that maintain that difference is not a universalizable category. These perspectives have taught us to understand difference not only as an inflection of social experience, a mode of subjection, or resistance to oppression but also as a moment of excess that puts subjectivity into action, generates political creativity, and prompts struggles for liberation (see, e.g., Davis 1983; Dominijanni 2001; Fanon 1967; Warner 1993). Struggles for racial and sexual liberation (and here we do not forget LGBTQI struggles, as contested and as insufficient as the multiple versions of this acronym may be) do not always align themselves with struggles against capitalism. But it is also the case that racism, sexism, heteronormativity, capitalism, and class rule are deeply entangled so that it is difficult to imagine one without the others. Thus, for us, understanding capital with respect to the politics of difference means returning to Marx, who saw capital as a "social relation" rather than as a thing or a substance. If we approach capital in this way, it becomes possible to see how its operations are inseparable from relations of social difference. We can also observe how these operations combine systematically without attributing to them a necessarily a priori coherence.

Affirming a view of capital as a dynamic, lived social relationship also means paying analytical attention to its relations with its multiple outsides. In this regard, it is important to note that capital is not all-encompassing. We mobilize the concept of "frontiers of capital" to register both the sense in which something always remains beyond capital's grasp—some activity or substance that has not yet been appropriated or capitalized—and the way in which capital requires an external dumping ground for its outputs. The dependency of capital on conditions that are not its own is the principal reason for the heterogeneity of its material operations. We agree with John Chalcraft (2005, 33) that "capitalist activity is always shaped and transformed by social relations more broadly conceived." We also concur with his recognition of the "seminal importance of diverse histories of labor" and the need to avoid a universal history that grants "historicity to a West that then spreads out and confers historicity on a non-West." Yet we are more cautious in the face of claims that the non-West, if such a reductive designation is plausible, provides a privileged ground or method for projects that challenge the "capital-driven forces which seek to penetrate or colonize all spaces on the earth with unchecked freedom" (Chen 2010, 4; for a similar argument, which even reduces the notions of capital and capitalism to an "enchantment with Western theory and philosophy," see Nigam 2016, 34).

As we show in this book, regions traditionally designated "non-Western"— such as Asia, Africa, and, more ambiguously, Latin America—not only have become sites of deep resistance to capitalism but also have furnished conditions for the reinvigoration and reinvention of the social relation of capital. Indeed, varieties of capitalism specific to these regions have become globally expansive, as evidenced, for instance, by the activities of the Taiwanese company Foxconn in countries such as Slovakia, Turkey, and Russia (Sacchetto and Andrijasevic 2015), the concession made by the Greek government in 2009 of part of the Port of Piraeus to the Chinese state-owned enterprise Cosco (Hatzopoulos et al. 2014), or more generally the massive growth of so-called emerging country multinational corporations (Cuervo-Cazurra and Ramamurti 2014). Far from suggesting that such activity involves a mere reversal of historical patterns of colonialism, we must recognize that capital's expansiveness was global from the start, even as it was also subject to processes of heterogenization and domination that made specific sites or regions ripe for its development across different historical periods. The question is not one about the unity of the concept of capital or the attribution of a universal or teleological bourn to European imperialism. Rather it is about investigating how the workings of capital generate a high degree of heterogeneity in the historical and spatial organization of capitalism.

It is important not to confuse our emphasis on heterogeneity with the discussion of varieties of capitalism carried out by a well-established school of "neo-institutionalist" thinkers dedicated to the comparative analysis of capitalism. Work conducted in this vein often takes its impetus from Michael Albert's well-known distinction between "American" and "Rhenish" capitalism (Albert 1993). As Bob Jessop (2012, 233) explains, such scholarship has developed influential analytical models of "institutional complementarities that promote efficient economic performance from the view point of representative firms and/or national economies." During the 1990s, this approach prompted sensitivity to alternatives and diversity in a climate that was generally dominated by global convergence arguments. Yet while focusing on the firm, the varieties of capitalism literature tends to take the nation as a privileged analytical unit and comparative tool. Such a privileging of the nation is a prominent feature of the volume *Varieties of Capitalism*, edited by Peter A. Hall and David Soskice. In their introduction to the collection, Hall and Soskice (2001, 7–8) explain that they compare "national political economies" with "reference to the way in which firms resolve the coordination problems they face." Without underestimating the extent to which states remain critical actors, this emphasis on national political economies needs to be reconsidered in the light of dynamics of capital, institutions, and territory discussed earlier. Even within the neo-institutionalist literature there is recognition that "the position of the nation-state as the definer of the boundaries of cases is not so fixed that it should be taken for granted *per definitionem*" (Crouch 2005, 42). The focus on national varieties of capitalism also tends to obscure the "commonalities" of contemporary capitalism (Streeck 2009), which we need to emphasize to better understand the meaning of "diversity" for capitalism on a world scale. Relevant commonalities in this regard include capitalism's dependence on its outsides, its need of powers of abstraction to spread globally, its embeddedness in social relations, and its tendency to amplify inequality. Indeed, we suggest that the current crisis intensifies these commonalities even as its spatial and temporal manifestations are extremely heterogeneous. The relation between capitalism's common characteristics and the geographical heterogeneity of its crises and transition thus emerges as an important object of analysis.

As discussed earlier in this chapter, processes of financialization play an important role in disarticulating the operations of capital from national economies. Recent investigations of the "geography of finance" further challenge the methodological nationalism implied by the literature on varieties of capitalism. Working on the German case, for instance, Gordon Clark and Dariusz Wójcik (2007) show that corporate governance in large firms is moving toward the mobilization of global standards demanded by capital markets (which means a more shareholder-dominated regime) as opposed to national institutional specifications. Clark and Wójcik also emphasize the existence of several corporate governance regimes in Germany, primarily along regional lines (meaning that some *Länder* foster models of corporate governance that are more consistent with the imperatives of global financial markets). The unity of the German model of capitalism (supposedly the quintessential "coordinated market economy") is thus exploded due to pressures placed on firms by global financial markets and institutional changes at the subnational level. In exploring the tension between convergence and divergence that characterizes the articulation of contemporary political and economic space, such work in the geography of finance demonstrates how the supposed "path dependence" of any model of capitalism is liable to change. With such susceptibility to change, there emerges, as Adam Dixon (2011, 203) succinctly puts it, the "risk of devising different models of capitalism when actually there is a single capitalism, but granted a variegated capitalism."

The concept of "variegated capitalism" proposed by the critical geographers Jamie Peck and Nick Theodore (2007) is useful for shedding light on the commonalities of capitalism in ways that are attentive to questions of territory and difference and thus to the tumultuous changes in capitalism's geography. For these thinkers, the spaces and scales of contemporary capitalist accumulation cannot be taken for granted or straightforwardly correlated with political borders or official administrative boundaries. Rather than pursuing a comparative approach, Peck and Theodore (2007, 760) emphasize dynamic and relational "principles, sources, and dimensions of *capitalist variegation*." They analyze the resulting "dynamic polymorphism" by combining a focus on the heterogeneity of capitalism with an attempt to grasp the "*systemic* production of geoinstitutional differentiation" (Brenner et al. 2010, 184). We see resonances between this approach and the vision of capitalist heterogeneity implicit in the concept of "axiomatic of capital" introduced by Gilles Deleuze and Félix Guattari. What strikes us as important about this concept—although it is not one we employ systemically throughout this book—is that it allows the continued deployment of a unitary concept of capital without affirming arguments about global convergence. Put simply, the concept "axiomatic of capital" shows why there is no need to equate the unity of capital with the homogenization of all the different sites and milieus in which capital operates. To "the extent that capitalism constitutes an axiomatic," the authors of *A Thousand Plateaus* write, "social formations tend to become *isomorphic* in their capacity as models of realization." However, "It would be wrong to confuse isomorphy with homogeneity," as it "allows, and even incites" a great deal of social, temporal, and spatial heterogeneity (Deleuze and Guattari 1987, 436). As in Peck and Theodore's vision of variegated capitalism, the deep heterogeneity of contemporary global space is the result of a continuous and systematic process of production that is adaptive, temporally variable, and constantly redefines its own boundaries.

The gap between axiomatic and heterogeneity—to maintain Deleuze and Guattari's terminology for now (although the entire problematic could be reformulated through a rereading of the Marxian category of subsumption, as we do in chapter 2)—is particularly evident today. The tension and divergence between these ways of describing how capital formats the world needs to be given analytical priority if we are to understand the most important transformations affecting contemporary capitalism, the geography of its crisis, and the unstable spatial coordinates of its transition. Capital does not function according to iron laws. To the contrary, its operations are flexible or pliable, capable of confronting the unexpected and thriving off contradictions and incompleteness. Deleuze and Guattari (1983, 250) explain that the "strength of capitalism resides in the fact that its axiomatic is never saturated, that it is always capable of adding a new axiom to the preceding ones." Just as isomorphy does not imply homogeneity, so the systematicity of capital's operations does not entail closure or an accomplished totality.

Capital, then, does not simply reckon with difference. Rather, difference is an internal feature of its operations. An important register of this is how capital seeks to gather the open flux of heterogeneity into what Gavin Walker (2016b, 79) calls "*specific* differences," which then become "equivalences" that can encounter and be compared with one another. Much of this book grapples with the nexus of capital and difference, analytically observing capital's operations in specific material circumstances, conceptually defining the logics that drive them, observing how these operations cross relations of racial and sexual difference, and examining the unhinging effects of differences manifest in social struggles and movements that contest capital's inexorable expansion. The challenge is to isolate a set of features and problems that shape the diverse domains and landscapes traversed by processes of capitalist accumulation and valorization without falling back on the "*specific* differences" of national-cultural contexts. Such isolation cannot be accomplished without a focus on the limits of these processes, which mark the impossibility of capital affirming itself as a self-sufficient totality at the same time as they produce an unbalanced configuration of forces. Once such an analysis is in place, we can ask questions about how capital and capitalism reshape their relation with politics. This means investigating the shifting roles of states and other institutions and agencies of governance, and bringing into relief the heterogeneous ways in which struggles of exploited subjects challenge and exceed the emerging formations of governance and capital in many parts of the world.

An Extractive Capitalism?

We have already discussed the sense in which we understand the operations of contemporary capital as extractive. To reiterate, when we describe these operations as extractive, we do not mean to reduce them to the literal removal of raw materials and life forms from the Earth's surface, depths, and biosphere. We certainly include such literally extractive activities in our analysis, noting the importance of mining, monocultural farming, and other practices of extracting wealth from the Earth for political and economic gain. Too often, at a time that critical analyses of capitalism emphasize the importance of supposedly immaterial relations and highly abstract forces, the ways in which such material extraction fuels the system are overlooked. Bringing these practices to the fore is crucial not just because of their effects on the environment, although this is clearly an urgent question for populations that live both near and far away from extraction sites, but also for the overall positioning of capitalism in what Jason W. Moore (2015) calls the "web of life." Attention to literally extractive practices is additionally important because the logics that impel them seem to be spreading to other realms of capitalist activity, prompting claims that capitalism has entered a new stage of extractivism.

Today we do not just mine coal, nickel, and other raw materials; we also mine data. Moreover, the forms of extraction implicit in data mining and other extractive activities that prey on human sociality are ever more at the edge of capital's expanding frontiers. In this book, we argue that extraction provides an appropriate way to name the processes by which capital draws on its multiple outsides to sustain and perpetuate itself, and we extend the term to apply particularly to the ways in which capital targets practices of social cooperation. However, we are hesitant to argue that extractivism constitutes a new paradigm of capitalism, a claim that is often implicit in Latin American debates about neo-extractivism that criticize

capitalism as a tool for exploit at

the continent's "progressive" governments for their role in facilitating mining, soy cultivation, and other literally extractive activities. This reluctance does not make us indifferent to the many resonances between "extraction" understood in the narrow sense and the wider implications of the term. As we write in an earlier article (Mezzadra and Neilson 2017, 4), "When we are attentive to the continuities and ruptures that characterize the relations between literal extraction and extraction in the expanded sense, it becomes possible to attend to the prevalence and strategic role of extractive operations in contemporary capitalism." The challenge is to remain sensitive to these continuities and cleavages and to track their relevance for social and political struggles that are cast against the historical and contemporary fronts of extractive capitalism.

It is no secret that Indigenous peoples across the world have borne the brunt of extractive activities. Dispossessed from their land and territories by colonial violence and the fictions of international law, their struggles continue to play out on the extractive frontier. This remains the case even in instances where legal judgment has revoked the principle of terra nullius, which in many colonial societies was used to justify the occupation of native lands—often retrospectively—on the basis that they were supposedly uninhabited. For instance, writing about the *Mabo* decision in Australia in 1992, a judgment holding that native title existed for all Indigenous people in Australia prior to colonization, Irene Watson (2015, 42) affirms that the "effect of terra nullius—its denial of the Indigenous being—is an historical process, which continues today." This continuation is evident in Indigenous struggles against the encroachment of extractive industries, particularly in settler colonial societies. Such struggles often contest the way governments and commercial bodies obtain consent for mining or other extractive activities from individuals rather than from appropriate Indigenous collectives. At other times, they question the limitation of Indigenous rights to cultural recognition, as opposed to self-determination or rights to land, water, and means of livelihood (Coulthard 2014). Watson gives the examples of Arabana struggles against the extension of the Roxby Downs uranium mine in South Australia and the opposition of Warlmanpa peoples to the building of a nuclear waste dump at Muckaty in Australia's Northern Territory, but the list can easily be expanded.

Most prominently, the Standing Rock struggles of 2016–17 against the construction of the Dakota Access oil pipeline combined tactics of encampment and blockading with sophisticated social media strategies that spread news of the standoff around the world (Dhillon and Estes 2016). Similarly, the Idle No More movement, which began as a reaction to Canadian legislation that eroded First Nations' sovereignty and rights, expanded rapidly and culminated with the signing of a Treaty Alliance against Tar Sands Expansion, signed by more than eighty-four First Nations and Native American tribes, including the Standing Rock Sioux (Johnson 2017). The capacity of these movements to enlist participants from around the world, and particularly from across the borders of the United States and Canada attests their passage beyond dynamics of international solidarity. For the Iroquois, Audra Simpson (2014, 155) writes, the US-Canada border is "an international border that cuts through their historical and contemporary territory and is, simply, in their space and in their way." Writing from a Mohawk perspective, Simpson explains how "Indigenous political orders prevail within and apart from settler governance," advocating a politics that, in refusing "to be on the other end of Patrick Wolfe's critical, comparative history" and "to go away, to cease to be," asserts "something beyond difference" (Simpson 2014, 11, 22).

In referring to Patrick Wolfe's (1999) understanding of settler colonialism as a process of elimination, Simpson grounds her approach to colonial extraction in a critical discourse that emphasizes the appropriation of territory as opposed to labor. This emphasis on the dispossession of territory is a feature of much work in Indigenous studies, which remains critically aware of the stakes of such an approach—as apparent, for instance, in Jodi Byrd's (2011, xxiv) reflections on the relations between settler colonialism and "the modern racialized division of labor" or in Robert Nichols's (2017) account of how Indigenous scholars' arguments about the dispossession of land deal recursively with the problem of prior possession. A concern with the removal of Indigenous territories also applies in many contexts where the doctrine of terra nullius was never formally applied or in colonial societies that cannot be easily brought under the interpretative frame of settler colonialism. Consider the colonization of Latin America, where the *encomienda* system "granted the conquerors rights over land areas as well as to the labour of the Indians" (Åhrén 2016, 16). Today, Indigenous struggles in Latin America, such as those against road building in Isiboro Sécure National Park and Indigenous Territory (TIPNIS) in Bolivia—which we examine in chapter 5—tend also to emphasize Indigenous relations to the land beyond logics of private property and opposition to mining, bioprospecting, or other extractive activities. A similar point can be made about many other Indigenous struggles occurring beyond the Anglophone societies that have tended to provide the empirical basis for arguments about settler colonialism (see Wolfe 1999, 2016; Veracini 2010), including battles against mineral extraction in India's northeast (Crowley 2011) or urban occupations for the return of traditional lands in Taiwan (Hioe 2017).

Indigenous struggles aimed primarily but not exclusively toward literally extractive activities are a first and last line of defense against the increasingly extractive operations of capital. The pains and agonies they involve—or what Simpson (2014, 3) calls "the hard labor of hanging on to territory"—haunt and enable the other struggles against extraction we examine in this book. Yet, as Robin D. G. Kelley (2017) argues, the elision of African peoples from arguments about the dispossessions brought about by settler colonialism—on the basis that they were colonized for their labor rather than their land—raises a series of questions. While Indigenous studies foreground issues of race, the erasure of African Indigeneity through the renaming of slaves as black Americans "severs any relationship to their land" and involves "a process of elimination: eliminate the culture, the identity, and consciousness while preserving the body for labor" (Kelley 2017, 268). Directing his arguments toward Wolfe's *Traces of History* (2016), Kelley contends that this elision sets aside "the long and tragic history of extractive processes like rubber production and mining in the Congo" and "*eliminates the settler* from African history" (Kelley 2017, 269). Here we arrive at another set of critical discourses, commonly glossed as *racial capitalism*, which are equally relevant for confronting the history and present of capital's extractive operations.

Often in dialogue with Indigenous activism and Indigenous critical theory (see, e.g., Melamed 2015, 83–84), the notion of racial capitalism figures prominently in contemporary North American debates, and most prominently in recent developments of African American radical thinking. It provides a productive angle on diverse questions such as the capitalist exploitation of "diversity" in the United States (Leong 2013) or the history and workings of the "racial capitalocene" (Vergès 2017), just to give two examples. Originally forged by Cedric Robinson in his path-breaking *Black Marxism* (2000) to describe, analytically and politically, the "development, organization, and expansion of capitalist society" along "racial directions" and the emergence of the "subsequent structure as a historical agency" (Robinson 2000, 2), the concept of racial capitalism had long been in gestation in the black radical tradition—for instance, in the writings of the authors systematically discussed by Robinson (W. E. B. Du Bois, C. L. R. James, and Richard Wright) but also in the important book by Eric Williams,

Capitalism and Slavery (1944). Crucial to these theoretical efforts is the attempt to shed light on the pivotal role played by the Middle Passage and Atlantic slavery in prompting and shaping the historical development of capitalism. Far from being marginal and exceptional to this development, or simply relegated to its inception (as a cursory reading of Marx's analysis of the so-called primitive accumulation may suggest; see Singh 2017), the experience of the Atlantic slave trade points to structural features of capitalism that are systematically underestimated by the mainstream of Marxism. The emergence of a specific "Black Marxism" takes race and racism as privileged cues to complicate and supplement the traditional Marxist critique of capitalism.

Robinson joins and foreshadows a wide array of materialist interpretations of racism in the history of North America, including the work of such thinkers as Theodore Allen (1994, 1997) and David Roediger (1991), who have laid new ground for the investigation of the relation between race and class through a challenging and thoroughly materialist use of the notion of "whiteness"—contrary to the popular meaning of phrases such as "white privilege" today (see Roediger 2017, 20–21). While it is important to continue such historical investigations of racial capitalism, it is even more important to stress, following the lead of Angela Davis (2017, 248), that "more recent developments linked to global capitalism cannot be adequately comprehended if the racial dimension of capitalism is ignored." This is particularly the case when one emphasizes the extractive dimension of such recent developments. The point is not simply to highlight once again the relation among extraction, dispossession, and racism across the whole history of capitalism, and particularly in the global geographies of its colonial moments. There is also a need to remain attentive to the ways in which the reproduction and mutations of race and racism intermingle with contemporary operations of capital, both when extraction takes place literally (as in the instances we mentioned earlier when speaking about Indigenous people and their struggles) and when it seems to take a more ethereal shape (as in the case of finance that we analyze in more detail in chapter 4). In all these cases, capital is far from targeting its subjects as formally equal "citizens." Instead, capital produces and works across a multiplicity of differences, among which race and gender figure prominently as particularly violent criteria of domination, which also often provide the ground for forms of resistance and subjectivation that occupy center stage in the global archive of liberation struggles. It is particularly from the angle of the link between race, racism, and subjectivity (which also means between race and class) that the notion of racial capitalism is a source of inspiration for the work we pursue in this book.

In the wake of Black struggles against police violence in the United States, which we analyze in some detail in chapter 5, the work of Robinson has attracted the interest of several activists and scholars engaged in an attempt to forge and further develop a heterogeneous "matrix of oppositional strategies, enlivening the intersection between domestic antiracism and global anti-imperialist struggles" (Johnson and Lubin 2017, 9). We do not want to enter here the discussion of Robinson's relation to Marxism or his discussion of the relevance of cultural factors within and against the Eurocentric history of capital's expansion at the global level. What is more interesting to us is the fact that Robinson's analysis of forms of racialization in medieval Europe (through a method that often resonates with that of Foucault) allows him to sketch the ways in which a specific civilization ("Western civilization"), whose "social and ideological composition" had assumed its fundamental perspectives during feudalism, determined "in form" the development of capitalism (Robinson 2000, 24; see also Harney and Moten 2017). "The tendency of European civilization through capitalism," Robinson (2000, 26) writes, "was thus not to homogenize but to differentiate—to exaggerate regional, subcultural, and dialectical differences into 'racial' ones." We are convinced that this tendency has become even more pronounced with the global expansion of capitalism, which made the production of difference one of its defining features as we explain in the preceding section. Within this global expansion the very articulation of race and class that distinguishes racial capitalism took more and more heterogeneous forms, including ones very different from those that characterize the Atlantic space. Just think, to make a couple of important examples, of the intertwining of race and caste in the Indian subcontinent (Rao 2009), or of the emergence of a specific Han racism across the Chinese world (Chen 2010, 257–68). And this is even more true today, when capitalism seems able to reproduce itself well beyond the primacy of a distinct "Western civilization."

These patterns of differentiation are pronounced when one considers extractive operations in the expanded sense, particularly with regard to finance but also in the logistical workings of supply chains and production networks. There has been much discussion of how the subprime crisis in the United States reproduced the hierarchies of previous racial, sexist, and colonial discourses and practices. Paula Chakravartty and Denise Ferreira da Silva (2012, 372), for instance, point to "the temporal discursive continuities—between the 'welfare queen' and the prototypical subprime borrower as the 'single African American woman.'" Aloysha Goldstein (2014) argues that financialization and the subprime crisis extend and reproduce the territorial seizures of settler colonialism while also "foreclosing" the lineages of this historical injustice. Yet it is also necessary to recognize how such reproduction involves discontinuities with past histories of racial exploitation and colonial subjugation. Importantly, the subprime borrower does not find himself or herself in a system of social cooperation organized by capital, as was the case for the industrial worker or even the slave or indentured laborer on the modern plantation. Rather, he or she pays a monthly debt by entering into a series of relations of cooperation, dependence, and exploitation that are basically *indifferent* to finance capital. In this latter instance, capital *extracts* a quota of value produced within these relations. Extraction, in this expanded sense, names the forms and practices of valorization and exploitation that materialize when the operations of capital encounter patterns of human cooperation and sociality external to them.

Ten years after the subprime crisis, capital is finding new ways to prospect and incorporate subjects excluded from the space of financialization. Rob Aitken (2017) explains how big data techniques drawing on local public records, social networking patterns, academic records, mobile phone usage, non-financial payment histories, and even psychometric testing are used to construct credit ratings for the "unbanked," or those without credit records or files. Constituted by "contradictory processes marked by *both* absorption and expulsion," the unbanked are "rendered visible" as "a body that is legible to financial institutions" (Aitken 2017, 281, 286). Such scoring involves a "social sorting" that separates those who might be absorbed into formalized financial networks from bodies that are too risky to carry value. Moreover, these processes "racialize credit markets in novel ways," employing "data generated from racialized sources" alongside "data related to social media clusters or consumption patterns" that serve as "proxies for particular communities" (Aitken 2017, 289). Although employed across different parts of the world (Aitken mentions companies operating in Uganda, Poland, Russia, Turkey, Mexico, Malaysia, and South Africa), these techniques are not the only way in which financialization plays out unevenly across space.

In the Argentinean case, for instance, Verónica Gago (2015) argues that financialization is not just imposed from above by data mining or other techniques that seek to incorporate subaltern groups. It also expands through "popular economies" that bring together migrant populations, peripheral neighborhoods, and informally waged sectors. In China, by contrast, Giulia dal Maso (2015) shows how the state has played a central role in the orchestration of mass financialization, creating a class of disaggregated "scattered players," or *sanhu*, who make "irrational" and often imitative financial investments in a bid to manage the labor precarity and social uncertainty created by the dismantling of the *danwei* (the socialized work units of the communist era). In both cases, logics of extraction, gender subordination, and racialization work in concert, whether they involve capital's implication in the grassroots economic activities of predominantly migrant populations or the distorting effects of investments made by a heterogeneous mass of "players" whose activities are seen by financial experts and market regulators as ungovernable and disruptive. It is not by accident that, particularly in Latin America, the combined effects of financialization and extractive activities in prompting and sustaining violence against women are at the center of feminist thinking and struggles (see Colectivo Ni Una Menos 2017; Segato 2016).

Extraction writ large allows us to pursue an analysis of operations of capital in crucial domains, while it raises the question—that we begin to tackle in the next chapter—of the relations between these extractive operations and other capitalist operations, which appear to be shaped by other logics. In the case of activities driven by logistical processes of coordination, the organization of chains or networks of production, transport, and communication across an array of global differences is key. Anna Tsing (2012) insists on the fact that today, contrarily to the situation pertaining at the height of industrial capitalism, supply chain operations tend to exercise command over processes of production. This is an important circumstance, which is confirmed by studies of effects of the so-called retailing revolution in agriculture, where production chains, including canneries, have become *retailer-driven* (Perrotta 2017). The effects of this shift impinge on the condition of (often migrant) workers and lead to specific processes of zoning in many parts of the world, including Italy (Peano 2017). Examining the operations of inventory giants such as Walmart and Amazon, Tsing shows how they push costs back to producers, who are allowed to use "any methods they want" to keep prices at a minimum. Usually these methods involve "eliminating labor and environmental standards" (Tsing 2012, 521). But what is even more crucial for the practices of valorization pursued by companies such as Walmart and Amazon is the "logistical" capacity to synchronize diverse modes of production along the supply chain. That Tsing uses the term "piracy" (Tsing 2012, 520) to describe the relation between supply chain operations and their surrounding economic and social environments shows just how close her analysis is to the semantic field of extraction. Despite the constant refinement of techniques in supply chain management through code, data, algorithms, and other logistical technologies, their operations hinge on the mobilization of differences—of race, gender, nationality, citizenship status, and so on—that cannot be fully disciplined by internal governance standards. Consequently, the forms and practices of valorization and exploitation enabled by logistics are no less extractive than those applying to finance.

Recognizing how the extractive dynamics of contemporary capital operate over a wide array of economic practices and sectors (and not just those pertaining to the extraction of natural resources) offers a novel take on debates about neoliberalism, a concept that has guided so many critical analyses of globalization and economic crisis in the past twenty years that it verges on becoming an empty and absolutely generic term. Many critical discussions of neoliberalism point to the hegemonic circulation of economic doctrines or techniques of governance without really taking stock of the complex disjunctions of space and time that accompany the patterns of extraction and racialization we highlight. Even analyses strongly informed by the history of economic and political thought, such as those offered by Philip Mirowski (2013) and Pierre Dardot and Christian Laval (2014), and those strongly influenced by Michel Foucault's (2008) lectures on biopolitics, such as Wendy Brown's *Undoing the Demos* (2015), tend to base their arguments on an engagement with exclusively North Atlantic circuits of intellectual and institutional influence (from the Vienna School and the German Ordoliberals to the Chicago School, the International Monetary Fund [IMF], and Reaganomics). This is despite the fact that Wilhelm Röpke, one of the principal German Ordoliberals whose work Dardot and Laval examine, was a supporter of South African apartheid who led an international front against the "globalization of Keynesian policies of full employment and state-subsidized industrialization in the 'Bandung Era' of decolonization and national development" (Slobodian 2014, 64; see also Slobodian 2018). Authors such as Pierre Bourdieu (1998), David Harvey (2005), and Naomi Klein (2007) tell the story of neoliberal doctrines and policies developed in the North Atlantic being rolled out globally via the IMF and World Bank, structural adjustment programs, and the Washington Consensus. We lack a history of neoliberalism that is attentive both to its regional and spatial variegation and to the ways in which it has scrambled and exploded the logics of global space and time.

Fortunately, many authors have produced important works that critically analyze the contours of neoliberalism in different global and national environments. One thinks of the analyses of neoliberalism in China offered by Wang Hui (2003, 2009). Aihwa Ong's important theoretical and empirical contribution in *Neoliberalism as Exception* (2006) is largely based on ethnographic research in Southeast Asia. Studies by James Ferguson (2006) and Brenda Chalfin (2010) have complicated our understanding of neoliberalism by exploring its workings in "extraction enclaves" and along frontiers in Africa. Raewyn Connell and Nour Dados (2014, 132) emphasize "the social experience and intellectual production of the global South," examining the role of trade, agriculture, and other extractive industries in producing "a more diversified and chaotic economic process" than accounts based on narratives of neoliberal policy transfer from the North suggest (Connell and Dados 2014, 126). The list could go on. But the point is not to catalogue the production of critical works that confront the multiplication of forms and practices of neoliberalism beyond the Euro-Atlantic world. Rather, we suggest that an expanded concept of extraction can help us track the logics that animate this multiplication and the heterogenization of space and time implicit in it. In particular, an approach that takes seriously the extractive workings of contemporary processes of valorization and exploitation can shed light on the geographical variegation and temporal complexity that characterizes current capitalist crisis and transition.

The challenge is to cross the insights produced by critical geographers such as Jamie Peck—who seeks to "specify the *patterning* of contingencies across cases" of "neoliberalization" (Peck 2013, 143)—with an account of the extractive operations of contemporary capital that is attentive to the dynamics of racialization and disrupted continuities with colonialism that we highlight. Our approach is not to privilege examples from the global South over those from the North or to deliberately seek out instances of racism or Indigenous dispossession to underscore at every analytical turn. We are cautious about affirming the heuristic split between the global North and South, preferring to emphasize patterns of geographical disruption that unsettle this divide. We are also skeptical regarding the possibility for an "atrocity exhibition" that catalogues and denounces ongoing racialization to provide an analytical or organizational matrix adequate to the political needs of movements that seek to create a world that is more just and free. To be sure, we are no less indignant than the next decolonial or standpoint theorist, but we do not think that indignation in separation from a sustained analysis of the practices of dominance and oppression that continue to operate in this world—and particularly those enabled by the operations of capital—is sufficient to confront the situation at hand. With these considerations in mind, we continue our analysis of the politics of capitalist crisis and transition, always keeping in mind the urgencies of racism and colonialism, while often highlighting dynamics of exploitation and extraction that operate along different if related lines.

The Politics of Crisis and Transition

January 7, 2016, was the shortest trading day ever on the Shanghai stock exchange. Twelve minutes after the opening bell, the market had plunged by 7 percent, and a "circuit breaker" was activated for fifteen minutes. When trading reopened, values plunged a further 2 percent within a minute, and the circuit breaker closed the market for the day. Instituted by the China Securities Regulatory Commission (CSRC), a body directly administered by the State Council—the highest state body in the land—this automated market device had been introduced just four days earlier. On January 4, it had been activated twice: first, shortly after the opening of afternoon trading, then again when the 7 percent limit was reached only six minutes after transactions resumed. Otherwise known as a trading curb, the circuit breaker is a regulatory device that halts trading when losses reach a threshold. In this case, the mechanism exhibited a "magnet effect," meaning that prices gravitated toward the level at which the threshold had been set (Hao 2016). Investors did not behave like their counterparts in the New York Stock Exchange, which also has an automated circuit breaker, but massively divested once the curb had been lifted. Just four days after the introduction of the circuit breaker, the CSRC abandoned this mechanism.

What does this extreme volatility—not only of the financial market but also of the measures that are meant to regulate it—tell us about the relation of market to state in the turmoil of global crisis? It is no secret that China's stock exchange is heavily shaped by the presence of both state institutions and myriad individual investors, reversing the familiar narrative by which financialization implies a process of state withdrawal (Dal Maso 2015). The Chinese financial crashes of 2015–16 had ripples around the world and were responses to a market characterized by debt-funded trades and risky short-selling plays. The state's regulatory arm became evident not only through the automation of the circuit breaker but also through measures such as the limitation of short selling, a halt on initial public offerings, and even the supply of central bank-backed cash to brokers. Indeed, one of the hallmarks of state management of economic crisis over the past decade has been the sudden release of funds into the system—evident also in the US bailouts. Just as many states were declaring their retreat from big government, and the ethos of taxing and spending less had spread across diverse political systems, the crisis triggered a reaction that exhibited a wealth of monetary reserves. Bailouts and stimulus payments appeared as if from nowhere.

These regulatory and fiscal measures open up a different angle on the question of neoliberalism that we discussed earlier. There is no shortage of arguments that position neoliberalism as a form of laissez-faire market fundamentalism radically opposed to all state intervention. It is not difficult to understand why such a claim proliferates amid the rollbacks of health, education, and welfare provisions that have been characteristic policy maneuvers in many states over the past three decades. However, this view of neoliberalism discounts the role of state governance in producing, often forcefully, the conditions for market competition and the entrepreneurial subject who supposedly thrives in these circumstances. Recognizing the role of the state in the production of such conditions, as well as in the management of the challenges that become manifest when these conditions are destabilized, does not mean ignoring the wider array of government entities and actors involved in this process. However, the testing of government capacities within the crisis of the past decade has at once made states prominent again and revealed the limits of state actions and interventions as a means of restarting growth in a global situation characterized by the intermeshing and interdependence of economic systems. The state raises its hand as a protagonist of crisis management just as the turmoil and volatility of markets, trade, and debt seem to exceed its grip. While this is apparent in the case of states that have been hit particularly hard by the crisis in the south of Europe—most notably, Greece—it is no less true for states that have faced the crisis under very different conditions, as the example of the circuit breaker in the Shanghai market shows.

Quantitative easing, investments in infrastructure, "helicopter money," rescue packages, tax subsidies, negative interest rates—these are just some of the measures that states have experimented with across the variable geography of the global crisis. Despite the inventiveness of some of these techniques, none has delivered a perspective of stable recovery. The prospect of an exit from the crisis seems ever more remote as its effects continue to circulate in an uneven and syncopated manner. At the same time, the infectious rhetoric of crisis spreads from the economic sphere to other areas of human and social concern. All of a sudden we have an environmental crisis, a migration crisis, and multiple crises of social and demographic sustainability. Each of these predicaments has its own complex genealogy and dynamics, but their concatenation and articulation present a novel scenario in which the increasing governmental desire for an exit from these crises makes such a trajectory seem teasingly unattainable. Under these conditions, relations among states and nations change yet again, taking on articulations that are significantly different from the ones that emerged against the background of the globalizing tendencies of the 1990s. While critical debates of that time emphasized phenomena such as diaspora, mobile "ethnoscapes," and transnational flows to shed light on a growing disjunction between state and nation, the horizon of crisis complicates these vistas. This is not to point to a new convergence of state and nation. To the contrary, these processes continue to challenge the stability of both nations and states, altering the composition of the former and limiting the capabilities of the latter. The political fantasy of a full, or fuller, re-conjunction of state and nation is one symptom of such alteration and limitation. Nevertheless, this fantasy has powerful effects in many parts of the world, spurring imperial dreams, nationalist rhetoric and policies, secessionist projects, and "populist" politics.

Are these dreams, rhetoric, and politics merely compensatory offerings in the face of an entrenched crisis? We think the situation is more complex. These tendencies definitely point to a conjuncture in which the continuity of neoliberalism is matched by the exhaustion of its promises of growth and wealth. "Secular stagnation," the phrase popularized by Lawrence Summers (2014, 2016) to describe a long-term period of negligible or slow economic growth, is a hypothesis seriously discussed by economists these days. While states struggle to cope with this predicament, nations absorb it and work with it. In the face of crisis, national imagination and belonging are tested and troubled by any number of phantoms, from the figure of the foreigner to the cosmopolitan urbanite, from the unpredictability of finance to the steady march of global warming. This provides fertile ground for nationalism and its politics of anxiety and fear, as well as for correlate processes of social division and hierarchization. Such nationalism entrenches rather than alleviates crisis. This is so, first, because contemporary manifestations of nationalism, far from being the opposite of neoliberalism, are particularly adept at negotiating with and accommodating themselves to neoliberal conditions and the global processes associated with them. Various degrees of combination between nationalism and neoliberalism shape the conjuncture. Whether this combination pivots more around economic logics (nurturing protectionist or mercantilist policies), religious identifications, civilizational convictions, or other sources of legitimization, the nation multiplies the heterogeneity that characterizes neoliberalism at the same time that it provides a way to make sense of different neoliberal trajectories and positions within them. From India to Japan, Germany to Russia, Turkey to China, the Philippines to the United States, there are many examples of this trend, which would deserve careful investigation to flesh out the peculiarities of each case.

While these unstable dynamics of nationalism and neoliberalism are likely to follow different and, to a certain extent, unpredictable paths, they are clearly contributing to the remaking of world order and disorder. The rebalancing of power among global regions, the forging of new trade corridors, the proliferation of borders and migratory movements, competition and conflicts among emerging regional powers—these are all defining features of the geopolitical and geo-economic moment. New accords and conflicts are part of this scenario. In a landscape crisscrossed both by vectors of homogenization and processes of fragmentation, war continues to be a material reality and threat in many parts of the world. Intermingling with the mutations of terrorism and civil war, military operations and violence shape the turmoil of the Middle East, reaching into sub-Saharan Africa, as well as into Iraq and Afghanistan. Flashpoints such as the South China Sea introduce new specters of territorialism while conflicts such as the one in Kashmir entrench established geopolitical disputes. Movements of refugees from war-torn areas such as Syria, for instance, prompt the emergence of humanitarian interventions and their intermingling with military operations and rationalities. The paradigm of "just war" has firmly returned to the global scene, although it tends to be invoked by actors with conflicting interests. Moreover, deep transformations of warfare are connected with the increasing relevance of nonmilitary forms of war, such as financial destabilization, information breaches, and the deprivation of infrastructure in occupied territories. These developments complicate the articulation of nationalism to neoliberalism while raising the political stakes and dangers of this combination. Radical politics cannot afford to ignore these stakes and dangers.

To fully understand the nexus of nationalism and neoliberalism, we have to go a step further and focus, in both conceptual and empirical terms, on the relationship of capital to politics. This means taking stock of how this relationship has pivoted around the form of the modern state. It also means paying attention to the production of political and legal spaces across diverse geographical scales, which has been part of processes of colonial imperial expansion since the inception of modern capitalism. In chapter 3, we explore these processes in detail, framing and expanding a discussion of the Marxist problematic of state and capital within an analysis that is attentive to the fractured geographies and landscapes of colonial and postcolonial formations of power, law, and institutional arrangements. We are not the first to note the uncanny continuities between colonial concessions and contemporary economic zones, or between the operations of the chartered company and the power of transnational corporations. These parallels, for instance, did not escape for the sharp critical gaze of Gayatri Spivak. In *A Critique of Postcolonial Reason* (1999, 220), she formulates the "easy" surmise that the "East India Company prefigured the shifting relationship between state-formation and economic crisis management within which we live today." However, we seek to provide an analysis that explains such continuities within a frame that emphasizes how the forging and unfolding of the world market have implications that extend beyond the reach of established theories of imperialism. While we are well aware of the relevance of the state in the history of capitalism, our analysis highlights the limits of the state's capacity to fully contain and articulate the relationship between capital and politics, not just in the contemporary era, but also in the period of the state's supposed heyday. Both in the social relations that constitute capital and in capital's aggregate operations, the inability of the state to fully control or regulate the nexus of capital and politics becomes evident, providing an analytical thread that allows us not only to trace the variegated and uneven expansion of capital's frontiers but also to rethink the very notion of politics. The acknowledgment of political moments inherent to the operations of capital provides a basis both for an analysis of how capital crosses existing political forms and for the forging of a politics adequate to negotiate the challenges of opening a path beyond capital's rule.

The role of states within the prolongation and variegated dynamics of capitalist crisis projects both their persisting presence within processes of globalization and the limits that constrain their actions. Clearly, the political moments inherent to the operations of capital—particularly apparent in the domains of extraction, logistics, and finance we analyze in this book—are among the main factors that constrain the action of states in what appears an extended and never accomplished transition. An investigation of these constraints is important because states continue to attract the investment of desires and expectations of emancipation and transformation. Such investment is evident both looking at critical debates on politics and capitalism and considering developments such as the emergence of "progressive" governments in Latin America over the past decade. The current crisis and turmoil of many of these governments should make us cautious regarding the prospects of a politics of social transformation centered on the state (see Gago and Mezzadra 2017b; Gago and Sztulwark 2016). For us, making this point is a matter of political realism, which does not mean that we dismiss the possibility that the state itself can play a role within such politics. But to understand how such a politics might emerge, as well as the conditions under which it might become effective, we have to focus on the contemporary realities of statehood. Many thinkers have shown how these realities have shifted with the transformations of capitalism since the 1970s (see, e.g., Brenner 2004; Hardt and Negri 2000; Sassen 2006). The exigencies of the crisis point to the need to continue and update this analysis. Four trajectories of investigation suggest themselves as salient in this regard.

The first concerns what we have called the aggregate operations of capital and the ways in which they traverse states; negotiate policies both within and among states; and establish entities that increasingly dictate the terms on which states act, particularly in the economic sphere. The second involves the shifting formations of territory, power, and law that we discussed earlier in the chapter and that destabilize the notion of territoriality characteristic of the modern state. The third regards the growing tensions between the legitimization of the state through a persistent reference to the "nation" and processes that continually erode the unity and transformation of the composition of the "people"—particularly due to movements of migration, communication technology, and the deepening of social polarizations. The fourth pivots around various governmental challenges to and gaps within the institutional unity of the state, whether they stem from the involvement of non-state actors in the machinery of governance or from the unbalancing of powers among different branches of the state, which are increasingly shaped by different rationalities, logics, and pressures. Taken together, these four trajectories enable not only an analysis that points to transformations in the political form of the state but also a tracing of what states are actually doing. At the crossing point of these transformations and processes, the limits and excesses that characterize the contemporary state's interaction with capital become apparent.

This book trains its analysis at this crossing point within a wider investigation of the shifting relations between capital and politics in the contemporary conjuncture of crisis, transition, and struggle. Although we more fully develop the concept of operations in the next chapter, it should already be possible to see how this notion provides a means for us to work through these shifting relations. Whether the reference is to the operative dimensions of human activity, the automated execution of algorithms and other machinic routines, or institutional procedures, the significance of operations is plain to see but often under-analyzed in discussions of global capitalism and its political contestations. Our specific use of the notion of *operations of capital* aims to open up a conceptual and analytical space within which it becomes possible both to shed light on the ways in which capital emerges as a political actor and to investigate its articulation to and frictions with a diverse array of institutions and political forms. This approach implies a radical challenge to the established borders of politics because it involves an emphasis on political processes and conflicts that are played out in domains that are usually considered nonpolitical and enables an analysis of the persisting roles of the state while accounting for its displacement from the center of the political scene. The notion of operations, once applied to the analysis of capital, provides a new angle from which to broach vexed questions regarding the unity of capital, the relations among its constitutive "fractions," and the antagonistic nature of the social relation that composes it. It is to these questions that we now turn.

Operations of Capital

The Unity of Capital

Most accounts of the origins of the current crisis of capitalism point to a crucial point of turmoil and transition in the 1970s. Often, as the story runs, the oil crisis and the fall of the Bretton Woods system based on the convertibility of the US dollar into gold are the pivotal moments. We do not want to underestimate the importance of these events, which unleash a sense of vertigo in which old certainties about historical progress and the centrality of a US-defined West seem to crumble. Although prominent in the arguments of Anglo-American critics such as David Harvey (1989) and Fredric Jameson (1991), this emphasis on uncertainty and crisis finds resonances in European debates on late capitalism, state, and democracy, which tended to stress the role of governments in managing the postwar period of stable growth. Writing about the contribution of German thinkers such as Jürgen Habermas and Claus Offe, Wolfgang Streeck (2014) notes that these debates represented an early attempt to grasp the deep transformations and dislocations that inaugurated a new era in the history of capitalism. But Streeck adds further detail to his account that is relevant for our consideration of the operations of capital. Such arguments, he claims, were characterized by a kind of overestimation of the range of action of state policies and planning in steering the development of capitalism. The resulting emphasis on the "legitimation crisis" led to systematic underestimation of the role of capital "as a political actor and a strategic social force" (Streeck 2014, 32). This role became clear in what Streeck terms a "revolt" of capital against the "postwar mixed economy" in the West (32), which became the leading thread of the neoliberal reorganization of capitalism in the decades to come.

In this chapter, we critically interrogate the multiple ways in which capital not only disseminates specific forms of power in the social fabric but also emerges as a crucial political actor. We do not think, as do some versions of contemporary network and assemblage theory, that speaking of capital in this sense (or, indeed, employing the very word "capital" as an analytical category) necessarily leads to essentializing it as a kind of "Unspecified Enemy" (Easterling 2014, 212) that forecloses the multiplicity of techniques of power and forms of resistance that constitute the social. To put our argument simply, the endless accumulation of capital constitutes the crucial juncture and principle of articulation through which this multiplicity of techniques and forms is organized in the contemporary world. The resulting constraints for social action and cooperation, the specific forms of violence, domination, and exploitation connected to the pervasive spread of the logics of endless accumulation of capital, require specific conceptual and analytical tools to be accounted for critically. But how does capital act as a mode of power so dispersed and distributed across the social body? How does this action connect to the deployment of specific forms of social power? And even more radically, how does capital constitute itself as a unitary actor, given its capacity to disperse, multiply, and, as we saw in the previous chapter, proliferate and grapple with difference? To tackle these questions, we start with a general discussion of the unity of capital, then introduce the notion of operations as a means to revisit questions about the relations between capital and capitalism, abstraction and materiality, and capital and politics.

There are many capitalists in the world. They meet regularly, and they form powerful associations that act at the national, as well as at the transnational and global, level. But you will never meet *monsieur le Capital*. Cinema has often dealt with this gap. Hollywood films on finance, from Oliver Stone's *Wall Street* (1987) to Martin Scorsese's *The Wolf of Wall Street* (2013), have provided us with powerful instantiations of the personification of greed that rules financial markets, although this topic is not at all new in the history of cinema, as the memorable *Greed* of Erich von Stroheim (1925) reminds us. Characters such as Gordon Gekko, Bud Fox, and Jordan Belfort definitely act, and their action contributes to the workings of capitalism and to the deployment and entrenchment of its specific forms of social power. But clearly they are also acted on by the logics of a system that they cannot completely control—logics that might better be registered, to take another recent cinematic example, by the surfacing of a crocodile in the swimming pool of a Florida housing estate that is nearly abandoned as a result of the subprime crisis in *The Big Short* (2015). Or take one of the many films on the social consequences of the crisis of capitalism that came out in recent years—for instance, the Dardenne brothers' *Two Days, One Night* (2014). The action of capital is clearly at stake in the film. Far from being exhaustively represented by one character—for instance, by the manager or by the foreman of the small solar panel factory where Sandra, the protagonist, works—the action circulates around the plot, splitting the personality of her co-workers and crystallizing in Sandra's deep depression. Capital presents itself as always in excess over the action of specific capitalist actors, its power is rooted in abstraction and characterized by a profound elusiveness.

The great Soviet director Sergei Eisenstein, who in the 1920s undertook the never accomplished project of filming Marx's *Capital*, was fully aware of this predicament and proposed to develop his narrative precisely by working the gap between abstraction and materiality that characterizes capital (see Jameson 2009; Toscano and Kinkle 2015, 81–82). "The maximum abstractness of an expanding idea," he entered into his notebook on April 6, 1928, "appears particularly bold when presented as an offshoot from extreme concreteness—the banality of life" (Eisenstein 1976, 15). Not surprisingly, he found in James Joyce's *Ulysses* a source of inspiration for the "associative unfolding" through which alone he thought the montage of a representation of capital would be possible (22). "The ideology of the unequivocal frame," he added, "must be thoroughly reconsidered" (24). In order to represent capital, the linearity of the narrative must be continuously interrupted, "the continuity of a series should by no means be 'sequential' as in a plot—unfolding in a logically progressive manner, etc." (22). Take the scene, imagined by Eisenstein, in which a German worker's wife cooks soup for her returning husband. The "associative unfolding" moves from the pepper, which she uses to season the food: "pepper. Cayenne. Devil's Island. Dreyfus. French Chauvinism. *Figaro* in Krupp's hands. War. Ships sunk in the port" (17). Needless to say, other associations would be possible, producing alternative although equally compelling frames for the representation of the unity of capital and of what we can call, with Marx, its "phantom-like objectivity" (Marx 1977, 128). Again, there is always a moment of excess over representation when we deal with the unity of capital, which cannot be easily grasped with models of linear causality that pretend to trace visible effects to visible causes. Gaps, ruptures, discontinuities are constitutive of capital once we try to think of it as a unity.

Part of the enigma of capital depends on the fact that it "is not a thing but a process in which money is perpetually sent in search for more money. Capitalists—those who set this process in motion—take on very different personae," ranging from merchant, industrial, and finance capitalists to landlords and a huge variety of rentiers (Harvey 2011, 40). But this picture of capital as a process, although descriptively compelling and useful, can be only a starting point for an investigation that aims at highlighting, on the one hand, the ways in which the circulation of money becomes the circulation of power, and on the other hand, the moments of friction, violence, racism, and resistance that crisscross this process. Marx himself, as we recalled in chapter 1, was decidedly convinced that capital "is not a thing." While David Ricardo had basically defined capital as the means of production, even in their simplest historical forms, Marx had a different aim in mind. What interested him was not a merely formal definition of capital. He sought instead to grasp the specific historical novelty of capital as a power capable of dominating the whole social fabric in the capitalist mode of production. Following the thread of his analysis of the value form and its metamorphosis, Marx stressed that this can happen only when the "possessor of money" finds on the market "a commodity whose use-value possesses the peculiar property of being a source of value" (Marx 1977, 240). We know the name of this commodity: labor power. Only the encounter between the possessor of money (the potential capitalist) and the possessor of labor power (the potential worker) transforms the means of production held by the former into capital. From this point of view, Marx (1977, 932) contended that "capital is not a thing, but a social relation between persons which is mediated through things."

The very definition of "capital" provided by Marx opens it onto a social relation in which power is always at stake (e.g., in shaping the conditions of the encounter between the possessor of money and the possessor of labor power, as well as in the command of the former over the latter in the production process). This is a crucial point, even beyond the specific form of this relation analyzed by Marx in the chapter of *Capital*, volume 1, titled "The Sale and Purchase of Labor Power," which is dedicated to the workings of the "free" wage labor contract. It is important to realize that, while capital is identified with a social relation, it represents for Marx one of the poles of this very relation. First, capital represents the individual capitalist, the "personification" of the "objective conditions" of labor opposed to the worker as an alien will (Marx 1973, 452). But it also registers a whole set of conditions (e.g., legal and political arrangements) without which the individual capitalist could not exist and the capitalist mode of production could not reproduce itself. While the establishment and defense of these conditions can present themselves as a kind of general (class) interest for all individual capitalists, different branches of capital and different capitalist actors frequently diverge in their interests and needs, and the representation of a general capitalist interest therefore becomes a field of struggle and negotiation. This conflict and divergence becomes evident in Marx's analysis of the regulation of the working day, again in volume 1 of *Capital* (Marx 1977, 340–416).

There is something more to be noted here. If we look at capital from the point of view of its circulation process and pay particular attention to the production process of capital as a whole, as Marx does in the manuscripts of volumes 2 and 3 of *Capital*, the unity of capital as one of the poles of the social relation that constitutes it becomes both more compelling and more problematic. Marx elaborates here on such concepts as *Gesamtkapital* and *gesellschaftliches Gesamtkapital*, which are usually translated as "total capital" and "social total capital." To stress the dynamic, unstable, and open character of the composition of parts that gives rise to *Gesamtkapital*, we prefer to translate the term as "aggregate capital," a phrase that is also used occasionally in English translations of Marxist works. Marx points to the crystallization of a logic of movement of capital that can (and often does) revolve against individual capitals (and, of course, against their personifications as individual capitalists). It is certainly possible to view each particular capital as "a fragment of the aggregate capital and each capitalist in fact as a shareholder in the whole social enterprise, partaking in the overall profit in proportion to the size of his share of capital" (Marx 1981, 312). But we should recall, as Marx ironically notes in writing about the "collective capitalist" in *Capital*, volume 2, that "this joint-stock company has in common with many other joint-stock companies that everyone knows what they put into it, but *not* what they will get out of it" (Marx 1978, 509). Even more important is that the speeding up of capital's turnover and the widening of the scale of its reproduction nurture the process of "autonomization of value." Marx (1978, 185) writes, "The more acute and frequent these revolutions in value become, the more the movement of the independent value, acting with the force of an elemental natural process, prevails over the foresight and calculation of the individual capitalist, the more the course of normal production is subject to abnormal speculation, and the greater becomes the danger to the existence of the individual capitals."

Although it was not fully developed by Marx, the concept of aggregate capital played an important role in early twentieth-century Marxist debates. One can even say that it haunted the contemporary development of bourgeois social sciences. In 1913, Rosa Luxemburg wrote in the first chapter of *Accumulation of Capital* that Marx had "made a contribution of lasting service to the theory of economics when he drew attention to the problem of the reproduction of the social aggregate capital (*gesellschaftliches Gesamtkapital*)" (Luxemburg [1913] 2003, 3). The end of laissez-faire capitalism and the incipient decline of British hegemony at the world scale signaled the need to investigate the changing shape of capitalism. Within this investigation, the figure of the individual capitalist was displaced by an emerging focus on processes of organization of what Werner Sombart and Max Weber termed "high capitalism" or "late capitalism." The formation of cartels, trusts, and monopolies; the transformations of the firm and of the relation between property and management against the background of the rise of the joint-stock company; new relations between capital and state; the heyday of imperialism; and dramatic labor struggles and the rise of the unions are all part of this new constellation, which began to emerge at the end of the nineteenth century, particularly in Germany and the United States.

The analysis of these and other forms of restriction of free competition was a crucial aspect of such important Marxist interventions as Rudolf Hilferding's *Finance Capital* (1910) and Vladimir Lenin's *Imperialism* (1917). "The old capitalism, the capitalism of free competition with its indispensable regulator, the Stock Exchange, is passing away," wrote Lenin ([1917] 1975, 52). "A new capitalism has come to take its place, bearing obvious features of something transient, a mixture of free competition and monopoly. The question naturally arises: *into what* is this new capitalism 'developing'?" "Organized capitalism" and "state monopoly capitalism," the two labels coined by Lenin and Hilferding, respectively, to answer this question ended up becoming two opposed slogans in the violent clash that pitted communists against social democrats after the division of the labor movement in the 1920s (see Altvater 1980; Kocka 1974; Puhle 1984). The political consequences drawn from the analysis, particularly the evaluation of the chances of a steady movement toward socialism from within capitalism, were indeed opposed. But from the angle provided by the concept of aggregate capital, Hilferding and Lenin converged on a number of important points.

First, they both stressed that, as Lenin put it, the immediate result of the emerging limits to free competition was an "immense progress in the socialization of production": "In particular, the process of technical invention and improvement becomes socialized" (Lenin [1917] 1975, 40). The resulting increase in the productivity of labor, in Hilferding's ([1910] 2006, 183) analysis, had led to a dramatic transformation of the "organic composition of capital," which means the relation between constant and variable capital. This, for him, was one of the main reasons that "present-day industry is carried on with an amount of capital far exceeding that which is owned by the industrial capitalists." The resulting fusion of "bank capital" and "industrial capital" into the emerging formation of "finance capital" (Hilferding [1910] 2006, 224–25) and the intensification of its functions of abstraction, centralization, and equalization signaled a major shift in the composition and in the very unitary logics of aggregate capital.

Under these conditions, the state was bound to play completely different, active and proactive roles with respect to the classical liberal age of capitalism. Friedrich Engels's definition of the state in the *Anti-Dühring* as the "ideal collective capitalist" nicely anticipates the important roles played by the state in the twentieth century in the representation of aggregate capital and in the mediation of the clashes and frictions among the fractions that constitute it (Engels [1878] 1975, 260). This development was, of course, far from linear: the ideal was always remote from the reality. Nevertheless, it provided a blueprint for the formation of compelling national frames for the representation of aggregate capital within a shifting world order and a changing international division of labor. During World War I, this tendency took a particularly harsh shape in the light of a process of "state penetration of the economy" that appeared to an acute observer such as the German social scientist Emil Lederer (1918–19, 18) to run parallel to a "capitalist penetration of the state." Against the background of the existential challenge raised by the success of the Russian Revolution, the dramatic transformations of capitalism connected with the ascent of mass production laid the basis for the crisis of 1929 and for the Great Depression that followed. Both in forms of European fascism and the democratic experiment of the New Deal, although in very different ways, the relation between state and capital became the crucial axis along which even the concept of the plan, closely associated with socialism, began to be considered compatible with capitalism.

From the point of view of the analysis we are pursuing here, the importance of John Maynard Keynes lies in his attempt to reformulate the theory of the state to come to grips with the two aspects of the definition of capital we highlighted in Marx (Negri, in Hardt and Negri 1994, chap. 2). On the one hand, Keynes's theory of effective demand—the "aggregate income (or proceeds) which the entrepreneurs expect to receive, inclusive of the incomes which they will hand on to the other factors of production, from the amount of current employment which they decide to give" (Keynes [1916] 2013, 55)—lays the basis for state intervention in the field of the reproduction of labor power, which means, first of all, the reproduction of the industrial working class. On the other hand, the state, far from being limited to "a merely monetary policy directed towards influencing the rate of interest," emerges as a power capable of synchronizing "the fluctuations in the market estimation of the marginal efficiency of different types of capital," because it "is in a position to calculate the marginal efficiency of capital-goods on long views and on the basis of the general social advantage" (Keynes [1916] 2013, 164). The state, which Keynes expects to take "an ever greater responsibility for directly organizing investment" (Keynes [1916] 2013, 164), is therefore bound to represent the unity of "social aggregate capital" at the national level, occasionally acting against the interest of particular capitalists.

Keynes's theory foreshadowed a significant shift in the organization of capitalism. This shift was described, for instance, by the Italian Marxist Raniero Panzieri in the early 1960s as the emergence of a "collective capitalism" in which "the main mode of working" is no longer "the immediate search for the maximum profit" but, rather, "the guarantee of the continuous growth, in time, of the mass of profit" (Panzieri 1973, 280). After World War II, in the framework of the Bretton Woods Agreement, this new capitalism became dominant in the West and led to structural transformations in the very form and organization of the state. While the representation of social aggregate capital at the national level led to the establishment of specific forms of planning, which blurred the boundary between factory and society, the state's role in the reproduction of labor power was performed within multiple varieties of welfare structures. In very general terms, this was the point of departure for the critical debates on late capitalism and the state that we mentioned at the beginning of this section—as well as, for instance, for the elaboration of the influential concept of "democratic corporatism" by Philippe C. Schmitter (1974). From our point of view, it is important to note that this moment in the history of capitalism had its important counterpart outside the West in theories and political practices of "development" (Sanyal 2007). We will come back to the concept of "developmental state" in the next chapter. But we can anticipate here that the project of development was, in many parts of the so-called Third World, interpreted as a means of consolidating a national representation of capital and of its mediation with a working class emerging from the process of industrialization.

The crisis of these complex arrangements of state and capital had multiple roots. Michael Kalecki anticipated in 1943 that full employment, as a crucial policy goal, would become a key point of contention in Keynesian economics. Discussing the reasons for the opposition of "business leaders" to "the policy of creating employment by government spending," he focused particularly on the challenges to "discipline in the factories" and the "political stability" related to the growth of "the self-assurance and class-consciousness of the working class" in a regime of full employment (Kalecki 1943, 326; see also Streeck 2014). The dramatic rise of workers' struggles in Western countries in the 1960s would confirm this forecast, challenging the very continuity of the growth of the "mass of profit," to pick up again on Panzieri's words. Beyond the interest of individual capitalists, the very stability of the reproduction of social aggregate capital at the national level was called into question. At the same time, anti-colonial and anti-imperialist struggles were threatening to disrupt the complex fabric of relations between center and periphery that built the real script of development, as stressed, for instance, by dependency theorists in Latin America beginning in the 1960s.

The representation of social aggregate capital at the national level by the state therefore became a limit to the further development of capitalism. New monetary and financial arrangements, a new geography of production, as well as the emergence of new logistical devices for the establishment, stretching, and governance of supply chains, signaled that, as Marx had emphatically contended, the spatial horizon of social aggregate capital is the world market. This does not mean that we are confronted with the emergence of a global capital, with unified institutions and decision-making bodies. Aggregate capital is not a totality, although capital is characterized by totalizing tendencies. Even regarding individual capitals as fractions of aggregate capital (Marx 1978, 468) does not mean that these fractions necessarily coincide with the capital owned by individual capitalists. Emerging crystallizations of capitalist interests in the form of fractions of capital are not necessarily limited to specific sectors of economic activity, and even in this case, their unity is always unstable and challenged by underlying divergences and clashes of interest (Sablowski 2008). Once understood in this way, the concept of fractions of capital reminds us that aggregate capital can never be reduced to the mere algebraic sum of its constitutive fractions. Aggregate capital today cannot be analyzed without taking into account the global dimension of the representation of its logics, of its operative principles, and of its frame. There is also a need to stress what can be called its mixed constitution. This is particularly important if we want to understand how capital emerges as a political actor and deploys a specific form of social power. At stake here is the question of the relation between capital and the political beyond the historical moment of the nationalization of capital and of the international world.

Operations of Capital

By contending that aggregate capital is not a totality, as should be clear by now, we do not intend to deny that capitalism is characterized by systemic and unitary logics, which manifest themselves in many different ways in the contemporary world. Nor do we want to rehearse the "war on totality" waged some decades ago by Jean-François Lyotard (1984, 82). We simply ask whether "the point of view of totality," celebrated in Georg Lukács's *History and Class Consciousness* as "the bearer of the principle of revolution in science" (Lukács [1923] 1971, 27), is really able to grasp those very systemic and unitary logics or whether it risks obscuring some of their crucial distinctive features. As we wrote earlier, we fully acknowledge the moment of unity that pertains to the concept and logic of capital, as well as the resulting limits and determinations for any domain of activity and experience in a capitalist society. We are also fully aware of the peculiarity of the dialectical concept of totality, as well as of the sophisticated elaborations surrounding it in the works of such powerful thinkers as, say, Theodor Adorno, Jean-Paul Sartre, and Fredric Jameson. "A social theory of capitalism as a totality," write Alberto Toscano and Jeff Kinkle (2015, 55), takes "the incoherence, the trouble in its object" as a crucial point of departure.

Nevertheless, we are convinced that precisely to grasp this incoherence and trouble the dialectical language of totality can be misleading. One of the reasons for this is its link with a set of other notions, ranging from reification and commodification to totally administered society, which haunted the discussion of the concept of totality in Marxism and critical theory in the twentieth century. The image of capitalism as a full-fledged and accomplished totality has therefore ended up concealing and, in a way, freezing the dialectical movement that was originally constitutive of the concept. It has also obscured the gaps, tensions, and aleatory aspects that crisscross capital both from the point of view of the social relation that constitutes it and, as we saw in the previous section, from the point of view of the production and representation of the unity of aggregate capital. To highlight these gaps and tensions, we explore the productivity of a different conceptual language that takes the notion of operations of capital as one of its cornerstones. Here we insist on the plural—operations—to mark the heterogeneity that composes capital as a difference machine and lies at the heart of the historical and conceptual variability of capitalism. Crucial to our attempt is the idea that capital is characterized by totalizing tendencies, by a drive to reorganize the whole social fabric according to the logics and imperative of its valorization. But the full accomplishment of these tendencies, the production of a totality in the literal sense of the word, would be simply impossible. This is so not only because of the relational nature of capital, which means it permanently confronts its other, including the "living labor" that Marx describes in the *Grundrisse* as "non-capital" (Marx 1973, 272–74), but also because capital, as we stressed in chapter 1, structurally needs to find or open up *new* spaces (literal and metaphorical) to expand what we call the frontiers of its valorization. From this point of view, a new assessment of the distinction between capital and capitalism becomes useful. This is a topic to which we turn in the next section.

The question that emerges at this point of our analysis concerns the relation of capital with its multiple outsides. Engagements with this question have shaped great and passionate debates on the transition to capitalism in many parts of the world (see, e.g., Harootunian 2015; Walker 2016b). Over the past few years, new readings of the Marxian analysis of so-called primitive accumulation have demonstrated that a set of key problems that emerge in historical transitions to capitalism continue to haunt the workings of capital throughout its development (see Mezzadra 2018, appendix; Mezzadra and Neilson 2013a, chap. 8). A different, although related strand of critical thought has harked back to Karl Polanyi's *The Great Transformation* ([1948] 2001) to rework his notion of the dependence of capital (or what Polanyi calls the "self-regulating market") on a set of conditions of possibility it is able neither to produce nor to maintain. The reference to Polanyi is particularly important for the work of feminist critics of political economy such as J. K. Gibson-Graham (2006), as well as for the investigation of blossoming popular, social, and community economies in many parts of the world (see, e.g., Coraggio et al. 2011). Bringing together these diverse theoretical developments, Nancy Fraser has recently argued for an "expanded conception of capitalism," taking as a crucial point of reference the impossibility of a total commodification of society. "That view," she writes, "leads down a blind alley, I think, to dystopian fantasies of a totally commodified world" (Fraser 2014, 59).

We will come back in chapter 5 to the work of Fraser, discussing her challenging notion of boundary struggles. We can anticipate here that we do not fully share her idea that what she calls "social, ecological, and political . . . non-commodified zones" necessarily "embody distinctive normative and ontological grammars of their own," irreducible to the "commodity logic" (Fraser 2014, 66). We are not convinced of the stability of the boundaries that circumscribe different spheres or subsystems of capitalism (e.g., Fraser's examples of the sphere of reproduction, the polity, and nonhuman nature). But we agree with her on the crucial relevance of the tension between the commodity logic—and, more generally, the logic of capital's valorization—and a social world that, even when it is fully shaped by that logic, continually reproduces spaces external to its domination. At the same time, capital, in expanding its frontiers to produce its outsides, disrupts forms of regulation that were key to former periods of its history. The three examples mentioned by Fraser (again, reproduction, the polity, nonhuman nature) nicely illustrate this point. The multiple outsides of capital take on a rather paradoxical character against the background of this conceptual analysis. Far from being limited to spaces (which also means forms of economic and social activity) that have not yet been subdued to the domination of capital, they are also continually produced *from within* capital, both through its initiative and through resistance to its logic. These outsides are privileged sites for the investigation of the operations of capital and their contestation.

What is an operation? In which sense do we employ the word? Finance, logistics, and extraction—the three domains of economic activity to which we turn our attention in chapter 4—are important points of reference for our understanding of operations. The use of such phrases as financial operations and logistical operations is particularly widespread even in the media and in everyday language, while the reference to extractive operations is a prominent feature of debates about mining, data skimming, and other activities that highlight capital's continuous need to draw on resources that are not of its own making. The concept of operations, taken in a naïve light, implies a straightforward relation of cause and effect, input and output, that can be tracked according to the model of classical mechanics. By this understanding, operations themselves take place in what is often referred to as a black box, or a zone in which their actual deployment is masked or obscured by what they accomplish. The widespread enthusiasm for the category of the performative in contemporary critical theory is one register of this so-called black-boxing of operations (see Mezzadra and Neilson 2013b).

Our approach is somewhat different. Keeping in mind the etymological origins of the word "operation" in the Latin *opus*—which, according to the eighteenth-century polymath Egidio Forcellini (1771, 275), signifies that which has been operated on (*id quod fit operando*)—we emphasize not the causal or effectual attributes of the operation but its own dynamics. We characterize the space and time of such dynamics by invoking the heuristic point of view of the interval that separates the operation's trigger from its outcome. Within this interval, the operation acquires an uneven and broken patterning of opening and closure that is constitutive of its unfolding. However automatic or given the results of an operation might appear to be, when we look at it from this perspective, there is always a back story, a drama of frictions and tensions in which the efficacy of the operation appears far more fragile and elusive than might otherwise be assumed. Approaching the operation from the heuristic point of view of this interval provides a kind of freeze-frame that brings into relief the combination of social activities, technical codes, and devices that make an operation possible. Such an approach also allows us to look at the outcome of the operation without taking it for granted. For us, then, an operation is a process with a beginning and an end; a process that accomplishes something without necessarily yielding a material thing; and a process that impinges on others, affecting possibilities and establishing multifarious and not necessarily predictable connections. This is why, in the analysis that follows, we are not merely interested in focusing on operations in their singular moments but also consider how they concatenate to link up and contribute to the fabrication of the world.

Once this notion of operations is in place, we can return to the question of capital—its unity and its relation to its outsides. What we call operations of capital take particularly apparent forms in the turbulence and transitions of capitalism over the past decades. Take the prominent role of operative logics in the development of logistics as a privileged field of capitalist activity. Deborah Cowen (2014, 32) has recently emphasized the importance of the shift from "physical distribution" to the "whole process of business," as epitomized by the writings of Peter Drucker in the 1960s, for the "revolution in logistics." It is interesting to note that the notion of operations played an important role in the elaboration of the theory of the value chain that later would further expand and deepen the analytical and practical focus of management theories on the whole process of business. Writing in the 1980s, Michael Porter (1985, 1987) used the term "operations" to define the productive activities located at the strategic juncture between "inbound" and "outbound logistics" within a larger "value system" (see also Grappi 2016, 64–65). Since then, the use of the term "operations" has become ubiquitous in the language of logistics, well beyond the boundaries established by Porter's theory. While this usage relates to profound transformations in the very notion of production and productive activities, it is also important to register the role played (in logistics, but also in finance) by digitalization. This is another crucial point of reference for any contemporary use of the notion of operations.

From Leibniz to Turing, it is possible to identify a specific genealogy of the concept of operations, intimately associated with an emphasis on calculation and algorithms as distinctive features of "thinking" that blur the boundary between body and mind, ultimately testing the very distinction between human and nonhuman machines. Leibniz's emphasis in the seventeenth century on the abstract nature of calculation already pointed to the possibility of detaching the operations of thought from a human agent, paving the way for the debates on artificial intelligence that would run parallel to the development of informatics in the twentieth century. "Operationalism," the epistemological understanding that reduces a concept to the set of operations that determine it, was first proposed by the US physicist and philosopher Percy Bridgman in 1927 and in many ways was intertwined with the development of informatics. Its jargon ("operational definition," "operationalization") as well as its "total empiricism" attracted the criticism of Herbert Marcuse, who considered operationalism a paradigmatic instance of "one-dimensional thought" (Marcuse 2002, 14–15). Independently of this criticism, which remains in many senses valid, the success and spread of operationalism went hand in hand with a set of technological innovations predicated on a kind of primacy of operations. An important part of this story is the drift of the logistical and military paradigm of "operations research" into economic thought, particularly in the United States following World War II, when the blossoming discipline of cybernetics contributed to the forging of sophisticated models of economic behavior and processes. In the account of Philip Mirowski (2002, 127–28), operations research combined "thermodynamics, optimization, game theory, and the computer into a prodigious new scientific discipline absorbing literally thousands of technically trained workers." Influencing and consolidating the hold of neoclassical approaches in economics, these developments had consequences for future developments in machine-driven economic activity. There is a direct link between the Turing machine, defined by Matteo Pasquinelli (2014, 98) as a machine "for the accumulation of information, the extraction of metadata and the implementation of machine like intelligence," and contemporary algorithms that prompt high-frequency financial trading, as well as other forms of data mining and predictive analytics. Once the power of operations has been acknowledged, the need to investigate their internal structure, as well as their relations with their multiple outsides, becomes manifest.

Operationalism has become more and more entangled in the contemporary workings of capital, as is particularly apparent considering finance and logistics. Dystopic visions of "a generalized inscription of human life into duration without breaks, defined by a principle of continuous functioning" (Crary 2013, 8) capture something crucial in the transformation of the quality of time in a world put under pressure and dominated by the 24/7 pace of digitally mediated exchanges on global financial markets or by the speeding up of the logistical arrangement and coordination of the movement of stuff and people. Finance and logistics coincide in producing the impression of a kind of automatic machinery working according to its own standards and parameters of performance. Financial and logistical operations deploy constitutive effects on the world. They play crucial roles in defining what we can call the framework, or the skeleton of the world. This means that precisely due to their increasingly abstract character they produce specific sets of links and relations that shape human activity within and across different social spaces and geographical scales. If one considers financial and logistical operations from the angle of their constitutive effects, which means heuristically isolating the ways in which they arise from and interact with complex configurations of society and life, a more general notion of operations of capital begins to emerge. Analytically cutting through the appearance of a continuum of capitalist activity in finance and logistics, we can isolate specific operations to shed light on the role of specific capitalist actors, as well as on the multifarious forms of labor involved in the execution of operations and on their enabling and framing effects on the labor and action of subjects who may not be directly involved in this execution.

Such a notion of operations of capital opens a new angle on the question of the relation of capital with its multiple outsides. While the world is increasingly constituted by a web of operations of capital, each of these operations is predicated on a set of conditions that it cannot produce, since operations necessarily involve the labor and activity of subjects that cannot be reduced to capital. At the same time, they impinge on environments (human and nonhuman) that present themselves as other with regard to operations. These three moments play a crucial role in the valorization of capital. They also highlight specific frictions and conflicts that are inherent to the very notion of operations of capital. Moreover, the concept of operations points to a specific, syncopated temporality in which the continuity of the process of valorization and accumulation of capital is continually interrupted and punctuated by the moments in which operations of capital "hit the ground," which is to say, the moments in which they enter into complex relations (both generative and destructive) with different forms of life and matter. These interruptions and punctuations inscribe themselves on the very notion of aggregate capital, further troubling its unity in ways that are even more apparent once the spatial concatenation and distribution of operations of capital are taken into account. Capital, writes Gavin Walker (2016b, 190), "functions in such a way that its totality or spectral body is always in excess of the parts that compose it." What the notion of operations of capital allows us to add is that this spectral body has to be considered a kind of unitary matrix to which each operation refers while at the same time implementing it in heterogeneous ways.

An operation always refers to specific capitalist actors and material circumstances while also being embedded in a wider network of operations and relations that involve other actors, processes, and structures. This perspective gives us two analytical avenues through which to examine the work done by an operation. The first, with its reference to specific capitalist actors, reveals the workings of capital in particular material configurations, shedding light on processes of valorization, as well as on the frictions and tensions crisscrossing them in lived and grounded circumstances. Studying operations in this optic involves careful empirical work to understand how they interact with different experiences of embodiment and social life, not least those involving dynamics of race and gender. The second focuses on the articulation of operations into larger and changing formations that make up capitalism as a whole. In this latter view, questions of sociological description, ideology, the role of the state and other agencies of power and governance, and even cultural dynamics of hegemony remain relevant. It is from this point of view that a new consideration of the relation between capital and capitalism becomes necessary.

Take, for instance, the study of the Port of Piraeus in Athens, Greece, which we undertook as part of a project called *Logistical Worlds*. The circumstances surrounding the transformation of this container port relate to the leasing in 2009 by the port authority of two of its three piers to a local subsidiary of Cosco Pacific Ltd., a company listed on the Hong Kong Stock Exchange but largely controlled by the Chinese state-owned enterprise Cosco Group. This port concession, which was accomplished under conditions of severe economic crisis in Greece, led to considerable technological investment in the Cosco side of the port, which, along with the introduction of more precarious labor conditions, resulted in a productivity boost. By August 2016, Cosco had acquired majority ownership of the port authority, under the guidance of the Hellenic Republic Asset Development Fund, an agency for the privatization of Greek public assets run under the oversight of the "institutions" of the so-called troika responsible for the imposition of austerity on the Greek state: the European Commission, the European Central Bank, and the International Monetary Fund. At the time of our visits in 2014, operations were divided between Pier I, where the port authority, which was still majority-owned by the Greek government, employed a unionized labor force, and Piers II and III, where the Cosco subsidiary had introduced an elaborate system of labor subcontracting, which employed workers on privately negotiated contracts, some of them limited to a couple of weeks with extremely short notice of working times sent by text message (Vatikiotis 2013).

There is much to be said about the situation on the ground at Piraeus, including about the complex territorial arrangements in place. These arrangements combine various degrees of Greek territoriality mediated and controlled by the powers of the troika, European Commission Free Zone regulations that allow the port to act as a container transshipment hub, the corporate governance mechanisms of Cosco Group (which extend up to China's State Council and the Organization Committee of the Communist Party of China), and the rule-governed software routines of the terminal operating systems operative on both sides of the port. The ways in which capital hits the ground at Piraeus are clearly both mediated by these spatial relations and productive of them. To take the example of terminal operating software packages, the CATOS system operating on the Cosco side of the port in 2014 did not communicate with the NAVIS-SPARCS N4 system installed at Pier I. Despite the existence of electronic data interchange protocols that would allow interoperativity between these systems—the first of which was manufactured in South Korea and the second in Silicon Valley—all movements of containers between the two sides of the port were logged by hand. These software systems also had implications for labor. For instance, the capacity of CATOS to undertake "process mining" analyses that use event logs to reduce the downtime of cranes, reach stackers, and other kinds of material handling equipment meant that labor hiring practices on the Cosco side of the port were fashioned according to constraints that would minimize the idleness of hardware. Logistical operations clearly structured the social relation of capital at Piraeus, but, in so doing, they also became enmeshed in relations of social difference, as became obvious during a visit to the Greek side of the port.

Walls in this facility were covered with graffiti that read "Greek Only" and "Chinese Go Home." Like many ports around the world, Piraeus plays host to a masculinized and union-based politics that militantly opposes the encroachments of capital but also aligns itself with the nation and defends a traditional gendered division of labor. The trade unions active on the Greek side of the port trenchantly opposed further privatization, organizing protests and framing their struggle as one against the privatization of Greek public property dictated by the troika. They were also vocal in their opposition to Golden Dawn, the Greek neo-Nazi party and extreme right political movement. Nonetheless, the presence of the graffiti, as well as of feminized and racialized images posted on office walls, registers the complex plight of working populations threatened with loss of employment or other kinds of dispossession in a situation in which the relation between the state and trade unions has broken down. Such representations play into an overarching narrative that understands the lease of the Port of Piraeus as evidence of a process of Chinification, whereby Greece is downgraded in a hierarchy of nations. Although this rhetoric does not stand up to sustained comparison of labor relations at Piraeus with those at Chinese ports, it does serve to obscure the gendered and raced quality of the workforce at Piraeus, assuming a kind of global precarious "unit" or, as Nelli Kambouri (2014) puts it, "a timeless and universal subject of capitalist development." In 2014, the vast majority of workers at Piraeus were Greek men, but those employed in the Cosco facility were younger and educated, while those on the Greek side were older and less educated. This scenario suggests not only that Cosco's subcontractors recruit a particular profile of worker but also that the reproduction of the labor force has been interrupted by crisis and economic transformation. What was once a militantly unionized population has, within a generation, become a more pliable and precarious body of workers.

The Chinese investment in Piraeus, however, needs to be considered beyond the rhetoric of Chinification, because it articulates to larger shifts and transformations that mark the evolution of capital at the global scale. This perspective comes into view when we consider how logistical operations at Piraeus concatenate with others, which may be geographically distinct or locked into relations of path dependence. The rise of the port as a transshipment hub, for instance, requires the arrival of huge vessels from China, which unload containers that are then placed onto feeder ships that transport them elsewhere in the Mediterranean. As Nicky Gregson, Mike Crang, and Constantinos N. Antonopoulos (2017) point out, this means the operations of container ports are articulated to many other kinds of logistical operations, including those in place at warehouses and distribution centers where the containers eventually arrive. The unloading of the boxes can pose challenges for labor provision and organization due to the way in which some containers are packed without pallets in China, meaning they cannot be emptied using forklifts, conveyors, or other unloading equipment. In this instance, logistical operations multiply forms of labor intensity around the world. The cost of labor in China means that containers can be packed to the hilt, leading to transport savings as container moves are priced according to volume rather than weight. But this passes on the problem of unloading the container at the receiving end, with the additional difficulty that the ways in which containers are packed are often unknown until they are opened. The approach taken to this problem in European warehouses is unsurprising: precarious labor is called in at the last moment.

In this case, we see how operations of capital articulate and multiply patterns of labor intensity across vast geographical distances. The point is similar but also, in a way, inversely related to the one we made in chapter 1 about the interdependence of the Chinese and US economies through finance and technology. What we see here is how operations of capital concatenate to create wider formations of capitalism that are linked to geo-economic and geopolitical transformations. In the case of Piraeus, these transformations cannot be understood in separation from the depth of economic crisis in Europe and dynamics of over-accumulation in China, which have led to a process of "going out," or the making of international investments. Most notably represented in the Belt and Road Initiative of Chinese logistical, financial, and cultural expansion announced by Xi Jinping in 2013, in which Piraeus is often positioned as a "crown jewel," these are developments we will further discuss in chapter 6. For now, we want to register how the distinct labor regimes and territorial mutations produced on the ground at Piraeus exist at the nexus between specific operations of capital and the planetary vista of capitalism.

Capital and Capitalism

It is well known that Marx did not employ the word "capitalism" in his critique of political economy. His notion of a "capitalist mode of production" grasped and anticipated some of the key questions at stake in debates surrounding capitalism. Nevertheless, it is safe to contend that the concept of capitalism emerged in the last decades of the nineteenth century, partly as a reaction to the radical challenge posed both by Marx's work, and by the growth of working-class movements and power. The resonances across Europe of the battle cry of the Paris Commune, "Wage war on the palaces; peace to the shacks," was widely perceived as a threat to the bourgeois order and prompted lively debates on the legitimization of the relations prevailing in a society that had been disrupted and reshaped by capital's rule over the previous few decades. The notion of capitalism emerged out of these debates, which were also a founding chapter in the history of modern sociology, and could never really get rid of the polemical and critical imprint that characterized its origin. It is not by chance that most economists do not use the concept, opting for more neutral definitions, such as market economy. Even reading the work of important bourgeois social scientists such as Werner Sombart and Max Weber, who played a prominent role in the scholarly discussion of the topic in the early twentieth century, it is easy to see that the concept of capitalism assumes the material contestation of the rule of capital and therefore the possibility of an alternative social order as constitutive of the object that the concept itself aims to describe. This is the reason that questions of legitimization figure so prominently in early sociological theories of capitalism (see Hilger and Hölscher 1982; Kocka 2016, 7–24).

There is no need here to go into the details of these debates and theories. Suffice it to say that the concept of capitalism that was forged by the combined effort of bourgeois historians and social scientists between the end of the nineteenth century and the beginning of the twentieth century was deeply shaped by an emphasis on its societal and systemic characters. Particularly important from this point of view was the criticism of the economistic inflection of Marxism—and of the concept of the capitalist mode of production—in the age of the Second International. Behind important debates of this time—including those concerning the distinctiveness of *modern* capitalism; the relations between merchant and industrial capitalism; its early, high, and late phases; and the interplay among religion, ethics, and economy—there was an attempt to shed light on the preconditions for the birth and development of capitalism in fields such as politics, law, and culture. The very notion of a "spirit of capitalism," popularized by Weber, is part and parcel of this search for a wider perspective on the history and present of capitalism, which necessarily led to a genealogical investigation of the conditions for the birth of a specific form of (*bourgeois*) subjectivity. The main problem at stake in these early debates on capitalism was precisely the way in which the rule of capital in the realm of economy is accompanied and, in a way, at least potentially "balanced" by developments in other spheres, which were regarded as retaining a kind of relative autonomy. One could add that the ghost haunting these debates was precisely the de-bordering and totalizing tendency of capital, which found iconic representation in the generalization of Marx's theory of commodity fetishism proposed in the later writings of Georg Simmel (see Simmel 1968) or in the image of the "iron cage" in the final pages of Weber's *Protestant Ethic* (see Weber 1992, 123). Nevertheless, this concern about the relation between capital's rule in the economic realm and developments in other societal spheres was bound to remain a crucial aspect of debates on capitalism for the decades to come.

Even within Marxism, such problems came to play an increasingly important role in the course of the twentieth century. For instance, the theoretical elaboration of the notion of hegemony in Antonio Gramsci's *Prison Notebooks* (1971) can be taken as the outcome of an attempt to combine a basically Leninist notion of communist politics with insights coming from coeval sociological theories (see Filippini 2015). Even before that, important works such as those by Hilferding and Lenin, as discussed earlier, had attempted to come to grips with what we have called the societal and systemic characteristics of capitalism. However, for our discussion in this chapter, it is important to briefly discuss the contribution of Rosa Luxemburg. Her *Accumulation of Capital*, published in 1913, can be read as an attempt to forge a concept of capitalism expanding on three of the main questions that we have discussed thus far in this chapter. First, as we already noted, Luxemburg takes as point of departure the Marxian notion of aggregate capital, stressing the peculiarity of its reproduction with regard to the movement and reproduction of individual capitals. Second, she emphatically stresses that "from the very beginning the forms and laws of capitalist production aim to comprise the entire globe as a store of productive forces" (Luxemburg [1913] 2003, 338), positing the world market as a dimension internal to any and each scale of capitalist development. Third, Luxemburg takes the relation between capital and noncapital as a crucial aspect in the workings of capitalism as an economic and social formation. "The existence and development of capitalism," she writes, "requires an environment of non-capitalist forms of production, but not every one of these forms will serve its ends" (Luxemburg [1913] 2003, 348).

There is no need to discuss here the limits and shortcomings of *Accumulation of Capital*, which are particularly apparent in Luxemburg's literal interpretation of the noncapitalist environment in territorial terms (see Mezzadra and Neilson 2013a, chap. 3). Undoubtedly, Luxemburg's emphasis on the combination of the exploitation of wage labor and the penetration of noncapitalist territories as a distinctive feature of capitalism retains a heuristic productivity with regard to both capitalism's long-term development at a world scale (see, e.g., Schmidt 2012) and the more specific question of the relation between capital and capitalism. What is really important from this point of view is precisely the disconnection between the accumulation of individual capitals and that of aggregate capital (*Gesamtkapital*). While in the first case the "assumption that capitalist production has attained universal and exclusive domination and is the sole setting" of the process is perfectly plausible (Luxemburg [1913] 2003, 329), the reproduction of aggregate capital, according to Luxemburg, cannot be predicated on "a society which consists solely of workers and capitalists" (Luxemburg [1913] 2003, 330). Instead, it structurally requires a set of conditions that are external to capital to retain its stability and dynamism.

We do not need to follow and critically discuss the details of Luxemburg's analysis of the problem of the realization of surplus value. There are two points we want to flesh out of her discussion: first, that the disconnection between the reproduction of individual capitals and aggregate capital is a distinctive feature of capitalism; and second, her insistence on the absolute relevance of the opening of new spaces and environments for the valorization and accumulation of capital. While the management of the disconnection between individual capitals and aggregate capital produces bounded capitalist formations, contained within specific boundaries and articulated around multiple social spheres, the opening of new spaces and environments constitutively challenges the stability of these capitalist formations. Once the outside of capital is conceptually reframed in nonliteral and non-territorial terms, as we propose, capitalism appears to be characterized at each of its scales of development by a disruptive tendency that is pronounced in its moments of transition. In these moments, specific forms of capitalist economic activity (say, a specific industrial cycle) or specific societal arrangements (say, welfare systems) may be posited by capital as an outside and invested by a disruptive violence that is conceptually comparable to that of colonialism and eloquently described by Luxemburg in her analysis of capital's "struggle against natural economy" (Luxemburg [1913] 2003, chap. 27).

Moving beyond Luxemburg's work, we suggest that her analysis of the disconnection between individual capitals and aggregate capital allows us to grasp the limits of a merely economic understanding of capitalism. From the angle provided by our notion of operations of capital, we can say that each operation and, above all, the moment of concatenation between multiple operations is predicated on a set of conditions that cannot be produced by capital itself. Law and politics, ethics and culture, subjective behavior and nonhuman environments are placed under ever more duress by the tendency for the endless accumulation of capital to become a societal norm. Nevertheless, these practices and domains play constitutive roles in facilitating the stability of capitalist societies as they become sites of friction, conflict, and antagonism. Specific formations of capitalism can be precisely described as provisional arrangements of boundaries between several social spheres in ways that are compatible with the reproduction of aggregate capital. These arrangements are both conceptually and historically heterogeneous, corresponding to a principle of variegation that emerges out of the multiplicity of conditions that capital encounters in its expansion at the world scale. (And one could pick up a concept from Niklas Luhmann [1997] to suggest that, parallel to the formation of the world market, a "world society" is the sociological horizon of this development.) In his recent book *Marx after Marx*, Harry Harootunian (2015) notes that the variegation of capitalism is particularly apparent outside Europe and the West, where capital's encounter with heterogeneous forms of production, social organization, and culture can be effectively explained through the Marxian notion of the formal subsumption of labor under capital. What distinguishes this operative modality of capital, Harootunian (2015, 64) contends, is precisely "its capacity to situate practices from earlier modes alongside newer ones under the command of capital to constitute the force of temporal interruption, unevenness, fracturing, and heterogeneity" that translates capital's "homogeneous, unitary, and linear trajectory of time" into specific formations of capitalism.

Marx develops the distinction between formal and real subsumption in the draft chapter 6 of *Capital*, titled "Results of the Direct Production Process." This distinction, alongside with the one between "absolute" and "relative surplus value" to which it corresponds, immediately refers to different modalities in which capital organizes the process of exploitation of alien labor. In what Marx calls formal subsumption, previously existing productive processes are appropriated by capital and synchronized with the dynamics of valorization from an external position, without the direct intervention of the capitalist in the organization of labor. Real subsumption, by contrast, is characterized precisely by this intervention, through the enhancement of workers' productive cooperation and the mechanization of labor. While Marx explicitly writes that real subsumption corresponds to the "developed *mode of production which is specifically capitalist*," and thus refers to a transition from formal to real subsumption as the constitutive moment of capitalist development, he is also keen to specify that formal subsumption is "the *general* form of every capitalist process of production" (Marx 1977, 1019). This is an important point for us, since in the deployment of formal subsumption what is at stake is the relation of capital with its outside. We therefore agree with Harootunian's emphasis on the constitutive role played by formal subsumption—as well as "transitional" and "hybrid" forms (Harootunian 2015, 64)—in the development of capitalism writ large. Particularly important, from our point of view, is the appropriative aspect of formal subsumption that reproduces itself when capital is confronted with the necessity to *open up* new spaces for its valorization and accumulation, even in conditions that cannot be described as noncapitalist. In such conditions, what counts, to continue to use Marx's terminology, is the moment of articulation between the workings of formal and real subsumption. This means highlighting the capacity of capital to fill with specific capitalist modalities of organization and exploitation of labor and social cooperation the spaces opened up and appropriated through interventions that always bear the traces of formal subsumption and its constitutive violence.

Even beyond the realm of capital's relation with the production process, this interpretation of the notions of formal and real subsumption allows us to grasp both what we have called the totalizing tendency of capital— its constant interruptions and its impossible accomplishment. Capitalism can also be understood as a societal system that organizes and contains the tensions and conflicts that emerge out of this situation. This is a question that has been widely debated within the framework of the modes of production controversy, where the articulation of capitalist and noncapitalist forms of production has been variously discussed as a specific characteristic of "underdevelopment" (see, e.g., Banaji 2010). Contemporary theories of "postcolonial capitalism" elaborate on the legacy of this controversy, pointing to the structural coexistence in countries such as India of a specific capitalist sector of economic activity and of a "need economy" within which the reproduction of large masses of dispossessed people takes place (see Sanyal 2007). These theories thus move beyond the notion of underdevelopment, of a belatedness to be overcome through the deployment of developmental programs and policies, pointing to the constitutive character of this deep heterogeneity of capitalism in its postcolonial formation. While we acknowledge the importance of such contributions, we remain skeptical regarding the definition of the need economy as a "site of non-capital" (Sanyal 2007, 72). Instead, we emphasize that capital is able to deploy a huge array of operations and techniques to extract value from this need economy, as in the case of the financialization of popular economies in Latin America investigated by Verónica Gago (2015) and in that of microfinance in Bangladesh and elsewhere (Roy 2010). What characterizes postcolonial capitalism is therefore the combination of different forms of subsumption of labor, social cooperation, and life under capital, which also means the synchronicity of operations of capital that target their outside in profoundly heterogeneous ways.

This problem of combination and synchronization, to pick up Luxemburg's analysis again, emerges out of the gap and disconnection between the reproduction of individual capitals and aggregate capital and is far from being reducible to a merely economic question. The articulation of the capitalist mode of production across a multiplicity of levels and spheres plays crucial roles in the stabilization of a societal order within which operations of capital can proceed. The nationalization of this societal order has been particularly important in the history of industrial capitalism. As we have discussed, the state historically has provided both a framework for a bounded representation of aggregate capital in its national denomination and for the reproduction of labor power under the pressure of class struggle. Histories of colonial and imperial expansion in a way have anticipated and then run parallel to the development of what we can call the industrial and national moment in the history of capitalism, violently inscribing themselves onto the scale of the world market. But since the crisis of the early 1970s, the very national denomination of capitalism has been challenged by the emergence and increasing prominence of a set of operations of capital whose logics are resistant to being contained and organized even by the most powerful territorial states. Well-established internal boundaries between spheres of human activity have been tested by these operations, which have disrupted traditional social arrangements and opened up new and multiple outsides for the valorization and accumulation of capital. The heterogeneity of postcolonial capitalism therefore has become, under specific conditions that deserve detailed consideration, a characteristic of capitalism writ large. States continue to play prominent roles in the articulation of capitalism and in the synchronization of the heterogeneous operations of capital with the reproduction of aggregate capital. But they are increasingly enmeshed within larger assemblages of territory, authority, and rights (Sassen 2006), where the pressure of global forces of capital is always tangible. The power of abstraction, a distinctive feature of the operations of capital since the inception of its modern history, spreads its material effects in ways that are significantly different from those that characterized industrial capitalism in its multifarious instantiations.

The Power of Abstraction

Whatever happened to the working day? In the famous chapter 10 of *Capital*, volume 1, Marx provided an analysis of the parameters of control and measure that would make the working day the primary unit of production and contention from his time to the end of the industrial moment of capitalism. We have already mentioned such notions as absolute and relative surplus value, which allowed Marx to provide an analysis that, while based in the instance of the English factory, could be extended to wider vistas of capitalist activity. What we want to highlight here is what Marx called the "limiting conditions" of the working day, the "boundaries both physical and social," which he found to be "very elastic" and to allow "a tremendous amount of latitude" (Marx 1977, 341). In Marx's analysis, these boundaries set the terms in which the average, or socially necessary (for the repro-duction of labor power), labor time could be calculated and manipulated. Against this average, the capitalist was able to compel the "surplus labor time" from which surplus value could be extracted. This calculation and compulsion assumed the existence of "abstract labor" as the condition that allowed the measurement, comparison, and coordination among different working days in different sites and sectors of production. Today it is com-monplace to assert that the working day has become so elastic that it no longer provides a stable parameter for such calculation, comparison, and coordination. The very notion of an average labor time corresponding to the reproduction of labor power appears increasingly problematic in the face of a set of processes that have made labor at once more fragmented and more pervasive. These circumstances point to the need to interrogate the persistent validity and applicability of the concept of abstract labor.

Discussions of the contemporary transformations of labor have been legion, ranging from analyses of precarity and "wageless life" to explora-tions of the growing interpenetration of formal and informal labor (see, e.g., Denning 2010; Sanyal 2007; Standing 2011). With regard to recent evolutions in the measurement of abstract labor, the new frontiers of labor monitoring and exploitation introduced by logistical and algorithmic forms of control are particularly relevant. Consider the so-called gig economy in which workers use digital matching platforms to provide services with-out the protections of employment. Examples of such platforms include "crowdworking" websites such as Amazon Mechanical Turk and work-on-demand applications such as Uber, Foodora, or Deliveroo. Let us focus on Deliveroo for a moment. Workers using this smartphone application carry food prepared at restaurants between suppliers and consumers, providing their own means of transportation and devices on which to run the app. Im-portantly, these workers are not directly employed by Deliveroo, although they are obliged to display the company's branded clothing and parapher-nalia while making deliveries and must even agree when they sign on not to accept jobs from similar platforms. When they take on jobs through the app, workers remain unaware of the address to which they must deliver the food until after they collect the goods from the supplier. The system allows them to accept jobs at their convenience, and this means that the company does not pay for waiting time between gigs. Under these conditions, the unity of the working day is disrupted. Workers are paid by the task.

For each job, the algorithms that run the Deliveroo app calculate payment amounts based on parameters such as distance traveled and time-related requirements that supposedly allow for "reasonable delays." Furthermore, the workers' performance is measured against a series of estimates calculated by the app—for example, time to accept order, time to travel to restaurant, time to reach the client—which are then averaged to deliver monthly personalized "service level assessments" (O'Connor 2016). Abstraction and averages shape the lives of these workers even as their patterns of activity are not constrained by the unity of time and place that characterizes the classical industrial factory. The rule of abstract labor is effectively instantiated by the parameters and averages against which their payment is calculated, but they experience this rule, as well as the modes of intensification it demands, in fragmented and even elusive ways. Although the example of Deliveroo makes particularly evident the algorithmic calculations that mark these experiences, this tendency to organize labor and capital in ways that cannot be classified in terms of a direct employment relation shapes many different instances of contemporary work, including those structured by complex subcontracting arrangements. Far from spelling the end of abstract labor, such scenarios of precarity and labor hiring exhibit its continued grip on and tensions with the world of living labor.

Crowdworking and work-on-demand via app, the two forms of work usually associated with the gig economy, include highly different activities, regulations, and tasks, but they also "share non-negligible similarities" (De Stefano 2016, 472). While they potentially allow flexible working schedules and a subjective negotiation of the boundaries between labor and life, they also "pave the way to a severe commodification of work" (De Stefano 2016, 472). But this commodification takes place in ways that are significantly different from the ones historically experienced by industrial workers. If, on the one hand, catchphrases such as "gigs," "tasks," "rides," and so on tend to hide the reality of work, the classification of the majority of workers in the gig economy as independent contractors, on the other hand, obscures the reality of their dependence on the platforms that organize and command their activities. Significant problems and challenges for labor law and labor protection arise from this situation, since the acknowledgment of a shared and collective condition is made difficult for these workers by the very individual construction of their relationship to the platforms. Impressive mobilizations and struggles—for instance, in the "summer of wildcat strikes in London's gig economy" in 2016 (O'Connor 2016)—have made these problems and challenges dramatically visible (Ciccarelli 2018).

We are confronted here with a peculiar contradiction, which becomes particularly apparent in the world of the gig economy and so-called platform capitalism (Srnicek 2017) but is far from being limited to these spheres. While the operations of capitalist actors in this world result in a huge fragmentation of laboring tasks, attributed to specific individuals, these operations actually code society as a productive environment shaped by multifarious forms of cooperation from which they extract labor and value in an elusive way. The working of Amazon Mechanical Turk is paradigmatic in this regard. The posting of tasks by "requesters," significantly called "Human Intelligence Tasks," generates a "workflow" in which individual workers' participation is synchronized, evaluated, and managed by an algorithmic system of control (see, e.g., Irani and Silberman 2016). This control system manages the gap between the workflow, which means the collective and cooperative nature of labor and the contribution of workers as individuals, which is completely subordinated to the continuity and productivity of the flow. Each operation of algorithmic management thus performs a double abstraction of labor. On the one hand, it literally abstracts specific tasks and activities from the embodied experience of a single worker, inserting him or her into a workflow that obscures any subjectivity of labor. On the other hand, these measures of control reproduce in a fragmented but compelling way the measure of abstract labor as a normative grid for the assessment and remuneration of human activity, whether this involves averaged "service level assessments" or customer-driven ratings scales that can seal the reputation and future employability of workers.

Considering the fragmentation of the labor process and its segmentation into a panoply of single tasks that is associated with algorithmic management, several scholars and observers stress that "it has uncanny echoes from the past," specifically pointing to its continuities with Frederick W. Taylor's scientific management and speaking of a "digital Taylorism" (see, e.g., Altenried 2017; O'Connor 2016). This is a phrase that has been widely employed in recent years also to analyze the ways in which new technologies enable the standardization of formerly skilled work (Avis 2012) or the implications of digitalization for the organization of industrial labor (Westkämpfer 2007). We do not deny the analytical relevance of the notion of digital Taylorism in specific sectors and branches of the economy—for instance, to remain in the world of logistics, in the warehouses of Amazon (Apicella 2016; see also Golumbia 2015). Nevertheless, we maintain that as a general description of the emerging trends in labor organization and exploitation, this notion can be misleading. Consider again the case of Amazon Mechanical Turk. In his classical analysis of Taylorism, Harry Braverman (1998, 77) posits as its first principle what he calls "the dissociation of the labor process from the skills of the workers." This does not seem to characterize work on Amazon Mechanical Turk. Workers, rather, are encouraged and solicited to demonstrate and implement their skills and knowledge for the performance of specific tasks, while the assemblage of these tasks (and of the related skills and knowledges) within the workflow happens *ex post* through algorithmic operations. More generally, while Taylorism took for granted the stability of the boundary between labor and life, which means the unity of the working day, what characterizes algorithmic management is precisely the fact that, in its operations well beyond the walls of the factory, the office, or the warehouse, it blurs that boundary and thus explodes the working day. Under these conditions, the fragmentation of labor and its dissection into a potentially infinite multitude of tasks takes on completely new meanings, which require detailed investigation. For now, we want to emphasize how the dissemination of the abstract power of algorithmic operations within the fabric of social cooperation, so apparent in the gig economy, resonates with other crucial developments in contemporary capitalism.

Wherever we look in contemporary capitalism, we are confronted with the power of abstraction, whether it is in ever more sophisticated financial devices, in the preparation of raw materials (from grades of coal to human tissues) for commodification, or in systems of standardization that allow the modularization of production and labor processes. None of this is new. As Alfred Sohn-Rethel memorably argues, capitalism has been characterized since its inception by the power of a specific form of abstraction—what he calls, with reference to Marx's critique of political economy, "real abstraction." This is best instantiated, according to Sohn-Rethel, by the commodity form, by the abstraction of exchange value, in contrast to use value, of commodities, as well as by the abstraction of labor "when determining the magnitude and substance of value." Money, the form in which value takes on its concrete appearance, is in turn "an abstract *thing*," which, as Sohn-Rethel (1978, 19) keenly adds, is, strictly, "a contradiction in terms" (Sohn-Rethel 1978, 19). In a capitalist society, this abstraction is real because it is constitutive of a whole set of social relations, which are increasingly shaped by the power of the commodity form, of abstract labor, and of that uncanny abstract thing that is money. Even the world market, whose creation was for Marx (1973, 408) a tendency "directly given in the concept of capital itself," ultimately works as an axiomatic principle that enables the continuous reproduction of this constitutive power of abstraction, allowing money to become "world money," on the one hand, and "abstract labor" to become "social labor" (Marx 1971, 253), on the other. For Sohn-Rethel (1978, 20), real abstraction is "not thought-induced; it does not originate in men's minds but in their actions." This opens up, even beyond Sohn-Rethel's intentions, the problem of the production of real abstraction, positing it as a fundamental field of struggle and antagonism. Far from being conceivable in terms of a mere opposition of the concrete and the abstract, a radical critique of capitalism has to take seriously the power of abstraction and to ask questions about the possibility for abstract powers to multiply the common characteristics of social cooperation against private appropriation and exploitation.

Such an understanding of abstraction and abstract labor allows us to place the concept of operations in relation to what, in chapter 1, we called the axiomatic of capital. Writing about this axiomatic provides us with a way to link the unity of capital to its multiple operations. It is tempting to think of this relation in linear terms, as if abstraction is the process that unifies capital. Although this view is not entirely mistaken, we already sought to problematize its linear and programmatic aspects earlier in this chapter, when we revisited Eisenstein's unrealized attempt to film Marx's *Capital*, to highlight the gap between abstraction and materiality that characterizes the social relation of capital. Sohn-Rethel's discussion of real abstraction allows us to take this point further. By emphasizing that abstraction is a process defined by material and spatial relations, even as it tends to elide them, Sohn-Rethel stresses the active or operative aspects of abstraction above its conceptual qualities. With the example of the "abstract thing" of money, it becomes clear that real abstraction is linked as much to processes of exchange, distribution, and circulation as it is to those of equalization, centralization, or totalization. We might even say that abstraction is a particular operation of capital, although it would be necessary to add, in analogy to Marx's famous comment about the status of labor power as a commodity, that it is an operation like no other. More pointedly, we can identify processes of abstraction at work across many different operations of capital. We should caution, however, against concluding that abstraction pertains merely to the concatenative axis of operations, which stitches them into wider capitalist arrangements. Abstraction and materiality intertwine in capital's operations, often in unpredictable and uneven ways. It is not as if the material can be equated with the outside of the operation, pushing back and shaping it in a purely physical way, as if the deployment and effects of an operation were somehow ontologically separated from the active production of society and space that unfolds on the ground. Equally, abstraction does not provide some kind of immaterial ether that connects different operations into capitalism. Understanding the complex interplay between abstraction and materiality in capital's operations is crucial to appreciating how the unity of capital cuts across its functioning as a difference machine.

When the question of labor is added, these dynamics of abstraction and materiality become even more complicated. The intensification of the split between abstract and living labor is a signal feature of contemporary capitalism, registering both the increasingly elusive application of norms and standards of temporal measure and the fragmentation and multiplication of labor across proliferating borders and processes of financialization. The example of work in the gig economy provides only one instance of this intensification, but it is worth commenting on further if only because its workings map so neatly over the algorithmic functioning of computerized applications. Recent years have seen an explosion of writings about "algorithmic capitalism" (see, e.g., Grindsted 2016; Pasquinelli 2014; Rossiter 2016), often with an emphasis on high-frequency financial trading or the logistical coordination of labor and mobility within supply chains. Indeed, the accelerated pace of algorithmic calculations, which with current computing capacities exceed the rhythms of human cognition, maps out an important new frontier for capital. This remains the case even if, as Jesse LeCavalier (2016, 174) explains in describing the data-rich environment of the Walmart warehouse, "The economy of human labor for carrying out simple tasks, like moving small boxes, continues to trump that of machines, which could do these jobs but only at considerable cost and possible obsolescence." It would be a mistake to reduce the operation to the algorithmic calculation or, even more broadly, to the technical procedure. Certainly, technical procedures perform an important function in assembling and composing labor forces. The organization of the labor process through machinery, skills, disciplinary devices, and other factors that structure the spaces and times in which work is distributed are all relevant in this regard. But the political or subjective element of labor is not captured through an exclusive emphasis on technical operations, even as they clearly intersect and establish the conditions for the production of subjectivity.

To inquire into the relation between operations of capital and the political composition of living labor is to revisit the question we posed earlier about the possibility for abstract powers to multiply conditions for the production of the common. Needless to say, there are important and sophisticated theoretical discourses that seek to describe the operations that undergird the production of subjectivity, from Hegel's master-slave dialectic through to Marx's hesitant and unfinished ruminations at the end of volume 3 of *Capital* on the impossibility of correlating class formation with sources of income. The psychoanalytic edifice built on Freudianism and its aftermath must also be acknowledged. We reserve a full discussion of operations and the production of subjectivity for the final chapter of the book, where we approach this matter in the context of an assessment of the changing fortunes of the state in capitalist globalization. For now, we want only to note the political potentiality inherent in what Jason Read (2014) calls the "real abstraction of subjectivity." Noting that for Sohn-Rethel "the form of thought is irreducibly social," Read understands "real abstraction less as a criticism of epistemology than as a description of subjectivity in capitalism." In so doing, he seeks to trace the transformations that accompany the shift from industrial capitalism to present-day conditions of production, which he understands to be based in social knowledge. At stake is a "migration of real abstraction into the center of production," which has "profound effects for subjectivity" as it "alters the relation between thought and existence." Read quotes Paolo Virno, who argues that the subjective form of the *general intellect* "distinguishes itself from the 'real abstractions' typical of modernity, which are all anchored to the *principle of equivalence*" (Virno 2003, 87). Virno contends that "the models of social knowledge" that drive contemporary production "are not units of measurement; instead, they constitute the premise for operative heterogeneous possibilities . . . They do not equalize anything; instead, they act as premise to every type of action" (Virno 2003, 87). Such a perspective is perhaps overly based in an approach to contemporary capitalism that emphasizes cognition over affect, but it does begin to account for relations between the production of subjectivity and the operations of capital. It is worth keeping these relations in mind as we move on to interrogate the politics of capital at the cusp of its continual need to internalize its multiple outsides and its production of subjects who have to negotiate its constant spilling over into social relations that exceed the economic.

The Politics of Capital

In recent critical debates on capitalism, as we have noted, the question of capital's multiple outsides has been rehearsed and tested from several points of view. "Capitalism," writes David Harvey (2003, 141), "necessarily creates its own 'other.' The idea that some sort of 'outside' is necessary for the stabilization of capitalism therefore has relevance." He is keen to add that this "outside" is not merely to be conceived of as "pre-existing," coinciding with noncapitalist social formations or with sectors within capitalism that have not yet been commoditized. Capitalism "can actively manufacture" its outsides (Harvey 2003, 141). Harvey emphasizes the spatial implications of this dialectic relationship between inside and outside in capitalist development and accumulation, whose dynamics inherently include the "necessity to build whole landscapes only to tear them down and build anew in the future" (Harvey 2001b, 76). More generally, he contends, referring indirectly back to the work of Rosa Luxemburg and attempting to update it, that "capitalism can escape its own contradiction only through expanding." Such expansion must be understood as a simultaneous dynamic of "*intensification* (of social wants and needs, of population totals, and the like) and *geographical extension*." He concludes, "Fresh room for accumulation must exist or be created if capitalism is to survive" (Harvey 2001b, 257).

It is this drive to expansion that opens up for Harvey the spaces within which capital necessarily operates through *dispossession*. The violent appropriation of land that characterizes the so-called primitive accumulation (the *Landnahme*, to use a word employed by Carl Schmitt in his theory of the *nomos* of the Earth) thus becomes a distinguishing feature of capitalism writ large, in its literal and, perhaps more important, in its metaphorical sense. It is above all in moments of crisis and transition that this becomes apparent. Klaus Dörre, who recently revisited the notion of *Landnahme* to make sense of the turmoil and dynamics of financial capitalism, effectively shows how, since the 1970s, the regulative mechanisms that had been integral to welfare capitalism in the post–World War II age (accomplishing a certain degree of institutionalization of "workers' power") began to appear as a "crucial obstacle to the accumulation of capital." One of the most important aspects of the transition to financial capitalism was therefore their transformation into a "specific 'outside,'" which became "the object of a new capitalist *Landnahme*"—a *Landnahme* of the social (Dörre, in Dörre et al. 2009, 52; see also Walker 2016a).

This book joins this strand of critical theory in acknowledging the relevance of these violent ruptures that punctuate and fracture the continuity of capitalist development. For us, the continued reproduction of the question of the outside points to the tensions between the totalizing tendencies inherent to the very concept of capital and the impossible accomplishment of capital as a totality. Our way to understand capital's outsides is predicated on a specific reading of a famous passage in the *Grundrisse* that we recalled in the introduction, in which Marx writes about the world market that, to capital, "every limit appears as a barrier to be overcome" (Marx 1973, 408). We understand this encounter with limits and their transformation into barriers to be overcome as a structural character of capital's expansion. What interests us more in this perspective is the multiplication of frictions and actual as well as potential conflicts that emerge on the heterogeneous frontiers of capital's expansion. We emphasize that capital's outsides should not be understood in terms of untouched physical or social territories. What characterizes contemporary capitalism is, rather, an opening of outsides that proceeds in parallel to the full deployment of capital's rule. The notion of operations of capital allows us to track how the ghostly or material presence of the outside haunts capital even in "sectors" such as finance and logistics—through the manifold forms in which it hits the ground no less than in the actual unfolding of its operations.

The expanded notion of extraction that we discussed earlier and elaborate in chapter 4 further clarifies our understanding of this point. Working with the notion of extraction helps us to make sense of the ways in which established capitalist formations and arrangements are turned into specific outsides. "We can characterize the relationship of advanced to traditional capitalism in our current period," writes Saskia Sassen (2014, 10), "as one marked by extraction and destruction, not unlike the relationship of traditional capitalism to precapitalist economies." Sassen's work over the past few years has been important in shedding light on the emergence of an extractive logic that crisscrosses the operations of capital and extends into the seemingly ethereal realm of finance. While we acknowledge the relevance of her contribution and share her emphasis on the brutality of the global economy, our investigation of operations of capital aims to open a conceptual space in which it becomes possible to critically interrogate her analysis of expulsions as a key consequence of the contemporary operations of capital. This is not to deny the dramatic phenomenology of expulsions in many parts of the world today, which is "marked by extremes in unemployment, poverty, suicide, displacement from home and land, incarceration, or suicide" (Sassen 2014, 76). The point, instead, is to analyze carefully the multifarious ways in which even expelled populations are targeted by a panoply of mechanisms and devices that differentially include them in the scope of capital's operations. Going beyond the incorporation-expulsion binary, which guides Sassen's analysis, and exploring the mobility and increasing elusiveness of the boundaries between these poles offers us a way to grasp both the operative logics of contemporary capitalism and the sites of its potential contestation.

Writing about the operations of capital, we have emphasized that each of these operations depends on a set of conditions that it cannot produce. This is particularly true from the angle of the necessary concatenation and articulation of operations into larger and shifting capitalist formations—that is, from the angle of the distinction and relation between capital and capitalism. Here again we are confronted with the problem of capital's multiple outsides. The "expanded conception of capitalism" advanced by Nancy Fraser and briefly discussed earlier in this chapter is particularly important in this regard. Fraser's analysis of the "functional imbrication" of the market dynamics of capitalist societies with "non-marketized aspects" (Fraser 2014, 59) is a welcome reminder of the complexity of market relations, whose constitution involves a set of arrangements that always exceed the traditional domain of the economic. These arrangements, which involve the very formation of subjects and their *habitus*, are nevertheless in a precarious position with respect to capital. They remain in a position of exteriority but they develop under the increasing pressure of capital's drive to unlimited accumulation.

The example of social reproduction, which is key to Fraser's analysis (see Fraser 2016), is particularly important in this respect. While it is clear that social reproduction could never be entirely predicated on logics of commodification and monetization, since it involves a huge quantity of affects, care, and reciprocity, it is also true that even the household tends to be more and more penetrated by capitalist logics—from the explosion of migrant care and domestic labor (Mezzadra and Neilson 2013a, chap. 4) to processes of financialization (Cooper and Mitropoulos 2009). These logics structurally alter the conditions under which social reproduction, even in its "non-marketized" aspects, takes shape. This is no less true regarding analyses that underscore, from a point of view quite different from Fraser's, the persisting role of the state in the creation of markets, in providing "positive externalities," in the facilitation of technological innovation, or even as a major risk-taker and entrepreneur (see, e.g., Mazzucato 2013). In all of these capacities, contemporary states may retain a position of relative externality to capital while being conducive to the articulation of specific capitalist formations. But in doing so, they are increasingly subdued to capitalist logics and rationality, whether through public-private partnerships, the pressure of powerful private actors, or simply the adoption of market standards and rules.

Under these conditions, there is a need to ask whether capital itself is not characterized in its operations by a specific politics, by the deployment of political effects that have become particularly apparent in our time. This is a question that appears especially urgent considering the critical discussions of neoliberalism we examined in the previous chapter. Even reading the most interesting and sophisticated Foucauldian writings on the topic—for instance, the recent works by Pierre Dardot and Christian Laval (2014) and by Wendy Brown (2015)—one has the impression that politics tends to be considered capital's "other," while capital tends to be relegated to the mere economic sphere. To be clear, we repeat that these works are of paramount importance, since they shift the critical focus on neoliberalism from an exclusive attention to economic policies to the production of subjectivity. Indeed, these analyses recast neoliberalism as a "governing rationality that extends a specific formulation of economic values, practices, and metrics to every dimension of human life" (Brown 2015, 30). Nevertheless, they pursue the critique of neoliberalism from an angle that maintains a firm boundary between economy and politics. Brown contends that the ubiquity of "neoliberal reason . . . is converting the distinctly *political* character, meaning, and operation of democracy's constituent elements into *economic* ones" (Brown 2015, 17). What remains hidden in this formulation is the possibility that contemporary forms of capitalist accumulation, prompted and molded by neoliberalism, have challenged the boundary between politics and economy, radically transforming the very notion of politics. In our view, it is particularly important for radical politics to take this possibility seriously.

As Ellen Meiksins Wood argues, there was always a sense in which the economic sphere in capitalism, which was supposedly separated from politics with the monopolization of coercive and legal powers by the state, remained political. Capitalism entailed a vast privatization of political power, leading to the integration of private appropriation with the authoritative organization of production. The maintenance of contractual relations between "free" producers and private appropriators not only required the juridical and coercive support of the state. It also generated new relations of authority, domination, and subjection between capitalists and workers. Wood (2012, 20) calls this power over social production and the human beings who perform it "appropriative power." She explains, "The differentiation of the economic and the political in capitalism is, more precisely, a differentiation of political functions themselves and their separate allocation to the private economic sphere and the public sphere of the state" (21). She thus distinguishes "political functions immediately concerned with extraction and appropriation of surplus-labour from those with a more general, communal purpose" (21). This is a classical rendition of the relation of capital to state in its insistence on "the differentiation of the economic and the political." But Wood's contention that the appropriative power of the capitalist be understood as properly political offers an important point of departure for our analysis of the troubling of the boundary between economy and politics in neoliberalism. Her observation that "coercion in capitalist societies . . . is exercised not only personally and directly by means of superior force but also indirectly and impersonally by the compulsions of the market" (Wood 2005, 11) takes this argument further to suggest how the coercive powers of the state are becoming increasingly indistinct from market processes.

In stressing how the capitalist class combines "the power of surplus-extraction" with "the capacity to organize and intensify production" (Wood 2005, 34), Wood identifies the extractive operations of capital as crucially intertwined with its capacity for subsumption. It is precisely this nexus of extraction and subsumption that we understand to have been tightened and displaced under contemporary capitalist conditions of variegation and accumulation. At stake is no longer simply the extraction of surplus labor, although this remains an important factor in many situations of industrial production and even in algorithmically mediated situations of "indirect" exploitation. What we earlier called the *Landnahme* of the social extends across many diverse spaces and scales as capital prospects, appropriates, and internalizes its multiple outsides. To highlight the articulation of formal and real subsumption in these dynamics is to explore the mutations of what Wood calls appropriative power. The politics of capital shift under conditions in which the organization and exploitation of social cooperation are not directly attributable to the particular fraction of capital that benefits from these processes. Whether in the financial logic of the derivative, which generates value by speculating on underlying assets that are never transacted, or the logistical organization of labor in the gig economy, capital's operations remain appropriative. But to accomplish this appropriation, they must increasingly impinge on the organization of society, the production of subjectivity, and even decision making with direct public consequences. Consider the automated decisions made by software about the routing of electronic communications or the decisions of engineers, software architects, and protocol designers who build and maintain the software and network systems run by large and opaque corporations such as Google, Amazon, and Facebook. These are nondemocratic decisions made in the name of operative efficiency and distribution, but they increasingly produce the communicative grounds for public disputes, and on these same grounds a new kind of political rationality emerges based in infrastructural and protocological relations. It is not simply a matter of politics being overcome by economy—particularly once we understand politics in a broad sense, including the production of subjectivity. Nor is it a question of imagining the conditions under which politics might seize back what it has ceded to the economic sphere of life. Rather, the challenge is to radically rethink both politics and economy under conditions in which the boundary between the two has been continuously tested and breached.

The concept of operations guides our analysis in this regard, providing a pivot around which our attempt to recast the relation of politics to capital turns. We are not interested in fashioning the concept of operations to provide a general or neutral ground on which interactions between politics and capital can be mapped. As becomes clear in chapter 6, the concept of operations allows us to rethink the political in ways that both confirm and question currently dominant strands of political theory that emphasize the role of performativity and the event in the constitution of political life. With regard to capital, as this chapter shows, the concept of operations allows an analysis that is attentive to both how it emerges through specific spatial and social situations and how it concatenates into wider arrangements of capitalism. Bringing these aspects of our argument together requires renewed attention to the category and the institutional forms of the state, because the state has provided the historical "container" and "articulator" of the politics of capital. We cannot but agree with Wood when she writes, "The state remains a vital point of concentration of capitalist power, even, or especially, in today's global capitalism" (Wood 2005, 14). Yet, with Sassen (2006; 2014), we also want to register how global capitalism has transformed the state and, to add the crucial point we are emphasizing here, how the economic operations of capital increasingly acquire political qualities. We fully develop this argument in the final chapter of the book, but to foreshadow an important aspect of our approach, it would seem that the state has lost its ability to represent the operations of aggregate capital and likewise to regulate the reproduction and socialization of labor power. These are changes that were already augured in debates of the 1970s about the state and capital. As we argue in the next chapter, however, they have a longer genealogy that extends back to capital's interaction with the legal and territorial forms of modern imperialism. To fully understand the contemporary institutional and infrastructural forms of the politics of capital, it is necessary to historically interrogate not only capital's relation to the state but also its relation to empire.

3

Capital, State, Empire

Empires of Capital

Is there a political moment inherent to the very notion of operations of capital? Even more generally, what is the relation of capital to politics? These are the questions that we asked in the closing moments of the previous chapter, where we argued that once politics is understood in broad terms as collective action that establishes, manages, and challenges the conditions of associative life, the political dimensions of capital become clear. Central to discerning the political contours of capital is an examination of how it prompts and sustains the production of subjectivity. Paying attention to these processes of production makes it possible to see how the operations of capital have specific political effects that circumscribe and structure the field of collective action while disseminating specific lines of antagonism across the social fabric. At the same time, such an investigation makes it clear that capital by itself cannot orchestrate its penetration into heterogeneous social formations, the variegations of capitalism, or the organization of markets, societies, and cultures in ways consistent with its logics of valorization and accumulation. It is by working this gap between capital's operations and its wider social effects that the modern state enters into variable relations with capital—relations that become an important distinguishing character of different formations of capitalism. Making this argument does not imply reducing the history of the modern state—its struggle in Europe since early modernity to gain a monopoly on institutional politics or its transformations, deformations, and even degenerations—to its relations with capital (see Schiera 2004). Rather, it means shedding light on a constitutive field of tension, which is nonetheless shaped by the de-bordering and totalizing tendency of capital—a tendency that appears particularly clear from the retrospective vantage point of the present. In this chapter, we investigate this field of tension from both a conceptual and a historical angle, placing emphasis on the global geographies within which both capital and the state have been enmeshed since the beginning of the modern age.

Within Marxism, discussion of the state has always been a point of controversy and, in many ways, a site of paradox. Marxism is often criticized for undermining the autonomy of the state—for simply reducing government ("the executive of the modern state") to a "committee for managing the common affairs of the whole bourgeoisie" (Marx and Engels 2008, 36) or imagining in naïve ways the "withering away of the state" and its replacement by the "administration of things" (Engels [1878] 1975, 262). But Marxism has also nurtured political movements that have become associated with an emphasis on and trust in the state as the main actor of social transformation. This is true for actually existing socialism, as well as for Western social democracy and several variants of anticolonial socialist movements in the twentieth century. We will return to this point in the final chapter of this book. For now, we want to stress that the image of the state prevailing in these various political movements was deeply influenced by transformations that reshaped the state itself in the transition of capitalism between the end of the nineteenth century and World War I. The processes of organization of capitalism that characterized that transition, the emergence of planning and rationalization as keywords of the time, and the pressure exerted by the organized working class through trade unions and other political organizations seemed to foster a process that, in the words of Heinrich Cunow, an influential intellectual of German social democracy in the Weimar years, was bound to lead to the steady emergence of a "socialist economic and administrative state" (Cunow 1921, 319). While Cunow's analysis focused on the emergence of a new communitarian dimension of the state, challenging and steadily displacing the relevance of domination in its constitution, it also emphasized the neutral nature of the emerging administrative functions of the state, which supposedly made it a privileged tool of social transformation. Regardless of political and historical differences, this putative neutrality was also an aspect of the state doomed to be underscored in orthodox Soviet theories of the state, particularly as far as discussions of "state monopoly capitalism"—which ended up elaborating a "purely instrumental theory of the state" (see Negri, in Hardt and Negri 1994, 141)—are concerned.

The global uprisings of 1968 laid the basis not only for the emergence of new approaches to the questions of power and the state but also for a deep transformation in the agenda of Marxist debates on the state. Particularly in the United States and Western Europe, the development of radical struggles against factory discipline, the refusal of war abroad and repression at home, and the role of what Louis Althusser (1971) called "ideological state apparatuses" prompted the development of new ways to analyze the relation between state and capital. The Marxist debates on the state that emerged in the wake of 1968 combined a new reading of Marx's texts with the appraisal of some of the most recent accomplishments of sociology. The relation of the state with aggregate capital, nicely captured by Friedrich Engels's definition of the state as the "ideal collective capitalist" (Engels [1878] 1975, 260), was investigated in ways that went beyond the merely economic dimension of the mediation among different capitalist interests. This relation instead emerged as a crucial problem crisscrossing the reproduction of the societal order as a whole. The resulting theoretical developments implied that the analysis of the state's representation of aggregate capital was more and more intertwined with a critical investigation of its roles in the framing of the reproduction and socialization of labor power, which had been a key aspect of its activities at least since the economic shocks of 1929. In his important chapter on the working day in *Capital*, volume 1, Marx (1977, 412–13) had already pointed to this function of the state in regulating the "protracted and more or less concealed civil war between the capitalist class and the working class." As the state confronted increasing barriers to its regulative functions in the 1970s, the socialization of labor power became inextricably linked to processes of subjectivation and struggle that neither capital nor the state could contain. At the same time, feminist struggles challenged the very definition of the reproduction of labor power, as well as the boundaries among productive, reproductive, and unproductive labor (see Weeks 2011). The critique of the institution of the family that was nurtured by these struggles powerfully contributed to pushing state theory beyond its traditional boundaries.

Marxists undoubtedly played an important role in efforts to "bring the state back in" to social sciences and history—efforts that became particularly visible in the early 1980s (see, e.g., Evans et al. 1985). However, the epochal sign under which the (capitalist) state was placed in Marxist debates of the previous decade was a sign of crisis. It is important to add that in the United States and Western Europe, this was not a generic crisis. Rather, it was the anticipation of the crisis of a specific political arrangement of the class compromise that had built the framework of capitalist development in the long decades following World War II. On both shores of the Atlantic, diverse forms of insurance, collective labor contracts and agreements, and welfare systems had aimed to acknowledge the Fordist working class, its movements, and its reproduction as a crucial element in the new dynamics of capitalist development. What characterizes Marxist debates on the state in this specific conjuncture is the awareness of the fact that the contradiction constitutive of the capitalist mode of production had thus become internal to the institutional structure of the state. At the same time, the continuity of working-class struggles at the point of production, combined with new forms of politicization that challenged and disrupted the very juncture between the state's representation of aggregate capital and its regulative role in the reproduction and socialization of labor power, raised the real political stakes of those debates (see, e.g., Piven and Cloward 1998).

Important controversies such as those between Nicos Poulantzas and Ralph Miliband (1972) and between Jürgen Habermas (1975) and Claus Offe (1984), as well as the critique of state monopoly theory formulated by different strands of "state derivation theory" (see Das 1996, 36–39; Demirović 2008, 30–36), revolved precisely around the possibility of inscribing the new challenges posited by social movements and struggles within the continuity of the political developments inaugurated by the New Deal in the United States and the defeat of fascism in Western Europe. Independently of the different positions held in these discussions, it is safe to contend that the combination of the "legitimation crisis" analyzed by Habermas with the "fiscal crisis" of the state (O'Connor 1973)—which in a way was symbolically instantiated by the default of New York City in 1975—announced the emergence of a new constellation. In the same year, a report written for the Trilateral Commission by Michel Crozier, Samuel P. Huntington and Jōji Watanuki (1975, 12) set the agenda for an interpretation of the "crisis of democracy" in terms of an overload of "participants and demands," which made the question of governability central for the rearrangement of the relations between capital and the state in the decades that followed.

We are convinced that Marxist debates of the 1970s, well beyond their theoretical and political shortcomings, remain relevant for an analysis of capital's relations to the state and, more generally, to politics. The two axes of the representation of aggregate capital and the reproduction of labor power continue to provide privileged entry points for such an analysis. However, there is a need to recognize that the aforementioned discussions in the United States and Western Europe remained quite provincial in their geographical scope. These debates took for granted a specific geopolitical and geo-economic organization of capitalism at the world scale that was beginning to be challenged and disrupted in the 1970s by anti-imperialist struggles and would change in profound and unexpected ways in the following decade with the crisis and incipient collapse of the USSR and really existing socialism in Eastern Europe. The discussion of these developments in studies of imperialism, as well as in the fields of dependency and world systems theory, only rarely intersected with Marxist debates on the state. At the same time, the new wave of financialization and the transformations of the banking system enabled by the delinking of the US dollar from gold in 1971 did not figure prominently in these debates (see Streeck 2014).

Needless to say, there were exceptions in this regard. In the tradition of Italian *operaismo*, for instance, there was a rapid appreciation of the epoch-making relevance of these processes and of their implication for the relations between capital and the state. The *operaista* discussion of the state in the 1970s focused on the crisis of planning as a strategic juncture between the state's activities in targeting the reproduction and socialization of labor power (which also means the articulation of capital's command over these processes) and its labor in the field of the representation of aggregate capital (see Negri 1974, 1977). While this debate was characterized by a political emphasis on struggles and the transformations of class composition underlying the crisis of the state, there was also an acute awareness of the reactive strategies of capital at both the national and the international level. The role of money and finance in these strategies was particularly emphasized (see, e.g., Berti 1978). The analysis of the crisis of the "planner state" (*Stato-piano*) pointed therefore to a set of violent dislocations of the reproduction of labor power and the representation of aggregate capital, which in many ways anticipated the trends later discussed in debates on neoliberalism and globalization.

Although this narrative of the crisis of the planner state remains seminal, it is not the only disruption that marks the political and economic turmoil that inaugurates the global era. To fully apprehend the depth and range of the crisis faced by the state since the 1970s, it is necessary to widen the geographical scope of analysis and confront the deep processes of heterogenization that remake political spaces in their tense entanglement with spaces of capital. It is in this regard that our interest in the operations of capital becomes relevant. There is also a need to provide different genealogies of the relation between capital and the state that take the opening and articulation of the world market as a crucial aspect in the political history of that relation since the inception of modernity. Colonial and imperial histories are particularly relevant in this regard. As integral parts of what Marx analyzes as so-called primitive accumulation, these histories open up original angles for an analysis of the ways in which capital entered multifarious relations with territorial powers in the process of its expansion at the world scale. They also allow us to grasp the constitutive relevance of global entanglements—which also means of the violence of conquest and the extraction of raw materials and forced labor—for the history of the modern state in Europe, as well as for the formation of a "law of nations" that came to encapsulate the whole world within its international order. As we argued in chapter 1, we are confronted today with the crucial relevance of a set of operations of capital that put the territorial norm of this international order increasingly under duress, producing their own spaces and deploying political effects that can hardly be tamed or simply contained by the state and its legal order. Both the representation of aggregate capital and the reproduction of labor power take place in forms that escape and continually displace the monopoly of the state. In coming to grips with this predicament, a consideration of the history of the relations between state and capital from a colonial and imperial perspective is particularly productive.

We take the lively debates surrounding empire and imperialism over recent years as symptoms and registrations of the moment of geographical disruption that lies at the core of the contemporary capitalist transition. The role of war and military power figures prominently in these debates, particularly as regards the analysis of the US reaction to the attacks of 9/11 and related plans of a "new American century" in the years of the George W. Bush administration. "New imperialism," the phrase popularized by David Harvey (2003), circulated widely in the early years of the twenty-first century. Nevertheless, subsequent developments in Afghanistan and Iraq, as well as the current situation in the "Greater Middle East," amply demonstrate that a traditional understanding of imperialism centered on plans of stabilization of territorial control through the action of a dominant power do not help much to understand the current predicament of world politics. Even such a brilliant book as Ellen Meiksins Wood's *Empire of Capital* (2003) frames the discussion of the relation between political and economic power in capitalism within a perspective that takes nation-states and nationally denominated capitals as the basic unities of the world order. Wood (2003, 127) emphatically states that, nowadays, "all international relations are internal to capitalism and governed by capitalist imperatives," but the rigid demarcation of the boundary between capital and state (between economy and politics) on which her analysis is predicated does not allow her to come to grips with the processes of globalization and transnationalization that are reshaping the very relation between them (see Robinson 2007).

"The political form of globalization," Wood (2003, 5–6) writes, "is not a global state but a global system of multiple states, and the new imperialism takes its specific shape from the complex and contradictory relationship between capital's expansive economic power and the more limited reach of the extra-economic force that sustains it." It is definitely true that no "global state" is in sight on the horizon of globalization. But it is equally true that global processes are testing the boundaries between capital's "expansive economic power" and "extra-economic force." This does not mean that states do not continue to play important roles in the contemporary world. But it does mean recognizing that states are increasingly traversed, pressed, and disarticulated by processes of capitalist production, valorization, and accumulation whose logics and even denomination they are no longer able to fully control and contain. New emerging assemblages of territory, authority, and rights (Sassen 2006) combine states and their legal orders with heterogeneous actors and orders that often represent the interests of capital and even include its direct participation. The political and legal form of globalization is characterized by the emergence of these assemblages, by the conflicts and tensions within and among them, and by the peculiar forms of instability that these conflicts and tensions disseminate at the national and global scale.

More than fifteen years after its publication, Michael Hardt and Antonio Negri's *Empire* (2000) remains a crucial reference in this regard. We do not think, as some passages of this book may seem to suggest, that the tensions between politics and capital can be regarded as having been smoothly overcome through the emergence of a new "capitalist sovereignty" (see, e.g., Hardt and Negri 2000, 325–28). Rather, we are convinced that the

problem of the reproduction of the general conditions for the endless accumulation of capital, which is also the problem of capital's relations with
the living labor and social cooperation it commands, cannot be solved by
capital itself. This problem continues to emerge across a diverse array of
geographical spaces and scales, raising again the questions of subsumption
and variegation that we discussed in the previous chapter from the angle
of the distinction between capital and capitalism. Moreover, it is important
to note that, as no "global state" is emerging, there is no "global capital"
that acts as a concrete subject capable of ruling the world. The elusiveness of the concept of aggregate capital that we discussed earlier is further
entrenched by the global scope of many contemporary operations of capital, which corresponds to the existence of several transnational capitalist actors but does not find any stable form of general organization and
representation. Hardt and Negri are fully aware of this when they write,
"Although transnational corporations and global networks of production
and circulation have undermined the powers of nation-states, state functions and constitutional elements have effectively been displaced to other
levels and domains" (Hardt and Negri 2000, 307).

What *Empire* was able to grasp are the new political dimensions and
implications of the existence of a network of capitalist activities and actors
directly operating at the global level. The concept of a "mixed constitution"
of empire that Hardt and Negri (2000, 304–23) propose nicely captures
both the heterogeneity of actors and orders that characterizes the political
and legal form of globalization and the directly political role capital plays
within it. If the concept of mixed constitution is read in a way that emphasizes its elasticity and openness, it allows us to understand the position
of contemporary states, which continue to be important players—and are
capable of expanding their margins of action and performing crucial tasks,
as has happened in different ways over recent years—without ceasing to
be subject to specific limits and transformative processes. What remains
to be investigated are, on the one hand, the multiple forms of intertwining
between capital and state that crisscross this mixed constitution, and, on
the other hand, the gaps, connections, and disconnections between the operative spaces of capital and the political and legal spaces that continue to
join and divide the world. While we have been emphasizing thus far the
novelty of the contemporary situation, an excursus through the legal and
political history of empire leads to the discovery of an uncanny element of
continuity.

Scattered Geographies of State and Empire

Classical histories of the modern state emphasize a transition from empires to nation-states. Take the influential work of Gianfranco Poggi (1978), which begins with the crowning of Charlemagne as Holy Roman Emperor in 800. Poggi offers a detailed sociological and juridical analysis of the various twists, turns, and reactions that marked the transition in continental Europe from the feudal system to the nineteenth-century constitutional state, emphasizing the transitionary phases of the corporative state (*Ständestaat*) and absolutist rule in France and Prussia. Leaving aside for the moment the exclusively European focus of this account, we can note that the distinctiveness of the modern state appears in contrast to the "heterocephalic" composition of ancient and early modern empires (and particularly of the Holy Roman Empire). As opposed to a configuration in which "semi-sovereign components [were] tied to an imperial center by relations of subordination," the modern state emerges as a "self-originating, self-empowered unit operating exclusively in pursuit of its own interests." Modern "states do not *presuppose* the system" of which they are part; "they *generate* it" (Poggi 1978, 87–88). We find similar versions of this claim in the histories of state formation presented by figures as diverse as Perry Anderson (1974), Otto Hintze ([1902] 1975), Georg Jellinek ([1914] 1900), Pierangelo Schiera (2004), Charles Tilly (1975), and Max Weber ([1919] 2008). States rise from the ashes of empire, mediated by the concentrated power of the monarchy and characterized by an ordering and arrangement of the powers of government along a center-periphery axis. These powers of government must negotiate the persistence of the old corporative society and confront peasants' rebellions, as well as the incipient insurgency of the urban proletariat. Modern imperialism, in turn, offers a vehicle by which the state form and the state system spread throughout the world.

The ubiquity of this narrative in studied canons of politics and international relations should not obscure the variability that strikes it. Of the thinkers of state formation listed (it would be easy to add more), Tilly is perhaps most attentive to variations in the emergence of modern European states. Emphasizing differences, setbacks, and failures in the formation of the French, English, Spanish, Prussian, and Italian states, he argues that histories of modern state making "do not fit together into any single pattern we could confidently call 'political development'" (Tilly 1975, 38). Nonetheless, Tilly (1975, 32) measures variations among these states against an ideal quality that he calls "stateness," which seems to derive from the most conventional of sociological understandings: "an organization which controls the population occupying a defined territory is a state *in so far as* (1) it is differentiated from other organizations operating in the same territory; (2) it is autonomous; (3) it is centralized; and (4) its divisions are formally coordinated with one another" (Tilly 1975, 70). It is not difficult here to hear the echo of Max Weber's famous definition of the state as "the human community that, within a defined territory—and the key word here is 'territory'—(successfully) claims the *monopoly of legitimate force* for itself" (Weber [1919] 2008, 156). Indeed, Weber's understanding of the state provides a template for many subsequent debates, even if he never develops a consistent theory of the state and describes it variously as "a machine," "a specific joint human action," a "legal order," and "a tangle of value ideas" (Weber, quoted in Anter 2014, 3). Influential in Marxian approaches as much as in mainstream sociology, Weber's definition has acquired an almost axiomatic status, providing a baseline model against which many claims for state transformation, crisis, development, variability, and failure have been assessed. But to what extent can the classicism of this definition stand the test of space and time? Can it persist amid a variability measured not against itself but against the ruptures of globalization, the operations of capital, and the ongoing dynamics of empire?

States today seem to falter on all three axes of Weber's definition: territory, community, and legitimacy. As we argued in chapter 1, states are still territorial entities, but the contiguity and legal foundation of their territoriality has been vexed by the vacillation of borders and the emergence of new kinds of territories both within and across their boundaries (Sassen 2013). At the same time, the communal aspect of human life has become more complex and diversified due to large-scale migration, information flows, and diaspora, meaning that in many instances the state's conjunction to the national configuration of community has been severed or rendered unstable (see, e.g., Appadurai 1996; Balibar 1990). In addition, the articulation of nationalism to crisis and neoliberalism, as we also noted in chapter 1, contributes to processes of diversification and fragmentation that further complicate the relation of nation to state. In the juridical sphere, the emergence of globally extensive but sector-specific legal regimes (from *lex constructionis* to *lex informatica*) has challenged the state's monopoly on the production of law (Fischer-Lescano and Teubner 2004). Many states have willingly ceded their monopoly on the legitimate use of force by outsourcing operations to organizations such as private military companies whose actions they can authorize but not fully control (Eckert 2016, 1–29).

In any case, Weber's emphasis on rational legal legitimacy—the idea that the state's commands are binding because they are legal—always turned the focus inward. As Poggi (1978, 132) remarks, such a "notion is relatively weak because it does not evoke a strong substantive ideal, a universally shared standard of intrinsic validity, but instead refers to purely formal, contentless considerations of procedural correctness." Compared with Carl Schmitt's emphasis on the necessity of the state for the preservation of the existence and integrity of the collectivity, Weber's understanding seems rooted in notions of functional specificity.

Perhaps it is no accident, then, that Schmitt's writings, despite the insidious and unavoidable danger posed by his National Socialist affiliations, have drawn increasing attention in recent years. Interest in Schmitt has grown as the state's claim to legitimacy has been eroded by institutional changes—for example, the shifting role of parliaments and the increasing autonomy of executive power. Displacements of the state-society division that have increased the political leverage of social forces and capitalist interests have also contributed to renewed interest in Schmitt. This is not the occasion to rehearse the fundamentals of Schmitt's political thought: the tension between liberalism and democracy, the primacy of decision and friend-enemy relations, or the centrality of exception to sovereign rule (for a useful reconstruction of Schmitt's intellectual trajectory, see Galli 2015). We are primarily interested in how an appreciation of the interdependence of empire and international law shapes Schmitt's understanding of the state. In *The* Nomos *of the Earth in the International Law of the* Jus Publicum Europaeum ([1950] 2003), Schmitt argues that the formation of modern European states went hand in hand with legal and political arrangements that were meant to organize an already global space. Two factors were crucial to the perseverance of the Eurocentric legal order that he called the *jus publicum Europaeum*. First was the formal equilibrium resulting from the reciprocal recognition between European states as *justi hostes* (just enemies), which allowed a "taming" and regulation of war in the old continent. Second was the designation of an extra-European space where the tension and conflict banished from Europe could have free rein. Colonialism, in Schmitt's view and consistently with the doctrine of terra nullius that we mentioned in chapter 1, was a lawmaking occupation of putatively free and empty space by means of conquest, land grabbing, and coercive entitlement. The dual articulation of colonial space and globally projected political space described by Schmitt allowed him to view the colony, as he wrote in 1941, as "the fundamental spatial data of international law until World War II" (Schmitt 2015, 171).

Although *The* Nomos *of the Earth* laments the waning of the jus publi-cum Europaeum, which Schmitt dates to the end of the nineteenth century and particularly to World War I, the text maintains many elements of his previous work. In particular, the notion of Großraum developed in a series of writings that lent support to the expansionist policies of Germany in the late 1930s and early 1940s, provides a way to describe the extended sphere of spatial influence exercised by dominant state powers. The concept of Großraum initially emerged to describe how "a consistent 'operative space'" could be created to provide critical utilities such as gas and electricity to a large-scale spatial economy; Schmitt (2015, 107–10), however, elaborated the notion with a geopolitical eye. Dismayed at the universalization of in-ternational law, which he saw as the dissolution of the established global order, he began to see the introduction of an international law specific to Großräume as desirable. Although the notion of Großraum, as employed in *The* Nomos *of the Earth*, does not necessarily imply territorial annexa-tion, Schmitt was alarmed at post–World War II developments, particularly the expansion of the US and Soviet spheres of influence and the role of economic power in reshaping the sphere of international law. "*Cujus oeco-nomia, ejus regio*," he writes bitterly—economic domination gives political control (Schmitt [1950] 2003, 308). Yet while Schmitt was able to explain this situation juridically and geopolitically, taking the "technical-economic-industrial sphere" as a point of departure for the elaboration of the notion of Großraum (Schmitt 2015, 109), he was unable (or, perhaps, reluctant) to offer an analysis that grasped the importance of the operations of capital within this new configuration of states and empire. For us, this is a seri-ous political limit of Schmitt's thought. It is not a matter of adding supple-mental economic detail to an otherwise accurate political analysis. Rather, Schmitt's failure to recognize the properly political dimensions of capital impedes his ability to understand and diagnose the new forms of spatial heterogeneity and the mutations in expression of political power that were already beginning to emerge in the wake of the Nazi defeat. What may be added to this is that a different conceptualization of Großraum, elaborated by so-called Ordoliberals beginning in the 1930s, provided a much more effective and influential framework in Europe at this point.

Despite these limits, Schmitt's non-sociological account of the legal and political intertwining of European state formation and European colonial expansion offers a powerful countercurrent to conventional sociological understandings of state making. Maintaining an uncompromisingly Euro-centric perspective—and, indeed, defending this perspective as the source of an international law free from moral postulates—Schmitt reinserts the history of the state into the history of empire in ways that do not simply imply the export of European state models through colonialism. In Schmitt's perspective, colonial expansion and conquest were also important conditions for the rise of the territorial state in Europe. In this way, his work provides an uncanny precedent for modes of critical postcolonial thought that recognize the centrality of the colony to the fabrication of the modern world and provide alternative ways to think about the making of borders, the role of violence in imperial and postcolonial contexts, and the translation of colonial power relations into metropolitan settings (see Blanco and del Valle 2014). As early as 1883, the British historian John Seeley attacked his peers for concentrating so much on domestic constitutional history by writing that the "history of England is not in England but in America and Asia" (Seeley 1883, 12). Quipping on this point, Salman Rushdie (1988, 343) writes that the "trouble with the English is that their history happened overseas, so they don't know what it means." Applying this principle more generally to the history of modern European state making, however, draws attention to an aspect of Schmitt's thought that works against the insights of postcolonial theory: his tendency to consign all colonial activities to an indistinct and empty extra-European legal space. Such a perspective, although by no means isolable to Schmitt's work, fails to recognize the heterogeneous geographical and legal arrangements that shot through European adventures of conquest and colonization. It also fails to trouble the coherence of European political and legal understandings of international society and the non-European world, assuming instead a unified and consistent body of thought that reinforces precisely the kind of rational universalism that postcolonial thinking decries.

A questioning of the central division between European and extra-European space that constructs Schmitt's vision of the jus publicum Europaeum is a prominent feature of the work of historians who argue for "the centrality and persistence of empires in world history" (Benton and Ross 2013, 1). Emphasizing the importance of peculiar forms of legal pluralism to empires, this work deliberately contrasts the narrative by which empires smoothly give way to states and opens up new vistas on the intertwining of the histories of empire and states. These historians do not simply trace colonial influences on processes regarded as central to the legal development of European states. Nor does their work limit itself to questioning the notion that state law is central to all legal orders or disabusing the myth that non-state law is somehow more egalitarian and less coercive than state law. Rather, historians working in this vein explore how empires "were legally plural in their core regions as well as in their overseas or distant possessions" and ask how empires "assembled political communities boasting divergent constitutional traditions" (Benton and Ross 2013, 1). There is an emphasis on jurisdictional conflicts, where the term "jurisdiction" refers to "the exercise by sometimes vaguely defined legal authorities of the power to regulate and administer sanctions over particular actions or people, defined by personal status, territorial boundaries, and corporate membership." Consequently, attention focuses on "clusters of conflicts" rather than the procedural application of rules and norms (Benton and Ross 2013, 6).

In the work of Lauren Benton, there is a foregrounding of case studies that examine the fractured geographies of empire, concentrating on difficult terrains such as islands and riverine regions, where the myth of central control was largely absent and activities of mutiny, marronage, piracy, and privateering often ran rife. Benton (2010, 9) traces how law "formed an important epistemological framework for the production and dissemination of geographic knowledge, while geographic descriptions encoded ideas about law and sovereignty." The result is a vision of empire as consisting of "layered sovereignties" and "variegated legal spaces" (Benton 2010, 31–33). Far from affirming a binary distinction between European and extra-European legal zones, this line of historical analysis shows how patterns "of divided and layered sovereignty . . . posed a sharp challenge to claims about the basis of international law in the agreements formed by separate and equal sovereign states." Furthermore, Benton (2010, 280) argues that these arrangements "developed not merely in opposition to imperial centers but also in response to shifting interimperial relations and cross-imperial comparisons, forming in the process part of a broader, geographically uneven regulatory web, or another source of international law."

In Benton's account, we find an element of continuity that allows us to trace connections between the political and legal spaces of the past and those that populate the scene of contemporary capitalist globalization. Importantly, this involves a detour through the history of empire rather than a working through of the state form and state system as understood in mainstream discourses of sociology, political science, and international relations. However, we must be emphatic that this is not to deny the continuing importance of the state, its internal transformations, or the incontrovertible historical processes by which, beginning in the eighteenth century, the association between empire and bounded territories became stronger. To the contrary, we seek to affirm the ongoing relevance of the state in shaping the operations of capital and providing a political terrain on which those operations can be played out. As much as we question a vision of the state as the sole horizon of politics, we are not iconoclasts of the state form or victims of what Michel Foucault (2008, 76) provocatively called "state phobia" (see also Dean and Villadsen 2016). The stance we take diverges from the dominant Weberian baseline and sees possibilities for the state beyond the restricted vision of coincidence between sovereignty, territory, and population or the abstract and idealized notion of "state-ness." A first step is to recognize how the wide array of "quasi-sovereign" or "partially sovereign" colonial polities that had emerged by the end of the nineteenth century posed challenges for defining political membership and limiting authority, despite the presence of an international order based on sovereign nation-states. As Benton (2010, 297) writes, attention to the "fluid discourse merging geography and law" in colonialism "helps us to move beyond the expectation that varieties of imperial territories awaited incorporation into sovereign states." In this perspective, the evolution of the modern state does not run directly through the coordinates of nation and citizenship but, instead, passes through commercial and legal arrangements that complicate and subvert the narrative by which a fully formed metropolitan sovereignty was exported and imposed beyond the center. The result is a more fragmented view of the history of the modern state, which we consider much richer and more fecund for a critical understanding of the relation of politics to capital. But before we can begin the work of forging an adequate account of this relation, we must complete the story by also tracing how the history of capital intersects the history of empire.

Formations of Capital and Empire

Toward the end of Amitav Ghosh's historical novel *Flood of Fire* (2015), the factories of Canton go up in flames. Although the novel is set in the nineteenth century, these factories are not sites of industrial manufacture like those described in such classic texts as Friedrich Engels's *The Condition of the Working Class in England* ([1845] 1887). Rather, they are colonial outposts or fortified structures serving as trading establishments, warehouses, and merchants' accommodation. With precedents in the *kontors* of the Hanseatic League and the Portuguese *feitorias*, which by the sixteenth century dotted an entire hemisphere, such trading posts were central to the activities of chartered companies and other commercial agents of empire throughout the world. In Canton (today the city of Guangzhou), mid-eighteenth-century Chinese imperial decrees limited foreign residence to a set of Chinese-constructed factories on the banks of the Pearl River. Known as the thirteen factories or Fanqui Town, this foreign quarter remained the principal site of Western trade in China well into the nineteenth century. After repeated trading seasons, which were initially limited to a period of only four months, the dwellings acquired names that reflected the nationalities of the merchants that lodged in them. Ghosh picks up the action in May 1841 in the midst of the First Opium War. Whisked away from the British factory onto a schooner anchored in the river, a group of merchants witnesses the havoc visited on the city by the iron gunboat *Nemesis* and the storming of the foreign enclave by an angry Chinese crowd. Noting the lavish woodwork inside the buildings and the tears of merchants who had frequented these factories for decades, Ghosh (2015, 541) writes, "They burned mightily, with upcurling plumes of fire shooting out of their doorways and windows."

We might take this burning of the factories as a moment of colonial resistance, which, although carried out in the face of superior British firepower, portends the fall of the factory trade system in Canton. Although the foreign enclave would continue to exist until 1856, when it would burn again during the Second Opium War, the Treaty of Nanking, signed in 1842, granted the British the right to trade in five treaty ports, ceded the territory of Hong Kong, set favorable trading duties, and established an indemnity to pay for opium confiscated in 1839. A supplementary treaty granted rights of extraterritorial jurisdiction. Similar treaties signed with the United States and France allowed the establishment of foreign concessions in treaty ports up and down China's coast, and most favored nation clauses extended privileges granted to one nation to other treaty powers. These were the outcomes of an uneven military struggle in which the imperial forces of the British state and the East India Company interceded to enforce principles of free trade that were purportedly distinct from the protection and enforcement of the opium trade. Here as elsewhere, modern imperialism had a commercial and even military basis that predated and exceeded the diverse forms of jurisdictional and territorial control established by sovereign states.

That the state was a latecomer to the imperial adventure is no historical revelation. In chapter 1, we mentioned how, during the same period in which the modern European state was under formation, chartered companies acted as sovereign entities across vast stretches of territory. Settler colonial claims to possession, by contrast, involved "a scattershot legal approach, with multiple, overlapping, and even conflicting arguments being addressed to various, sometimes imagined, audiences" (Benton and Straumann 2010, 29). Furthermore, "justifications for colonial settlement" were often elaborated well after settlers themselves had affirmed the seizure or purchase of land as "the central mode for legitimately acquiring territory" (Benton and Straumann 2010, 8). Far from asserting an inner incompatibility between empire and state, the historical record ascertains the variability of state forms, commercial enterprises, and legal claims at stake in Europe's imperial expansion. Working through the analytical matrix provided by this variability provides a way to trace the shifting formations of empire and capital as they intersect the opening and articulation of the world market from early modernity.

The political relations surrounding the establishment and operation of colonial factories offer a strategic starting point for such analysis. Part of the logistical infrastructure of modern European empires, factories were often administered by charted companies and thus linked to the development of finance, as many of these organizations were joint stock companies. Alongside the various proprietorships, encomiendas, seigneuries, captaincies, and patroonships granted by imperial authorities, chartered companies provided a formidable form of imperial agency that mixed commercial and political imperatives. The Dutch East India Company (VOC) was the first organization to conduct what today would be called an initial public offering, issuing stock in 1602 to finance the outfitting of its fleet and making subsequent use of bonds to raise capital for individual voyages. As early as 1607, a secondary trade in derivatives based on VOC shares arose. Instruments such as forwards, options, and repos "allowed traders to participate in the share trade without necessarily having to pay the full value of the shares they traded" (Petram 2011, 20). In 1657, the English East India Company, which, like its Dutch counterpart before its establishment as a joint stock company raised capital by issuing stock for each voyage, followed suit by raising a permanent joint stock. Other examples could be given. From these two instances alone, however, it is possible to see how the logistical expansion of empire through the founding of factories in sites such as Surat, Batavia, Bombay, and Calcutta was deeply intertwined with the financial operations of capital. The same can be said for the logistical organization of the Atlantic slave trade, which is another crucial moment in the historical formations of capital and empire (see, e.g., Baucom 2005) and laid the basis for the accumulation of finance that enabled British industrial expansion, as Eric Williams noted in the early 1940s (see Williams 1944, 98–107).

Needless to say, chartered companies themselves took on a variety of forms. Aside from juggernauts such as the VOC, the British East India Company, and the Hudson's Bay Company, which acted as political organizations in their own right across different territories and vast stretches of time, a great many chartered companies were short-lived or absorbed more quickly into other forms of colonial government. Colonizing companies such as the Virginia Company (1606), the Massachusetts Bay Company (1629), the French Royal West Indian Company (1664–74), the Santo Domingo Company (1698), and the Dutch West India Company (1621) were dissolved relatively quickly. Late nineteenth-century companies such as the British North Borneo Company (1881), Royal Niger Company (1886), British South Africa Company (1888), and German East Africa Company (1884) had more restricted powers and tended to limit their activities to the initial stages of colonization (Robert 1969). Nonetheless, it would be mistaken to view chartered companies as merely commercial bodies that were secondary or instrumental to the political will of a "pre-formed imperial center." These organizations display in an early form the means by which operations of capital take on directly political implications.

In his history of the early British East India Company (before its nationalization in the wake of the Sepoy Rebellion in 1857), Philip Stern cautions against characterizing the political activity of this organization as "state-like," "semi-sovereign," or "quasi-governmental." Instead, he approaches the company as "a body politic on its own terms, neither tethered to supposedly broader national histories nor as an imitation, extension, or reflection of the national state, which was itself still in formation" (Stern 2011, 6; see also Spivak 1999, 220–23). The company's charter, which encompassed "all the trade and traffic between the Cape of Good Hope and the Strait of Magellan, translated into a claim to jurisdiction over all English subjects in Asia and the Eurasian populations resident in its growing network of settlements." By the late seventeenth century, the British East India Company had acquired "leave to establish fortifications, make law, erect courts, issue punishment, coin money, conduct diplomacy, wage war, arrest English subjects, and plant colonies" (Stern 2011, 12). While the company's factories were led by councils that supposedly were answerable to the central Court of Committees in London, the actual practice of governance was shaped not only by charters and mandates from England but also by "grants, treaties, alliances, and agreements with Asian polities establishing an array of commercial and political powers and immunities" (13). As Stern comments, "The ability to borrow and balance these various sources of authority and legitimacy potentially offered a remarkably flexible and robust form of political power" (13).

Following Stern in characterizing the British East India Company and others like it as "company-states" means not only decentering our understanding of what constitutes a state away from Weberian or Schmittian conceptions but also reorienting our understanding of the political operations of capital. Chartered companies are usually seen as an important part of mercantilist capitalism by which European states sought to monopolize profits produced in their empires by controlling trade and accumulating capital in the form of gold and silver. As the story normally goes, the mercantilist system was supplanted by physiocracy and the ideas of Adam Smith in the eighteenth century, meaning that practices of free trade gradually replaced the building of state monopolies, and an emphasis on production and the division of labor emerged. In *The Wealth of Nations*, Smith ([1776] 1904, 111) wrote, "The monopoly of the colony trade, therefore, like all the other means and malignant expedients of the mercantile system, depresses the industry of all other countries, but chiefly that of the colonies, without in the least increasing, but on the contrary diminishing, that of the country in whose favour it is established." Indeed, merchants active in the early nineteenth-century opium trade in Canton, such as James Matheson and Lancelot Dent, were active exponents of Smith's ideas (Le Pichon 2006).

As Lisa Lowe emphasizes, such a prominent advocate of free trade as John Stuart Mill was an employee of the British East India Company for thirty-five years. Lowe (2015, 105) writes, "Mill's embellishments of Ricardo's laws of international trade may well have been describing the East India Company's strategy that had successfully balanced the China tea trade by increasing the export of British India-manufactured opium to China." The reference to David Ricardo is important here because his development of the theory of comparative advantages in "On Foreign Trade," chapter 7 in *On the Principles of Political Economy and Taxation* ([1817] 1821), provides the seminal nineteenth-century theorization of international trade in the context of geographical division and specialization of production. Yet all these understandings of foreign trade, whether mercantilist or liberal in orientation, tend to assume the existence of bounded state spaces that could be approached as analytical units. The notion of the company state provides a very different perspective, suggesting not only a more dispersed and scattered spatiality of capital, but also a more complex articulation of empire and capital that decenters and questions the analytical primacy and centralized power of the European sovereign state. We have already discussed how Marx's arguments concerning the tendency of capital to create the world market display a tension between the frontiers of capital and political borders (primarily those of territorial states). The concept of the company state allows us to add something more: an analysis of how this tension manifests itself in the institutional forms that articulated empire to the operations of capital and provided ways to represent order, authority, and rights that were necessarily open to jurisdictional conflict, territorial uncertainty, and the pursuit of sovereignty as a loose, incomplete, but also corporate project.

Narratives of a smooth transition from mercantilism to free trade are illusory and should be approached with suspicion. The nationalization of the British East India Company in 1858, as well as counterexamples and tendencies such as the protectionist policies of the United States under Abraham Lincoln (and successive administrations) and the anti–free trade writings of American School economists such as Henry Charles Carey, suggest other trajectories of transition and means of managing the unstable relations between empire and state. Through a rigorous analysis of historical tariff rates and trade policies, Paul Bairoch unseats the myth of the nineteenth century as the golden era of European free trade. He shows how in "those parts of the world which gradually became part of the developed world, protectionism was the dominant commercial policy." In "those countries that were colonized," by contrast, "liberalism prevailed, but it was not by choice; it was enforced liberal commercial policy" (Bairoch 1993, 30). Furthermore, Bairoch questions the dogma that relates trade liberalization to economic growth, pointing out that the "great European depression of 1870–2 to 1891–3" coincided with the point "when trade policies reached their most liberal" (Bairoch 1993, 44). Although Bairoch's analysis rests in state-centered notions of development, it provides a firm quantitative basis to illustrate what Lowe (2015, 101–33) calls "the ruses of liberty."

Lowe shows how the enforcement of free trade in the colonies aimed not only to "lift mercantilist trade barriers" but also offered "the means for expansion of the opium and 'coolie' trades in India and coastal China" (Lowe 2015, 110). She argues that "liberal notions of education, trade, and government grew out of the conditions of colonial encounter, and were themselves precisely philosophical attempts to grapple with and manage *colonial difference* within an expanding empire" (106). Furthermore, she contends that the forms of government enabled by these notions "consisted in the power to adapt and combine the projects of earlier colonial conquest with forms of transportable migrant labor, monopoly with laissez-faire, and historic territorial rule with new powers over circulation and mobility of goods and people" (108). Such government also supplied conditions that enabled processes of capital accumulation which, as we explored in the discussion of Rosa Luxemburg in chapter 2, required "an environment of non-capitalist forms of production" (Luxemburg [1913] 2003, 348). Furthermore, their mixing of "monopoly with laissez-faire" (Lowe 2015, 108), as well as their variegated operations across the expanding scope of the world market, provided the precedent and impetus for the transitions of the "new capitalism" that Vladimir Lenin would characterize as involving a "mixture of free competition and monopoly" and "the domination of finance capital" (Lenin [1917] 1999, 45–57).

If Luxemburg was too hasty in identifying imperialism as the "final phase of capitalism" (Luxemburg [1913] 2003, 427), Lenin did not hesitate to predict—in the 1920 preface to the French and German editions of *Imperialism*—a "worldwide revolutionary crisis" involving the uprising of "*a thousand million* people (in the colonies and semicolonies)" (Lenin [1917] 1999, 3). Regardless of whether we read these claims as analytical or rhetorical, the history of the changing formations of empire and capital is incomplete without an account of the resistance of the colonized, for whom the question of whether imperialism was imposed by commercial or political entities was often irrelevant. From the burning of Canton's thirteen factories to the Sanyuanli incident involving the siege of sixty British troops by a crowd of ten thousand Chinese a few days later, from the long Maori resistance against colonial settlement in New Zealand to the Haitian Revolution and the marronage of African slaves in the Caribbean, from the Sepoy Rebellion in India to the wars in Algeria and Vietnam, the history of anticolonial resistance is varied and multiform. Likewise, the intellectual production surrounding it is diverse, including the cultured internationalism of Rabindrinath Tagore, W. E. B. Du Bois's linking of slave rebellions to transcontinental anticolonial movements, Frantz Fanon's reflections on the violence of decolonization in *The Wretched of the Earth* (1963), the political speeches of Amílcar Cabral (1973), and more recent interventions such as the work of the subaltern studies group (Guha 1997) and the Indigenous epistemologies of Linda Tuhiwai Smith (1999). Whether one emphasizes moments of coming together such as the Bandung Conference of 1955 (Chakrabarty 2005) or the longer and often bloody trajectory of nationalist struggles that resulted in the founding of newly independent states (usually within the bounds of former colonial territories), the advent of decolonization is an irrevocable episode of global political history.

John A. Hobson, whose seminal *Imperialism: A Study* provided the point of departure for Lenin's 1917 tract, argued that the political significance of imperialism lay in the threat that techniques of colonial rule posed for home politics—that is, how "the arts and crafts of tyranny, acquired and exercised in our unfree Empire, should be turned against our liberties at home" (Hobson [1902] 1965, 151–52). In identifying this threat, Hobson foresaw what Aimé Césaire and Hannah Arendt, as well as Michel Foucault after them, would call the "boomerang effect" (Césaire [1950] 2000, 36; Arendt 1951, 155; Foucault 2003, 103)—a phenomenon also noted by Du Bois in *The World and Africa* (1946), where, like Césaire in *Discourse on Colonialism* ([1950] 2000), he characterized Nazism as a form of internal colonialism visited on Europe. We wish to make a related but almost opposite point. Recognizing the crucial role of decolonization and anti-imperial struggles in the global diffusion of the modern state as it unfolded across the twentieth century means not only asking how colonial tyranny rebounded on Europe but also tracing how the multiple forms taken by and pressures exerted on the colonial state led to trajectories of liberation and entanglements with capital that opened a vast field of heterogeneity. Charting the terms and transformations of this heterogeneity means understanding why the twentieth century can be seen at once as the time of the state's maximum diffusion and domination and as the time of its maximum crisis.

Figures of the Twentieth-Century State

A global history of the modern state cannot be written without taking into account the constitutive relevance of colonial and imperial expansion. In the preceding two sections we attempted to test the productivity of this statement by multiplying the gazes from outside Europe and the West on state and imperial formations, as well as on their multifarious entanglements with capital. Following Benton (2010), we suggested that Schmitt's introduction of a binary distinction between European and non-European legal zones in *The Nomos of the Earth* ([1950] 2003) was insensitive to patterns of variation within, across, and among European empires. While recognizing the validity of Benton's argument, there is a need to acknowledge the relevance of Schmitt's reference to the global scope of the development of "European public law" (which also means of the territorial state in

Europe) from the very inception of modernity. Schmitt was keen to emphasize that a basic condition for that global development was the existence of a qualitative difference, constructed and legitimized by law, between European and other spaces—a qualitative difference that remains relevant even if we emphasize the limits of considering non-European spaces legally "empty." The further foundation of this qualitative difference, before a growing intertwining of metropolitan and colonial developments, was the primary factor in the blossoming discipline of colonial law in several European countries between the nineteenth and twentieth centuries (see, e.g., Center for Studies of the History of Modern Legal Thought 2004–2005).

Although the influential German jurist Georg Jellinek ([1914] 1990) provided a majestic reconstruction of the development of the modern state in Europe at the crossing point of powerful processes of steady homogenization of its three constitutive elements—territory, people, and sovereignty—the legal and political condition of the colonies, dependencies, and protectorates raised several problems. The variable geometry of territorial control and bordering, the distinction between citizen and subject (Mamdani 1996), the French construction of the Indigénat (Le Cour Grandmaison 2010), and the growing heterogeneity of legal conditions built the backdrop against which questions of civilization, culture, and even race became internal elements of European legal theories and orders. As Dipesh Chakrabarty (2000, 8–9) demonstrates in an engagement with the writings of John Stuart Mill, the qualitative "meta-border" circumscribing the European space started to become inscribed onto time. The Italian jurist Santi Romano, who published his *Corso di diritto coloniale* (Course of Colonial Law) in 1918, did not limit himself to arguing for supplementary conditions for the naturalization of colonial subjects, due to the fact that they were of "non-European race" (Romano [1918] 1969, 126). He also explained that the "diversity of civilization" did not allow the introduction of principles of "constitutional government" in the colonies; rather it imposed the construction of the metropolis-colony relation according to the figure of the "patrimonial state, which prevailed *before* the constitutional state." This figure posited the state, "at least according to a much widespread opinion, as the object of domination of the power of the monarch" (Romano [1918] 1969, 104).

Viewed from the angle of decolonization, the twentieth century is the century in which the state form reaches its widest scope of diffusion. The time of "the majority of the inhabitants of the earth, who happen for the most part to be colored," has come, Du Bois wrote soon after the conference at Dumbarton Oaks in 1944, which laid the basis for the foundation of the United Nations (Du Bois 1946, v). The claim of the colonized to share in "that democracy which alone can ensure peace among men, by the abolition of poverty, the education of the masses, protection form disease, and the scientific treatment of crime" (Du Bois 1946, v), was also a powerful challenge to the existence of the qualitative meta-border that supposedly separated Europe and, later, the West from the rest of the world. The success of decolonization movements led to a multiplication of states and to the production of the familiar political map of the world in which discrete territories are separated by linear boundaries all over the globe. This is not the place to rehearse the critical discussion of how state formation in the postcolonial world took place within the territorial and national boundaries established by colonialism and imperialism (see, e.g., Chatterjee 1986; Winichakul 1994). Instead, we are interested in asking whether the globalization of the state form brought about by anticolonial and decolonial struggles contributed to setting the stage on which a set of transformations and deformations of the state form began to take place in the early 1970s, in a way foreshadowing the double crisis of Eurocentrism and "state-centrism" in the international world that looms today (Colombo 2014, 193).

The early twentieth century, in any case, was dominated in Europe by lively debates on the incipient crisis of the modern state. Santi Romano dedicated his inaugural address for the academic year 1909–10 at the University of Pisa to this topic. The main problem for Santi Romano, who was in dialogue with "institutionalist" theories of law emerging particularly in France (one thinks of names such as Maurice Hauriou and Léon Duguit), resulted from the fact that "modern public law does not dominate but is rather dominated by a social movement, which governs itself according to its own laws" (Romano [1918] 1969, 15). This was a clear reference to the new forms of organization of capitalism that had been emerging since the 1890s, as well as to the challenge posited by the growth of the labor movement and by a syndicalism that threatened to disrupt the unitary form of the state (see Elliott [1928] 1968). The crisis of "parliamentarism," famously discussed by Schmitt in 1923 (see Schmitt 1988), needs to be understood against the same backdrop, which was characterized by the emergence of new, extra-parliamentarian forms of negotiation among organized interests, processes of bureaucratization, and an increasing autonomy of executive power. Needless to say, the mutation of the relation between state and capital was a crucial factor in these developments, particularly after the success of the Russian Revolution in 1917 and the revolutionary movements and great waves of labor struggle at the end of World War I.

As we discussed in chapter 2, the Great War itself was a laboratory for the organization of the economy and the emergence of new patterns of relationship between capital and state. Such a crucial concept as "planning" began to be detached from its exclusive link to socialist and Marxist theories, and its variable combination with capitalism began to be tested. This is a tendency that became even more pronounced after the economic shocks of 1929 in European fascism, in Roosevelt's New Deal, in the social-democratic experiment in Sweden, and even in colonial settings such as India. To note this emphasis on planning is not to equate such radically heterogeneous political experiences but to point to a set of structural problems and tendencies that coalesced in the new space of experience opened up by the Great Depression. Schmitt was fully aware of this when, as a convinced supporter of the German *Führerstaat*, he criticized the decision of the US Supreme Court against Roosevelt's National Recovery Act (see Schmitt 1935). What Schmitt stressed was that the court had decided according to a "constitutional concept of law" predicated on a rigid distinction between legislation and government, which had been made obsolete by the imperatives of planning—in the United States, no less than in Germany (Schmitt 1935; see also Schmitt [1936] 1899, 219–20). As perfidious as it is, considering Schmitt's political proximity to Nazism at that time, his remark definitely grasps some of the tendencies at play in the early 1930s that led James Burnham, former leader of the American Trotskyist movement, to emphasize in his wartime bestseller *The Managerial Revolution* (1941) commonalities between the economic and political formations of Nazi Germany, Stalinist Russia, and the United States in Roosevelt's New Deal. As challenging as it is for a historical understanding of the state in the twentieth century, an analysis of European fascism and of the related controversies about totalitarianism (see Traverso 2002) exceeds the scope of this chapter.

Between world wars, anticolonial uprisings, and economic turmoil, what had been described in the early years of the twentieth century as the incipient crisis of the modern state was overcome by a set of processes that reinstated the state itself at the very center of global political developments over the following decades. Planning played crucial, although very diverse, roles in these developments. In his influential *The Economic Lessons of the 1930s*, Heinz Wolfgang Arndt ([1944] 1963, 93) wrote, "A large measure of conscious control, or, if we like, planning, both national and international, had become the precondition of any return to a beneficial system of multi-lateral trade." He was quick to add, "We must reckon with the fact that the tendency toward planning and State control in the domestic economies of most countries, which was already pronounced during the inter-war period, will continue at an accelerated pace after the war" (Arndt [1944] 1963, 301). This is a key point for us, since it provides a guiding thread for fleshing out some characteristics of the three main figures of the state that emerged after the end of World War II: the democratic welfare state, the socialist state, and the "developmental" state. Needless to say, what we aim to provide here is a very general typology, in the awareness of the great variety of instances that we subsume under each of these figures, as well as the mixed and hybrid forms they would take. Nevertheless, elaborating on this typology can be useful for grasping the multiple ways in which the state came to play crucial roles in the mid- to late twentieth century at the junction between the representation of aggregate capital and the reproduction of labor power. Such an approach can also help in providing multiple points of entry into the analysis of the crisis that opened up the political history of globalization.

In the United States, "the post–World War II social compact," write Frances Fox Piven and Richard A. Cloward (1998, 3), "brought unprecedented prosperity to many workers. Big industry negotiated with big labor, with the result that unionized workers won regular improvements in their wage and benefit packages, making them partners not only as production workers but as consumers of the new homes, refrigerators, cars and television sets spilling off the assembly line." It is this explicit acknowledgment of the role of the working class as a properly "constitutional" element (see Negri, in Hardt and Negri 1994, chap. 3) that makes up the peculiarity of the democratic social and welfare state in the twentieth century, distinguishing its policies from the multifarious forms of paternalistic poverty management that have been critically investigated by Foucauldian scholars over the past few decades (see, e.g., Castel 2003; Ewald 1986; Procacci 1993). This is not to deny the relevance of continuities in this regard, which are particularly apparent in the disciplinary aspects of the democratic social state. Nevertheless, it is impossible to make sense of this specific form of state—from its violently interrupted experimentation in the German Republic of Weimar to the New Deal in the United States and its heterogeneous instantiations in Western Europe after the war—without taking into account the new position of the working class. A new figure of the citizen, the "citizen-worker," emerged as the main character dominating subsequent political developments. The emergence of this new figure was a result of workers' struggles that, in the case of the New Deal, were powerful enough to dictate the pace and nature of Roosevelt's social and economic policies (see Ferrari Bravo 1972). Citizenship was qualitatively transformed by the entrenchment of "social rights" (Marshall 1950), and a peculiar dynamic reshaped constitutional law itself. As Alain Supiot (2013, 34) writes, this is so because the social state acknowledges the relevance of the dimension of "collective social determination," which troubles—particularly through collective labor bargaining—the binary relation between the "horizontal dimension" of private law and the "vertical dimension" of public law.

Although the democratic social state took very heterogeneous forms, which have been amply described by sociologists and political scientists (see, e.g., Flora and Heidenheimer 1981), we propose a very general definition of its form. The social qualification of the state becomes crucial to its legitimization under the pressure of workers' struggles in conditions of mass production that require the expansion of workers' demands and consumption as a crucial element for the general equilibrium and pace of capitalist development. Recognizing this situation involves taking a position that combines elements of the interpretation of the social state, which stresses the role of conflict in its origin, with elements of a more "systemic" interpretation, which emphasizes matters of stability and political legitimization (often referring to the role of warfare). To again pick up the Marxian terms we elaborated on in chapter 2, the state became social in an attempt to mediate the reproduction of labor power with the representation of aggregate capital—or, even more precisely, in an attempt to posit the reproduction of labor power as a crucial aspect of the representation and dynamics of aggregate capital (in a different perspective, see also Gough 1979; Walker 2016a). What has been called the Keynesian revolution (Klein 1947) established the general framework for this attempt in the second half of the twentieth century. This wave of economic restructuring required complex architectures of money, credit, and securitization; the expansion of "social insurances and allied services," to recall the title of the report released in 1942 by William Beveridge ([1942] 1969); programs of public housing; a varying mixture of economic planning and competition; as well as the establishment of a wide array of labor bargaining systems and "industrial democracy." The ensuing institutionalization of class conflict (see Dahrendorf 1959) was predicated, as Melinda Cooper (2015, 400) writes regarding the United States, on an attempt to sustain "a core workforce of standard, long-term, insured workers—a workforce that excluded minorities and women of all races." It is important to stress that these exclusions had their counterpart in all instantiations of the democratic social state. At the same time, the acknowledgment of the founding role of labor implied the reproduction of class struggle within the very structure of the state. Class struggle would also prove to be at the root of the state's fundamental instability, as became apparent through the social struggles and insurgent practices of the years around 1968.

The acknowledgment and rhetorical celebration of the central position of labor were, of course, crucial aspects of the socialist state. During the years of Stalin in the Soviet Union, the state took a form that established a kind of model against which the "popular democracies" established in Eastern Europe after 1945 had to be measured. This was particularly the case after the constitutional reform inspired by Andrey Vyshinsky in 1936. From the point of view of legal theory and practice, this constitutional reform sealed the violent closure of the extraordinary period of experimentation opened up in Russia by the radical break of the Russian Revolution. Such important Marxist jurists as Pëtr I. Stucka and Evgeny Pashukanis (himself a victim of Stalin's terror in 1937) had emphasized in the 1920s the relevance of the critique of civil law and, more generally, had made law, conceived of as a system of social relations, a crucial element of class struggle in the socialist transition (see Cerroni 1964; Negri 1977, chap. 5). In the wake of the reform of 1936, and under the guidance of Vyshinsky, Stalin's "crown jurist," the emphasis on socialist legality and rule of law led to a prevalence of normative legal theories that had been so radically criticized by Stucka and Pashukanis in the previous decade (see Bobbio 1955, 155).

The brutal accomplishment in the 1930s of what the Soviet economist Yevgeny Preobrazhensky (1965) termed "primitive socialist accumulation" laid the basis for a new role of the state, which became the indisputable center of economic planning and social development in the USSR (and, with significant variants, in the popular democracies of Eastern Europe after the war). The "socialist property of the state," to translate the title of an influential book by A. V. Venediktov published in 1948, was founded in terms that took the exclusive interest of the individual proprietor in classical bourgeois theories of property and projected it onto the state as representative of the "whole socialist society" (see Venediktov [1948] 1953, 39). This was particularly the case as far as the means of production were concerned. Positing labor as the source of all property, Soviet law and political economy acknowledged the entitlement of individual workers to use the means of production and to take part of the social product. But this entitlement was attributed to individual workers only as part of the collective of workers, whose exclusive representative was the socialist state. And it was the state that, through its planning and economic calculation, dictated the pace and quality of economic development while allocating the "consumption fund" that built the material basis of a set of entitlements and rights of Soviet citizens that ranged from social services to the "personal property rights" acknowledged by Article 10 of the Constitution of 1936 (see Malfliet 1987, 81–82). The socialist state after World War II was definitely authoritarian, but it was continuously challenged by workers' struggles in the USSR and elsewhere in the Eastern bloc. Although accumulation was led by the state, and not by private capital, the stabilization that followed Stalin's years built on the "solution" to the problems of "socialist transition" epitomized by the Constitution of 1936 and laid the basis for economic development that shared many aspects of capitalist rationality. This was even more the case in the years of the so-called peaceful competition with the West, when the USSR and the Eastern bloc became steadily integrated into the world market—up to the point at which they faced a set of transformations they were unable to sustain (see Castells 1998, chap. 1).

If talking about the democratic welfare state and even the socialist state implies a high degree of generalization and abstraction, this is even more the case for the third form of state mentioned earlier: what we call the developmental state. As Iain Pirie (2013, 148) wrote in a recent review of the uses of this label, there is a significant "lack of consistency" in the ways in which the developmental state is defined in political and economic literature. This has to do with the fact that, as he writes, "Any state that demonstrates a capacity to intervene effectively in the economic process can, in practice, be considered developmental." Consequently, while the notion is often primarily applied in this literature to East Asian countries such as Japan, South Korea, and Taiwan, it is possible to find analyses that underscore the presence of a more or less hidden developmental state even in the United States, where it takes the form of the huge investments in research and development that enable innovation in such cutting-edge industrial sectors as biotechnology or information technology (see Block 2008; Mazzucato 2013). The way in which we speak of the developmental state is significantly different, and although it is somewhat general, it aims at a certain degree of historical and conceptual precision. With this label we seek to name a huge variety of political regimes that emerged out of decolonization in the second half of the twentieth century, as well as those established in Latin America within the framework of theories of dependency and *desarrollismo* (developmentalism) that blossomed from the 1950s, particularly within the framework provided by the activities of the Economic Commission for Latin America of the United Nations (CEPAL; see Miguez and Santarcángelo 2015). The history of the developmental state intersects with the rise of the important movement of nonaligned countries that arose in the wake of the Bandung Conference of 1955 but cannot be restricted to this particular development. It intertwines with the turmoil of partition in the Indian subcontinent, revolution in China, and anti-imperialist war in Vietnam, but it also includes political developments in countries that were under the US sphere of influence, such as Indonesia after Suharto's coup in 1967. This history comprises nationalist, democratic, and authoritarian regimes and brutal dictatorships. Even limiting our analysis to a single country—say, Argentina—such heterogeneous experiences as the first government of Juan Domingo Perón and that of Arturo Frondizi (1958–62) can be considered instantiations of the developmental state. To hazard a general definition, the developmental state includes political regimes in which the perception of a "gap" or belatedness in economic development is constructed as the main problem to be addressed through policies that actively promote development itself. Planning had important roles to play here, as is clear in one of the most important instances of the developmental state: Nehru's India (see Escobar 2010; Sanyal 2007, 151–66).

The figure of the developmental state is predicated on the new conceptualization of development that emerged after the end of World War II, at the crossing point between Western theories epitomized by the "noncommunist manifesto" of Walt Whitman Rostow, *The Stages of Economic Growth* (1960), and theories of desarrollismo, which posited industrialization, import substitution, and generalization of wage labor as a privileged channel of inclusion in national citizenship, and socialist theories of planning (Sanyal 2007). These were radically different and even antagonistic theories and political projects (often literally at war with one another), but they all contributed to make the promotion of development a key criterion of legitimization of the state in vast parts of Asia, Latin America, and Africa. There were important precedents to this change in the perception of development in colonial history. Arndt stressed the relevance of the British Colonial Development Act of 1929 in shifting the meaning of development from a process of economic transformation that "a society undergoes (the economy develops)" to a "discrete structural change in the economy to be brought about by purposeful intervention (the economy has to be developed)" (Sanyal 2007, 105; see Arndt 1981). The developmental state negotiated its formation within the international environment of the post–World War II era, as established by the Bretton Woods system, on the one hand, and by the convolutions of the Cold War, on the other. If the political history of globalization was opened up by a triple crisis—that is, by the crisis of the three figures of the state we have sketched in this section—the disruption experienced by the developmental state provides a particularly effective angle from which to analyze the shifting entanglements of state and capital at the global level.

After Development

While the social state involved the mediation of the reproduction of labor power with the representation of aggregate capital and the socialist state sought to collectivize labor as the source of property, the developmental state faced severe difficulty in reproducing labor power according to the norm of the "free" wage. Such difficulty emerged from the pronounced presence of informal, coerced, and mobile labor forces, as well as by household conditions and gender regimes that could not easily be managed by technologies such as the Fordist family wage or the social consumption fund. In addition, the script of so-called primitive accumulation in developmental states did not easily follow the narrative of transition from agrarian to industrial work, creating myriad surplus populations that could not readily be corralled into standard regimes of reproduction. At the same time, the reality of aggregate capital took on imperial and neocolonial guises, generating comprador classes and weakening the state's powers of intervention and negotiation. These circumstances, which were met in many parts of the world by powerful social struggles and revolutionary movements, provided conditions for experimentation with new kinds of governmental and economic intervention, all with their precise political correlates. The structural adjustment programs initiated by the World Bank and International Monetary Fund are probably the most widespread and best known of such interventions, imposing debt repayment and economic restructuring that led to myriad patterns of dependency and impoverishment. But the crisis of the developmental state took many forms, not all of them necessarily associated with a diminution of state power. Writing about the land-locked African country of Lesotho, for instance, James Ferguson (1990) argues that technocratic imperatives of development aimed to reinforce and expand bureaucratic state power, with poverty alleviation as only an incidental goal. The Latin American country of Chile was a particularly important site of experimentation. Under the government of Salvador Allende (1970–73), the British cyberneticist Stafford Beer assisted in the design of Project Cybersyn, a computer-based system that aimed to manage the national economy through the monitoring and coordination of industrial production (Medina 2011). Beer viewed this system as a way to involve workers in decentralized practices of planning that would change the internal organization of government. However, this experiment was fast abandoned with the coup of September 11, 1973, which brought to power the military junta led by Augusto Pinochet (1973–80) and began a period of social repression, disappearances, and the emergence of Chile as a neoliberal laboratory where the economic principles of the Chicago School could be put to the test. Argentina followed in 1976 when a military coup initiated the so-called Proceso de Reorganización Nacional (National Reorganization Process), which was more brutal, criminal, and even "genocidal" in repressing forms of political opposition and social militancy. Differently from military dictatorships of the past, the new military junta decidedly broke with any kind of developmentalist path. Instead, the coup opened the path for audacious measures, such as the financial reform of 1977 that abolished state control of interest rates and laid the foundation for ongoing processes of liberalization and financialization that would spur the privatizations of the Carlos Menem era and eventually lead to the economic meltdown and social unrest of 2001 (Nápoli et al. 2014).

These Latin American precedents illustrate the tendency for the crisis of the developmental state to become entangled with coercive rule, neocolonial debt relations, and neoliberal styles of governance. Yet it would be a mistake to emphasize this tendency to the point that it becomes just another narrative about the Washington consensus or the export of neoliberal styles of thought and practice from the center to the periphery. Neoliberal currents were present in developmental states such as Argentina, Brazil, Chile, Turkey, and Uruguay well before they took hold in the Euro-Atlantic world in the era of Ronald Reagan and Margaret Thatcher. In Chile, the Chicago doctrines offered Pinochet a developmental strategy that contrasted with the previous emphasis on planning and industrialization and reoriented the economy to international trade (particularly the export of raw materials and agricultural products) in ways that appeased his wealthy backers, ensured US support, and kept his political opponents in the labor movement at bay. The swerve from policies of import substitution industrialization, which were a centerpiece of the desarrollismo advocated by CEPAL, to extractive economies based on mining and agriculture had important colonial and postcolonial precedents. It is also important to note that this swerve was a hallmark of the post-developmental turn not only in Latin America, where it is currently reflected in lively debates on "neo-extractivism," but also in many African states. In other parts of the world, particularly China and the Asian "Tiger" economies—but also, for instance, in Turkey and Mexico—export-led industrialization played a similar role. These changes tended to concentrate rents in the hands of predatory elites and, at the geographical level, gave rise to export processing and other kinds of economic zones that provided the basis for the "graduated sovereignty" that Aihwa Ong (2000) identifies as constitutive for the post-developmental state in Southeast Asia. This is true also for India, where the "liberalization" of the economy initiated in 1991 took place under the pressure of "economic leaders' demands that the post-independence social contract of formal-sector employment security and benefits be dismantled" (Goldman 2015, 141). Here, the dispossession of lands from peasant and sharecropping communities became a pronounced feature of such zoning exercises, giving rise to displaced and underemployed populations whose struggles for livelihood propelled the emergence of what Partha Chatterjee (2004) calls political society. Wherever agriculture took an extractive turn oriented toward export and the building of comparative advantage, informal economies thrived. Mass migrations, land grabbing, business criminalization, informality, securitization, and the rise of mega-cities—these were all features of the post-developmental state that took uneven and unbalanced combinations in different regions and under different political hues (Connell and Dados 2014). In Latin America, at least since the publication of Hernando de Soto's influential *The Other Path: The Invisible Revolution in the Third World* (1990), the valorization of "human capital" involved in informal economies and migration has been a key feature of regional neoliberalism (see Gago 2018). More generally, the relations between processes of neoliberalization and informalization of labor are topics of lively discussion in many regions of the post-developmental world (see Borghi and Routh 2016; Mitra et al. 2017).

Searching for a single logic to explain these variegated changes is a vexing and likely unfulfillable task. Characterized by more flexible political technologies of rule, heterogeneous territorial arrangements, and increasingly decentered ways to mediate the relation between capital and the state, this post-developmental scenario—as we anticipated in chapter 1—offers a very different perspective on the rise of neoliberalism than familiar stories of "thought collective" meetings at Mount Pelerin (Mirowski and Plehwe 2009), the Volcker shock that restricted monetary supply in the United States during the early 1980s (Klein 2007), the tensions between the Chicago School economists and German Ordoliberals (Dardot and Laval 2014), or the efforts of financial institutions to assert their primacy in the capitalist order (Duménil and Lévy 2004). Emphasizing the politics of extraction and the material weight of trade, to which processes of logistical coordination would prove crucial, this gaze from Asia, Africa, and Latin America places finance and financialization very differently from accounts that propose the emergence of a "weightless economy." Far from assuming a functional separation of finance from the "real economy," the challenge becomes to confront the deep intertwining of the operations of finance capital with other forms and operations of capital, and this means focusing on how financial processes interact with existing institutional, urban, and class relations, as well as approaching financialization itself as an uneven geographical process. Our conviction is that the neoliberal turn of capitalism cannot be understood in separation from the conditions of heterogeneity that it confronts and produces (see Gago 2015; 2017). Within this vista, the post-developmental tendencies outlined earlier appear not as mere irregularities with respect to a supposed norm or "ideal type" of the modern state but, rather, as mutations that adapt to but also motivate the tumultuous and asynchronous temporality, expansion, and intensification of contemporary capitalist accumulation.

We have already mentioned the concept of "accumulation by dispossession" introduced by Harvey and discussed by many other thinkers. Harvey's claim that accumulation by dispossession has "moved to the fore as the primary contradiction within the imperialist organization of capitalist accumulation" (Harvey 2003, 172) needs to be considered with an analytical eye turned toward processes of exploitation that continue to drive accumulation. Although Harvey's argument usefully captures some of the post-developmental tendencies outlined earlier, there are always instances in which its utility becomes contestable. Most controversially, Giovanni Arrighi (2007, 361–67) characterizes the developmental path of China as "accumulation without dispossession," describing a situation in which domestic markets expand, reproduction costs decrease, and the labor force is raised by rural development and industrialization that do not displace people from the land. Arrighi has been criticized for ignoring the integration of Chinese farmers into the world market as de facto wage workers (Chase-Dunn 2010, 47–48), the rise of unequal class relations within town and village enterprises (Panitch 2010, 84), and the growth of speculative real estate markets in Chinese cities (Walker 2010). A similar point could be made about the stock fever that, as we discussed in chapter 1, gripped Chinese financial markets in the lead-up to the meltdown of 2015–16 (Dal Maso 2015). One could also mention the global extension of Chinese economic interests through commodity-backed finance and state-owned enterprises in Africa and Latin America (Bräutigam and Gallagher 2014) or Xi Jinping's promotion of the so-called Belt and Road Initiative that aims to bolster logistical connections between Asia and Europe through the financial medium of the Asia Infrastructure Investment Bank (Akhter 2015; Callahan 2016). Yet our interest lies not in questioning the accuracy of Arrighi's argument as much as in registering the dissonance that marks the post-developmental scenario as it extends across different spatial and political formations.

In earlier writings (see, e.g., Mezzadra and Neilson 2013b) we have tried to capture this dissonance and variability in the mediation of the relation between capital and state through the concept of *differential accumulation*. What we had in mind was a perspective that went beyond the concern with institutional and regulatory arrangements that characterizes the varieties of capitalism approach (see chapter 1) to consider the material fabric of subjective antagonisms and struggles that shape strategies of accumulation across time and space. While this requires an investigation of labor and social struggles that we will complete in chapter 5, we can note for now that differential patterns of accumulation were always a feature of the formal subsumption of capital as theorized by Marx. In *Marx after Marx* (2015, 58), Harry Harootunian notes how primitive accumulation followed many different paths to that classically described by Marx for England and how "the logic of formal subsumption" has "acted to interrupt the temporal continuum of the very process of capitalist production it also fuelled."

We discussed Harootunian's work and the question of formal subsumption in chapter 2. Important to stress in this regard are the spatial and geographical implications of the intertwining of real and formal subsumption in the development of capitalism beyond the Euro-Atlantic. Heterogeneity seems to be the norm rather than the exception here. Antonio Gramsci's analysis of the "Southern Question" in Italy (see Gramsci 2005) provides a standard reference for the critical investigation of such heterogeneity from the perspective of a latecomer European country, but the history of Marxism in other parts of the world provides us with several instances of analysis of geographical unevenness as a hallmark of colonial and postcolonial capitalism. *Seven Interpretative Essays on Peruvian Reality* (Mariátegui [1928] 1988) is particularly relevant in this regard. Focusing on the tensions between the coast, characterized by modern forms of capitalist development, and the Andean highlands, where *latifundia* and peasants' servitude prevailed, Mariátegui was able to flesh out both the geographical contrast that shaped Peru's economic and social reality and the unifying principle underlying it from the angle of its subordination to capital and the world market (see Harootunian 2015, 135–52). From this point of view, it is important to note that he proposed the notion of "semi-feudalism" to denote the conditions prevailing in the *sierra* (in the highlands), taking a critical distance from the view commonly held by liberal and democratic intellectuals of his age in Peru, who spoke instead of an "integral feudalism" (see Quijano 1979, lxxviii–lxxxv). It was precisely capital's role even in the sierra that cautioned Mariátegui not to use the concept of feudalism in the analysis of Peruvian reality without further qualification. While this question has remained crucial in Marxist debates on the reproduction of "feudal remnants" particularly in Asia, from India to Japan (see Harootunian 2015, chap. 4), Mariátegui included in his picture of the temporal as well as spatial stratification of development in Peru in the 1920s the persistence of forms of communal organization of the Incas. At the same time, he emphasized, consistently with his general analysis, that the Incas could play a political role in anticapitalist struggles only through the establishment of forms of alliance with the emerging proletariat of the coast.

The conditions analyzed by Mariátegui are peculiar. Nevertheless, it is striking to note that such spatial and temporal heterogeneity has been a characteristic of capitalism outside the West since its "take-off" through colonization. Far from homogenizing space and time, as well as forms of economic activity, the "universalization" of capitalism has gone hand in hand with the production of conditions of heterogeneity that require careful investigation from a political, legal, and social angle. Fanon grasped this point in *The Wretched of the Earth* when he described colonial capitalism as "real life with all its infinite variations and lack of balance, where slavery, serfdom, barter, a skilled working class, and high finance exist side by side" (Fanon 1963, 107). One can say that the project of the developmental state, in all of its infinite variations, has been an attempt to overcome this heterogeneity, accomplishing the process of nation building, positing the national territory as a unified scale for economic development, and reorganizing both the labor market and citizenship around the standard of "free" wage labor. Accordingly, the crisis of the developmental state has set the conditions for the reemergence of conditions of heterogeneity, from both a spatial and an economic and social point of view. Interruptions and connections shape "post-developmental" geographies (see Sidaway 2007), stitching together a wide array of territorial pockets and heterogeneous forms of production and exchange, as well as forms of life. Our use of the concept of differential accumulation attempts to grasp precisely this emerging constellation of heterogeneity, which has to be analyzed—in a way following Mariátegui's methodological advice—against the background of the shifting principles of its articulation with capital's accumulation at the scale of the world market and of the ensuing frictions and conflicts. This question becomes more and more crucial well beyond the limits of the former Third World, which makes a notion such as postcolonial capitalism analytically relevant for the analysis of global capitalism as a whole.

Speaking about post-developmental geographies and the crisis of the developmental state does not imply a denial of the persistent, even intensified relevance of development and growth as rhetorical and material references for economic policies around the globe today. A "view from the South" demonstrates, instead, that neoliberalism presented itself from its very beginning as a "development strategy" that challenged some of the key elements of what we have broadly termed the "developmental state" (Connell and Dados 2014, 122). The abandonment of industrialization strategies; the weakening of the working class and the labor movement; the reorientation of the economy to international trade and its opening to global capital are all hallmarks of neoliberalism that altered the very meaning of development and growth. They eventually laid the basis for a new form of integration of economies and societies within the framework of a world market increasingly reshaped by processes of financialization. Within this process, what was severed was precisely the link between nation-state building and development that had characterized multifarious experiences of the developmental state.

The state has crucial roles to play in this new scenario, but the national scale of development reproduces itself more as a resource for political rhetoric than as a relevant reference for policy. Processes of spatial heterogenization explode this scale from below, while global dynamics and logics of accumulation penetrate the national territory from above. This is apparent even in those cases where the state has greater regulatory capability, which means in cases that are good candidates for demonstrating the persistent relevance of the national scale as an analytical unity of contemporary capitalism. Take the example of China. In the aftermath of the financial crisis, Wang Hui (2016, 287) writes, the fact that China "is vast and regions are unevenly developed has ironically acted as a buffer." The framing of the Chinese transition in terms of "upgrading and updating" and industrial transfer has fostered the continuity of processes of industrialization and urbanization. But it has also deepened processes of territorial heterogenization, spurred social unrest, and failed to spare the country the financial turmoil of 2015–16, as we noted earlier. At the same time, the further intensification of what Wang calls the degeneration of politics into "management" (Wang 2016, 172) and the "corporatization of government" (Wang 2016, 155) have led to the emergence of completely new forms of articulation between economic interests and administration. Even the leadership of the Chinese "state-party" (Wang 2009) has to negotiate its regulatory capability with such forms of articulation, which also represent the fragmented and uneven ways in which global capitalist logics intermingle with Chinese administration and government.

This is not to say that the national denomination of capital and capitalism does not make any sense at all nowadays. It is perfectly meaningful to speak, for instance, of a specific Chinese capitalist formation, which results from the peculiar history of China and from the peculiar assemblage of state and capital in that country. This peculiarity can be traced also in the ways in which Chinese state-owned enterprises and finance operate abroad and in the logistical projects that connect China to markets across the globe. But it is even more important to emphasize the limits of any contemporary representation of aggregate capital at the national level, the intermingling between the action of the state and the logics of global capital that challenge the very unitary articulation of the state, and the resulting disruption of any form of general mediation of the reproduction of labor power through the regulatory power of the state. This is apparent even in Latin America, where in the last long decade several political projects have attempted to requalify the state as the crucial actor of emancipation. We do not intend to deny that these projects, which developed under the push of powerful social movements and struggles, as well as within the framework of a regional dynamic of integration, were able to effect social change and, particularly in such cases as Bolivia and Ecuador, foster processes of decolonization. But the continuity of processes of extraction and financialization eventually gave rise to a mixture of neo-developmentalism and neoliberalism that led to a political impasse, as well as to ruptures and tensions within the state (see Gago 2015 and 2017; Gago and Mezzadra 2017a and 2017b; Gago et al. 2014; Mezzadra and Sztulwark 2015).

Looking at the contemporary global landscape from the angle of the relation between state and capital presents us with a scattered and contradictory picture. The notion of empire remains relevant because it grasps the powerful push of global capital on the development of states and legal systems. But this empire does not succeed in even alluding to the horizon of peace that, according to many accounts, ought to characterize its planetary rule (see, e.g., Hardt and Negri 2000, xv). While war inflames large portions of the Earth, processes of integration of regional and continental economic spaces are under way. But these processes, as we noted in chapter 1, are continuously interrupted by the emergence of old and new forms of economic nationalism—from India to Japan, from Germany to South Africa, from China to the United States. No new world order is in sight; nevertheless, capital continues to rule the world, displaying a unitary logic that enters multifarious forms of negotiation with states and even disarticulates states by reproducing the conditions for its accumulation and valorization within a variety of global legal and political assemblages. Geographical and institutional entities such as the concession and the chartered company make multiple returns in new clothes in this scenario. These are phenomena to which we turn our attention in the last chapter of the book. But before doing so, we need to deepen our analysis of the logics of contemporary capitalist accumulation and analyze in further detail the new shape taken by class struggle in the present.

Extraction, Logistics, Finance

Cuts

The mutating scenarios of empire, state, and capital that we discussed at the end of the previous chapter generate distinct and asymmetrical arrangements of space and time within which the operative dimensions of contemporary economy and politics can be discerned. Whether we speak of post-developmental geographies, postcolonial capitalism, or neo-extractivism, the unearthing of systemic logics that underlie the workings of capitalism in the present is a crucial task. We are convinced that such logics exist and that it is worthwhile not only to conceptually define them but also to empirically map the variable geometry and geographies of their steady expansion. This chapter shifts focus from the large-scale conceptual nomenclatures that have channeled debates on these topics in various parts of the world to examine the operative spaces within which these logics unfold. We are interested in processes and concatenations that cut across the unstable and heterogeneous vistas of contemporary capitalist development and crisis. At the center of our analysis are the intertwined themes of extraction, logistics, and finance that we have already hinted at several times in this book.

Although extraction, logistics, and finance are important and strategic domains of economic activity, we do not limit ourselves to a detailed investigation of the operations of capital in these three "sectors." Of interest to us, rather, are the divisions and connections that become evident when operations in these domains are considered together, paying attention to the multiple resonances and divergences among them. Moreover, we focus on the ways in which the deployment of extraction, logistics, and finance intermingles with the heterogeneity of global space and time, particularly as regards emergent patterns of state and capital. In their own ways, each of these domains provides strategic points of entry for a critical analysis of these changing patterns. They are all characterized by globally extensive logics, regulations, and parameters while compelled at the same time to come to terms with grounded and intensive dynamics that shape and interrupt their axiomatic workings. Beyond its literal reference to mining, commodities, and the plundering of earth and sea, extraction describes any form of economic activity that relies on or benefits from resources or relations that are external to it. The logistical coordination of capital's valorization and accumulation provides a framework not only for enterprises of transport and communication but also, more generally, for the reorganization of production and the social relations that enable production. Speculation, debt, and the technical frontiers of finance reach into the interstices of daily life, but they also require sophisticated and abstruse products and processes that push market logics and rationalities to ever more abstract heights. Taken together, extraction, logistics, and finance provide some of the most important conduits for tracking and understanding transitions of capitalism and operations of capital that are currently reshaping the world.

Not surprisingly, these domains have been central to recent critical debates. As we have already mentioned, the discussion of extraction is particularly virulent in Latin America, where the concept of neo-extractivism has provided a critical lens with which to view wider transformations of capitalism even under "progressive" governments (see Svampa 2015; Svampa and Viale 2014). Speaking of neo-extractivism implies a reference to the continuity of a long history of the region's insertion within the capitalist world system through violent forms of raw material extraction and related processes of dispossession—as well as to the dictatorships of the 1970s, as we noted in chapter 3. What the prefix "neo" signals, on the one hand, is a shift toward Asia as the main market for Latin American commodities, and, on the other hand, the fact that the "re-primarization" of the economy is connected to the state's ability to use and direct a certain part of the extraordinary rent from natural resources to finance social policies. Critics of neo-extractivism make strong arguments against the quality of development connected to this primacy of extractive rent, shedding light on environmental pillaging, land grabbing, and the disruption and dispossession of Indigenous and peasant economies. Beyond Latin America, these topics also figure prominently in the critical analysis and practical contestation of economic activities related to the expansion of the extractive frontier. An important chapter in the history of social struggles of the past decades has been written along this frontier, intertwining environmental questions with the battle for the commons, as well as building impressive trans-local and transnational coalitions. One thinks, for instance, of the struggle against Eldorado Gold's gold mine in the Skouries forest in northern Greece (Klein 2014, chap. 9); the negotiations, tensions, and contestations surrounding offshore oil extraction in the deep water of West Africa's Gulf of Guinea (Chalfin 2015); or the operations of the Denver-based Newmont Mining Corporation and its Batu Hijau Copper and Gold Mine in Sumbawa, Indonesia (Welker 2014).

In the field of logistics, there has also been a mounting of critical debates and struggles. Geographers such as Deborah Cowen (2014) and Craig Martin (2016) have explored the multifarious tensions and conflicts between the logistical production of space and established territorial and political formations. Keller Easterling (2014) has drawn attention to the infrastructural skeleton that supports and enables logistical processes, arguing that this layer of organization has a political force and meaning that rivals and parallels that of the contemporary state. A parallel debate on "logistical media" emphasizes the digital and software dimensions of logistical practices, organizing and orienting the relations among people, property, and things (Peters 2015; Rossiter 2016). More generally, the critical investigation of logistics is connected to the analysis of so-called supply chain capitalism and to the synchronization of heterogeneous forms of production and distribution (Tsing 2009, 2012). Stefano Harney and Fred Moten (2013) investigate the historical relation between logistics and the slave trade to argue that logistical processes redefine relations of property and subjectivity, producing "logistical populations" that extend circuits through "new adaptions, translations, governances, scales, and approximations" (Harney 2010). Taken together, these approaches present logistics as a key set of techniques and technologies for the orchestration and execution of contemporary capitalist operations, with consequences for the control of labor, the production of space, and even the emergence of new imaginaries in culture and art (Toscano and Kinkle 2015, chap. 6). Importantly, these debates have developed in parallel to a series of struggles in the logistical industries, extending, for example, from the ports of California (Bologna 2012) to the warehouses of Amazon in Germany (Apicella 2016) and the inland ports of northern Italy (Cuppini et al. 2015). The processes of zoning and the carving out of corridors stemming from logistical developments have also spurred intense struggles, as in the case of the projected establishment of the so-called Delhi-Mumbai Industrial Corridor (Dey and Grappi 2015; Grappi 2016).

As far as finance is concerned, recent years have witnessed an efflorescence of critical studies and theories, which became even more pronounced after the crisis of 2007–2008. "No account of contemporary capitalist development," Robin Blackburn (2006, 39) writes, "can ignore the scale of the financial sector's recent expansion." *Financialization of Daily Life*, the title of a book by Randy Martin published in 2002, nicely captures the pervasive nature of contemporary finance, signaling also its new dimensions with respect to classical discussions of the topic. The very notion of financialization posits a process by which the logics and workings of finance come to superimpose themselves on and dominate other realms of economic activity and life. Christian Marazzi (2010, 2015) has taken this new quality of financialization as the most distinctive feature of contemporary capitalism, investigating, from this angle, transformations in the composition of labor and changes in the relations between labor and capital. The relevance of these processes is also emphasized by scholars who consider financialization a stage in historical economic cycles that are specified according to the model developed by world systems theory (see, e.g., Durand 2017). The rise of new forms and technical arrangements of financial trading has likewise inspired a new wave of critical commentary, which has focused on the role of derivatives (Bryan and Rafferty 2006; LiPuma and Lee 2004) and the changing logics of commensuration and valuation (Grossberg 2010; Grossberg et al. 2014) as well as on phenomena such as high-frequency trading (HFT; MacKenzie 2014; Toscano 2013) and shadow banking (Cooper 2015). Other approaches have emphasized the popular dimensions of speculation, the ethics of greed, or the competition to attract financial capital through the establishment of fiscal havens. Regardless of the theoretical slant of these diverse works and approaches, it is difficult to deny the power of finance in making and ruling the world in which we live. Correspondingly, finance has been at the center of the development of several social and political struggles over recent years, whether in a targeted campaign such as *Strike Debt!* (Ross 2014), the continuing disputes over Argentinian state debt, or the violent and protracted turmoil and resistance that have characterized the economic crisis in a country such as Greece.

Far from seeing bodies of thought and argument that have developed separately around extraction, logistics, and finance as mutually exclusive critical paradigms, we see opportunities for them to work in consonance. To conduct an analysis that cuts across and moves among these domains of capitalist activity means questioning our earlier characterization of them as sectors. This is not to deny that the languages and technologies that divide economies into sectors have an efficacy that affects how they operate and develop, as well as the labor and regulatory regimes that apply to them. However, there is much to be gained from an attempt to produce resonances among extraction, logistics, and finance—both looking at material intersections between them and investigating the logics that underlie and animate their workings. Doubtless, these are not the only possible analytical levers that can be applied to the present situation. There have been many attempts to identify similar sectoral domains or fractions of capital to motivate and guide the investigation of the changing systemic logics of capitalism. More than a decade ago, Beverly Silver (2003) singled out a number of emerging industries that promised to provide a leading product cycle after the decline of the global prominence of automobile production: the semiconductor industry, producer services, the education industry, and personal services. We do not want to deny the importance of such branches of economic activity. We also acknowledge the relevance of attempts to define contemporary capitalism pointing to the role played by knowledge and knowledge production in its cognitive fabric (see, e.g., Fumagalli and Morini 2010; Lucarelli and Vercellone 2013; Moulier Boutang 2012).

What we seek to carve out of an analysis of extraction, finance, and logistics is not solely an understanding of the workings of crucial economic sectors or cycles. Rather, we aim to shed light on a set of principles or logics that increasingly play an important role in driving the development of other sectors, including those mentioned by Silver. In this regard, our perspective is quite close to the recent work of Saskia Sassen. "Are there a few logics," Sassen (2014, 220) asks, "that drive what on the surface becomes present as enormously diverse worlds—the world of fracking, the world of finance, the world of the logistics for outsourcing?" We share Sassen's concern with identifying and analyzing such logics. However, while she isolates these worlds almost incidentally, in this chapter we undertake a systematic investigation of their mutual implication and crosscutting. What Sassen (2014,

211) terms the "systemic edge," or "the site where general conditions take extreme forms," is also important for our inquiry. In our understanding, as we pointed out in chapter 2, the site of this systemic edge is also where the expanding frontiers of capital impinge on the materiality of space and life in violent ways that involve processes of *differential inclusion* as much as the processes of expulsion to which Sassen gives analytical priority (see Mezzadra and Neilson 2015, 4–5). Again, by employing our central notion of operations of capital, we seek to show how these underlying or "subterranean" logics create patterns of inter-referencing among extraction, logistics, and finance on what Sassen (2014, 5) calls the "surface" or "the localized shape . . . of deeper systemic dynamics that articulate much of what now appears as unconnected." By highlighting the tensions between the ways in which capital hits the ground and its concatenation into larger formations of capitalism, we move from the subterranean to the surface level and back again to show how the systemic edge is always caught in a dense fabric of frictions, conflicts, and resistances.

Taking the understanding of extraction, logistics, and finance beyond a sectoral definition does not have even or equivalent consequences for an analysis of operations of capital as they unfold in relation to each of these domains. In chapter 1, we discussed how lifting the concept of extraction away from its sectoral or literal association with mining and other forms of resource extraction allows an analysis that is attentive not only to Indigenous and antiracist struggles but also to more general predations of capital. It is not only when the operations of capital plunder the materiality of the Earth and biosphere, but also when they encounter and draw on forms and practices of human cooperation and sociality that are external to them, that we can say that extraction is at stake. This expanded notion of extraction has not only important consequences for the analysis of logistics and finance but also conceptual implications for critically grasping the core logics and principles that drive the syncopated rhythm of crisis and transition that characterizes contemporary capitalism (Gago and Mezzadra 2017a). We are, indeed, convinced that the composition and logics of the processes that we analyzed earlier in the book using the Marxian notion of aggregate capital are characterized more and more by the prevalence and strategic role of *extractive* operations. The figure of rent is consequently more and more important to understanding the forms and practices of capitalist valorization and accumulation (see Vercellone 2013), although there is a need to stress that the extraction of rent continues to articulate with heterogeneous forms of profit in ways that deserve detailed analysis. At the same time, far from being limited to what David Harvey (2005) calls "accumulation by dispossession," an extractive logic permeates widespread practices of exploitation, making a new consideration of this surprisingly somewhat forgotten concept an urgent task.

On the Frontiers of Extraction

At base, extraction is a simple notion. More often than not, it refers to the forced removal of raw materials and life forms from the Earth's surface, depths, and biosphere. From precious metals to fossil fuels, from copper to uranium, from tungsten to cobalt and the rare-earth minerals essential to today's miniaturized electronics, the history of mining has always opened new frontiers and continues to find untapped substances to turn into commodities. The digging up of the earth's surface has both ancient mythological and contemporary resonances. There is a scrambling of time at stake in mineral extraction. Sedimented in the deep time of geological processes, extracted minerals are thrust into industrial applications and have become essential elements in the devices and infrastructures that enable even the most recent developments in new media (Parikka 2015). As immaterial a metaphor as "the cloud" may be to describe current technologies of data storage, processing, and transmission, its very existence is predicated on an unprecedented intensification of extractive dynamics and related processes of dispossession (Bratton 2015, 75–108; Mosco 2014). Fracking in particular presents a cutting edge of extraction, allowing it to continue beyond the point at which the gases it seeks to remove from the earth have been otherwise depleted. It asserts the demise of the carbon economy, with all of the promise of a new beginning. If fracking were the protagonist of a twentieth-century novel, it would be Beckett's Murphy: "I can't go on. I'll go on" (quoted in Neilson 2012, 87). Chasing down the chain of mineral extraction, whether it leads to coal, gas, or the "gray gold" lithium that powers rechargeable batteries, is a means of discerning the shifting operations of capital, as well as the multifarious forms of resistance that surround them.

Extraction is not limited to mining and drilling for minerals, oil, and gas. Since the days of the so-called green revolution, involving an intensification of technological and even industrial methods of farming, agriculture has taken a more extractive turn, with dramatic implications for the "food industry" and for questions of land use and property relations (Liberti 2016). Importantly, these developments have intertwined with and enabled processes of financialization that, as Stefan Ouma (2016) contends, deserve a detailed investigation from the angle of "operations of capital." The extractive turn in agriculture, for instance, becomes apparent in the case of the extensive soy cultivation in ever more marginal areas of the Latin American pampas (Cáceres 2014), as mentioned in the introduction. These soy crops are destined not only for alimentary purposes but also for a variety of industrial applications, from the production of polyurethane foam to the making of cleaning supplies and adhesives. Soy cultivation has dramatically transformed rural landscapes in many parts of the world, with a disruptive impact on economies and populations. One has only to remember the role played by genetically modified seeds and the fertilizers and pesticides manufactured to work specifically with them to get an idea of the wider implications of the extractive turn in agricultural activities. The names of agribusiness giants such as Monsanto, Dow, and DuPont are synonymous with the global expansion of such farming techniques, which are highly destructive of biodiversity and have spread particularly rapidly in post-conflict societies where the edge of primitive accumulation is focused on agriculture (see, e.g., Brown 2015, chap. 4). An extractive turn can also be witnessed on the new frontiers of aquaculture—for instance, in shrimp farming in Southeast Asia (Horstmann 2007, 150–51). Correspondingly, new logics of accumulation are evident in the oceans. The krill harvest in Antarctica provides fish meal for use in aquaculture, as well as health products consumed by overfed human populations that suffer from high cholesterol (Ziegelmayer 2014). Life-forms are more and more tested and put under pressure by the invasive action of extractive techniques, which do not stop at the border of the human body.

In all of these examples, whether they involve minerals or life-forms, extraction is understood in a literal sense. In an interesting discussion of the proceeds of such literal extraction, James Ferguson asks why they seem to be more susceptible to collective claims than those resulting from other economic activities. He hypothesizes that this is because "the value" derived from literal extraction "is so out of proportion to the effort; in some sense, we recognize that the value was 'already there'—stumbled upon, not created . . . from labor," but emerging "fabulously, almost magically, as if from nowhere" (Ferguson 2015, 184). This simple understanding, which Ferguson uses to highlight popular attitudes, clearly derives from John Locke's famous discussion of labor and property. Ferguson uses this hypothesis to draw attention to the violence implied in extraction, as well as its reliance on contingencies that make it feasible as a revenue-generating activity. In reality, as Ferguson himself is well aware, the situation is always more complex. Speaking of coal extraction, Anna Tsing (2005, 51) outlines how the process involves not only the substance's coercion from the earth but also practices of transportation, storage, sorting, and grading. Only when these practices are operative can the raw material of coal be turned into a commodity. All of this is part of extraction, too. Extractive activities always have their productive sides, which in some of the instances mentioned earlier involve the deployment of sophisticated technical and knowledge practices.

Nevertheless, it is important to stress the moments of appropriation and expropriation without which extraction cannot proceed. If we think of the extractive operations of capital, the point we made earlier regarding capital's relation with its multiple outsides takes on particularly salient forms. Capital is so dependent on its outsides that it is prepared to make considerable investments—for instance, in prospecting and research—to ensure the constant reproduction of these outsides. Just think of the efforts trained on mineral discovery or the constant expansion of soy cultivation into ever more marginal areas. In both cases, there is a complex interplay among technological advances, knowledge production, and financial manipulation that allows capital to prepare the ground for further extraction. This does not mean that capital's operations are homogeneous along the extractive frontier. Capital's reliance on heterogeneous conditions and materials that are not of its own making corresponds with a proliferation of different operations that impinge on its multiple outsides. To be sure, the mobilization or application of these operations involves a kind of projective logic by which these outsides are already constructed as susceptible to appropriation by capital. The heterogeneity of operations that surround and prepare the ground for extraction concatenate in ways that are constitutive of a particular fraction of capital that we might call extractive capital. Equally, any one of these operations—take, for example, the financial dimension of mineral prospecting—can mesh into other concatenations that both support extractive activities and are part of the formation of other fractions of capital. These concatenations and crossovers must be analyzed in ways that are attentive to human inputs and property relations that sustain and perpetuate capital's drive for endless accumulation.

The traditional story about these human inputs and property relations is well known. The extractive zeal of European imperialism emptied the world's pits and mountains and lined the mints and museums of the metropole with metals and artifacts that barely conceal the scars of slavery and indentured labor. As Achille Mbembe memorably argues, the connection between forced labor and extraction is so strong that it allows an understanding of the slave trade in extractive terms. Mbembe writes about a process by which "African peoples are transformed into living minerals from which metal is extracted," giving rise to a transition from "*homme-minerai* to *homme-métal* and from *homme-métal* to *homme-monnaie*" (Mbembe 2013, 67–68). A similar logic applies in other instances of forced labor that were central to the continuity of extractive activities throughout the long centuries of colonialism and imperialism. One thinks of the mines of Potosí, in contemporary Bolivia, where Indigenous people were compelled to work according to the *mita* system for the silver extraction that sustained the circulation of the first global currency (Mezzadra and Neilson 2013a, 32–33; Tándeter 1993). Michael Taussig (1984) has eloquently traced the "culture of terror" surrounding the labor regimes that enabled rubber extraction in the Putumayo territories of the Amazon. Resonances of this coercive and fear-generating culture can be found in other theaters and periods of colonialism where the extraction of this same precious "milk" took place— from the Congo to Burma, Indonesia to Madagascar (Tully 2011). Throughout the globe, a complex composition of labor enabled extractive activities in heterogeneous colonial and other fringe landscapes. A global history of this labor force would include Welsh coal miners (Williams 1960), "coolies" who plied the rubber plantations of Malaya (Tully 2011, chap. 16), and the Quechua and Aymara who negotiated with the "devil" in the tin mines around the city of Oruro, Bolivia (Taussig 1980, 143–228). Part of this history would also encompass the multifarious struggles and rebellions that made the miner an iconic figure for the labor movement in many parts of the world. The mutinous foment in the worlds of coolies and other forced laborers would supply another chapter in this global history.

Our interest here is not to write another volume in the immensely important archive of global labor history. Rather, we want to remember and question the justifying narratives and juridical regimes that sustained and enabled colonial extraction—narratives and regimes that have mutated but also maintain continuity in the present day. Ingrained in practices and techniques of extraction is a kind of colonial imprint that becomes particularly apparent when new fields and quarries are opened in the landscapes and spreadsheets of contemporary capital. The violence of this opening often manifests in controversies surrounding property and land rights. To take just one example from the panoply of cases from around the world, the opening of the Porgera gold mine in Papua New Guinea exhibits multilayered property relations that at once facilitate and impede the extractive process (Golub 2014). This multiplicity of layers is evident in the juridical regimes governing the relation between the land's surface and depths, the former of which belongs putatively to the Indigenous Ipili, themselves a kind of indistinct "hinge" between two much larger Indigenous groups, and the latter belonging to the national government. In this instance, the government has power to issue a lease to outsiders "if it decides that such a lease is in the best interest of its citizens—whether they consent or not" (Golub 2014, 10). This arrangement then obliges a series of legal agreements, foremost among them a "compensation agreement" by which the mine must "pay for land and plants damaged by its activities" (Golub 2014, 10). The agreement struck with the mine operator Porgera Joint Venture, primarily owned by the Canadian transnational Placer Dome, has resulted in an uneven trickling of revenues to the Ipili, among whom the "big men" of the group have been the primary beneficiaries. The upheaval resulting from the establishment of the mine has clearly led to a situation in which "the Ipili are the losers" (Golub 2014, 213). Catherine Coumans (2011) describes the environmental damage, shooting of trespassers, worsening subsistence crises, and social disorder. With due respect to Alex Golub's ambition to "get beyond dualist stereotypes of ecologically noble savages fighting the good fight against global capital" (Golub 2014, 212), the case illustrates how property regimes are tested and manipulated in ways that allow the violence of extraction to proceed amid contemporary cultural and economic sensitivities.

It would be easy to locate landscapes of extraction where this violence is much more pronounced and unmediated by compensation agreements and the like. Tales of dispossession and displacement are the flip side of the expansion of extractive activities. Indigenous groups are often the protagonists of these tales, sometimes negotiating benefits around the edges of extractive enterprises or astutely deploying the tools of capital to their own ends but always seemingly ending up on the vanquished side. While the groups that bear the brunt of drilling, mining, and agribusiness are multiple and scattered, the agents that pursue these activities display a surprising level of corporate concentration. In the mining sector, a limited number of companies control an increasing share of the industry globally (Ericsson 2012). Although massive players such as Vale, BHP Billiton, and Rio Tinto are being joined by companies based in countries such as Russia, South Africa, Mexico, and Chile, the industry is extremely polarized between major producers and small-scale exploration companies. Within this hierarchized scenario, states are not innocent actors. Whether engaged in juridical or territorial negotiations that allow the advance of extractive enterprises, as in the case of the Porgera mine, or directly involved in partnerships or state-owned enterprises (as is the case increasingly in Russia, China, and India, as well as in many sub-Saharan African countries), the entanglement of states with extractive activities is an important aspect of their changing relations to capital. On the ground, this entanglement often involves multifarious and changing forms of patronage, from petty corruption through political complicities with transnational actors and companies whose weight in national economies is rapidly increasing. Further complicating these scenarios are new trends in extraction such as mega-mining, fracking, green washing, oil sand processing, and the growing disputes surrounding conflict resources. These and other trends, not least among them the activation of discourses and practices of sustainability and corporate social responsibility (Welker 2014), ensure that the world's extraction activities continue along an open frontier.

The mapping of this frontier cannot be restricted to sites of literal extraction. Over recent years there has been a marked dissemination of the language of mining into other spheres of human activity. This applies not only to the "mining" of bitcoins (Maurer et al. 2013) but also to the practice of "gold farming" by which young Chinese workers spend hours upon hours in warehouse sweatshops playing games to accumulate points and high scores that can be sold to players in other latitudes who are external to the rounds of play in which the points have been generated (Dyer-Witheford and De Peuter 2009). In these instances, we can discern the expanded sense of extraction we discussed earlier, involving not only the appropriation and expropriation of natural resources but also, and in ever more pronounced ways, cutting through patterns of human cooperation and even trespassing on the very sinews of the human body. The expanding panoply of practices in data mining is another register of this pervasive penetration of extraction across different spheres of human and economic activity. From security to social media, purchasing patterns to financial practices, the collection, storage, and analysis of massive amounts of data enable correlations that at once are highly individualized and sort populations into a range of diverse categories: drivers, pedestrians, consumers of tuna fish, potential terrorists, mortgagees, viewers of Brazilian soap operas, and so on. This logic of profiling produces fungible schemes and relies on algorithmic operations that scan and aggregate data gathered through processes of what can be called digital excavation and extraction (Pasquinelli

2014; Rossiter 2016). The extension of data-mining techniques across a diverse range of economic activities corresponds with an entrenchment of extractive operations within contemporary regimes of capitalist valorization and accumulation. The resulting extractive imprint is apparent in enterprises such as Google and in practices such as HFT, which mobilize data-driven commerce and arbitrage to accomplish openings that are no less violent than those associated with literal extraction.

The role of data mining is also prominent in another important domain that deploys extractive logics to trespass on the sinews of the human body. We have in mind what Kaushik Sunder Rajan (2006) has called biocapital, whose multiple logics are importantly layered "on logics of globalizing, speculative financial capital, manufacturing capital, and knowledge and innovation economies" (Sunder Rajan 2012, 335), as well as the clinical labor (Cooper and Waldby 2014) necessary for its development. At stake here is not only the extraction of tissues and other biological substances from the human body but also the generation and patenting of knowledge derived from genomic manipulations that break down and recast genetic materials according to logics of risk and speculation—enabling the "*metaphor* of life-as-information to become *material* reality that can be commodified" (Sunder Rajan 2006, 16). These operations require the input of bio-informatic data that are generated through the pain and tolerance of experimental subjects who are usually recruited according to specific parameters of gender, race, and class (Cooper and Waldby 2014). As Kalindi Vora (2015) argues, this opening of the human body as a site for annexation, harvest, and production has strong resonances and continuities with land plundering and natural resource dispossession under European territorial colonialism. The sophisticated techniques that link the generation of bio-informatic data to processes of genomic sequencing enable a continuous process of innovation that is also a continuous process of extraction. The most recent developments in biocapital are driven by improvements in the speed and functionality of data collection, storage, and analysis that have dramatically lowered the costs of and time required for the sequencing of genetic materials (Mosco 2014, 182). The resulting processes of innovation and extraction continually test the boundaries of property, once again generating disputes that require new juridical arrangements and a stretching of old ones.

The productive front of data mining is particularly amplified in urban environments, which have been reshaped in many parts of the world by the stretching of work beyond traditional points of production. The urban landscape has become a site for new processes of data extraction that function through various "smart city" and remote-sensing technologies (McNeill 2015). The debates and practices that have sprung up around the ride-sharing application Uber are a familiar example here. The rapid rollout and local infiltration of this app across many world cities has created an echelon of precarious workers who respond to the "click and ride" demands of users while also displacing traditional forms of labor and organization in the taxi industry. Importantly, as we have noted in the case of other capitalist platforms in the gig economy, Uber drivers are not employees of the company that launched the app. Uber works as a kind of flexible and time-space-sensitive device for the collection and mining of data that enable the extraction of skills and labor power from these drivers. In a wider perspective, Uber and other major sharing economy players are laying the ground for new forms of data-driven urban governance that combine logics of privatization with service economy models of networked provision and decision-making practices that widen participation along speculative fronts (Sadowski and Gregory 2015). They are, to quote from a recent text by Trebor Scholz (2016, 4), "'digital bridge builders' who insert themselves between those who offer services and others who are looking for them, thereby embedding extractive processes into social interaction." In a city such as Barcelona, the "progressive" government led since 2015 by Ada Colau has been compelled to come to terms with the profound transformations in tourism and urban space produced in a limited span of time by the invasive operations of Airbnb (see Arias 2015; Martínez Moreno 2016). Needless to say, these transformations are far from being limited to Barcelona. Although the uses of Airbnb are diverse across cities, in many contexts the platform provides a source of income for a generation that has inherited property but is unable to obtain stable employment in an environment of generalized precarity and thus functions as a kind of privatized welfare.

These activities and operations, as the case of Airbnb makes clear, also extend and deepen the reach of a well-established form of property—real estate—that works as a properly extractive device in processes of urban gentrification. Although this is by now an old story (Smith 1996), the "new urban frontier" is continually opening in diverse contexts (Bojadžijev 2015), prompted by the appropriation and expropriation of spaces, values, infrastructures, and forms of life that are submitted to capitalist valorization. Although it is provocatively hyperbolic, Fredric Jameson's (2015, 130) statement that "in our time all politics is about real estate" registers the political stakes at play here. Especially when these processes of "planetary gentrification" (Lees et al. 2016) become enmeshed in new technological environments—one thinks, for instance, of real estate apps that combine locative media routines with pricing and other speculative mechanisms—the city once again becomes a privileged site of accumulation. New strategies of urban governance intertwine with software and database techniques that intersect with the booming world of logistics. It is to this sphere that we now turn.

The Elasticity of Logistics

Like the concept of operations itself, logistics has strong military resonances. According to the military historian Martin van Creveld, logistics arose in the years 1560–1715 as a means for armies to liberate themselves from the "tyranny of plunder" (Van Creveld 1977, 5), by which he means the need to obtain food and other supplies by pillaging and looting from populations in their vicinity. Although the concept of logistics is not developed directly in Carl von Clausewitz's classic *On War* ([1832] 2007), it is possible to derive an understanding of logistical practice from this work (Proença and Duarte 2005). Clausewitz describes what today would be understood as logistics as "preparatory activities" ([1832] 2007, 75) for war. These activities include recruitment, training, marching, eating, and other pursuits considered prior and extraneous to actual military engagement. There can be no doubt that Clausewitz's reflections on war and politics have been influential on subsequent generations of thinkers. Michel Foucault's (1978) famous reversal of Clausewitz's dictum that war is the continuation of politics by other means is only the most recent and celebrated instance of this influence. However, it is a less well known nineteenth-century military thinker who is credited with recognizing the growing importance of logistics in modern warfare. In *The Art of War* ([1838] 2008, 200), Antoine-Henri Jomini, a Swiss officer who served with Napoleon at Jena, asks whether logistics is becoming a "general science, forming one of the most essential parts of the art of war." Today the proposition that military operations, like those in other spheres of human activity, are limited by lines of information and supply seems a truism. But these were notions that were violently forged in the face of material developments and historical transformations. Present-day thinkers (Cowen 2010; LeCavalier 2016) who trace the diffusion of logistical practices into civilian economic life are fond of quoting Jomini as a predecessor who recognizes the leading role of logistics in the organization and execution of war.

Discussions of the so-called logistics revolution of the mid- to late twentieth century explore continuities between the history of logistics as a military art and its more recent history as a means of managing the movement of people and things to achieve economic, communication, and transport efficiencies. In this respect, the study of logistics is haunted by the thesis of the militarization of society. The expansion of business logistics and its related infrastructures is frequently hedged by fears regarding military and geopolitical ambitions. Consider China's recent investments in deepwater shipping ports in countries such as Myanmar, Bangladesh, Sri Lanka, and Pakistan. US and Indian military planners have argued that these commercial ventures form a "string of pearls" that could be converted into a series of naval bases that surround the Indian subcontinent (Dixon 2014). The line between economic and military activity remains thin, at least in the eyes of parties with vested interests. As in the case of the Internet, which also evolved from military technologies, the prospect that logistics advances or intensifies the relation between war and capital cannot simply be conjured away. Indeed, contemporary logistical systems not only offer a means of securing supplies for capitalist enterprise but are also crucial in instituting networked forms of geopolitical security that aim at channeling and monitoring flows rather than interrupting or blocking them (Cowen 2014).

The emergence of logistics as a business proposition and civilian practice dates to the post–World War II period. The logistics revolution culminated in the 1960s, when the introduction of a systems analysis approach to transport and distribution dynamics began to reshape the world of production (Allen 1997). Changes that occurred in this period and its aftermath include the spatial reorganization of the firm, the interlinking of logistics science with computing and software design, the introduction of the shipping container, the formation of business organizations and academic programs for the production and dissemination of logistical knowledge, the development of real-time technologies for monitoring labor, the emergence of global supply chains, and the search for cheap labor rates in poor areas of the world. Logistics moved from being an exercise in cost minimization to becoming an integrated part of global production systems and a means of maximizing profit. The myth that production stopped at the factory gates, challenged in feminist theory and politics, as well as in the celebrated thesis of the "social factory," was shattered with the evolution of more sophisticated management systems that made the practice of trading labor and transport costs off against each other a more exact science. The assembly and marketing of goods across different global locations, with objects and knowledge constantly moving among them, served to blur processes of production, distribution, and consumption. Logistics also made the organization of global space more complicated and differentiated. Geographical entities such as special economic zones and logistics hubs sprang up to attract investment and organize the business of global production. Increasingly, logistics also came to play a role in service economies and production processes in the media and digital industries.

"If you think of Wall Street as capitalism's symbolic headquarters," writes Kalvin Henely (2012) in a review of Allan Sekula and Nöel Burch's film *The Forgotten Space* (2010), "the sea is capitalism's trading floor writ large." In choosing the world of container shipping to explore the often forgotten logistical conduits and circuits that sustain and contribute to current systems of trade and production, Sekula and Burch join a long line of thinkers who take the empty bulk of the shipping container as a potent symbol of the changes logistics has introduced to contemporary economic and labor practices. Supposedly introduced by the entrepreneur Malcolm McLean in the early 1950s (Levinson 2006) and given an important fillip by the US military's development of the CONEX (Container Express) system, which was put to effective use in the Vietnam War, it was not until 1968 that the International Organization for Standardization corralled key shipping, railroad, and trucking companies to agree on global standards. The container's global diffusion through the spread of intermodal transport systems was marked by labor struggles and attendant changes in economic geography, including the decline of industrial ports such as New York and London and the opening of East Asia as a major site for industrial production. Shifting the object of measure in shipping from weight to volume and introducing a modular logic by which transport costs could be submitted to processes of financialization, the container remains the icon of logistical standardization and efficiency. Yet the imbalances of trade that are characteristic of capitalism's variegation mean that the global movement of containers is uneven, and much logistical energy today is devoted to the shipping and storage of empty containers (Neilson 2015). As Tsing (2009) observes, logistical systems produce as well as eliminate frictions and inefficiencies. Their negotiation and exploitation of geographical, societal, and other differences that they cannot fully control by means of internal governance mechanisms is a key factor to take into account when asking how logistics has changed the conduct of production and trade.

Although Marx did not use the term "logistics," its importance to capitalist enterprise was already specified in *Capital*, volume 2 (Marx 1978). According to the argument advanced in that volume, capitalist production needs to reduce the circulatory time of capital as much as possible, because during that interval the capitalist cannot convert surplus value into profit. Although the turnover time of capital consists of both production and circulation time, logistical processes tend to dissolve the heuristic division between these two. "Transportation," Marx writes, "is distinguished by its appearance as the continuation of a production process within the circulation process and for the circulation process" (Marx 1978, 229). Logistical efficiency is thus an important part of profit maximization. More than a matter of cost reduction, or the mere transportation to consumers of goods to which surplus value has already been added, logistical modes of coordination are integral to production itself. This analytical frame still provides a powerful way to understand the role of logistics within the heterogeneous landscapes of contemporary capitalism. Logistical operations are important to the reduction of capital's turnover time, whether deployed in economic domains strongly identified with logistics such as transport and communication or applied more generally—for instance, in activities associated with literal extraction and finance.

Crucially, however, such reduction of turnover time does not necessarily mean that processes of production, circulation, and exchange necessarily become faster. Despite the elegant theorizations of Paul Virilio ([1977] 2006), logistics is not the fetishization of speed. Certainly, in many domains of current economic activity, the increased 24/7 pace of production and trade is legion. The instance of high-frequency trading, discussed in chapter 1, is a particularly redolent example. Yet while HFT in many ways represents the becoming logistical of finance, the reduction of capital's turnover time also paradoxically commands strange forms of slowness. Perhaps this is most evident in that form of economic activity that we have identified as the most iconic of contemporary logistical practices: container shipping. In this field, the cutting edge of efficiency is so-called slow steaming. Container ships are becoming both larger (and thus capable of carrying more boxes) and slower in their cruising speeds (a factor that introduces savings and efficiencies due to reduced energy costs). This tendency, which is closely linked with processes of financialization of shipping and consequently of shipbuilding that have made the sector highly unstable in recent years (see Bologna 2013, 131–47), is driving many logistical developments in commercial shipping, including the refitting of many ports with cranes and other kinds of equipment capable of handling the largest class of post-Panamax craft, the subsequent opening and closing of shipping routes, and the investment in large infrastructural projects such as the widening of the Panama Canal. But it is not these changes on which we want to remark. Rather, we emphasize the *making elastic* of time and temporality mandated by logistical operations that aim to reduce capital's turnover time—the command to both speed up and slow down that is characteristic of current capitalist development and crisis. This paradoxical and contradictory temporal movement accompanies and supports the spatial stretching of production processes and supply chain operations that signal an economic predicament in which, as Tsing puts it, "deviations from older models of capitalism are not just defects of the system [but] have become the system" (Tsing 2015, 330).

As we have argued many times, such temporal and spatial elasticity is a crucial aspect of how the operations of capital are currently reconfiguring the world. It would be a mistake, however, to understand logistics merely as a system for searching out and connecting diverse firms and labor forces on the basis of cost or other parameters. Deborah Cowen (2014, 3) argues that "logistics is not just about circulating *stuff* but sustaining life." Logistics actively produces environments and subjectivities, including those of workers and labor forces, through techniques of measurement, coordination, and optimization. This is to say, it is not simply a socio-technical system that adapts to existing economic and material conditions. As Brian Larkin (2013, 329) writes about infrastructures more generally, they "also exist as forms separate from their purely technical functioning" and show "how the political can be constituted through different means." A prominent instance of such infrastructural power can be found in the logistical production of spaces that are not only economic but also political in their constitution—territories, we might say. In *Border as Method* (Mezzadra and Neilson 2013a, chap. 7), we provided a preliminary framework for understanding the global proliferation of multiple kinds of zones and corridors, as well as for analyzing the "lateral" practices of arbitrage and circulation that link and move among them. In chapter 3 of this book, we explored the precedents for this expansion of zones and corridors in early modern processes of colonization and trade. The role of chartered companies and privateers in establishing far-flung "factories," concessions, and trading routes provides a fascinating history that parallels and troubles the formation of the nation-state while also illustrating how imperial geographies evolved through the mixing of commercial and political violence. Cowen's (2014, 8) claim that logistics "maps the form of contemporary imperialism" registers the continuation of this amalgam of commerce and politics in current expressions of logistical power.

Our intention is not to catalogue or explain how, beginning in the 1970s, zones began to spread rapidly in both number and type. Others have accomplished this task with more detail (Meng 2005) and style (Easterling 2014) than we can hope to muster here. Suffice it to say that we understand zones not primarily as spaces of sovereign exception, although clearly a sovereign gesture is involved in their establishment, but as sites where a multiplicity of normative orders (some of them legal in the hard sense, but others less so, such as corporate social responsibility protocols or the rule-governed scripts than run logistical software packages) interact and conflict in ways that firms and governments can manipulate to their advantage. Thus, a specific politics characterizes zones as well as infrastructural places such as corridors (Grappi 2016, 115–30). While zones classically are spaces in which state-sanctioned labor, tax, and industrial safety legislation are suspended or relaxed, they remain susceptible to strategies of supply chain governance that increasingly adhere to the imperatives of what Joshua Barkan (2013) calls corporate sovereignty. In this sense, zones are part of what we call in chapter 6 the state of capitalist globalization. Far from being sites that necessarily facilitate the establishment of labor conditions or logistical practices that are radically different from those that exist outside them, they tend to make obvious and singularly manifest that which is often hidden or obscure in wider social economic domains. In other words, zones render visible and legitimize arrangements that are frequently informal or emergent in the economy at large (Neilson 2014).

One way to conceive the zone is to emphasize how it makes clear the connection among different operations of capital. This becomes particularly obvious in large-scale planning or infrastructure projects that aim to link up or articulate zones into larger spatial-logistical formations. In their account of the Delhi-Mumbai Industrial Corridor, Ishita Dey and Giorgio Grappi (2015) emphasize how logistical operations join extractive exercises of land grabbing and financial arrangements of private-public partnership to establish new relations among the state form, neoliberal politics, and processes of market governance. Particularly important to Dey and Grappi's analysis is an investigation of how these arrangements produce labor power and labor struggles along the way. Their account of the Maruti-Suzuki strike of 2012 shows how this seemingly traditional industrial struggle is connected to the development of the corridor model and heterogeneous dimensions of labor that extend far beyond the factory site where the shutdown occurred. Crucial here is "the need to think the industrial dispute in places such as Maruti-Suzuki together with struggles around land or other resources along the corridor without disavowing the relevance of the wage or considering the struggles of peasants and informal workers as radically separated from it" (Dey and Grappi 2015, 164). As Ferguson (2015, 94–102) argues in the South African context, the prospect of separating formal from informal labor is increasingly fraught (see also Du Toit and Neves 2007). In this perspective, logistical labor can be understood not only as the production and circulation of commodities, whether material or immaterial, but also as various forms of hustling, tapping into flows, or distributive labor that spring up, and in many cases dominate, in situations where capital has done its work of dispossession.

The nexus of logistics and labor is an intense site of struggle and connection. Stefano Harney and Fred Moten contend that logistics "was founded in the Atlantic slave trade, founded against the Atlantic slave." Although they recognize that "logistics could not contain what it had relegated to the hold," they argue that it is in the slave trade that logistics finds its "ambition to connect bodies, objects, affects, information, without subjects" (Harney and Moten 2013, 92). The status of the slave as "not just labor but commodity" (93) impels and inspires the dream of logistics "to dispense with the subject altogether" (87), "to move objects and move through objects" (92), to pacify and eliminate the subject, to substitute the subject with "human capital" (90). These are politically potent claims that provide a tragic historical precedent to explain an important feature of contemporary logistical systems: their striving for resilience, or "fault tolerance," for an ability to go on operating despite breakdowns or interruptions, for the accommodation or avoidance of hindrances, whether they result from natural disasters or labor stoppages. Classically, logistical labor is understood to hold a double position, subject to forms of monitoring and measurement (just think of the real-time labor management systems in place in the contemporary warehouse) but also holding a "strategic position," which means that even minor industrial actions can have effects that ricochet down the supply chain (just think of the masculinized militancy of the dockworker). Harney and Moten's argument finds in the figure of the Atlantic slave a kind of historical imprint that marks current logistical efforts to route around the double bind of this subjectivity, to render it redundant, superfluous, or even just precarious by choosing another path, an ontological passage that attributes to the object an unassailable priority.

Importantly, this argument should not be understood to imply that the contemporary logistics worker is a slave in the juridical sense. As Harney and Moten are aware, current logistical operations are driven by software packages and algorithmic processes that themselves rely on such possibilities of switching and rerouting. Florian Sprenger (2015) explains how technologies of data transmission function by breaking data into small "packets" that are sent by different routes and recomposed at their point of arrival. If a packet cannot travel by one route, or encounters an unexpected delay, it is simply handled by another server. Through this system of bursts and flows, communication appears smooth and instantaneous. The same logic applies in the domain of logistical coordination and transport. The movement of people and things appears smooth, but this smoothness is an illusion created by the bursting of information and materials across diverse systems and locations that do not necessarily piece together seamlessly. Realizing that such seamlessness is an illusion is crucial to understanding the logic that animates contemporary logistical operations. As Ned Rossiter (2016) argues, what we colloquially call logistical nightmares arise at points in the network where the interoperability among different systems breaks down. By locating such points and addressing our research and political efforts to them, we obtain a powerful perspective on how capital hits the ground, observing technological mismatches, labor struggles, social inequalities, and even cultural conflicts that spill over into the operations of extraction and finance. Nowhere is this more evident than in the world of finance, where the logistical introduction of HFT has made possible new forms of volatility and crisis.

Finance beyond Finance

"On May 6, 2010, the prices of many US-based equity products experienced an extraordinarily rapid decline and recovery. That afternoon, major equity indices in both the futures and securities markets, each already down over 4% from their prior-day close, suddenly plummeted a further 5–6% in a matter of minutes before rebounding almost as quickly." This is the beginning of the joint report by the Commodity Futures Trading Commission and Securities and Exchange Commission on what has come to be known as the flash crash of 2010. A large trade of E-Mini contracts executed by a "large fundamental trader (a mutual fund complex)" via an automated execution algorithm prompted a series of chain effects that resulted in "severe dislocations" in many securities and in a double "liquidity crisis"—"one at the broad index level in the E-Mini, the other with respect to individual stocks" (Commodity Futures Trading Commission and Securities and Exchange Commission 2010, 1–6). Our interest here is not in the technicalities of flash crashes, which were, in a way, anticipated in 1995 when Juan Pablo Dávila, a Chilean trader of financial futures, instructed his computer to buy when he meant to sell, prompting a concatenation of trades that eventually resulted in losses in the amount of 0.5 percent of his country's gross national product—leading to the coining of a new verb in Chile, *davilar*, meaning to botch things up royally (see Malvaldi and Leporini 2014, 51). Flash crashes have occurred on other occasions since 2010— for instance, in April 2013 on Wall Street; again in October of the same year on the Singapore Exchange; and, more recently, in October 2016 with the flash crash of the British pound. We take the disrupted temporality of the flash crash as a symptom of the peculiar temporal scrambling of crisis and recovery that permeates financial capital and markets in an age of algorithmic trading and fiscal cliffs. Similar to the temporal elasticity of logistics that we noted in the previous section, this volatility does not confine itself to financial markets but reaches into the wider social fabric, where it produces experiences of uncertainty and precarity with deep effects for labor and other forms of life. The very idea of recovery seems to be shattered when the rationality of capitalism is dominated by financial instability and by the attempt to make it productive.

The position of finance in contemporary capitalism cannot be adequately explained by cyclical analytical models—whether according to the "long waves" detected in the 1920s by the Soviet economist Nikolai Kondratieff or the "systemic cycles of accumulation" eloquently discussed by Giovanni Arrighi, each associated with the hegemony of a particular territorial state— with more or less turbulent transitions from Genoa (1340s–1630) to the Netherlands (1560–1780s) to Britain (1740s–1930s) and the United States (1870s–2000s). Despite the differences among these theoretical frameworks, what they have in common is the idea that the prevalence of finance is not merely "a sign of autumn," to recall Fernand Braudel's (1984, 246) famous definition often invoked in contemporary debates. Financial expansions, Arrighi writes, must be seen "as announcing not just the maturity of a particular stage of development of the capitalist world-economy, but also the beginning of a new stage," because financial expansions lay the basis for the "'organizational revolution' in processes of capital accumulation" that runs parallel to the "change of guard at the commanding heights of the capitalist world-economy" (Arrighi 2010, 88). From this point of view, Kondratieff's theory, although it has a quite different focus, is at least formally similar. Kondratieff's fifty-year cycles are prompted by "the deployment of new technologies and high capital investment" and are divided into an up phase, characterized by capital flows to "productive industries" and a down phase, in which capital "gets trapped in the finance system" (Mason 2015, 53). While this moment of financialization is marked by the multiplication of recessions that eventually lead to the end of the cycle, it also plays a crucial role in the accumulation, centralization, and mobilization of capital that facilitate the takeoff of the next cycle.

Arrighi's and Kondratieff's theories are predicated on a clear-cut boundary among material and financial expansion, productive industries, and the financial system. To make sense of Kondratieff's approach, it is important to stress that he aimed to understand the dynamics of economic development in *industrial* capitalism. The lively controversy that surrounded Kondratieff's work from the 1920s, which was particularly virulent in Soviet Marxist debates and anticipated his execution in 1937 by a Stalinist firing squad, revolved around the ability of capitalism to overcome its inherent tendency to crisis, and eventually around the plausibility of the idea that capitalism would inevitably encounter a "final crisis." At stake in these debates was, furthermore, the main cause of the long waves he detected, whether they were traceable to the rhythms of capital investment, to technological innovations, to class struggle, or to some kind of external shock. What interests us here is the peculiarity of the financial moment in industrial capitalism and the distinction between finance and productive industries. In chapter 2, we discussed Rudolf Hilferding's interpretation of the role of financial capital in a crucial moment of the transition of capitalism, coinciding with the beginning of the third long cycle identified by Kondratieff. Crucial to Hilferding's analysis was the fact that, in the age of incipient mass production and monopolist concentration, the amount of capital needed to start and carry on industrial activities exceeded by far what individual capitalists owned. While he was interested in tracing the fusion of "bank capital" and "industrial capital," epitomized by the expansion of industrial credit that was made available by banks, it is easy to see that industry remained at the root of the whole process, dictating the rhythms and scope of investments.

In general terms, a cyclical explanation of capitalist development seems to work quite effectively as far as the workings of industrial capitalism are concerned. In a different and wider perspective, world systems theory can claim the same for previous moments in the history of this mode of production. The question is whether this scheme remains valid as a tool with which to analyze contemporary capitalism. We do not think this is the case. As Paul Mason (2015, 43), who recently provided a challenging reassessment of Kondratieff's theory, put it, "If industrial capitalism has produced a sequence of fifty-year waves over a period of more than 200 years, then maybe at some point this too breaks down, inaugurating a regime change that leads to a whole different pattern." This does not mean denying that specific business cycles, to take a phrase popularized by Joseph Schumpeter, or product cycles, to hark back to the work of Beverly Silver (2003), continue to play important roles in economic dynamics anymore. The point is, rather, that they do not allow us to make sense of the movements and composition of aggregate capital. Nor do they allow us to distinguish crisis and recovery or material from financial expansion. This has to do with the completely different position of finance within capitalism as a whole, which in turn is connected with dramatic changes in the world of production. From this point of view, it is important to stress once again that contemporary processes of financialization were prompted by a series of measures taken by the US government and Federal Reserve in the 1970s, starting with the decoupling of the dollar from gold in 1971, which laid the basis for a general reorganization of capitalism. It was the continuity and radical nature of working-class struggle that challenged industrial profits and compelled capital to break the walls of the factory and expand its circuits of valorization to the whole society. At the same time, the continuity of anti-imperialist struggles challenged the center-periphery relations on which capitalism as a world system was based in the postwar age. From both of these angles, the new financial practices that began to emerge in the 1970s provided effective "solutions." They provided new chances for profits, a new scheme for the synchronization and command of processes of socialization of production, and new instruments to discipline unruly populations and even states (as would become clear, for example, with the Mexican debt crisis in 1982 and with structural adjustment programs in the following years).

The deregulation of financial markets has fostered a process of displacement and reorientation of capitalist accumulation that Greta Krippner, for instance, has documented for the United States in *Capitalizing on Crisis*

(2011). This process is far from being limited to the United States and has involved a dramatic increase in the weight of the financial sector, a corresponding boom in the profits of financial companies, as well as a growing financialization of the incomes of non-financial corporations and activities (Durand 2017, 75–82). The latter point is perhaps the most important. Finance is characterized by a specific form of rationality, which can be described as a speculative, risk-based, promissory, and "mimetic" rationality (Orléan 1999). This rationality nowadays permeates capitalism writ large and tends to act as the orchestrating and unifying principle of its workings. In terms of our discussion of the notion of operations of capital, this means that the rationality of finance, besides shaping specific financial operations, plays an increasingly crucial role in the determination of other operations—say, for instance, an industrial investment, the launch of a new mining project, or the further stretching of a logistical supply chain. Far from being guided by the needs and logics of production, or what is often called the real economy, finance increasingly interpenetrates production itself, disseminating its rationality, devices, and logics within the social fabric. In so doing, finance loses the self-referential character often ascribed to it by critics and becomes completely enmeshed within the "real economy" and social life.

This new position of finance has far-reaching implications for basic economic notions and related processes. The increasing sophistication and diffusion of financial instruments such as derivatives gives new meanings to the very notion of the commodity. Following the analysis pursued by Randy Martin, the contrast with industrial capitalism is again striking here. Where the assembly line gathers all the elements in one site to construct an integrated commodity, financial engineering reverses the process. Such engineering disassembles "a commodity into its constituent and variable elements and disperses these attributes" (Martin 2013, 89). The derivative is "the very paradigm of heterogeneity, even the heterogeneity at the heart of that homogeneous process we call capitalism" (Jameson 2015, 119). The volatility of financial markets thus infiltrates the markets for goods and services. In the framework of the financialization processes initiated in the 1970s, the form of money has also undergone deep changes. The emergence of "shadow money" is particularly relevant in this regard. Melinda Cooper has recently analyzed the ways in which the restriction of money supply effected by the so-called Volcker shock in 1979 laid the ground for the rise of this "private, parallel system of money creation" through the extension of "money market mutual funds" and "various money market instruments" (Cooper 2015, 413). This alternative monetary system offered an alternative to traditional deposits. Derivative instruments such as the "credit default swap" played a very important role in facilitating the emergence of shadow money. Even more importantly, Cooper (2015, 416) calls attention to "the evolving, symbiotic relationship between the organization of labor, the form of money, and the terms of credit," focusing first of all on the formal analogies between the derivative contract, which is oriented toward nonstandard risk, and the emerging nonstandard contractual forms for precarious labor. "What is equally at stake in the credit derivative and the zero-hour contract," Cooper (2015, 399) writes, "is the absolute contingency of post-Fordist work time—labor that will be performed at some unspecified place and time—and the challenge this poses to actuarial modes of risk management."

The rise of shadow money can therefore be understood as a crucial aspect of the dismantling of the New Deal compromise in the United States, which also spelled the end of "free" wage labor as a standard and led to the formation of a huge and heterogeneous "shadow workforce" (Cooper 2015, 414–15). Here we can see the close relation between processes of financialization and deep transformations occurring in the realm of the so-called real economy—or, more precisely, in the monetary form of the mediation of the capital-labor relation (see also Dörre, in Dörre et al. 2009, 54, 58). Concurrently, the change in "terms of credit"—particularly in the management of long-term loans by commercial banks—led to the emergence of new instruments, epitomized by subprime mortgages, whose target was again what Cooper calls the shadow workforce. Part of a more general process of financialization of social rights (Crouch 2009), the spread of subprime mortgages seemed indeed to offer to targeted groups of marginalized people a chance to solve the housing problem. But the price for this expansion of credit, as became dramatically clear in the crisis of 2007–2008, was that such a basic condition of social life as housing was made dependent for the poor on the volatility of financial markets—and on the susceptibility of such markets to ever more unpredictable patterns of bubble formation and bursting. The ensuing wave of evictions and foreclosures has been described by Sassen as a process of violent dispossession and expulsion that resembles Marx's analysis of so-called primitive accumulation (Sassen 2010; Sassen 2014, 128). We are indeed again confronted here with the problem of capital's relation with its multiple outsides. While familiar images of finance focus on the sparkling and seemingly self-referential world of financial markets and the stock exchange, some of the most important financial innovations of the past decades are driven by an attempt to "expand the operational space of advanced capitalism" (Sassen 2010, 25). Such expansion not only disrupts and reorganizes traditional forms of capitalism. It also targets ever more marginal territories and populations. Important instances of this tendency are micro-credit, banking for the poor in many parts of the world, and the role of consumer credit in the financialization of so-called popular economies in Latin America (Gago 2015). In such cases, the evolution of new financial instruments and innovations is manifest. More important for our purposes, the adaptions and strategies deployed by populations in these situations allow us to study in an effective way the gritty realities that accompany capital's entanglement with spaces, social practices, and forms of life.

The prominence of finance today involves a dissemination of patterns of volatility and risk across the entire fabric of economy and society. Finance clearly has effects that extend beyond the financial sector as narrowly defined. Examples such as the subprime mortgage, structural adjustment programs, and the harsh imposition of austerity on entire populations (e.g., the recent case of Greece) show that volatility and risk go hand in hand with a huge amount of violence. At the same time, the specific forms taken by financialization since the 1970s, which led to huge flows of foreign investments into the market for US securities, eventually led to a situation of global instability, characterized by the risk of unpredictable shifts and turbulences in the geographies of financial power. These are important references for a critique of contemporary financialization. Such a critique, however, must also necessarily acknowledge the deep entrenchment of such financialization in wider processes that have reshaped capitalism over the past decades. Financialization corresponds to a situation in which the heterogeneous composition of labor and social cooperation emerges as the main productive force. From this point of view, the question of the "source" of financial value becomes important. In very general terms, we can define "finance," quoting from a recent book by Cédric Durand (2017, 151), as "an accumulation of drawing rights on wealth that is yet to be produced, which takes the form of private and public indebtedness, stock exchange capitalization and various financial products." This is not an entirely new story. In his important discussion in *Capital*, volume 3, of finance capital (which he calls "interest bearing capital" and is defined elsewhere as "capital *par excellence*" [Marx 1981, 499]), Marx (1981, 599, 641) actually provides the basic terms of this definition, stressing the accumulation of "claims or titles" to "future production" as a distinctive feature of the specificity of the financial moment in the series of transformations effected by capital.

This emphasis on the relevance of the wealth *to be produced in the future* seems crucial to us because it challenges any interpretation of finance as self-referential, of financial capital as merely fictitious and opposed to productive capital. Picking up again our notion of operations of capital, this perspective allows us to highlight the crucial role played by financial operations in contemporary capitalism while stressing that they cannot be abstracted from the promise of future production, which also means from other operations of capital that shape and organize social cooperation according to heterogeneous logics. In this regard, the recent critical move to place debt at the center of an analysis of the workings of capital (Graeber 2011; Lazzarato 2012) must be qualified by an emphasis on the compulsion to work that corresponds to the widening and further entrenchment of the logics of debt. An abstract figure of future cooperation traversed and constricted by this compulsion looms as the main "source" of financial value, regardless of the forms and arrangements that this future cooperation may assume. What is produced and crystallized in financial operations is the measure and norm of this future cooperation in a situation in which, differently from that pertaining in industrial capitalism, there is no longer a single branch of the economy or a single standard employment relation that can be taken as a reference for the calculation of the average rate of profit and as a standard for the mediation of the relation between capital and labor.

Resonances

Our skepticism regarding the possibility of identifying a single branch or sector of the economy as providing a dominant paradigm for capitalist activity today does not exclude recognition of the orchestrating role played by finance. Similarly, the pervasiveness of logistical modes of economic coordination and the reliance of enterprise and social life on substances and energy obtained from literal extraction does not license totalizing arguments for the dominance of these sectors. Rather than searching for a particular branch of the economy that trumps all others, we think it is more important to specify empirically and conceptually how relations of power and dominance are forged through the intertwining of different kinds of operations.

This implies two levels of investigation. The first is a grounded and detailed analysis of how the operations of extraction, logistics, and finance interact and collide across diverse spaces and scales. The second is a more abstract and conceptual exercise that aims to identify commonalities and underlying logics that manifest themselves in the many resonances that emerge among operations of capital in these domains. As we outlined in chapter 2, operations of capital can be isolated only heuristically because in practice they concatenate with one another, confront frictions and discontinuities, and are deployed within larger formations of capitalism. Identifying the underlying logics of capital's operations means excavating or unearthing the principles that drive such concatenation and conflict. Needless to say, such principles are not iron laws. They are sensitive to the contingencies of history and geography and, to this extent, work in accord with what we earlier called the axiomatic of capital, which is never exhausted in any single empirical situation. An investigation of this type allows us to chart the temporal and spatial variegations and transitions of capitalism while remaining attentive to the question of capital's conceptual unity and necessary embeddedness in social relations.

The notion of operations of capital inspires an inquiry that aims to shed light on an emerging set of operative principles that become apparent in material interventions of capital on the ground. These interventions not only require concerted efforts of coordination and foresight but also have to negotiate specific and often unpredictable circumstances of difference and heterogeneity. This is why, for us, the unity of capital is not merely a conceptual matter, given from the skies or from some past dogma, but a question of capital in action, of its restless movement between conceptual skies and empirical battlegrounds, of its cutting through of space and human activity in ways that are both devastating and productive. The operative principles we referred to earlier are always subject to variation and change. Nonetheless, they also exhibit a stubbornness and resilience that, as many movements and struggles that have challenged capital have discovered, are difficult to shift. Identifying the specific variabilities and dislocations to which these principles are subject, particularly on the cusp of historical change, opens an effective angle from which to analyze capital's composition and active form, its multiple relations with its shifting outsides, and the qualities and nature of the social relationship that constitutes it. In this perspective, the operations of extraction, logistics, and finance discussed in this chapter begin to take on different hues. While it is clearly possible to detail the peculiarity of operations of capital in each of these domains, it is even more important to delineate the principles that transect them and thus emerge as distinctive criteria of capitalism in its present global formation. Extraction, in this light, stands out in ways that go beyond its literal and expanded terms of operation.

We have already hinted at the ways in which the operations of extraction, logistics, and finance intertwine on the ground. Whether in our description of HFT as the becoming logistical of finance, our attention to the infrastructural conduits of extractive activities, or our comments concerning the speculative dimensions of mineral prospecting and the pricing of commodities, the overlapping and mutual implication of capital's operations in these three domains become apparent. While it would be interesting to explore this intertwining further (Mezzadra and Neilson 2017), the point we want to make here is more specific. We previously highlighted how the composition and logics of aggregate capital are increasingly marked by the prevalence and pivotal status of *extractive* operations. It should by now be clear that the operations of contemporary finance take on a specifically extractive character in their constitutive relationship with a wealth to be produced in the future through social cooperation that finance itself does not directly organize. The well-rehearsed formula that profit is increasingly becoming rent is one way to describe this tendency. Other approaches, as we have seen, stress the imbrication of contemporary finance with the continuous working of primitive accumulation or point to the long-term "historical constitution of private property, resource extraction, and speculative investment in and through colonialism and slavery" as crucial for addressing the "present day displacement of risk, accountability, and culpability from the wealthy to the poor" (Goldstein 2014, 44). From a different angle, Ferguson extends the point we quoted earlier about the seemingly magical and fabulous appearance of wealth through literal extraction by remarking that also "other forms of wealth" in the contemporary conjuncture seem to materialize "as if from nowhere" (Ferguson 2015, 185). Needless to say, wealth generated from finance figures prominently among Ferguson's examples of such other forms. These kinds of analysis delineate a more conceptual sense of extraction, which remains tied to the literal and expanded meanings of the term but also encompasses a wider and necessarily critical perspective on the operations of capital.

As we have intimated, the extractive operations of capital are also evident in the workings of logistics and supply chains. In chapter 1, we discuss how the spatial stretching of global production systems means that logistical processes have a capacity to shape and guide productive activities. The role of logistics in synchronizing diverse forms of production along supply chains, often commanding only that producers keep their prices as low as possible, means that wealth can be generated through forms of coordination that connect and valorize the relative spatial positioning of different points of production above the methods of production deployed at any one of these points. The logistical moment in the operations of capital assumes an external position with respect to the multiplicity of productive environments and differences that it exploits (although it is important to note that many of these environments are in turn reshaped by logistical arrangements in the organization of labor). It thus becomes possible to speak of a properly extractive dynamics of logistics, since logistical operations exercise a kind of drawing power over diverse labor regimes and meshes of social cooperation that they do not directly organize or mandate. Like the operations of finance, which draw on a future wealth whose production is forever deferred, logistical operations thus display an extractive dynamic. As we stated earlier, this theoretical emphasis on extraction does not mean that extractive activities in the literal sense come to control and command activities in these other domains. We remain skeptical of so-called neo-extractivist positions that find narrow extractive practices to provide a privileged key for analyzing the contemporary capitalist moment. Instead, we point to a predicament in which the operations of capital within and across different domains become increasingly oriented to an outside that sustains and enables them. Whether this outside takes the form of mineral deposits, land, biological materials, or social cooperation, the increasing reliance of capital on materials, reserves, and conditions external to it means that the operations of capital acquire a distinctively extractive edge. Along this edge we can begin to identify the systemic aspects of contemporary capitalism, specifying the common characteristics that hold together an array of practices, forms, and relations that find coherence in their capacity to traverse, interrupt, and exploit a multiplicity of outsides.

It should be evident by now that the multiple outsides of capital cannot be reduced to spaces (which also means forms of economic and social activity) or materials "not yet" subdued to domination and appropriation by capital. As we argued in chapter 2, this leads to a situation that can be described through a reframing of the Marxian concept of formal subsumption. Particularly when looking at the operations of finance and logistics, it becomes clear that the social and economic spaces they target and exploit cannot be considered noncapitalist. They are instead permeated and shaped by other operations of capital, which concatenate with financial and logistical operations in specific ways. While this realization provides an effective angle from which to describe the composition of capital critically in the present, it also calls for an analysis of the modalities that tie these heterogeneous operations of capital into different formations of capitalism. The role of the state in the production of these variegated formations of capitalism is particularly important, although there is a need to emphasize that the logics of the extractive operations of capital are increasingly articulated at levels that cannot be captured at the national scale. More important for us is the question of how the relation between capital and labor is reworked in the face of the crucial role played by these extractive logics.

Speaking of the composition of capital involves something more than listing different fractions of capital that supposedly combine to make up a whole. Although we might safely claim that capital today has become more and more financial capital (this is basically the tendency described by the concept of financialization), it is a more tenuous proposition to nominate other candidates to play support or cameo roles alongside this protagonist. But this is not really the point. Contemporary capital is composed through a continuous process of formation and deformation. More often than not, capital these days is disproportioned and struggles to assert its unity amid multiple internal conflicts and heterogeneous relations with its different outsides. What the notion of the operations of capital allows us to do is to cut through different sectors or branches of economic activity in a way that is attentive to ensuing resonances. The extractive logics that we have mapped in this chapter through an investigation of extraction, logistics, and finance emerge precisely out of these resonances and provide a blueprint for discerning the evolving and unstable principles that undergird the composition of contemporary capital. These are principles manifest in the immanent deployment of specific operations of capital. At the same time, due to their pervasiveness and guiding role, they spread across the variegated fabric of capitalism as such. These principles thus play a pivotal role in the organization and structuring of capitalist activities outside the domains of extraction, logistics, and finance. This is particularly the case regarding industrial activities, which continue to expand in many parts of the world but no longer guide capitalist development writ large. We emphasize the role of extraction, understood in a more conceptual sense, in shaping the guiding principles of capitalist valorization and accumulation in the present. A new *tableau économique* emerges against this background and deserves further investigation.

While much of the discussion in this chapter has revolved around the dynamics of financialization and the peculiar forms of capitalist activity that have also emerged with the expansion of logistics and the new frontiers of extraction, we need to remember that the processes that drive speculation, investment, and valorization across these fields are subject to the patterns of variegation we addressed in chapter 1. The role of spatial and scalar arrangements in contributing to this variegation is far from passive. Perhaps this shows one of the main limitations of the metaphor we deploy continually in our analysis of how specific operations of capital take shape in and impinge on diverse situations. When we speak of capital hitting the ground, it might be possible to misunderstand us as building a contrast between capital's operative dimensions and its existence as a social relation that unfolds in and across distinct spaces and historical vistas. The metaphor seems to imply that capital is somehow fully formed before it hits the ground. It should be clear from the discussion of finance that we do not consider the operative space of capital to be so ethereal, just as our dealings with logistics and extraction should make it evident that we understand capital's operations to be deeply enmeshed with material configurations of flesh and earth. In this sense, we do not separate the operations of capital from capital's relational or social qualities, which, as we emphasize in chapter 1, always unfold over landscapes and experiences of difference. Nor do we simply equate the grounds on which capital operates with its multiple outsides, rendering geographical space an external, inert, or residual element. Our emphasis on the production and heterogeneity of global space, as well as its intertwining with techniques and technologies of power in the making of territory, should make it clear that we consider capital's operations to work in and through the active articulation of historical forces and geographical relations. However, something more needs to be said about how labor fits (or does not fit) into this nexus of space, ground, and operations.

The operations of extraction, logistics, and finance clearly require and tie up significant components of contemporary living labor. As we have shown in this chapter, these operations also target and exploit other forms of activity and labor that are not directly connected to the kinds of employment that have evolved in these domains. While it is important to talk about the histories and struggles of prominent figures such as miners, dock workers, and traders, it is perhaps more necessary to map and interrogate the ways in which the operations of capital involve extractive logics that affect other figures of labor and life. Far from any nostalgia for wage labor, we can point to a panoply of expulsions, exclusions, and differential inclusions that generate a range of subject positions that are unevenly intersected by the extractive operations of capital. Although these subject positions and the populations that occupy them are also exposed to other operations of capital, we need to ask how the logics of extraction play out in relation to transformations in labor relations, the composition of wages and other forms of income, and changing patterns of welfare and distributive social policy. The relation of capital to labor within forms of capitalism marked by the prevalence of extraction raises problems both for the possibility of a political mediation of this relation and for the ways in which labor and social struggles can confront capital. Extraction is certainly connected with processes of dispossession. But in its current forms, it alters and intensifies the social dimensions of exploitation, which is to say that it overlays and infiltrates the multiple ways in which living labor confronts and works through capital's drive to generate and appropriate surplus value. The conceptual expansion of extraction that we propose is made possible by the amazing continuity of struggles that have developed along the multiple frontiers of extraction. It is also part of the continuing search for forms of organization, institutional arrangements, and sources of sustenance and connection capable of effectively confronting the increasingly invasive and extractive dimensions of current forms of capitalist activity and valorization.

Vistas of Struggle

Snapshots

On June 7, 2013 five hundred protestors gathered in São Paolo. The protestors, members of the Movimento Passe Livre (Free Fare Movement), a
small but well-organized collective campaigning for free public transport,
had assembled to protest an increase in bus fares. Within ten days, the dis-
quiet had spread to other Brazilian cities. On July 20, one million protesters
lined Rio de Janeiro's President Vargas Avenue. By then, the movement had
mutated beyond its concern with the logistical conditions of urban life,
manifest in dissatisfaction with crowded and expensive public transport.
Various tributaries of discontent—Indigenous resistance against dams, the
rage of the poor at the clearing of *favelas*, hostility toward the planning of
mega-events such as the 2014 World Cup and the Rio 2016 Olympics, youth
despair at precarious employment—coalesced to form what commentators
called a *pororoca*, a word that means "great roar" in the Tupi language and
describes a tidal bore on the Amazon River (see Cava 2014; Cocco 2014).
The protests were given fillip by solidarity against police violence, which
became epitomized by the disappearance of a bricklayer named Amarildo
de Souza from Rio's Rocinha favela. Tortured and suffocated with plastic
bags, De Souza had been detained by the Unidade de Polícia Pacificadora, a

special force introduced in 2008 to "integrate" slums into the city (Mendes 2014). Poised on the cusp among logistical transformations of the metropolis, the nexus of finance and real estate, and the extractive logics of forced eviction and mega-event planning, the protests in Brazil in 2013 unleashed a massive and painful roar in the face of capital's hitting of the ground in some of Latin America's largest and most complex cities.

Amid the fracas on the streets of Rio some of the most familiar chants were "Nao Vai Ter Copa" (There Won't Be a World Cup) and "Acabou a Mordomia, o Rio Vai Virar uma Turquia" (The comfortable life is over, Rio will be another Turkey). The latter slogan was an explicit reference to the Gezi Park movement that had exploded in Istanbul just weeks earlier. Sparked by efforts to make way for a shopping mall by bulldozing a rare green space adjacent to the city's Taksim Square, the Gezi Park unrest spread rapidly to other Turkish cities. Like the events in Brazil, the Turkish protests faced harsh police repression while gathering together different subjects, perspectives, worlds, and points of departure. Called *çapulcu* (plunderers) by Turkish Prime Minister Recep Tayyip Erdoğan, whose Justice and Development Party government had overseen the transformation of Istanbul at the hands of developers and other actors of so-called neoliberalism with Islamic characteristics (Karaman 2013b), the protestors willingly embraced this label as part of their resistance to the modes of extraction and financialization involved in the city's remaking. As in Brazil, the Gezi Park movement faced the accusation of being a largely middle-class affair, pursued by youth disenchanted with employment prospects but otherwise held in the grip of consumerist culture. As Bülent Eken (2014) argues, such characterizations not only ignore the multiplicity of actors involved in the protests but also reduce class to a question of social stratification by subtracting the question of political agency. Eken (2014, 431) writes, "The middle class designates what people ceased to be when they started participating in the insurrection," since Gezi was properly a "'proletarian' movement" based on "the commonality of those who, in their antagonism to the state, share the same fate, since the state is integrated with a plundering bourgeoisie that seeks to expropriate immense urban wealth." Similar claims are evident in the Brazilian context. Bruno Cava (2014) suggests that even sociologists such as Jessé Souza (2012), who argues that the new middle class that supposedly arose under the government of Luiz Inácio Lula da Silva is actually a new type of proletariat, fail to heed the "productive and political dimensions" of class. Cava (2014, 850–51) explains that, although Lulism conserved a "classist (and racist) social contract," it also "opened a constituent breach" that, after the ascension of Dilma Rousseff to the presidency in 2011, reached a "saturation point." In both Turkey and Brazil, then, the insurrections of 2013 involved kinds of social composition and modes of political expression that cannot be easily classified or accounted for within sociological typologies of class stratification.

Importantly, the Gezi Park movement was not only a moment of insurrection. It also involved occupation of the park and experimentation with ways to be political and build the commons. From the final days of May, hundreds of tents were pitched in the park, which was thus transformed into a "primary infrastructure" and "facilitated a kind of federalist assembly, enabling encounters between different sections, groups and identities who could thereby relate positively to each other, in the first step towards recomposition," toward "a kind of *commoning*" (Karakayalí and Yaka 2014, 124–25). Among the occupiers were environmentalists, feminists, communists, anticapitalist Muslims, anarchists, LGBT groups, nationalists, Kurds, soccer fans, and unaffiliated women and youth. As Eken (2014, 434) explains, the remarkable thing about the Gezi occupation "was not the diversity of its identities" but "the realization on the part of the people that their identities that were so complete and functional outside the park proved utterly inadequate during the commune." Until the violent clearing of the park on June 15, this "unscripted co-presence of differences *in space*, and the day-to-day urgency of collectively holding the *commoned* territory" generated experiments in "actively producing a different kind of urban life" (Karaman 2013a). Contrary to arguments that maintain that such a generation of different forms of life is hindered by a politics that focuses on capital and its operations, the Gezi occupation was strongly articulated to urban struggles that explicitly pit themselves against the modes of accumulation at stake in the transformations of Istanbul. This combination of anticapitalist politics with the building of commons is an important feature of the struggles that have swept the world since 2011, connecting Tahrir Square in Cairo, Puerta del Sol in Madrid, Syntagma Square in Athens, and Occupy Wall Street.

Another example of such combination can be found in the Spanish movement Plataforma de Afectados por la Hipoteca (Mortgage Victims' Platform; PAH), a "transversal social union" agitating for tenant and mortgage rights, working against evictions and in defense of housing occupations, and undertaking civil disobedience and direct action for constitutional recognition of the right to housing. Politicizing indebtedness and contesting the legitimacy of the creditor banks, the PAH's struggle has a materially "ethical" dimension aimed at establishing a new practice of "common, or communal property" (Pirita Tenhunen and Sáncez Cedillo 2016, 123). Manuela Zechner and Bue Rübner Hansen, thinkers and activists who have worked closely with PAH in Barcelona, emphasize how "struggles around social reproduction" can "become a field for reorganizing social relations, for building social power." Citing other instances, such as the creation of solidarity clinics in Greece after the withdrawal of state health provision, they propose the building of "relations and infrastructures for struggle and change" that "generate resistance" without forgoing "antagonism between actors in different fields or within one field" (Zechner and Hansen 2015). Further examples could be mentioned here—for instance, the impressive number of solidarity structures that blossomed in Greece and elsewhere in the wake of the crisis of the European border regime in 2015 (Bojadžijev and Mezzadra 2015). These structures include occupations such as the one that began in late April 2016 at the City Plaza Hotel in Athens, an occupation that aimed "to create a co-operative refuge for hundreds of families, many of them women and children" (Connelly 2016). In such cases, migrants and refugees have often been at the forefront of struggle, laying the basis for the building of new and original coalitions, as well as for the material forging of new social relations. While it may be difficult to theoretically reconcile such social antagonism with perspectives that emphasize difference, performativity, or the decentering of the human, these are relations that are actively being negotiated and worked out within the movements themselves. In situations where the production of the common is sustained by committed, and even violent, struggle, the idea that the generation of diverse economies is incompatible with an anticapitalist politics appears increasingly fraught.

According to Emre Ongün (2016), one of the principal legacies of the Gezi Park movement was the democratization of social sectors hostile to the Justice and Development Party and a greater awareness of the Kurdish question, especially among Turkish youth. The Kurdish struggle itself has been a potent locus of social experimentation, both in the Turkish southeast—where new forms of politicization, insurgency, and resistance were invented particularly by urban youth, and a new political party, the Democratic Party of the People, was founded in 2012—and in the cantons of Rojava, which lie along Syria's border with Turkey and Iraq. Widely known for the role of women in the militias that have been fighting the Islamic State and the Syrian as well as the Turkish army, Rojava since 2012 has been governed under a charter that prioritizes rule by people's assemblies and embodies minority rights, gender equality, and ecological principles (Knapp et al. 2016). It is dangerous to idealize the social and political experimentation that is occurring in Rojava, since it is enabled by a geopolitically precarious situation in which US air cover has been a significant factor in sustaining the republic, despite growing hostility from the Turkish regime and the ruling party in Iraqi Kurdistan. As Bülent Küçük and Ceren Özselçuk write, celebrations of the struggle in Rojava can project "a civilizational narrative . . . that divides the world into good (Kurd) versus evil (Islamists)." Such projections can also enable "the West to displace into another context the highly pressing and conflictual problems shaping the global and postcolonial environment it confronts and fails to adequately address (such as the rampant racism that finds expression in the 'Muslim immigrant problem')" (Küçük and Özselçuk 2016, 185). Nonetheless, the political movement in Rojava joins a critique of patriarchy and the nation-state to a framework of "democratic autonomy" and "confederalism" that recognizes how operations of capital exploit and colonize cultures, ecologies, and women's bodies. Resonant with the thought of Abdullah Öcalan (2015), the leader of the Kurdistan Workers' Party (PKK) imprisoned in Turkey since 1999, this framework presents itself as a method of decolonization and *politicization of the social* through bottom-up, locally based governance grounded in institutions such as assemblies, cooperatives, and academies. Comparisons with historical instances of popular resistance such as the Paris Commune, the Battle of Stalingrad, the Spanish Civil War, and the Zapatista uprising of 2006 in Oaxaca abound (see, e.g., Dirik 2016). The Rojava revolution faces the challenge of sustaining itself in a conflict zone given to high volatility and historical irresolution, but it offers yet another example of how anticapitalist struggle can articulate itself to the building of common spaces and forms of life.

Brazil, Turkey, and Rojava—the three snapshots of struggle we just provided—must be considered against the backdrop of recent developments in those regions. The impeachment of Brazil's President Dilma Rousseff in August 2016, widely described as a coup of a new type and part of a general turn in Latin American politics, has dramatically changed the landscape and conditions of struggle in that country (see, e.g., Tible 2016). Retrospectively, it is possible to see that this crisis was triggered partly by the blindness and repressive attitude of Brazil's Partido dos Trabalhadores (Workers' Party) toward the uprisings of June 2013, which offered a chance for the party to renew its politics in ways that would link it with popular movements. Another coup, this time attempted and failed in July 2016, has laid the basis for a further entrenchment and seeming consolidation of the authoritarian and nationalist regime of Recep Tayyip Erdoğan in Turkey (see, e.g., Medico International 2016). This, in turn, has dramatic implications for the struggle in Rojava, which now has to fight not only against the Islamic State and the regime of Bashar Hafez al-Assad but also against the Turkish Army (see, e.g., Biehl 2016). Nevertheless, we are convinced that struggles such as those we have briefly described retain an exemplary value, and their successes, as well as their limits and even defeats, are part of a wider history of struggle—of its "ontological" fabric and legacy (see Negri 2016a).

At first consideration, forms of struggle and experimentation such as those in Rojava seem to be a far cry from the more spontaneous outbursts of anger and pain that characterize many contemporary urban conflagrations. Take the protests and riots that broke out in the US city of Ferguson, Missouri, following the shooting by a white policeman of Michael Brown, an eighteen-year-old black man, in August 2014. The pattern of revolt, in this instance, seems to embody the "indignation" that Michael Hardt and Antonio Negri associate with self-organized rebellions, or jacqueries: "from the ferocious sixteenth- and seventeenth-century European peasant uprisings to the spontaneous worker revolts of the nineteenth and twentieth centuries, from anticolonial insurgencies to race riots, various forms of urban rebellion, food riots, and so forth" (Hardt and Negri 2009, 236). As Robert Stephens (2014) notes about the outrage that followed Brown's death, the "crowd was not irrational or apolitical" but attempted to use the "opportunity to express their broader political needs." The indignation in Ferguson spread rapidly, turning the city and the greater St. Louis metropolitan area into "a laboratory and genesis point for a new generation of activists against state-sanctioned violence" (Murch 2015). Protests continued for more than a year, attracting allies from other racial and ethnic communities, more affluent US cities, and international solidarity groups. Prevalent forms of expression were the blocking of freeways and staging of "die-ins" in shopping malls—actions that disrupted practices of logistical circulation and coordination that, as we saw in previous chapters, are central to the workings of contemporary capitalism. The Black Lives Matter movement, initiated in 2013 after the acquittal of a neighborhood watch officer responsible for the death in Florida of a black teenager named Trayvon Martin, gained momentum in the wake of these events (see Taylor 2016). Black Lives Matter organized rallies that highlighted the connection of racial violence to feminist and queer issues and intertwined with the Boycott, Divestment, and Sanctions movement against Israel's occupation of Palestine. With these developments, the path from spontaneity to organization was seemingly traversed. Since the murder of Trayvon Martin, countless episodes of often lethal police violence against blacks, for which such names as Eric Garner, Renisha McBride, John Crawford, and Philando Castile are iconic and tragic instantiations, have demonstrated once again that the "destruction of black bodies" is the daily form of "terror" on which the reproduction of racism in the United States ultimately relies (Coates 2015, 44, 87). These episodes have also spurred a new conjuncture of African American activism and organizing, which had to confront complex issues in the wake of the shootings in Dallas of July 2016 but nevertheless continue to evolve in multiple ways.

Stefano Harney and Fred Moten (2015, 82) link the insurrection in Ferguson with "modernity's constitution in the transatlantic slave trade, settler colonialism and capital's emergence in and with the state." Harney takes this further by describing Brown's jaywalking, the offense for which the teenager was apprehended before his shooting, as "an act of sabotage" or a "pursuit of other forms of movement" that come into "direct conflict" with contemporary "logistical capitalism." At stake in this understanding of Brown's actions is the interruption of a system of production that requires "connection, flexibility, availability, reorganization on demand, translatability, in short access, radical access to labour . . . and indeed to capital . . . a radical openness to being financialised" (Harney 2015). Arguments that point to the role of "structural violence" in perpetuating the processes of dispossession and extraction that bring cities such as Ferguson to the boil foreground "the slow violence perpetrated by unemployment, educational inequality, environmental racism, housing and food insecurity, and aggressive and oppressive police harassment and brutality" (Lipsitz 2015, 123–24). But, as Jared Sexton (2015, 164) provocatively asks, "Can the structural form of violence be delimited and, if so, how?" Sexton's question is relevant in a situation where, consistently with Cedric Robinson's analysis of racial capitalism, which we discussed in chapter 1, racial ordering has become integral to forms of production that are increasingly inseparable from the making of social relations and forms of life. The reaching down of racialized forms of power into the capillaries of social life means that the structural becomes ever more indistinguishable from the incidental, whether we are discussing state-sanctioned violence or acts such as jaywalking. This predicament, in turn, has implications for how we understand the political dimensions of a situation such as Ferguson. Writing about the riots in London of 2011, Rodrigo Nunes (2013, 570) suggests that the attempt to impose "an all-or-nothing analytical grid—*revolutionary subject or bust!*—

flattens the different dimensions of rational decision and subjectivation that are always present." What matters, instead, is "what takes place between the occasional cause that will retrospectively appear as having been so and the different layers of material causes" (Nunes 2013, 571). In this gap between the apparent trigger of an uprising such as Ferguson and its complex material causes we discern the specter of class in contemporary vistas of struggle.

An important concern about struggles that materialize around a trigger point or event is that they become subject to what Vladimir Lenin ([1902] 1978, 52–53) called *khvostism*, or "tailism." The term, which is well known due to Georg Lukács's use of it in his essay "Tailism and the Dialectic" (Lukács 2002), refers to the philosophy of those who argued that the Communist Party should not take the lead in a revolutionary situation but, rather, wait to take advantage of events such as strikes, crises, and uprisings that would unfold on their own. One of the senses in which we develop the concept of operations in this book is to contrast such a politics of the event, turning attention instead to operations of capital that in different ways catalyze events without arguing in any way that such operations cause events according to a mechanical or linear logic. This does not mean that we advocate a vanguard perspective by which the traditional institutions of the working class—the political party and the trade union—must take the lead in educating, agitating, and waiting for opportunities. While the proletariat has not disappeared, there is "a new proletariat which has very different characteristics from the traditional one the left used to identify as the vanguard of the working class" (Harvey 2015, 271).

In the next section of this chapter, we discuss how this new proletariat is shaped in the relation and tension between social cooperation and living labor, between the disrupting effects of what Nick Dyer-Witheford (2015) calls the "capitalist vortex" and grounded as well as specific experiences of exploitation. For now, and in keeping with the snapshots of struggles presented earlier, we want to mention some exemplary struggles that have been organized in the space defined by this tension. Immanuel Ness (2016) traces how the decline of the traditional working class in Europe and North America has been accompanied by the appearance of a vast proletariat in the global South. Although this narrative needs to be supplemented by an account of how such changes also produce surplus populations that are not integrated into productive circuits, Ness's explorations of labor agitation in India, China, and South Africa demonstrate how direct struggle in the workplace and beyond has been successful in breaking the integration of political parties and unions into the nexus of capital and state. From the Maruti struggle of 2011–12 in India to the Yue Yuen shoe factory agitations in China in 2014 and the South African miners' strike that followed the killing by the police of thirty-four workers at Marikana in 2012, a pattern emerges of struggles organized by worker-led bodies and networks testing the role of official party- or firm-aligned trade unions and fighting for the rights of precariously employed contract workers. We return to these instances later in the chapter, but it is important at this stage to note the problem of the translatability of struggles and the challenge of moving beyond grassroots action to create organizations capable of assembling and enforcing social change on a wider scale. With this problem in mind, we turn to the question of labor in the frame of social cooperation.

Cooperation

In the previous chapter we demonstrated that an abstract figure of social cooperation constitutes the main source of financial value. Considering the paramount roles played by financial operations in articulating and synchronizing contemporary processes of valorization and accumulation of capital, in shaping the logics of aggregate capital, it should be clear that social cooperation, at this abstract level, emerges as the main productive force driving these processes. The emphasis we placed on the abstract character of this social cooperation should, however, caution us against any representation of its composition in homogeneous terms. We instead showed that the articulation of financial and "productive" operations of capital intensifies the heterogeneity of subject positions, labor relations, and working activities that make up the fabric of social cooperation. Contemporary living labor is exploited in multiple ways and by a wide array of capitalist actors, which correspond to heterogeneous operations of capital, as well as to their overarching articulation and synchronization through finance. This gap between social cooperation and living labor is a crucial starting point for any attempt to rethink class struggle and the question of a political subjectivation of labor in front of the extractive features of global capitalism. This was nowhere so clear as in the light of the fires that illuminated Paris and many other French cities in the long spring of 2016 during the extraordinary movement *contre la loi travail et son monde*—that is, against the new labor act proposed by the socialist government "and its world" (see Assennato 2016; Gallo Lassere 2016). It is important to remember that this movement developed within and against the *état d'urgence* (state of emergency) declared after the terrorist attacks of November 13, 2015 and not revoked until almost two years later. While much attention focused on the so-called *nuit debout* (the occupation of Place de la République in Paris) and its links with the 2011 struggles, and on the aesthetics of an eventually accomplished insurrection, the crucial aspect in that movement for us was precisely the combination, the encounters, tensions, divergences, and convergence among a radical unionist militancy; a new rebellious spirit of sections of the youth; and the mobilization of the wider social fabric of precarious, mobile, and cognitive labor. Blockades of key logistical sites and the metropolitan scale of strikes and political action vividly instantiated—at least in some moments—the potentialities and actual power of contemporary living labor in its diverse composition. At the same time, the fact that the law was ultimately passed (although through recourse to an emergency procedure in Parliament) can be taken as an effective and painful reminder of the limits and pitfalls that continue to haunt any attempt to politicize social cooperation under the conditions of contemporary capitalism.

"A large number of workers working together at the same time, in one place (or, if you like, in the same field of labor), in order to produce the same type of commodity under the command of the same capitalist, constitutes the starting point of capitalist production," Marx writes at the beginning of his chapter titled "Co-operation" in *Capital*, volume 1 (Marx 1977, 439). At stake in Marx's analysis of cooperation in the factory is the "fusion of many forces into a single force," the "creation of a new productive power, which is intrinsically a collective one" (Marx 1977, 443). Cooperation works the boundary between the singular dimension of labor power—its connection with an individual body, with a "living personality" as its "bearer"—and its social, or common dimension—epitomized by the fact that it is defined in terms of general human potentialities (see Macherey 2014, 164–65; Virno 1999, 121). In the framework of a grounded analysis of the combined organization of labor in the large-scale industry of his time, Marx reframes basic philosophical and political problems that continue to haunt any discussion of the concept of cooperation, ranging from the empowering effect of "mere social contact" to the very conditions for the emergence of a collective subject (see Mezzadra 2018, chap. 7). Crucial to his investigation of the "special productive power of the combined working day" (of the "social productive power of labor, or the productive power of social labor") is precisely the latter question. "When the worker cooperates in a planned way with others," Marx (1977, 447) writes, "he strips off the fetters of his individuality, and develops the capabilities of his species."

This potentially enhancing and liberating experience develops in Marx's analysis under the exclusive and "despotic" command of capital. In *Grundrisse*, we read, "All social powers of production are productive powers of capital, and it appears as itself their subject. The association of the workers, as it appears in the factory, is therefore not posited by them but by capital. Their combination is not *their* being, but the *being (Dasein)* of capital. *Vis-à-vis* the individual worker, the combination appears accidental. He relates to his own combination and cooperation with other workers as *alien*, as modes of capital's effectiveness" (Marx 1973, 585). A radical split traverses the subjectivity of workers, who are at once incorporated into a collective body and separated from its social productive power, which is crystallized in and represented by "the powerful will of a being outside them, who subjects their activity to his purpose" (Marx 1977, 450). This is so because the industrial capitalist entirely performs the organization of cooperation, which means the establishment of the objective conditions of the process that enables the emergence of the new, collective subjectivity of labor.

In many parts of the world and in many workplaces, living labor continues to be subjected to forms of organization of productive cooperation that are strikingly similar to those described by Marx in *Capital*. However, significant transformations have occurred even in the field of industrial labor. One has only to think, for instance, of the logistical coordination of production and the stretching of supply chains we described in chapter 4 to grasp this point. While Marx writes that as a "general rule" the assembly of workers "in one place is a necessary condition for their co-operation" (Marx 1977, 447), things have become much more complicated. This predicament posits difficult and well-known challenges for the organization of effective labor struggles. The situation looks even more puzzling if we focus on the abstract figure of social cooperation that constitutes the main source of value for finance. On the one hand, as we argued in the previous chapter, this abstract figure describes social cooperation linked to future production. On the other hand, while this figure is traversed and organized by multiple figures and operations of capital, the one that exploits it in the whole—that is, financial capital—does not directly organize future social cooperation. It takes a position of relative exteriority to it, reproducing in a way the conditions of formal subsumption of labor while prefiguring and reproducing the capitalist command over cooperation through the dissemination across the social fabric of what we have called the compulsion to work. Under these conditions, the combination of forces appears even more accidental to the individual worker, widening the gap between living labor and cooperation. The domination of capital thus takes on even more elusive characteristics, particularly in the many instances in which cooperation takes shape outside capital's immediate grip.

We are again confronted with the quite paradoxical position of the "outside" with regard to capital. In chapter 2, we pointed to the relevance of the work of Karl Polanyi in contemporary critical discussions of capitalism. According to him, capitalism is characterized by an expansive tendency that is best described in terms of commodification and related "cultural degradation" (see Polanyi [1944] 2001, 166). Contemporary processes of financialization accordingly can be interpreted as processes of steady colonization of social cooperation, which is organized by a multiplicity of principles that are not reducible to the market rationality of exchange. It is important to note that these processes are predicated on the disruption of a whole set of institutional arrangements that had enabled at the level of nation-states what Polanyi calls a partial "de-commodification" of labor (see Arrighi and Silver 2003). Central to his understanding of capitalism is the idea that the unleashing of the movement of commodification paradoxically challenges the very existence of the social and cultural premises of "market society." A "counter-movement" from society, for him, is indeed the necessary reaction to the "de-bordering" of market relations, which leads to the "embedment" of the market and to the establishment of novel forms of social protection. Does this theoretical perspective provide us with effective tools to forge alternative political projects in the face of contemporary capitalism? And is it possible to imagine such a counter-movement at the global level at which operations of capital work today?

Polanyi's theory is challenging, particularly insofar as it questions any merely economistic understanding of capitalism and points to the relevance of the juncture between the economic and other spheres—from the institutional to the social and the cultural—as a crucial site of conflict and tension. Nevertheless, there is a need to highlight, among other limits of Polanyi's work, that his notion of society is thoroughly organic, meaning that it is conceived as bearer of a kind of general interest beyond any class division. Furthermore, he tends to approach the state and its institutions as neutral, again ruling out the question of their class nature (Burawoy 2003; Selwyn and Miyamura 2014). Moreover, as the very notion of cultural degradation suggests, his critique of market society is predicated on an external criterion of moral evaluation and "a nostalgia for community, land, and family" that "seeks to transform these institutions into conduits for state-based forms of social protection" (Cooper 2017, 15). Polanyi himself claims these values as the basis of his struggle against "economistic prejudice" and the related primacy of exploitation in the analysis of capitalism. "It is precisely this emphasis on exploitation," he writes, "which tends to hide from our view the even greater issue of cultural degradation" (Polanyi [1944] 2001, 166). While we are sure that there is still much to be learned from Polanyi's work, we take critical distance from his understanding of exploitation "in strictly economic terms as a permanent inadequacy of ratios of exchange" (Polanyi [1944] 2001, 166). We will come back to this point later in this chapter. For now, suffice it to say that, following Marx, we conceive of exploitation in terms that cannot be reduced to the sphere of exchange but, rather refer, to put it shortly, to the production and appropriation of surplus. From this angle, we contend that exploitation is not merely an economistic category because it includes a constitutive reference to the social, political, and even cultural conditions that enable it.

Nevertheless, there is a need to reframe the notion of exploitation in relation to the new extractive characteristics of capitalism—and particularly with regard to what we have described as a widening gap between living labor and social cooperation. A narrow understanding of productive labor has led, in the history of Marxism and the labor movement, to the prevalence of an economistic understanding of exploitation, tailored to the experience of specific figures of workers at the point of production (which usually meant in factories). Movements and struggles of a multiplicity of subjects—from women to the unemployed, from racialized people to casual workers—have effectively challenged this notion of exploitation, highlighting the need to expand and alter it. In this challenge we can identify one of the subjective roots of the contemporary crisis of the labor movement, which is one of the defining features of the current global predicament from the perspective of social movements and struggles against capitalism. This is not to deny that labor organizations and unions continue to play important roles and even grow in many parts of the world (for a discussion of the predicament and challenges confronted by unions in the United States, see "Rank and File" 2016). What seems to be radically challenged is the existence of the labor movement as a political form capable of combining (through the action of unions and parties, as well as a wide array of associations) the unitary representation of wage labor and a hegemonic project at the societal level. The transformations of capitalism and related processes of multiplication of labor have clearly played a crucial role in bringing about this crisis, which is avidly interrogated within and subjectively expressed by movements and struggles of laboring subjects who challenge the ways in which labor is understood and represented by the labor movement.

Parallel to this crisis of the labor movement, we can observe that the concept of the working class has lost most of its power in practical politics. In previous writings, we examine the multiple meanings, pitfalls, and ambiguities that characterize the very concept of class (Mezzadra and Neilson 2013a, 95–103). What we need to add here from the analytical perspective provided by the crisis of the labor movement is that the concept of class is structurally linked to *class politics*. It is interesting in this respect to turn our attention to China, a country that undoubtedly has its own peculiarities but may help in illuminating broader tendencies. What makes the Chinese situation so interesting is the dramatic contradiction between the predicament in the early twentieth century, when the working class was "small and weak" but proletarian politics swept the whole region, and today's conjuncture, when China, the "'world's factory' with almost 300 million workers," is apparently "unable to generate a working-class politics" (Wang 2016, 215). Again, the point is not to deny the intensity, continuity, and even radical nature of workers' struggles in contemporary China. We have referred briefly to these struggles in the opening section of this chapter. What matters here is to highlight—following the analysis provided by Wang Hui—how these struggles do not coalesce into a coherent working-class politics and identity. The weakening and vanishing of class politics have paved the way for a shift in social analysis and public discourse from questions of class structure to issues of social stratification, with absolutely concrete political implications. This is particularly true for the group that Wang calls "new workers": internal migrants floating among different forms of employment and, in this way, preserving links with the countryside and agricultural production from which they departed. These new workers far exceed "China's twentieth-century working class in number and scale, yet as a group they have almost no position within the realm of politics or culture" (Wang 2016, 188). They make up the "largest portion of the new poor" (Wang 2016, 185), the group in China that embodies the emerging dimensions and politicization of poverty at the global scale.

Poverty over the past few decades has been a crucial field of politicization and struggle in many parts of the world. Movements of the poor have been on the rise from South Africa to India, from Brazil to Argentina. Without delving into the details of these heterogeneous movements, we limit ourselves to noting that they have forged a very distinct practice of political organization and struggle. What in South Africa is called "living politics" (Chance 2017) resonates with what Arjun Appadurai (2002) terms "deep democracy" in his investigation of forms of activism related to urban poverty in Mumbai. Self-organization at the daily level; dealing with situations of emergency in slums, as well as metropolitan peripheries and rural landscapes; opposing evictions through localized struggles; and efforts to build coalitions beyond national borders are common features of these movements. What characterizes them is often an offensive claim to politicize the very identity of the poor (Desai 2002), which nurtures a politics capable of combining confrontational attitudes with a surprising ability to enter negotiations with a panoply of institutions and organizations, ranging from municipal and national governments to nongovernmental organizations. This form of politics has its origins in the South, but it is important to emphasize that—particularly in the wake of the crisis of 2007–2008—this living politics has also reached the streets of many cities of the North and has been an aspect of struggles against austerity. The explosion of the standard of "free wage labor" and the related multiplication of labor have run parallel to the spread of multifarious forms of "wageless life" across diverse geographical scales (Denning 2010). Movements, struggles, and the claims of subjects of this life, which extend well beyond the traditional limits of unemployment, are a crucial aspect of contemporary vistas of social struggle and posit further challenges to the language and political horizon of the labor movement.

Contrary to its conventional association with marginality and lack of employment, contemporary poverty tends to be highly productive. This is true even in an ontological sense, which is apparent in struggles and movements that demonstrate "the innovation, the subjectivity, and the power of the poor to intervene in the established reality and create being" (Hardt and Negri 2009, 50). But it is also true in the sense that poverty today appears to be the site of forms of governmentality that spread their effects across the social fabric (Gupta 2012; Sanyal 2007). Moreover, as we mentioned in chapter 4, poverty has become a crucial site for experimentation with financial innovations that range from subprime mortgages to microcredit and consumer credit (Rankin 2013). Far from being conceivable as an "absolute outside," poverty today—even in the extreme forms manifest in slums and shantytowns—is a field of struggle in which economic, social, and political efforts to self-organize the reproduction of impoverished lives are constantly confronted by heterogeneous forms of governmentality and capital. In many of these efforts—for instance, in the multifarious experiences of the "social and solidarity economy" that have blossomed in recent years in Latin America—we can see an attempt to "produce society," privileging the generation of "use values to satisfy the needs of the producers and their communities" over "profit and endless accumulation of capital" (Coraggio et al. 2011, 45). Nevertheless, these experiences are far from free from the drive of capital to expand its frontiers, particularly through processes of financialization (see Gago 2015). Even in the case of the workers' cooperatives popularized in Avi Lewis and Naomi Klein's film *The Take* (2004), the partial appropriation of the surplus by the workers does not solve the problem of funding, supply, and distribution of the surplus itself in the wider society, which continue to be ruled by capitalist logics (see Ruccio 2011). This is, of course, a question that haunts the very form of the cooperative, as well as experiences of mutualism that, in many parts of the world, including Europe and the United States, have been and continue to be essential tools of resistance and self-organization for precarious workers and the unemployed (De Nicola and Quattrocchi 2016).

It is not only in the "global South," as Jean Comaroff and John L. Comaroff (2012, 121) write, that "old margins are becoming new frontiers, places where mobile, globally-competitive capital finds minimally regulated zones in which to vest its operations." This is also true for new forms of poverty emerging out of the explosion of the standard of free wage labor wherever a partial de-commodification of labor had been achieved as a result of a long history of struggles. The dismantling of institutional arrangements stemming from such de-commodification has opened up spaces for the further expansion of capital's frontiers by means of the intensification and exploitation of forms of social cooperation whose logics and organizing principles continue to appear as "accidental," to quote again from Marx (1973, 585), with respect to living labor. Here, as well as in the valorization of multifarious forms of popular pragmatism and vitalism that build the fabric of new and old instantiations of poverty (Gago 2017), the expansion of capital's frontiers continually encounters what Nancy Fraser (2014, 69) calls "distinctive ontologies of social practice and normative ideals." As we discussed in chapter 2, Fraser (2014, 68) uses the term "boundary struggles" to describe conflicts around "capitalism's institutional divisions," separating, for instance, "economy from polity, production from reproduction, human from non-human nature." Proposing to shift attention from such established boundaries between normative realms and their institutional arrangements, we propose to supplement this perspective with the conceptual thread established by our own, earlier reflections on border struggles (Mezzadra and Neilson 2013a). What interests us are the ways in which boundary struggles crisscross the fabric of social cooperation and living labor, becoming a crucial aspect of related forms of production of subjectivity. This is a point to which we return in the last section of this chapter, where we tackle the need to reframe the concept of exploitation. But before turning to this task a further exploration of contemporary vistas of struggle is needed.

Subjects of Struggle

We are now in a position to return to the discussion of workers' struggles in China, India, and South Africa that we left in the closing paragraph of the first section of this chapter. At that point, we followed Immanuel Ness in noting the role of direct and autonomously organized action in unsettling the stranglehold of political parties and trade unions on the organization and conduct of labor struggles. In the case of the Maruti Suzuki strike that rocked India in 2011–12, the struggle was led by the Maruti Suzuki Employees Union (MSEU), an independent organization that was denied registration by the Haryana Labor Department due to the presence of a company-allied union in the plant. Significantly, the MSEU sought to mobilize workers in all classifications—including apprentices, trainees, and contract workers—and among its demands was the reclassification of informal workers as permanent employees (Ness 2016, 97). These are significant goals in a country where most employees "are hired through contractors or as casual workers" and—as revealed by a report commissioned by the government in 2009—93 percent of workers "are 'unorganized' (government's term) or 'informal' (academic term), which means workers are without formal representation and without job-based protection and benefits" (Goldman 2015, 141–42). Similar conditions are confronted by contemporary labor struggles across different geographical scales and social spaces, in and beyond the so-called global South. Speaking of South Korea, Su-Dol Kang (2016) describes a "four-faceted dualization between regular and non-regular workers, between male and female workers, between 'chaebol' and 'non-chaebol' workers, and between native and migrant workers," which emerged from the way in which governments and corporations reacted to the challenges posed by the surge of labor militancy in the wake of what is commonly referred to as the Great Workers' Struggle of 1987. Such divisions are nevertheless often successfully challenged. In 2014, during the strike at the Yue Yuen shoe factory in China's Pearl River Delta, for instance, rank-and-file organization was crucial to forcing the company to update social-security payments. Ness argues that the absence of a union affiliated to the All-China Federation of Trade Unions, China's only authorized national labor federation, was "a major cause for the strength of the worker mobilization and the durability of the strike" (Ness 2016, 139). In the South African miners' strike at Marikana in 2012, it was again rank-and-file workers, after making an explicit break with the National Union of Mineworkers (NUM), who spearheaded a struggle that resulted in a 22 percent wage settlement. Indeed, NUM operatives perpetrated violence against the strikers, some of whom were members of the same union (Ness 2016, 166–73).

We mention these struggles because the tensions and cleavages that characterize them effectively illustrate the growing gap between living labor and social cooperation. When capitalist valorization takes place in forms that are seemingly ever more abstracted from labor processes, the autonomy of living labor becomes at once a source for extractive processes of exploitation and registers the sense in which capital's orchestration of social cooperation functions increasingly by the imposition of command. Although the struggles described by Ness take place in traditional industrial settings, they register the heightened political stakes of challenging such command, and, in so doing, demonstrate how strikes articulate to other forms of political action and organization. They also make evident the boundary struggles that increasingly crisscross the institutionalized order of capitalist society. That union operatives shot wildcat strikers in South Africa, for instance, shows how the background conditions for capital accumulation are entangled with political contests that in themselves have become a "major site and flashpoint of capitalist crisis" (Fraser 2014, 65). At stake in this tragic incident are the very boundaries separating economy from politics, labor struggles from questions of autonomy and collective self-determination.

It should be clear by now that what Fraser calls boundary struggles occur not only along the boundaries of economy and politics but also along lines that separate production from reproduction (crisscrossing at the same time both fields) and human from nonhuman natures. We share Fraser's interest in clarifying relations between the disparate struggles of our time. However, we take a different path. Where she emphasizes the normative differentiations of capitalist society, we turn to the question of struggle itself, which also provides us with a way to inquire into the constitution of what too often are taken for granted as social movements. What is a struggle? The question seems banal. Unlike, say, the concepts of conflict or resistance, the notion of struggle has not been made to carry a great deal of theoretical weight, relating to, say, the state of nature, the progress of the dialectic, or the Freudian unconscious. This is so because struggle does not designate a pre-political condition that is superseded by the foundation of a political or normative order, as modern philosophers from Hobbes to Hegel would have it. Rather, struggle describes a field of action that is itself deeply political insofar as it is necessarily partial and cannot be apprehended, experienced, or occupied from a neutral position. Struggle opens an arena in which political actors encounter power relations, natural elements, and contingencies that they negotiate and attempt to turn to their advantage, violently or otherwise, without ever fully mastering the situation. Such an understanding of struggle derives in part from readings of Niccolò Machiavelli that approach material struggle not as a destabilizing factor but as the grounding and animating force of political collectivity and subjectivity (see, e.g., Del Lucchese 2014; Negri 1999). As Roberto Esposito (2012, 53) explains, Machiavelli offers an understanding of struggle as a form of conflict "viewed not as a residue or opposite of order, but as a form of order." Furthermore, Machiavelli places struggle on a plane of immanence, which never reaches a moment of sovereign transcendence and, in this regard, provides a powerful precedent for what we can call, following the postcolonial elaboration of Ranabir Samaddar (2007), the materiality of politics. Struggle for Machiavelli is indeed constitutive of any historical conjuncture precisely because it is the material aspect that links together real or potential forces and thus seals their relations (see Althusser 1999, 19).

The point to underscore is that struggle does not precede or follow the establishment of political order, as normative visions would have it, but equally it does not turn on a sovereign decision that creates an exception. While Carl Schmitt's vision of politics as predicated on the distinction of friend and enemy involves recognition of struggle as a fundamental criterion of politics, the question of sovereignty introduces to his thought a theological dimension that is at odds with the approach to struggle that we have just outlined. Doubtless, there can be a more restricted understanding of struggle that describes conflicts played out within the ambit of sovereignty, whether under normative or exceptional conditions. Or struggle can be understood, following the lead of Max Weber, as a basic sociological concept that describes a specific form of social action oriented toward the imposition of an actor's will against the resistance of others—a form of violence that can be violent or peaceful, including economic competition and social selection as instances of the second type. However, these are not the senses in which we intend the term. One could say that our understanding of struggle is closer to what Chantal Mouffe (2005, 20) calls "antagonism," which describes a situation in which adversaries have no common ground, than what she calls "agonism," which designates a struggle where the legitimacy of an enemy is established by an existing political order. We are cautious regarding Mouffe's central proposition that "the task of democracy is to transform antagonism into agonism" (Mouffe 2005, 20), since this peculiar and influential variant of "radical democracy" takes for granted the institutional framework of the nation-state and eventually strips antagonism of any political productivity. On the contrary, it is precisely the moment of political productivity and creativity inherent to struggle that we want to emphasize.

There can be no doubt that Carl von Clausewitz's ([1832] 2007) understanding of struggle as a relation of enmity framed by a balance of forces has had immense influence. In his book *On Resistance* (2013), Howard Caygill shows how Clausewitz's nineteenth-century understanding of struggle as a Newtonian opposition of forces in which one side attempts to reduce the other's capacity to resist influences subsequent visions. These perspectives on struggle include Marx's understanding of class war, Schmitt's friend-or-enemy view of politics, Mao Zedong's theory of revolutionary struggle, Frantz Fanon's arguments about anticolonial violence, and Michel Foucault's analysis of power relations. Running parallel and counter to this Clausewitzian influence is the Hegelian notion of a struggle for recognition, equally conceived as an opposition of forces but resolving itself not in total opposition but in the production of consciousness and the institution of freedom under law. The Marxian inversion of Hegel and understanding of proletarian struggle as a fight for the new political form of communism frees this vision from an idealist and narrowly state-bound legacy, allowing Lenin, for instance, to adapt the Hegelian theory of consciousness as a means of understanding revolutionary struggle. Contested by Rosa Luxemburg and pushed to an extreme in Lukács's analysis of reification and the commodity form, this focus on consciousness becomes, for Harry Harootunian (2015, 1–2, 235–36), the signature of a Western Marxism that privileges the analysis of thought and culture above attention to labor, production, and uneven development. By approaching struggle through the question of political subjectivity and its production, we seek to move away from such a focus on consciousness, foregrounding how the making of subjects who struggle is deeply connected to the organization of labor and production across the uneven and changing space and time of contemporary capitalism.

In this view, the subject of struggle does not necessarily enjoy a constituted freedom. Instead, this subject faces conditions of chance and enmity under which it is compelled to act. It is certainly possible to turn such an understanding of struggle back to a reading of Lenin, emphasizing the emergence of a revolutionary political subject embodied in the reality and material processes of class composition above the dialectic of consciousness (see, e.g., Negri 2014). Toward the end of his life, Marx replied to a "question touching upon the final law of being" in an interview with the New York journalist John Swinton (1880) by identifying it "in deep and solemn tone" with "struggle!" Marx famously writes in *The Poverty of Philosophy* that "the struggle of class against class is a political struggle" precisely because "in the struggle" the mass of workers constitutes itself as a political subject (Marx 1937, 145). Our concern with current vistas of struggle directs our attention to how struggle is driven by a production of subjectivity that is something more than a reaction to the contradictions and operations of capital or a practice of resistance that is determined by the forces that oppose it. In this regard, the problem of the form of struggle emerges alongside and above the issue of its conceptual framing, drawing us back to questions concerning the waning of working-class politics, the productivity of poverty, and the growing gap between living labor and social cooperation.

The weakening of working-class politics is usually explained in two ways. The first explanation concerns the displacement of class as the central social antagonism and the emergence of a more general bifurcation centered on relations of domination and resistance, which can include aspects of class, race, and gender. On this we need to be absolutely clear: we understand race and gender as productive and destructive in their own right, and not as secondary divisions that qualify class struggle or name the modalities in which it is experienced. While in chapter 2 we discussed the distinction and connections between capital and capitalism, we are far from contending that race and gender should be analyzed from the angle of their role within capitalism and not within the logics of capital (for a critique of this position, see Roediger 2017). It is capital itself, in its constitutive relation with difference, that continually works and reworks hierarchies predicated on race and gender. In this perspective, the question of how class exploitation under capitalism is mutually constituted by other intersecting oppressions remains crucial to understanding contemporary struggles. To put it in the language of Michel Foucault (1982, 781), who distinguishes struggles "against forms of domination," against "forms of exploitation," and "against subjection, against forms of subjectivity and submission," we take struggles in the field of subjectivation as a key reference to reframe the very notions and manifestations of domination and exploitation.

The second explanation frequently offered for the apparent waning of working-class struggle is that it has been spatially displaced from the so-called global North with the shift of manufacturing, mining, and other labor-intensive industries to poorer parts of the world. This is, for instance, the position of Ness, who notes that "the industrial working class has not disappeared but has been relocated and reconstituted in the South in larger numbers than ever before" (Ness 2016, 2). By this view, working-class struggle remains prevalent in the global South, particularly through forms of direct action and participatory unionism that challenge "the system of capitalist domination far more successfully than existing unions in the West that are advanced by sanctimonious advocates of liberalism and corporate social responsibility" (Ness 2016, 24). However, as we noted earlier with reference to Wang's writings on China, the sheer number of workers and proliferation of struggles in the South have not resulted in a coherent working-class politics that can successfully challenge the institutions and governing rationalities of contemporary capitalism. Furthermore, as we have argued elsewhere, the nomenclature of "North" and "South" is unable to fully capture the complex spatiality of capitalist production and labor movements in the contemporary world, a fact that comes plainly into view once border struggles and migration politics are taken into account (Mezzadra and Neilson 2013a, 61–66). Under these circumstances, a consideration of the diverse forms assumed by social struggles provides a way to reenergize debate on the challenges and barriers facing anticapitalist politics today.

Strike, riot, occupation, blockade, sabotage, protest, boycott, disobedience, everyday resistance—these are among the forms of struggle that compose the repertoire of contemporary political action. How are we to understand how, when, and why they are deployed or the mode of their combination in specific material circumstances? Asking this question is a way to broach the issue of the translatability of struggles and inquire into the possibility for different struggles to work into broader fronts of organization and mass movement. This is so because the forms assumed by struggles—that is, how they are conceived and the practices they involve on the ground—determine the chances for their translation and confluence as much as the issues or claims they directly address. Struggles are defined not simply by their opposition to prevailing conditions or specific injustices but also in relation to one another, sometimes through careful study and learning about past failures and successes, and at other times through a breaking with traditions or a process of contagion that can spread like wildfire. In this invention and inter-referencing we can observe not only the possibility for struggles to connect but also their creative or constituent element.

It is tempting to impose a long-term historical logic on this variability, searching for correlations between capitalism's transformations and changes in the dominant practices of struggle. This is the gambit of Joshua Clover in *Riot. Strike. Riot* (2016). Clover draws on Giovanni Arrighi's account of systemic cycles of accumulation and Robert Brenner's periodization of capitalism to argue that the strike replaced the riot as the foremost form of collective struggle in the early nineteenth century, but new forms and experiences of riot have emerged to eclipse the strike with the transformations surrounding the "world-historical year of 1973" and "the waning of the labor movement" (Clover 2016, 9). Arguing that the "strike and riot are practical struggles over reproduction within production and circulation respectively" (Clover 2016, 46), Clover claims that the "strike ascends when the site of proletarian reproduction moves to the wage" (86) and declines when "the death of the wage demand spells the fading of production struggles" (151). In the riot, by contrast, "participants are not unified by their possession of jobs but by their more general dispossession" (151). The supposed return of the riot as the primary form of anticapitalist struggle thus links to an epochal shift in which capital "has shifted its hopes for profit into the space of circulation," leaving "the under- and unemployed" to "molder" in "informal economies" that are profoundly marked by the racialization of "deindustrialization" (151). Concentrating his analysis on the riots in Ferguson and the blockade of Oakland's port in 2011, Clover contends that the riot and associated forms of barricading and occupation have emerged as powerful practices of social antagonism in an era when "the economy as such has receded into planetary logistics and the global division of labor into the ether of finance" (124).

Clover's emphasis on logistics and finance brings his analysis close to ours. Yet his insistence, following the group Théorie Communiste, that labor has been forced to affirm "the domination of capital in return for its own preservation" (Clover 2016, 30) remains indifferent to the kinds of labor struggle highlighted by Ness in the global South—and to the persistence and shifting forms of such struggles in the global North. By limiting his analysis to what he calls "the early industrializing and now deindustrializing nations of the west" (7), Clover glosses over the heterogenization of global space and time that, for us, lies at the center of an analysis of the operations of capital. Clover's problem is thus the inverse of that which we have located in Ness. If the latter neglects the problem of labor struggles failing to converge into a coherent working-class politics and focuses his analysis exclusively on the South, the former sacrifices his sense that there are "multiple forms of collective action within a given conjuncture" (105) by limiting his investigation to the North. Even in countries of the so-called North, however, there have been important labor struggles in recent years, some of them in precisely the sectors that Clover sees as pivotal to capital's circulation. In chapter 4 we pointed to struggles in the logistics sector across diverse sites in Italy, Germany, and the United States. In these instances, we see various crossings of the traditional labor strike with forms of blockading and occupation, which are certainly not new in the history of working-class politics. Yet to fully appreciate how labor struggles articulate to riots, blockades, and occupations—or, as we phrased the problem earlier, how exploitation articulates to dispossession—we need an analysis that crosses and questions the North-South divide.

Such an approach has important implications for the analysis of struggles, which go beyond making easy points regarding the analytical limits or geographical indeterminacies of the categories of North and South. For a start, no form of struggle can be seen as paradigmatic, although many struggles have exemplary value, and some of them can play strategic roles at specific conjunctures. This realization is not merely the effect of an analysis that pays equal attention to the production and heterogeneity of space under capitalism as it does to historical transformations and cycles over the *longue durée*. Rather, it requires an investigation of how struggles cross and articulate to specific operations of capital as they converge and hit the ground. As we have argued, this kind of analysis means turning attention to the ways in which capital is sustained by its outsides, as well as to the question of how specific operations of capital relate to capitalism as a whole. Needless to say, such an approach involves an encounter with the extractive operations of capital, as well as the growing importance of finance and logistics explained by Clover as an effect of capital's new reliance on circulation, although there is a need to stress once again that this reliance involves not a diminishing relevance of production but, rather, the reorganization of its relations with circulation. Leaving aside the extractive dimension of capital is more than an effect of pursuing an analysis inattentive to the literal operations of extraction in the South. It also implies a bracketing of the whole question of capital's relation to its outsides, which, it is important to emphasize, are multiple and not restricted to labor or practices of social reproduction that sustain labor. In this regard, what we call boundary struggles come into view. As indicated by Fraser, these struggles are not equivalent to "the class struggles over control of commodity production and distribution of surplus value that Marx privileged" (Fraser 2014, 68), but equally they cannot be reduced to disputes arising on the lines of demarcation surrounding "non-commodified zones" and supposedly deemed to shield their "normative and ontological grammars" from the intrusion of the "commodity logic" (Fraser 2014, 66). At the same time, it should be clear that boundary struggles cannot be immediately equated with the riots privileged by Clover. Rather, such struggles challenge or defend boundaries that define established conceptions of polity, production, and the human. To see how these struggles cross and reconfigure the gap between social cooperation and living labor, giving rise to new forms of the production of subjectivity, it is necessary to further our analysis by investigating more precisely how social struggles articulate and respond to capital's operations.

Boundary Struggles

One of the most complex recent struggles surrounding the extractive operations of capital involved protests in 2011 against the building of a road through Bolivia's Isiboro Sécure National Park and Indigenous Territory (TIPNIS). Culminating in a violent episode in which police raided a group of Indigenous marchers, these protests marked a symbolic turning point in the political life of contemporary Bolivia due to "the support of a variety of youth, environmentalist, feminist, Indianist, and cultural activist organizations, as well as a good number of anarchist groups, which marched with their own flags and banners" (Rivera Cusicanqui 2015, 95; see also Arnez et al. 2013). The wide and heterogeneous composition of the struggle against the TIPNIS road-building project, connecting rural and urban movements, marked a new stage in the development of conflicts surrounding neo-extractivism in the framework of the Initiative for the Integration of South American Regional Infrastructure (see Martínez 2013). Due to the interests of the majority Brazilian government–owned oil corporation Petrobras in the project, the regional role of Brazil was politicized and contested.

The TIPNIS conflict was also a radical challenge for the "progressive" government of Bolivian President Evo Morales, which had prided itself on its respect for Indigenous autonomy and "Mother Earth" (see Arnez et al. 2013). Indeed, prominent authors have linked the Bolivian government's funding of social programs through resource extraction with the expansion of a so-called neo-extractivist agenda across the Latin American continent (see, e.g., Gudynas 2010), while the Morales government has also emphasized the need to recover "energetic sovereignty," linking the conflict surrounding TIPNIS with the polemic on the nationalization of hydrocarbons in 2006. These associations seem to have gotten stronger since September 2015, when the Morales government issued a decree allowing oil and gas exploration in nationally protected areas and returned to supporting the TIPNIS road after declaring the area out of bounds for state development in the wake of the protests. Following this, the project was approved by Parliament in August 2017, leading to further intensification of the conflict. Bolivia's Vice-President Álvaro García Linera has defended this model by referring to a supposed absolute rigidity of the world market and the international division of labor, which structurally limit the possibilities for Latin American countries (see García Linera 2012, 103–7). In chapter 4 we argued for an expanded understanding of extraction that extended beyond resource extraction to encompass an analysis of capital's relation with its multiple outsides. Here we explore how even struggles against resource extraction must be seen to unfold against the background of such an expanded sense of extraction once they are understood to involve boundary struggles that produce complex forms of subjectivity.

John-Andrew McNeish, a researcher present at the police raid in September 2011, has identified two prominent narratives in explaining the TIPNIS protests. The first describes "the action of a rural proletariat resisting the overly controlling action of an exploitative state." The second views the protests as "an environmental campaign where indigenous peoples and environmentalists are seen confronting the state together to secure a sustainable way of life" (McNeish 2013, 233). McNeish suggests that both of these narratives are oversimplified. The first plays down environmental aspects of the struggle by promoting an economistic viewpoint that separates nature from society and overlooks the complexity of relations between class and Indigeneity. The second risks homogenizing and idealizing Indigenous "*eco*-sophies" by ignoring the interests of some groups in territorial autonomy above environmental concerns and inadequately accounting for how Indigenous communities have been forced to build a relation to the extractivist state in ways that have transformed their understanding of resources, commodities, and markets. McNeish emphasizes diversity and fragmentation among the TIPNIS protestors, stressing the fragile alliance of interests that came together.

One way to gain a sense of how this complex subjectivity was composed is to explore the role of boundary struggles in the dispute. This means not only tracing the multiple axes along which the struggle unfolded—including race-ethnicity, class, rural-urban, and human-nonhuman relations—but also introducing an expanded sense of extraction and capitalism. Clearly, the potential for and intention of resource extraction associated with the project catalyzed struggles that not only converged around the political and legal conditions of land use but also gave new material meanings to environmental factors, linking them with questions surrounding landed property, the presence of multinational corporations, and the displacement of populations. The point is that these dimensions of struggle address operations of capital that are wider than economy and that cannot simply be dismissed as background conditions associated with the limited options for revenue generation on the part of a progressive government committed to poverty alleviation, Indigenous inclusion, and principles of *buen vivir* (living well). These factors are not wholly reducible to the role they play in enabling resource extraction and associated means of commodity production, labor exploitation, and capital accumulation, but they have peculiar characteristics that in specific conjunctures can contribute to widening, and even radicalizing, anticapitalist struggle. In the TIPNIS dispute, boundary struggles coalesce around environmental and legal-territorial matters in ways that give rise to a complex and multifaceted political subjectivity. They can be understood as struggles against operations of capital with extractive effects that go beyond the resource industries to encompass the erosion of legal-territorial rights, the dispossession of Indigenous knowledges, and the diminution of social capacities of reproduction and cooperation.

It is easy to see that these struggles end up questioning the anticolonial aspect of the mobilizations and class alliances that made the rise of the Evo Morales's progressive government possible, as they pitted the social forces that composed the autonomous struggles of the 2000s against the Morales government's actions (see Laing, forthcoming). But the wider question of how Indigenous struggles for self-determination relate to boundary struggles that articulate anticapitalist politics to the building of the common remains open. In chapter 1, we characterized such Indigenous struggles as a first and last line of defense against capital's extractive operations. But it is also well known that Indigenous groups in many parts of the world have adopted the strategies of capital to secure tenuous control over territories and ensure a means of living under economic and political circumstances not of their choosing. Moreover, the claim for Indigenous sovereignty, both as a horizon of struggle and as the very ground on which such struggle becomes possible, risks replicating a claim to exclusive power and authority that works at cross-purposes to the construction of the common. This problem is especially pronounced in places where Indigenous peoples had to confront the violence of settler colonialism that employed the figure of terra nullius (nobody's land) to legitimize conquest. Indigenous struggles can thus seem disconnected from struggles that seek to counter capitalism and its global formations. As one of us argued in a collectively written text exploring "the status of 'grounds' with respect to sovereignty and its politics" (Watson et al. 2002), globalization theorists stress how "the sovereignty of capital" has "been unleashed from its modern, nationalist constraints," while "Indigenous sovereignty theorists continue to claim the viability of 'grounds' as a means of asserting their rights."

The strategy of some Indigenous thinkers to anchor claims for sovereignty in Indigenous practices or "ways" of law, particularly in settler colonial countries such as Australia and Canada, suggests a way around this dilemma. Writing from the perspective of the South Australian Indigenous nations of Tanganekald and Meintangk, Irene Watson (2015, 8) refers to "raw law" or "a natural system of obligations and benefits, flowing from Aboriginal ontology." Such a body of law, or what Watson calls a "law way," is "unlike the colonial legal system . . . for it was not imposed, but rather lived" (Watson 2015, 12). As Robert Nichols (2017, 11) notes, such claims for sovereignty not as a relationship based on control of territory but as a lived relation of responsibility to land and country also frequently register the sense in which Indigenous communities "have experienced, and continue to experience, colonization as a form of theft." There is a dynamic peculiar to colonization that involves "not (only) the *transfer* of property" but the transformation of land "into property" (Nichols 2017, 12). Once this is realized, the project of Indigenous sovereignty can be joined to struggles for the making of the common, recognizing that the latter is a form of "*nonproperty*, that is, a fundamentally different means of organizing the use and management of wealth" (Hardt and Negri 2017, 97). This does not mean investing in myths of precontact Indigenous societies as instantiations of primitive communism; it means only pointing to the possibility of alliances (or better translatability) between different kinds of movements and struggles, as occurred in the TIPNIS protests. Such a realization also implies recognition that the making of the common is not necessarily a de-bordering project but one that can involve the institution and management of borders in ways that do not heed the social relation of capital, including the kind of territorial borders implied by Indigenous sovereignty claims.

Returning to the field of labor struggles, the notion of boundary struggles can also illuminate some of the complexities surrounding important and iconic recent disputes, such as the Maruti Suzuki strike of 2011–12, which we have already mentioned as an instance of working-class struggle in India. One of the puzzles surrounding the Maruti strike is the way it has emerged as a cause célèbre among labor activists despite the fact that the fledgling Maruti Suzuki Workers Union (formed after the leaders of the MSEU reached a settlement with the company in October 2011) was crushed by the Indian state (Ness 2016, 100–2). This situation can be understood only if the dispute is seen as more than an industrial struggle for wages and conditions. Significantly, many of the temporary contract workers at Maruti are migrants from elsewhere in India, whose presence in the factory has implications for gender relations and social reproduction in their home villages. While most permanent workers own houses and live with their families, thanks to a company loan scheme, these temporary workers share rooms or rent apartments in dormitory villages that were created when Maruti Suzuki moved into the Manesar area in 2001, clearing agrarian land and displacing peasant populations. The company absorbed some former village heads as workers, but many of these land-displaced peasants opened tea shops or other small businesses or built houses with the compensation money. Former peasants thus act as landlords or are otherwise dependent on earnings derived from the wages of temporary migrant workers, leading them sometimes to side with the company in industrial disputes to keep these wages flowing (Sen 2014, 85–86).

As Ishita Dey and Giorgio Grappi observe (Dey and Grappi 2015, 163), in the context of the Maruti Suzuki strike the "nexus of the capital-labor relation develops well beyond the simple production of wage laborers." It crosses not only the legal-political relations surrounding land acquisition and consequent peasant dispossession that are at stake but also the fabric of social reproduction in the surrounding villages. The vista becomes wider again when one considers that Maruti Suzuki outsources many activities, creating networks of informal labor "that are becoming constitutive for the formation and functioning of large supply chains necessary for the economic and social functioning of the factory" (Dey and Grappi 2015, 164).

Furthermore, the manufacturing plant in Manesar and the Gurgaon area of which it is part insert themselves into wider public-private partnership initiatives for a Delhi-Mumbai Industrial Corridor, which entails a reordering of land and labor relations in line with logistical imperatives. The point is that the Maruti Suzuki struggle cannot be understood in separation from boundary struggles occurring over the political arrangements that support land acquisition, the consequent environmental degradation and devastation of biodiversity, and the conditions of social reproduction within former peasant communities displaced from these acquired lands.

Here the articulation between labor struggles and the surplus populations created by dispossession becomes evident. Far from seeing surplus populations as "castaways of development" (Latouche 1993, 35) that sit entirely outside of productive relations, our interest is in how the ongoing processes of so-called primitive accumulation that generate such populations sit alongside and enable capitalist exploitation. In his investigation of the transformations of labor in the making of Bangalore into a global city, Michael Goldman (2015, 155) demonstrates that, while "speculative finance is the driving force" behind that process, slums and other "marginal spaces," as well as the physical spaces of households and neighborhoods more generally, "have become renewed sites of commodity production for informalized labor" in a "highly exploitative putting-out system" (141). Importantly, Goldman stresses the "socially cooperative" nature of the precarious and often "wageless" labor that crucially contributes to Bangalore's vitality and affordability and speaks of what he calls the "city as collateral" as a "place of collective *crowd sourcing*" (158), where intense struggles over the urban commons intersect and contest processes of dispossession and exploitation of labor. Under these conditions, he concludes, "Crowdsourcing in the need economy is underwriting surplus production in the speculative economy." It thus becomes possible to see that "the power of finance depends more and more on the participation of the majority—and not just their exclusion—to produce the financialized social relations that rock our cities. Herein lies the urban majority's growing source of power" (Goldman 2015, 159). This power translates across diverse urban landscapes into struggles for urban commons and the right to the city (see, e.g., Lefebvre 1968; Martinez 2017; Mitchell 2012).

To this it is necessary to add an account of how struggles over nature and the environment articulate to productive processes. Marking a "point of stress" in Marxian theory, Étienne Balibar (2012) suggests that an analysis of the exploitation of labor needs to be supplemented by recognition that "the exploitation of nature, or the natural 'things,' is also an intrinsic part of the creation and accumulation of capital." Balibar cites Marx's observation—also recently emphasized by Jason W. Moore (2015, 26)—that capitalist production "develops the techniques and degree of combination of the social process of production by simultaneously undermining the original sources of all wealth—the soil and the worker" (Marx 1977, 638). Although Balibar approaches this as a "moral judgement" rather than, like Moore, attempting to integrate it into Marxian value theory, his comment registers how and why environmental struggles articulate to labor struggles. The remark is even more resonant when one notes that the German word Marx uses for "soil" is *die Erde*, as this links the question of "the exploitation of nature" to our discussion in chapter 3 of the limits of Carl Schmitt's theorization of the *nomos* of the Earth (*die Erde*) for an analysis of the mutations of capital, empire, and state. The editors of the volume *The Anomie of the Earth* (Luisetti et al. 2015, 3) claim that critical engagement with Schmitt's propositions helps to document "the antagonistic forms of autonomy that are moving away from the Western coordinates of the planetary nomos, such as the indigenous, postcolonial, and naturalistic perspectives that are reconceptualizing traditional notions of the political in the Americas and Europe." Our own sense of the spatial and temporal disruption that crosses current planetary patterns of political and legal order similarly encompasses diverse struggles that reveal the articulation of expropriation, dispossession, and exploitation, as well as the deep heterogeneity of capital's operations.

It would be easy to expand the list of struggles we consider in this chapter. Other important recent struggles might include resistance against slum clearance in Kolkata (Chatterjee 2004), Islamabad (Hashmi 2015), or Cape Town (Benson 2016); the *campesino* and Indigenous movement against genetically modified soy cultivation in Argentina, which we mention in the introduction to this book (Leguizamón 2016); urban struggles and labor unrest in logistical export hubs such as Durban, Rio de Janeiro, and Hong Kong (Bond et al. 2016); the summer of wildcat strikes in London's gig economy (O'Connor 2016) and the mobilizations of Deliveroo riders in Italy (Pirone 2016); or struggles in the financial sphere such as the New York–based Strike Debt movement (Ross 2014) and the many protests staged by small investors after the collapse of the Chinese stock market in 2015 (Yap 2016). This multiplication of struggles is part of the scenario we face in looking for possibilities to translate between them. Our approach seeks to go beyond abstract notions of solidarity by treating struggles as relational even as they materialize in vastly heterogeneous circumstances. An emphasis on boundary struggles is part of this perspective, as it allows a focus on the common features of contemporary capitalism while throwing into relief the variable points at which tensions and conflicts condense around specific operations of capital. Although we do not want to privilege particular spaces or subjects of struggle, our argument is that the *extractive* dimension of capital sheds light on moments in which value is extracted from nature and social cooperation in ways that are not directly organized by the fraction of capital that benefits from this extraction. Needless to say, this extractive dynamic is observable in the domains of finance and logistics as much as in physical resource extraction. Our analysis does not seek to reduce contemporary capitalism to its extractive operations but instead to gain a sense of how these operations shape capitalism's workings across diverse scales and spaces. Corollary to this analysis is an investigation of how and why in some of these situations intense struggles crystallize.

This leads us to confront a problem that has been much debated in recent discussions of global struggles and that we already hinted at in this chapter: the production of surplus populations. Marx's observation that "the working population therefore produces both the accumulation of capital and the means by which it itself is made relatively superfluous" (Marx 1977, 783) has sparked a series of discussions concerning the role of populations that are excluded from the formal wage relation in contemporary upheavals and insurrections. Entwined with debates concerning primitive accumulation, informalization, deindustrialization, and racialization, the category of surplus populations goes beyond classical conceptions of an industrial reserve army to describe populations for which capitalist production has no need and who confront the impossibility of reproducing the wage relation. Writing about the politics of the poor in South Africa, for instance, James Ferguson (2015, 11) claims that "it has become more and more difficult to argue that the value produced at the region's industrial centers is generated by the suffering of those at its periphery; instead, the suffering of the poor and marginalized appears as functionally isolated from a production system that no longer has any use for them." Ferguson's observation underlies a passionate and reasoned support for the practice of governments making direct cash payments to the poor. For Théorie Communiste (2011), by contrast, the growing incapacity for capital to reproduce conditions for the exploitation of labor creates surplus populations whose political capacity to riot contrasts positively with the entrapment of wage workers in struggles that supposedly affirm and perpetuate capital. We suggest another view of surplus populations, which derives from our understanding of the articulation of dispossession to exploitation in the operations of capital.

In our discussion of the Maruti Suzuki strike, we sketched how the dispossession of peasant populations constrains them to modes of survival that are derivative of workers' wages. We do not want to suggest that the relation between surplus populations and productive workers is always so straightforward and compromised: even during the Maruti strike, some of the former peasants established a communal kitchen to support the workers (Dey and Grappi 2015, 163). Surplus populations are multilayered and diverse. Nonetheless, they are compelled to survive in extremely challenging circumstances. Their heterogeneous activities mesh with dense social and technical infrastructures within "flexibly configured landscapes" (Simone 2004, 409); thus, they engage in everyday struggles that are consequential, both economically and politically. Tatiana Thieme (2013) calls this the hustle economy, a notion that nicely resonates with Verónica Gago's (2017) exploration of the unruly composition and capitalist exploitation of the vitalism of popular economies in Latin America. The reference to hustling is particularly relevant in a historical conjuncture in which the neoliberal notion of human capital enables a reading of subaltern activities and life (as well as those of surplus populations) from the angle of the valorization of capital and the encroachment of its extractive operations even within the most destitute slums of the world. Thieme explores modes of survival, contestation, and opportunism among youth who work as informal waste collectors in Nairobi's "uncontrolled" settlements. In Thieme's account, hustling entails not only "getting by" but also a "spirit of struggle and insurgency" that contests municipal and generational authority and works the boundaries of the licit and legitimate (Thieme 2013, 391–98). Similarly, in Kristin Peterson's study of traders in the Lagos pharmaceutical market, there is an emphasis on how "the logic of the hustle" produces "a form of economic subjectivity" she calls "derivative life" (Peterson 2014, 105). Let us briefly explore this concept of derivative life, which has important implications for how we understand surplus populations in relation to operations of capital.

Peterson's *Speculative Markets* offers an ethnographic account of the lives and economic strategies of pharmaceutical traders in Lagos, many of whom operate in informal and fake drug markets that have sprung up with the abandonment of the Nigerian drug market by manufacturers of brand-name medicine. One of her concerns is how these small-time traders speculate on "chronic market volatility as well as life's chances" (Peterson 2014, 21), a situation that leads her to connect these speculative practices to the logic of the derivative in finance. Just as financial derivatives allow the pricing transfer of risk without the trading of underlying assets, so hustling in the Lagos pharmaceutical market "requires a repertoire of decision-making skills and is entirely separate from the economic rationalities that are hailed by regulation or other forms of governance" (108). The drugs traded are subject to "derivative price scaling," regardless of whether they "got their start from narcotics dealers who dumped 'licit' drugs into the market, from direct imports from a distributor, or from 'fakes' that are priced to outsell all others" 124). Moreover, she writes, "Cash and the market are not simply nodes at which exchanges take place; rather, they are profoundly socialized through their important derivative forms" (125).

Peterson's study allows us to see how populations that eke out an existence in the wake of market dispossession work within the logics and constraints of financialization. This financialization is quite separate from the formal financial sector and distinct from those modes of "poverty finance" that aim to extend financial services to those who are traditionally excluded from the financial system (Rankin 2013). Nonetheless, it registers how these populations, whatever their relation to productive labor, engage in everyday struggles to make the most of the devastation that can occur when capital hits the ground. The point is not to valorize these everyday struggles above traditional industrial disputes or even riots that explode when capital fails to generate the conditions for social reproduction. Let us affirm again that we are not interested in presenting any particular struggle as paradigmatic or essential for multiplying the power of others, although in the conditions of a specific conjuncture, a single struggle can definitely play a strategic role in this multiplication and concatenation. Rather, we are interested in translating between struggles in ways that are attentive to the vast heterogeneity of laboring and living conditions in the contemporary world. To chart a way to do this, we need to extend further our discussion of how exploitation articulates to dispossession in the face of an extractive capitalism that incites and continually reproduces the conditions for insurrection and struggle among the poor.

Bringing Exploitation Back In

In the opening sentence of his entry on *Ausbeutung* (exploitation) for the *Historisch-Kritisches Wörterbuch des Marxismus*, Johannes Berger (1994, 736) notes that "originally the word was meant to designate the extraction of mineral resources in ore, coal mines, etc." It is important to keep in mind this etymological link between the concept of exploitation and the world of extraction. One can find several traces of this link in Marx's *Capital*, particularly where the "production of surplus value" is equated with the "extraction of surplus labor" (Marx 1977, 411). This semantic proximity with extraction points to a crucial aspect of Marx's understanding of exploitation—that is, the constitutive role of the violence that operates in silent but nevertheless compelling ways at the juncture between the labor and valorization processes whose unity makes up the process of production in a capitalist society. We know that for Marx, exploitation is not a violation of formal rules of justice or some kind of trick used by capitalists to take advantage of workers. It is instead predicated on a "fair" labor contract, taking place according to a logic different from, although articulated to, the logic and rationality of law. Without dismissing the relevance of the legal concept of exploitation that has become entrenched in several national legislations and in international human rights law with regard to such topics as human trafficking, sex work, and child labor, we use the notion here in a way that is close to Marx's original intentions.

We are aware of the multiple problems that haunt Marx's theory of exploitation, ranging from its constitutive connection with his labor theory of value to the rigid distinction it presupposes between productive and unproductive labor, as well as between production and reproduction (see, e.g., Balibar 2012; Berger 1994). These limits were for instance tested in a specific and interesting—although for us problematic—way from the early 1980s within so-called analytical Marxism and, most notably, in the work of John Roemer (1982, 1984; for a critique see Dymski and Elliott 1988). We are not interested here in providing a full-fledged defense of Marx's position, since we have already taken a critical distance from some of its aspects. What we want to emphasize instead is the specificity of a notion of exploitation rooted in an analysis of the dramatic gap between the capacity of subjects to produce, the use (or nonuse) of this capacity, and the accumulation of wealth outside these subjects' control. The concept of exploitation is rooted in the materiality of the production of subjectivity; it works the boundary between the two meanings of the genitive in this phrase, which means between the exploitation of the subjective productive power and the forging of figures of subjectivity that facilitate exploitation (see Read 2003, 102).

Starting with this basic definition, we can easily see that exploitation is connected to a whole set of other concepts that enable it and are part and parcel of its workings. This is particularly the case with the notion of *dispossession*, which, in the wake of David Harvey's influential formulation, often tends to be opposed, even beyond Harvey's original intentions, to the concept of exploitation (see Harvey 2003). Once we disentangle the concept of exploitation from the narrow paradigm of the exploitation of "free" wage labor in the factory system described by Marx in *Capital*, it becomes clear that a moment of dispossession, or expropriation, is inherent to the very nature of exploitation. As far as *power* and *domination* are concerned, they come into play with the multifarious coercive techniques and the panoply of normative arrangements that rule and direct the capacity of subjects to produce—putting it at the disposal of others. The operations of gender and race as crucial and contested domains for the production of subjectivity are vitally important in this regard because they intervene in the fabrication of the bodies that are constructed as exploitable bearers of labor power. Moreover, there is a clear link between exploitation and *alienation*, which goes well beyond the instance of the reification and literal alienation of labor power by means of the legal device of the contract understood by Marx as the basis of "free" wage labor. This link, rather, refers more generally to the missing control by producing subjects of the objective conditions of their lives and labor, of the combination of their forces and capacities to produce within larger assemblages, where social cooperation meshes with machines, control devices, algorithmic protocols, and logistical coordination systems. It is within these larger assemblages that exploitation ultimately operates and enables the accumulation of wealth and capital.

Matters of measure and calculation figure prominently in Marx's theory of exploitation and in successive Marxist debates on the topic. It is important to emphasize that the blueprint for Marx's understanding of exploitation is the relationship between an individual bearer of labor power and an individual owner of money, which means an individual capitalist. It is with respect to this relationship between individuals, mediated by a "free" contract that is also an act of mutual, dialectical recognition, that exploitation emerges as an appropriation (without any corresponding equivalent) of the value produced during a period of labor time that exceeds the "socially necessary labor time" required to reproduce the value of (the individual's) labor power. Nevertheless, this theory of exploitation is predicated on a set of conditions that greatly exceed the individual dimensions of the relationship. The fact that "the owner of the means of production and subsistence finds the free worker available on the market as the seller of his labor power," Marx famously writes, "comprises a world's history" (Marx 1977,

274). But also independently of this, the value of the commodity of labor power, which regulates the extension of "socially necessary labor time," is far from being an objective parameter, existing outside the development of the drama of exploitation. It is, rather, crucially determined by what Marx calls "a historical and moral element," which means by the "level of civilization attained by a country" and, more specifically, by "the habits and expectations with which the class of free workers has been formed" (Marx 1977, 275). These elusive aspects become politicized by workers' struggles for wages.

At the same time, as we saw in the second section of this chapter, the labor process under capitalism is by its nature cooperative. In the chapter titled "Co-operation," Marx sets out, first, to show that the accidental differences among individual labor powers are equalized into an "average social quality" (Marx 1977, 440) that can be taken as a kind of individual statistical measure. But then he is confronted with the emergence of a social productive power, or a "social force," that cannot be considered "the sum total of the mechanical forces exerted by isolated workers" (Marx 1977, 443). There is a split between the individual dimension of labor power and the collective use of it in the labor process (see Virno 2008) that produces a differential of force. And since it targets this differential of force, exploitation in capitalism is always "exploitation of a social labor process." The "unavoidable antagonism between the exploiter and the raw material of his exploitation" crisscrosses the fabric of cooperation in the industrial setting analyzed by Marx. While "the number of cooperating workers increases," he writes, "so too does their resistance to the domination of capital, and, necessarily, the pressure put on by capital to overcome this resistance" (Marx 1977, 449). An unstable system of reciprocal limits emerges out of this parallelogram of forces, which lays the basis both for the further development of antagonism and for what can be called the "normalization" of exploitation (and the ruling out of "over-exploitation") through a dialectical process of recognition between capital and labor (see Balibar 2012). Marx's analysis of the "struggle for the normal working day" in *Capital* (Marx 1977, 389–416) can be read as a kind of blueprint for such a limitation and normalization of exploitation. To this one may add that the history of recent decades has shown the instability and historical contingency of this process.

While Marx's conceptual and empirical description of cooperation remains challenging and in many ways inspiring, we need, at this stage of our analysis, to underscore once more its historical conditions and limitations. When we talk about social cooperation as the main productive force in the present, we have in mind something different from Marx's factory system.

The split between the individual and social aspects of labor power is exploited in the factory system by the same capitalist through the whole set of operations at his or her disposal. Such an exploitation of productive cooperation continues to be performed and to shape laboring lives in a wide array of work sites in many parts of the world. Nevertheless, what marks the distinctiveness of the current situation is the fact that even these laboring lives, which means even the conditions and exploitation of traditional industrial workers, are influenced and altered by the vertical intervention of other operations of capital—by *extractive* operations of capital. This means that the notion of extraction that we are using in this book cannot be equated with the meaning given to the word by Marx when he speaks of "extraction of surplus value." By analyzing the ways in which financial operations synchronize and command the accumulation of capital and investigating the logistical coordination of social and productive environments and processes, we have singled out logics of "drawing" and capture of value that need to be grasped in their specificity. Logistical and financial operations of capital penetrate the fabric of social cooperation without directly organizing it. They extract value from the multiplication of labor they incite and, at the same time, enable labor relationships, even without being necessarily implied in them.

Exploitation takes on very specific characteristics once it is considered from the angle provided by these extractive operations of contemporary capital. The gap between the capacity of subjects to produce and the appropriation and distribution of wealth looms large—and beyond any measure—once the huge accumulation of capital (and power) enabled by such operations is considered. While it is becoming more and more difficult to reconstruct exploitation in terms that lead from the daily experience of subordinated individuals or collective groups to the identification of the specific operations of capital (and related capitalist actors) that are concretely responsible for it, the ghost of dispossession increasingly haunts experiences of exploitation. Processes of individualization, competition, and the production of subjectivity under the signs of self-entrepreneurship, human capital, and debt proliferate within these gaps and experiences. The struggles we map in this chapter are attempts to come to grips with this situation, both in cases where the confrontation with a specific figure of capital (or with specific capitalist actors) leads to an encounter with the wider assemblages of capitalism within which its operations are enmeshed and in cases where the metropolitan scale of an uprising is traversed and constituted by extractive operations characterized by a certain degree of elusiveness.

How is it possible to define the subject of these struggles, their social and political composition? Is the concept of class a working tool that allows us to grasp the heterogeneity and shifting nature of the convergences of forces that are manifest in today's most significant struggles at the global level? We tend to agree with Göran Therborn that this is definitely not the case if we work with a traditional understanding of class as a "structural category to be filled with 'consciousness.'" In the present, class instead becomes "a compass of orientation—towards the classes of the people, the exploited, oppressed and disadvantaged in all their variety" (Therborn 2012, 26). The compass of class not only allows recognition of "the inhuman, abstract and unearthly reductions forced onto people and planet" by capitalism (Dyer-Witheford 2015, 8). It also cuts through the composition of social cooperation and directs our attention to the crucial junctions of its articulation where exploitation becomes visible and embodied in the lives, joys, and pains of specific subjects. The struggles that erupt at these junctions are potential moments of politicization of social cooperation because they point at radical fractures that the operations of capital inscribe into its fabric. It is precisely where the singular, grounded, and lived experience of living labor, which means the subjective use of the capacity to produce, becomes concatenated and networked with other subjective uses of that capacity that exploitation operates in its most violent although often elusive forms nowadays. Contrary to the argument of Polanyi discussed earlier, exploitation is far from being reducible to an "economistic prejudice" or to the "inadequacy of ratios of exchange" (Polanyi [1944] 2001, 166). Rather, it splits the field of subjectivity, articulating its diverse forms in ways that correspond to the heterogeneity of the operations of contemporary capital and give rise to boundary struggles that penetrate the very composition of living labor in its social and cooperative dimensions.

Asking against the background of the struggles we analyze in this chapter whether it is possible to imagine and politically organize a social countermovement to the de-bordering of market relations in a way that is consistent with Polanyi's theory means asking important questions about the chances and limits of a reformist project in the present situation. The normalization of exploitation as an outcome of the dialectic between capital and labor can be considered a pretty accurate definition of historical reformism. From the angle of our discussion of the extractive characteristics of contemporary capitalism, we contend that such normalization is highly problematic today because crucial dimensions of exploitation operate precisely in an extractive mode, beyond any measure and dialectic.

The huge degree of power that is connected to the accumulation of capital enabled by such operations requires the formation of a counterpower adequate to confront capital in directly antagonistic terms. The boundary between reform and revolution seems to be blurred today, and one could even say that radical political action is the condition for the very possibility to test the effectiveness of a reformist project. This is a problem that has been recently tested in many parts of the world with reference to Polanyi. Writing about workers' insurgency and wildcat strikes in the Pearl River Delta, Eli Friedman raises the question regarding the possibility of such a countermovement in contemporary China. He identifies the main obstacle in the absence or weakness of "independent workers' organizations," as well as in the peculiar history and structure of the All-China Federation of Trade Unions, which we encountered earlier in this chapter (Friedman 2014, 162). "Whether or not dispersed worker insurgency will create enough political pressure to force changes in the union" is, for Friedman (2014, 166), a crucial variable for the future of labor. But the prospects for a reformist path in China also depend on the state's response to workers' mobilizations and on the position of labor within the state itself. These are questions that, alongside the issue of the capacity of unions to provide a general representation of labor, do not regard only China.

We reserve for the next and last chapter of the book a more detailed investigation into the role of the state in contemporary global capitalism, which will also be guided by a consideration of its possible roles within a project of social transformation aimed at taming or superseding capitalism. For now, what needs to be noted is that the most important social struggles of recent years, starting with the global cycle of occupations in 2011, seem to be characterized by a radical quest for a direct political articulation, through the invention of new institutions and forms of organization precisely capable of stabilizing and expressing a counterpower. This is apparent also in the most original and challenging manifestations of social unionism, in the reinvention of the tradition of mutualism that goes hand in hand with the development of struggles for housing or in more and less traditional labor struggles in many parts of the world—notably, when casual and precarious workers are involved (De Nicola and Quattrocchi 2016). Even the effectiveness and the conditions of the strike have been tested by social struggles, which, on the one hand, raise the question of how the abstention from work can actually lead to the interruption of the valorization of capital and, on the other hand, point to the need for a sophisticated fabric of infrastructure and even institutional devices that enable the participation in strikes (see Negri 2016b). Crucial from both points of view once again is the connection between living labor and social cooperation and the articulation between the singular experience of exploitation and its commonality (which is also the articulation of the singular use of the capacity to produce and its enmeshment in wider and shifting collective and cooperative arrangements).

Different forms of community building and popular economy, ranging from the establishment of cooperatives to the organization of subsistence networks, tackle the problem of politicizing social cooperation and instituting forms of defense and self-tutelage for the exploited and oppressed. We have seen that these forms are not at all free from the predations of capital, and particularly of financial capital. The same is true of experiences of co-working and the sharing economy that attempt to contest—or, at least, to limit—the logic of private appropriation within the field of knowledge-based capitalism or the gig economy. This is so because the common emerges here as the main productive force that is exploited by capital. Our own discussion of the gaps and articulation between living labor and social cooperation is to be understood in this sense as a contribution to the ongoing discussion on the common. A theory of exploitation makes sense today only if it can grasp the new dimensions of extraction introduced by the eminent role of the common as a productive force. But the common is not at all a homogeneous or organic subject. It is, rather, fractured by a multiplicity of fault and boundary lines. It exists in the abstract and mystified figure produced by capitalist exploitation (and is, in a way, represented on the global financial markets). But in political terms, it has to be produced and articulated through the hazardous action and struggle of the exploited to become the basis of a new democracy that develops in a tense relation with the extractive dimensions of contemporary capitalism.

This tension in the establishment and appropriation of the common emerges as the unifying thread that runs through the vistas of struggle we analyze in this chapter. In their development, these struggles encounter and confront multiple figures and operations of capital. Sometimes they raise the possibility of a radical rupture with the social relation of capital. At other times, they qualify in new ways the ground on which experimentations with a reformist rearrangement of this relation might be performed. These struggles must also reckon with the state, more often than not confronting its repressive capacities. But what is the position of the state within the variegated landscapes of contemporary capitalism? This is a question that has haunted our analysis from the beginning, and we turn to it in a systematic way in the final chapter of the book.

The State of Capitalist
Globalization

The State's Unity in Dispute

As the previous chapter demonstrates, the operations of contemporary capital are surrounded and contested by a huge array of struggles, which confront the interaction of these operations with diverse forms of society and life, as well as their concatenation into wider assemblages of capitalism. These struggles take multifarious forms, are characterized by highly heterogeneous dynamics as far as their social and political composition is concerned, and enter different relations with capital and state apparatuses. Our snapshots and analyses have combined industrial labor struggles and conflicts crisscrossing the development of cutting-edge sectors of capitalist activity. They have included new forms of social unionism, metropolitan uprisings, and disputes that can be grouped around the general topic of the right to the city, as well as struggles along the extractive frontier that relate to questions of Indigeneity, landed property, and environment. Moreover, writing about the "spirit of struggle and insurgency" that permeates the "hustle economy" (Thieme 2013), we have tested the boundary between what is usually acknowledged as a struggle and mundane practices of resistance connected to the reproduction of subaltern lives in many parts of the world (and once again, there is a need to add, well beyond the global

South). This is a particularly important point for us that becomes even clearer, considering daily fights against patriarchy and racism. Struggles of migration are an obvious instance in this regard (see De Genova et al. 2015, 80–83). In previous writings, we have taken inspiration from the daily practices by which migrants challenge, confront, and negotiate borders to forge the notion of "border struggles" (Mezzadra and Neilson 2013a, 264–70). The deeply political and even subversive nature of such border struggles was perhaps nowhere so apparent as in Europe in the summer of 2015, in what is aptly called the long summer of migration (Bojadžijev and Mezzadra 2015; De Genova 2017; Hess et al. 2017; Kasparek and Speer 2015).

Some of the struggles that we mention and analyze are seemingly related in only indirect ways to the operations of capital. This is even more the case if we consider other forms of mobilization and political activism, such as the crucially important new wave of feminist struggles that are sweeping many world regions and found a provisional culmination in late 2016 in the organization of impressive "women's strikes" in countries as diverse as Poland and Argentina—strikes which continued to spread transnationally in 2017 and 2018 as part of the March 8 celebration of International Women's Day. By pointing to links among these heterogeneous forms of struggle, mobilization, and activism to the contemporary workings of capitalism, we are far from proposing an "economistic" reduction of their meanings, implications, and potentialities. Our discussion of class and class politics in chapter 5 has, instead, made clear that we decidedly refuse to take race and gender, for instance, as "secondary aspects" of some fundamental contradiction between labor and capital. What we want to stress is that the production of subjectivity, which means the field within which gender and race operate as both productive and destructive, is increasingly placed under duress by the extractive logics of contemporary capitalism writ large. Our insistence on the relations and tensions between living labor and social cooperation as a general field of struggle is a way to conceptually register this. Such an insistence allows us to acknowledge the limits of specific struggles, pointing to the need for a political labor of translation to connect them with other struggles. It also cautions against the risk of taking social cooperation as an already constituted political subject. Boundary struggles, where capital confronts the multiple outsides that the expansion of its frontiers encounters and continually produces, become strategically important under such conditions.

The state is always involved in the struggles we describe, whether it is through its repressive action and apparatuses (as it is most often the case), as an addressee of more or less radical contestation or claims, as complicit with operations of capital, or as a negotiating and mediating actor. It is from the point of view of such struggles that we undertake an investigation of the contemporary transformations and roles of the state in this chapter. Our analysis of the state is framed within a more general interrogation of the political nowadays, which we think is important if we are to think of struggles beyond mere resistance—if we are to contribute to opening up, against the background of really existing struggles, a horizon of life beyond capitalism. What can the role of the state be in such efforts? And even more generally, what is the position of the state within a politics of emancipation and liberation? Needless to say, this is not a new question. But it takes new forms today as the rich, contradictory, and complex experiences of "progressive" governments in Latin America over the last long decade (and much more briefly in a European country such as Greece) demonstrate. A realistic analysis of the contemporary state and its multiple entanglements with the operations of capital is particularly urgent from this perspective.

As we mentioned at the end of chapter 1, such a realistic analysis cannot take the unity of its object as given. This is a crucial methodological caution that should characterize contemporary discussions of the state. While we have dwelled on the question of the unity of capital, on its elusive and complex character, an emphasis on the unity of the modern state has been characteristic of mainstream political and legal theories since the early formulations of sovereignty by Jean Bodin and Thomas Hobbes. This remains true even if the constitutional articulation of this unity, including federal arrangements and various degrees of decentralization, has been a prominent topic of discussion in the history of those theories, particularly in the wake of the "Atlantic revolutions" that shook the Americas and Europe in the late eighteenth century (Klooster 2009). The contemporary situation is significantly new in this regard. This is not to say that it is completely unprecedented. We have hinted at some uncanny elements of continuity with the political and legal histories of modern empires, which seem to us more intriguing than the widespread parallel with the European Middle Ages. We hint again at this point later in the chapter. For now, we want to stress the relevance of analyses that point to increasing processes of governmentalization of the state to demonstrate that its institutional unity is placed under duress by contemporary developments. Independently of their different genealogies, the notions of governance and governmental-ity have provided many scholars (critical and mainstream) with a privi-leged analytical perspective on the transformations of political processes and institutions within a neoliberal framework (see, e.g., Dardot and Laval 2014; Ives 2015; Jardim 2013; Walters 2012). Considering the prominent roles played in the analytical scope of such notions by risk management, "human capital," and public-private partnerships, it is easy to understand that operations of capital haunt the transformations they help us to grasp and describe. The very boundary between the political and the economic, between state and capital, becomes blurred in such a framework, as is ap-parent in the "anticipatory" governmental patterns that prevail in the field of security (see Amoore 2013). State agencies, institutional structures, and administrative branches are powerfully reshaped and often even frag-mented by such processes, which are at the root of a multiplication of gaps, tensions, and conflicts within and among them.

Anthropologists and ethnographers have made important contributions to a grounded study of such processes of governmentalization (see Fer-guson and Gupta 2002). "All claims about the state [today]," writes Akhil Gupta in *Red Tape* (2012, 52), an impressive work on the governance of poverty and structural violence in India, "should be countered with the question, Which state?" Sure, Gupta refers here specifically to India and the confounding proliferation of different levels of government; heteroge-neous agencies and bureaus; and the various policies, programs, and people that constitute the state in that context. But his question also has relevance beyond that particular case. Not only does it remind us of the wide array and heterogeneity of states that populate the present global landscape, but it also encourages, and even compels, an investigation of how the unity of all these different kinds of states, as we contend, cannot be taken for granted. A spatial take on the transformations of the state further en-trenches this point, shedding even more light on severe challenges to the unity of the state. More than ten years ago, the urban theorist Neil Brenner began to carefully map processes of "rescaling" state space. These processes have been under way since the 1970s and disrupt the "project of national territorial equalization" that ran parallel to the development of indus-trial capitalism. "It is no longer capital," Brenner (2004, 16) writes, "that is to be molded into the (territorially) geography of state space, but state space that is to be molded into the (territorially differentiated) geography of capital." This general point retains its validity, even beyond Brenner's theoretical framework. When one considers the multiple, heterogeneous, and fuzzy array of spatial arrangements that we have often mentioned in this book—from special economic zones to infrastructural and industrial corridors, from supply chains to extractive enclaves—the implications of the geographical variegation of contemporary capitalism for state space become even clearer. The notion of "extrastatecraft," recently elaborated by Keller Easterling (2014, 15) to grasp a set of spaces and "often undisclosed activities outside of, in addition to, and sometimes even in partnership with statecraft," nicely captures these implications, while at the same time highlighting the overlapping and collisions among jurisdictions, orders, and actors that characterize sites such as special economic zones.

Looking at contemporary debates on the state and sovereignty, the emphasis on states of exception that shape another series of arguments epitomized by the work of Giorgio Agamben (see, esp., Agamben 1998, 2005) seems, by contrast, to take the unity of the state for granted—although always on the verge of its renewed foundation through the moment of sovereign decision. We do not need to rehearse here our critique of such arguments (see Mezzadra and Neilson 2013a, 147–48, 189; Neilson 2010), which ultimately rely on a Schmittian understanding of the relation between norm and exception that is not able to grasp the contemporary operation of exception "through the norm itself, or more precisely, via the movements of a mobile norm" (Amoore 2013, 17). While this is a strategically important point, which has to do with the very meaning of "norm" and "normality" in the present, the emphasis on sovereignty in arguments surrounding states of exception is nevertheless important insofar as it registers the need to counterbalance the vanishing of sovereignty itself in many studies of governance and governmentality.

We suggest there is a need to grasp both the salience of processes of governmentalization and the persistence of sovereignty, as well as their mutations beyond the state to understand the evolution of political processes and institutions in the world today. Such an effort must take into account new formations of "legal pluralism" and the emergence of a fragmentary but no less effective "global law" along sectoral and functional lines, whose best-known and most discussed example is the *lex mercatoria* (see Teubner 2012). From a different theoretical angle, which effectively emphasizes the relation between law and boundaries, as well as between legal order and its constitutive outside, a recent book by Hans Lindahl (2013) takes the investigation of legal spaces of globalization a step further, pointing to the manifold "sharply demarcated spatial boundaries and other, more or less fuzzy boundary zones and borderlands" that proliferate within, across, and beyond states (Lindahl 2013, 75; see also Menga 2014). We could even say—to produce resonances with our conceptual language—that these boundaries and borderlands are produced by the multiple ways in which legal orders such as *lex mercatoria, lex constructionis,* and *lex digitalis* hit the ground. Within these border zones, struggles proliferate, often through practices of literal trespassing, as Lindahl is keen to show in his discussions of Indigenous resistance to oil drilling in Colombia and land occupations by Brazil's Movimento dos Trabalhadores Rurais sem Terra (Landless Workers' Movement; Lindahl 2013, 53, 60–64). These struggles, for Lindahl, take on crucial constitutive characters also from a legal point of view.

Lindahl argues that "spatial closure" defines not only legal orders constructed around political and legal borders (state law and international law) but also those that apply within operative spaces established by infrastructural and commercial connections. He gives the example of multinational corporations, which extend their operations across multiple state territories and whose "internal regulations," a number of legal theorists have found, constitute "legal orders which resist accommodation on either side of the correlation between municipal and international law" (Lindahl 2013, 56). Putting aside the issue of the private character of multinationals, Lindahl accepts that they challenge understandings of law based exclusively on state territoriality. But he also resists the notion that they produce forms of "global law," indicating that they "do not claim to regulate the whole face of the earth" and operate "more like movable enclaves" (Lindahl 2013, 57). The oil multinational Royal Dutch Shell, for instance, maintains buildings, laboratories, computer facilities, oil extraction rigs, refineries, service stations, and other infrastructure across many different global sites. Again employing our conceptual idiom, we can say that this disjointed territorial arrangement specifies the sites where the operations of capital that enable the company's extractive activities hit the ground, even if the effects of these activities can spiral beyond the point of impact. Shell is free to move its activities to different sites, but in legal terms it constitutes a "(more or less movable) spatial unity" linked to "a first-person plural perspective in terms of the normative point guiding its various activities" and "limited in terms of the inside/outside distinction" (Lindahl 2013, 57). Thus, when environmental activists occupied the Brent Spar oil platform operated by Shell in the North Sea, they disrupted this spatial unity, creating a "limit" among sites that come under the company's jurisdiction and a "strange outside" (Lindahl 2013, 58). Moreover, this outside "is not merely 'figurative' or 'metaphorical'" (Lindahl 2013, 74). It marks the "spatial limit" of legal order, even if such demarcation calls "forth altogether different sorts of scales of preciseness and impreciseness of legal boundaries" from those "governing state borders" (Lindahl 2013, 75–76).

It is tempting, but too easy, to correlate this constitutive legal "outside" with the multiple outsides we have associated with the prospective and extractive operations of capital. Although legal principles and actions can be understood in an operative sense, and operations can be limited by or transgress legal orders, these discrepant outsides cannot be consigned to some pure space of externality because they are always generated by boundary and border struggles in which the very difference between inclusion and exclusion is at stake (Mezzadra and Neilson 2012). As much as it would be a mistake to suggest that the movable "spatial unity" of a multinational corporation is more operative than legal in nature, so it would be wrong to emphasize the legal unity of the state at the expense of its operative capacities. Michael Mann's discussion of the state's "infrastructural power," which he describes as "the capacity to actually penetrate society and implement logistically political decisions" (Mann 1984, 170), is only one register of this. In her fascinating study of the Ghanaian customs authority, the anthropologist Brenda Chalfin (2010, 24–25) cites the state's capacity to extract revenue through taxation as a crucial instance of such infrastructural power. She quotes the economic historian Gabriel Ardant (see Chalfin 2010, 25), who stresses the financial basis of modern statehood and argues that "the fiscal system was the transformer of the economic infrastructure into political structure." Today this situation seems reversed, even in the midst of protracted financial crisis. Writing about the privatization of "public" finances, Wolfgang Streeck (2014) argues that the *Steuerstaat* (tax state) has been transformed into a *Schuldenstaat* (debt state). Financial institutions have become at once moneylenders for states, which rely more on credit than taxation to balance their budgets, and beneficiaries of state (public) money that prevents them from collapsing. As Étienne Balibar (2013) writes, these institutions "have an almost absolute command over the government *both* because they are creditors and because they are debtors." Understanding the changing position of the state in contemporary globalization means interrogating this command.

In chapter 2, we discussed how operations of capital increasingly collapse economic and political power. The question of how financial markets and institutions transform and limit the powers of the state challenges us to further specify the nature of this power. A key difficulty here is to register the manipulative and seemingly coercive qualities of this power while remaining attentive to the volatility and vulnerability of financial markets. Although governed by different kinds of institutions (some of them state apparatuses) and algorithmic processes, these markets are given to patterns of speculation and appropriation that are inherently unstable and, as we have seen in the instance of flash crashes, increasingly detached from cyclical rhythms of crisis and recovery. Balibar (2013, part 3) attempts to capture the "*conflictual*" and "*disseminated*" power of finance by describing it as a form of "*quasi-sovereignty.*" Working in analogy with the power exercised by modern empires over dependencies and protectorates—which we discussed in chapter 3—he suggests that the "new sovereignty" of the global financial market "substitutes (or subordinates) the old imperialist structures of the world-economy, and in this sense it could be called an Empire (or *imperium*) that—much more than any military power today (i.e., with less possibilities of resistance)—has restricted the independence of states and nations" (Balibar 2013, part 3). Yet Balibar (2013, part 2) also recognizes that sovereignty requires the "legitimation of power," which is a process undergoing "profound ideological transformation" in a situation where "credit mechanisms . . . have become in practice the 'regulators' of society." The production and stakes of legitimacy shift when states apply rules and strategies imposed by financial markets, instituting austerity, privatization, and welfare rollback measures that exacerbate inequalities and accelerate the general precariousness of populations. The "*decomposition of the people*" that results from the "*paradoxical organization, by the State itself, of its incapacity to resist pressures from the financial sector*" affects "not only the independence of the nation but also the legitimacy of the state" (Balibar 2013, part 3). At the same time, it illustrates how the quasi-sovereignty of finance capital is "negatively defined" rather than offering a "unified or effective power dictating positive behaviors to its 'subjects'" (Balibar 2013, part 3). This negative and paradoxical power characterizes what we call the state of capitalist globalization, a phrase that registers both the global condition pertaining under the rule of contemporary capital and the particular qualities and transformations of the state within this configuration. To further analyze the workings of this quasi-sovereign form of power, it is necessary not only to consider how it reaches beyond the operations of finance, but also to investigate how it multiplies and explodes the state form, creating new and hybrid experiences of state and extra-statehood that make even the post–World II state seem unfamiliar.

Figures of the Contemporary State

Globalization affects not only capitalism but also the state. We may be suspicious about the use of globalization as a portmanteau concept and aware of the uneven dynamics of denationalization and renationalization that have accompanied its unfolding, but as soon as one recognizes that the state itself has been transformed by globalization, it is necessary to take stock of its effects not only on economic processes but also on political institutions and environments. In other words, it is insufficient to approach the state as a stable entity defined within the parameters of territory, community, and legitimacy, which is then either augmented or diminished by globalizing forces. Such an approach has been a dominant tendency over the past few decades, leading to a series of prognostications concerning the decline or withering away of the state, on one hand, or its continued relevance and unchanged form, on the other. We do not find either of these prognoses convincing, since the interaction between state and capital is not a zero-sum game. Globalizing processes erode the borders between economics and politics, state and capital. Although it would seem otherwise from mainstream debates, this erosion occurs not simply because globalization is about more than the forging of free trade deals, the growth of direct foreign investment, the deregulation of financial markets, and the cross-border mobility of people. As discussed in chapter 2, the fabrication of the world market is inherent within operations of capital and is not a process that was initiated in the late twentieth century alone. To speak of the political dimensions of these operations requires something more than the identification of a sphere of political globalization, which sits alongside economic, cultural, and social globalization and is usually identified with the formation and influence of supranational and nongovernmental organizations. Working from the description of quasi-sovereignty offered earlier, we can begin to investigate mutations in the workings and articulation of power that reshape the very form of the state and multiply the different figures that it assumes on the world stage. Once the global history of the modern state is taken into consideration, uncanny continuities and mutations of older institutional arrangements abound.

One way to explain the political effects of globalization, especially during its most recent phase, is to say that it involves a defeat of politics by economics. Such a proposition captures something of the transformations that have accompanied a burgeoning but heterogeneous neoliberalism. However, it fails to recognize the political nature of the depoliticization that many critical thinkers associate with the increasing dominance of technical and managerial modes of governance (see, e.g., Bourdieu 2002; Swyngedouw 2016; Wang 2003). Depoliticization names the requirement for a political force and form capable of instituting and preserving the conditions for an ascendency of the economic. We might say that the state, under globalization, has provided such a force and form or that it has provided the political conditions under which the capacity for politics to resist or restrain the operations of capital has been diminished. But, again, this does not imply an exclusively negative process by which the state is stripped of powers it once possessed, or, inversely the possibility that the restoration of such powers might reverse or tame the capacity for capital itself to act politically. We are arguing not for the autonomy of the political under the powers of the state but, rather, for recognition that the state is not the only seat of politics and the need for an alternative radical politics capable of confronting capital to arise from political practices that mingle with economic, social, and cultural forms of life.

More than a decade ago, Saskia Sassen (2006) coined the term "denationalization" to describe how much of the global is constituted from within the national. Although the term sounds like it addresses a winding back in the communal dimension of national belonging—or the "decomposition of the people" (Balibar 2013, part 3) that we referred to earlier—its range of reference is actually wider. Sassen (2006, 22) uses it to describe multivalent dynamics that change "what is 'national' in . . . institutional components of states linked to the implementation and regulation of economic globalization." Denationalization "can function as a creative force rather than simply as a negative consequence of overwhelming external global power" (23) and affects realms as diverse as "policies, capital, political subjectivities, urban spaces, [and] temporal frames" (1). Furthermore, it has partial effects and can "feed nationalizing dynamics in separate though at times connected domains—for example, the denationalizing of certain components of our economy and the renationalizing in certain components of our immigration policy" (2). This is why renationalizing dynamics—evident, for instance, in the reintroduction of border controls in Europe's Schengen Area, Brexit, Donald Trump's policy preferences regarding tariffs and travel bans, the burgeoning of "mercantilism" in many parts of the world, and the promotion of return migration by Asian states—should be seen not as an undoing of globalization but, rather, as part of its uneven and multivalent effects. As Sassen writes, "What was bundled up and experienced as a unitary condition," the "national assemblage" of territory, authority and rights, reveals "itself to be a distinct set of elements, with variable capacities for becoming denationalized" (6)—and, we would add, renationalized.

Again, the unity of the state is at stake in its interactions with and internalization of globalizing dynamics. The effects of these processes are myriad and kaleidoscopic. Following Sassen, however, some tendencies can be identified. First is the reorganization of power within states, usually involving the shifting of power to the executive branch of government. Second is the emergence of privatized realms of authority for the governance of specialized domains, displacing and sitting alongside *raison d'état* in much the same way as the normative realms sketched out, although from different theoretical angles, by thinkers such as Gunther Teubner (2012) and Hans Lindahl (2013). Third is the circulation of the logics of global capital within state public spheres and their integration into policy. These tendencies may not necessarily dissolve the formal unity of statehood, but they disarticulate it internally. We think the observation and recognition of these changes is a matter of political realism. In so doing, we seek to steal the mantle of realism from those versions of international relations that posit the state as the fundamental unit of global politics—a rational actor within a field of power.

Ever since the publication of Rob Walker's *Inside/Outside* (1993), the problems with assuming a bounded state sovereignty have dominated critical debate in international studies. In debates about security, for instance, it is no longer possible to posit separate internal and external spheres of security—social security and national security—that come together in the post–World War II "welfare-warfare" state (Neocleous 2006). Didier Bigo (2001, 2016) uses the topological figure of the Möbius strip to illustrate how lines of internal and external state security and sovereignty have merged and become difficult to differentiate. The internal disarticulation of the state, which was always linked to its negotiation and incorporation of external factors, thus becomes increasingly hard to distinguish from its outward relations, whether they exist with states, markets, corporations, electronic networks, large-scale infrastructural installations, or other kinds of institutional bodies. The idea of an international order, whether rules-based or anarchic, is displaced or relativized by a complex set of power dynamics that are no longer strictly international in the sense that they are not exclusively articulated among states. But to recognize this is not yet to account for the changing role of the state, and, in particular—if we are always to ask, "Which state?"—the way in which the political form of the state has fragmented into many different figures, none of which seem able to supply a general theory or baseline model to inform theoretical arguments about the state's position in capitalist globalization.

Speaking of figures of the contemporary state, we cannot follow the same path as we did in chapter 3, where we provided a general typology composed of three prevailing figures of the state after World War II. Certainly, the historical gaze makes such typological exercises easier. But there is something more at stake here. To put it briefly, the blurring of the boundaries of the state and the powerful challenges to its unity hinder a clear identification of the main features that define it across different geographical, economic, and cultural settings. It is important to stress that we employ the word "boundaries" here in a very general sense, referring both to geopolitical borders and to the internal demarcations that distinguish the domain of the state from other domains—most notably, from those of capital's operations. One of the implications of such a conceptual predicament is the proliferation of labels, prefixes, and adjectives that populate discussions about the transformations of the state form today. Even in debates that are mainly focused on the West, such definitions as the ones we mentioned—from the debt to the security and surveillance state, from the workfare to the entrepreneurial state—point to relevant aspects of the contemporary state, but they are unable to grasp its "figure" in a unitary way.

Interestingly, and consistently with the point we made earlier discussing Walker and Bigo, analyses that attempt to bridge the securitization and neoliberalization of the state—for instance, in the United States—point to the fact that "the contemporary spatialization of security increasingly blurs notions of 'inside' and 'outside,' such that domestic and foreign policy might be seen to operate in a continuum rather than as discrete moments of policy" (MacLeavy and Peoples 2010, 740). This blurring of boundaries between the inside and the outside is even more evident if we consider other conceptual labels that circulate in the current critical discussion. Take the notion of a "logistical state," which has been proposed by several authors, often on the basis of Henri Lefebvre's work on the state in the 1970s (see, e.g., Grappi 2016, 25–28; Toscano 2014). In his elaboration of this concept, Ned Rossiter emphasizes the enmeshment of the logistical state within global networks of supply chains and its "fusing" with finance (Rossiter 2016, 170–71). He concludes that the "territorial imaginary of the logistical state is constituted through network topologies and infrastructures of extraction in ways that do not necessarily conform to the territorial logic of the nation-state" (Rossiter 2016, 173). We are again confronted with the blurring of the boundary between inside and outside, which means the blurring of a founding conceptual and political feature of the modern state.

Widening the analytical scope and taking a global perspective—as we try to do throughout this book—the multiplication of labels and the variegation of the state landscape they signal become more puzzling and confusing. Although their heyday seems to have passed, the use of terms such as "failed state"—to aggregate instances as diverse as Colombia, Haiti, Somalia, and Tajikistan (Call 2010)—and "rogue state" marked an important period of political debate and history in the 1990s and 2000s. Critical analyses of discourses of state failure effectively demonstrate their implication within colonial and postcolonial assemblages of power (Figueroa Helland and Borg 2014), while the notion of rogue states to denounce so-called state-sponsored terrorism has been part and parcel of US political strategies, justifying wars that—to say the least and to put in a sober way—have not been particularly successful. Writing in the early 2000s, Jacques Derrida was keen to shift attention from states designated rogue to those that claimed the monopoly of making this designation, noting that the latter—"namely, the United States and its allied states"—in "taking the initiative of war, of police or peacekeeping because they have the force to do so . . . are themselves, as sovereign, the first rogue states" (Derrida 2005, 102). Sure, one can think of a certain irony of history reading today, with the "Islamic State" in mind, Derrida's statement about the "overwhelming and all-too-obvious fact" that "after the Cold War, the absolute threat no longer took a state form" (Derrida 2005, 104). His *Rogues: Two Essays on Reason* is nevertheless a remarkable piece of political analysis, especially for its emphasis on the need to read the intensified use of the notion of rogue states, which had its roots in the Cold War, as a symptom of growing anxiety in the face of the blurring of political concepts that hitherto had built the scaffolding of the state form and of international relations.

Turning our attention to definitions of the state that are tailored to specific instances or regions, we encounter a wide array of developmental (in the mainstream sense that we discussed in chapter 3) and post-developmental (in a critical sense, which is closer to our conceptual language) state formations. These range from the "petro-modernist state" in the Persian Gulf—which balances the persistent privilege of royal families against its positioning in the global capitalist system through the exploitation of a huge mass of migrant workers (AlShebabi 2015, 10)—to the various instantiations of a "post-neoliberal" state over recent years in Latin America (Grugel and Riggirozzi 2012; for a critique, see Dávalos 2010).

In war-torn regions, "militia states" and "warlord politics" (Reno 1998) proliferate, with characteristics that resonate with the securitization of globally connected "extraction enclaves" in African "oil states" (Ferguson 2006, 204). As the case of Darfur, along the border between Sudan and Chad, tragically demonstrates, even when oil is just a rumor about a future possibility, it spurs conflicts and has socially and spatially disintegrative consequences (Behrends 2008). Needless to say, more variants should be taken into consideration when exploring the globally variegated state landscape of the present—for instance, religion, which plays crucial roles in state formation not merely in "extreme" (although completely different) cases such as the "theocratic republic" of Iran and the Islamic State but also in many other places, from Nigeria to Israel, India to the United States, the Middle East to Indonesia. Such a questionable notion as the "civilizational state" also circulates in analyses of India and China (Wei 2012, 24; Zhang 2012), while both of these countries can also be analyzed from a more interesting and productive angle as instances of "continental states," a category that also fits the United States.

Questions of democracy, authoritarianism, and even "totalitarianism" have also been tested by recent developments—for instance, in debates surrounding the rise of China. On this point we follow the position elaborated by Wang Hui, who has brilliantly analyzed the transformation of the relations between China's Communist Party and the state from the "party-state" to the "state-party" model (Wang 2009). He understands this transformation as a result of the interrelated dynamics of "bureaucratization of the party" in the wake of the failure of the cultural revolution and "the marriage of the party and capital in the process of the corporatization of government during market reform" (Wang 2016, 155). What makes Wang Hui's analysis particularly interesting for us is the fact that he takes the state-party model as a specific instantiation in China of a more general crisis of political representation and "statification" of parties, which are "common to all political systems" as "a product of neoliberalism in the political sphere" and as a consequence of ensuing depoliticization (Wang 2016, 296). From this point of view, while discussions of "post-democracy" (Crouch 2004) and "deconstitutionalization" (Amendola 2016) abound in the West, the whole question of a "democratic transition" in China is productively displaced from the realm of supposedly normative models of representative democracy to the search for new forms of "autonomy," social mobilization, and working-class politics that cannot be contained within "the model of traditional socialism based on the nation-state as a unit" (Wang 2016, 296).

What interests us here are precisely the kind of resonances produced by an analysis such as that offered by Wang Hui of the state party in China. We have pointed to Balibar's use of the notion of quasi-sovereignty to come to terms with the power of finance. As we show in chapter 3, this is a category that has its own history in colonialism and colonial law. It is closely connected with the notion of the "quasi-state," widely employed to refer to unrecognized "de facto states," "para-states," or "pseudo-states" often linked with the efforts of secessionist movements (Kolstø 2006) or to such entities as the Kurdistan Regional Government in post-Saddam Iraq (Natali 2010). It is interesting to note that the same label is also used in Europe, where several scholars define the European Union as an "unfinished federal quasi-state" (see, e.g., Pelinka 2011), while at the same time member states could be defined as quasi-states, given their enmeshment within an assemblage of power that radically limits their formal sovereignty in such crucial fields as monetary and fiscal politics. A final example that cannot go unanalyzed is the concept of the "gatekeeper state," whose origins can be traced back to the work of the Marxist and Pan-Africanist writer Walter Rodney (1972) and that was later formalized by Frederick Cooper in *Africa since 1940* (2002; see also Chari 2015). In the wake of incomplete decolonization in Africa, this notion was meant to emphasize the continuity between colonial administrations and postcolonial states on that continent, shedding light on their strategic roles in controlling and organizing the junctures between domestic economies and the world market. While carefully keeping in mind the peculiarity of African conditions after decolonization, we think there is something to be gained analytically by using the notion in different and unexpected contexts—for instance, by approaching the United Kingdom as a gatekeeper state, at least since the City of London situated itself in the Thatcher years "as a strategic refueling stop on the migration routes that the world's capital took to reach New York" (Varoufakis 2011, 139). More generally, we can even ask whether all contemporary states (although in crucially different ways) are not in some way gatekeeper states.

Reckoning with the State

As we have argued, powerful transformations are disrupting and reshaping each of the three constitutive elements of the state identified by traditional political and legal theories: territory, people, and sovereignty. While heterogeneous factors come into play in these transformations, operations of capital play prominent roles in prompting and orchestrating them. One has only to think about the many limits placed on the independence (and therefore the sovereignty) of states by a fabric of 24/7 global financial operations to get an intuitive image of these roles. As we amply demonstrated in earlier chapters, logistical operations both work the boundaries of the geopolitical borders of states, traversing their territories, and "seam" together sites that are unevenly distributed across the globe. The legal construct of territoriality characteristic of the state is increasingly placed under duress by such operations and by the related emergence of heterogeneous spatial formations—including the space of the "cloud," whose nomos is no less compelling for being named in such an ethereal way (Bratton 2015). As far as the "people" are concerned, processes of differential inclusion and exclusion connected to the neoliberalization and governmentalization of the state—which means the infiltration of the operative logic of capital into state apparatuses—profoundly alter the shape of citizenship, while migratory movements continue to challenge the boundaries of citizenship itself. What we have described as the disarticulation of the dyadic figure of the "citizen-worker" (Mezzadra and Neilson 2013a, 243–51) is particularly relevant here.

Nevertheless, states continue to exist and to perform important tasks in the global present. There is therefore a need to go beyond the boundaries of traditional state theory and its normative assumptions, as well as its baseline models. What we need to undertake is a more "positive" description (positive in analytical terms) of what states are actually doing today without presuming to know already what the state is or might be. In the previous section of this chapter we have outlined some general tendencies following Sassen (2006), but what we have in mind here is a less integrative approach. Take Sassen's discussion of the increase in executive power within states over past decades. This, again, is a tendency that is not completely new, since its manifestations can be traced at least back to the early twentieth century and figured prominently in debates on the incipient crisis of the modern state that we recalled in chapter 3. Sassen's observation is nonetheless acute and timely, based as it is on an analysis of the internal state reorganization of power in the United States, particularly during the presidency of George W. Bush. She notes that "elements of this shift are evident in a growing number of states around the world" (Sassen 2006, 168), but the absence of a wider investigation limits her understanding of some of the more striking manifestations of this trend, including those that have occurred in the decade since her intervention. The capitalist crisis of 2007–2008 has accelerated and mutated these changes by increasing social and economic polarization and displacing working populations in ways that have opened political opportunities for "populist" leaders and ideologies—not least, those revolving around race, gender, and migration. This is not the occasion to interrogate the suitability of the term "populism" to describe these developments, although it is interesting to note that most accounts of populism (see, e.g., Albertazzi and McDonnell 2008; Laclau 2005; Oudenampsen 2010) do not contemplate changes to the state form. If we consider the augmentations to executive power occurring in the world today, however, it is possible to discern a shift in the way states formally distribute power—internal changes that are often driven by attempts to reverse or deny the blurring of inside and outside that is such a prominent feature of the contemporary state.

Take, for example, Russia, where Vladimir Putin has extended the presidential pyramid, or *vertikal*, established by Boris Yeltsin with the constitutional crisis of 1993 to establish "a distinct form of state populism that is a response to the expectations of the majority of the population who self-identify as 'the people' by way of its leader" (Clément 2015). Or consider the administration of Narendra Modi in India, which operates under the slogan "Minimum Government, Maximum Governance." In this case, executive power has been bolstered by limiting parliamentary government, political transparency, and social dissent (Ruparelia 2015). In the case of Egypt's General Abdel Fattah el-Sisi, who seized power in a coup after the electoral victory of the Muslim Brotherhood following the uprisings of 2011, legislative power has been regularly bypassed—including on the occasion of the secretly negotiated ceding of the islands of Tiran and Sanafir to Saudi Arabia, an arrangement that has led one commentator to suggest that in Egypt there exists an "island of executive power" (Kaldas 2016). The chase for an "executive presidency" on the part of Turkey's Recep Tayyip Erdoğan, by contrast, has been reinforced by the failed coup of July 2016, an event that has buttressed rule by decree, imprisonment of political opponents, and attacks on the independent press (Cizre 2016). In Hungary, the constitution has already changed to limit the judiciary's power, and further anti-migrant amendments are under way, cementing the country's transition to what Prime Minister Viktor Orbán has called an "illiberal state" (Tóth 2014). Meanwhile, in the Philippines, Rodrigo Duterte's "war on drugs" provides a platform on which extensions to executive power achieved under the presidency of Benigno Aquino can be furthered (Curato 2017). Needless to say, these situations are diverse, and it is always possible to find counterexamples. In Brazil, for instance, the "parliamentary coup" against Dilma Rousseff has exposed limits to executive power in a state where the presidency is traditionally quite strong, although the right-wing mobilization in play has resonances with the dynamics observable in the situations noted earlier (Santos and Guarnieri 2016). The election of Donald Trump as president of the United States in November 2016, with the ensuing multiplication of conflicts with the judicial system, adds further and crucial nuances to this global political landscape. The point is that a vast undercurrent is reorganizing the institutional arrangement of power within states, and while it is possible to point to instances where it is less pronounced, this shift needs to be noted in any "positive" description of what states are doing in contemporary times.

In investigating this shift as a question of state form, we distance ourselves both from liberal outrage at the upsetting of balanced powers and its grotesque inversion in celebratory authoritarianism or bear-baiting accusations such as the charge of "judicial activism" that emerges when courts attempt to curb executive prerogative. Instances of the latter point abound, from Italy to Brazil, to mention just two cases. The question for us is how these changes relate to the operations of capital, and this means interrogating not the relation between national markets and individual states, but, as Bob Jessop put it in a recent interview, "the relation between the *Weltmarkt* (world market) and *Staatenwelt* (world of states)" (Flohr and Harrison 2016, 309). Notions such as the "transnational network state" (Demirović 2011) and the "global state" (Ricciardi 2013) point in the same direction. At stake here are not only the differences among states or the different figures they assume but also, as Jessop puts it, the need to analyze "how *variegation* in the world of states relates to the possibilities of capital accumulation on a world scale" (Flohr and Harrison 2016, 309). In this regard power differentials among states remain as important as interdependencies—such as the economic and financial links between the United States and China that we discussed in chapter 1. Although variegated capitalism also works off differences that exist above and below the level of the state, as well as off relations between states and non-state institutions, Jessop's approach is useful for thinking about what states are doing in the contemporary world. His observation registers both how states provide opportunities for capital to pursue its interests across different territories, spaces, and scales, and how, in turn, this pursuit rearranges state actions and forms. The role of the state in organizing its own incapacity to resist pressures exerted by the operations of capital is certainly a factor here and must register prominently in any account of what states are doing. The example of Greece looms large in this regard, particularly considering how, in July 2015, the country's government and Parliament were forced by the "institutions" of the troika to pass austerity measures that directly flouted the will of the people as expressed in a referendum result that had mobilized around political energies and enthusiasm in and beyond Greece. But it is also important to note that a limited number of states, primarily the United States and the United Kingdom, are producing "the design for the new standards and legalities needed to ensure protections and guarantees for global firms and markets" (Sassen 2007, 55). These standards and legalities, in turn, are "produced through the particular institutional and political structures of other states" (Sassen 2007, 55) within the framework of a general transformation of the meaning of "rule of law," which is increasingly reduced to the protection and implementation of "market rights" (Mattei and Nader 2008). This dynamic by which the world market mandates and relies for its own generation on protocols that are mediated by the uneven relations, policy transfers, and power expressions that compose the contemporary Staatenwelt is crucial to understanding the role of the state today.

A simple and inadequate way to explain what states are doing today is thus to say that they are doing what other states are doing. In stating this, we are only partially joking, since mimetic behavior has long been a feature of how states have organized their policy and political environments. Think about the historical spread of the welfare state policies from Otto von Bismarck's German Reich; the circulation of knowledge and technologies of domination and exploitation through "colonial conferences" in the late nineteenth century; and the prevalence of planning across the post–World War II socialist, developmental, and welfare states, which we discussed in chapter 3. Today, the movement of policies around the world is a much quicker affair, involving a complex array of actors, the development of best practice models, compressed times for design and experimentation, and increased referencing among sites. In our previous writings on migration and borders, we joined several other scholars in demonstrating how these trends are powerfully reshaping one of the essential sovereign "competences" that states still claim in the most jealous way—that is, the control of borders (see Mezzadra and Neilson 2013a, chap. 6). The literature on the "migration industry" further contributes to these analyses, shedding light on the roles played by a variety of commercial actors within the heterogeneous assemblage of power that facilitates, controls, and limits mobility across borders (see, e.g., Gammeltoft-Hansen and Nyberg Sørensen

2013). "Migration management" is more generally a crucial field for the investigation of processes of outsourcing to private actors of formerly public functions, as is particularly apparent if one considers the prominence of a panoply of agencies and brokers in the intermediation of labor migration in such diverse sites as China, Indonesia, and Germany (see Altenried et al. 2017; Lindquist and Xiang 2014).

In *Fast Policy* (2015), Jamie Peck and Nick Theodore take a different although no less important approach by following policy diffusion networks linked to the spread of conditional cash transfers and participatory budgeting models. Both of these policy currents find their origins in the global South—the former in Mexico, and the latter in Porto Alegre, Brazil—but are now encountered all over the world. Peck and Theodore (2015, 223) emphasize that "fast policy cannot be reduced to some measurement of the elapsed time between the occurrence of a policy at site A and its emulation at site B." Rather, they study the "inescapably social nature of those *continuous* processes of translation, intermediation, and contextualization/decontextualization/recontextualization, through which various forms of policy mobility are realized" (Peck and Theodore 2015, xxv). What they discover is the political malleability of policy as it adapts to various polity conditions. In its Brazilian context, for instance, participatory budgeting—a process by which community members contribute to decisions about how to allocate part of a public budget—was envisioned as a way to reclaim and repurpose the state while augmenting the capacities of social movements. When it traveled to cities in the United States, United Kingdom, and Canada, it became more about "customer satisfaction" and the augmentation of a "consultative approach consistent with the drive to reduce the scope of the state through the mechanisms of accountability, austerity, and restraint" (Peck and Theodore 2015, 216). Conditional cash transfers—where cash payments are paid to poor households on the basis of certain conditions being met (e.g., school attendance, health checkups)—have also had a politically ambiguous trajectory. Some see in them the potential for the transcendence of neoliberal forms of governance (see, notably, the account of the South African experience in Ferguson 2015), while others approach them as a means for achieving the financialization of poverty (see Lavinas 2013).

What interests us about the fast policy perspective is less the process of policy diffusion per se than the way in which Peck and Theodore understand it as a form of "experimental statecraft" at the "thresholds of neoliberalism" (a phrase present in the subtitle of their book but not developed at all in their analysis). The statecraft at stake might equally be conceptualized as a form of extrastatecraft (to recall the term from Easterling 2014), given the various non-state agencies, experts, and networks involved in such diffusion. More important, the placement of this statecraft at the thresholds of neoliberalism chimes with our analysis of the frontiers of capital and the dynamics of inclusion and exclusion that are always at stake when capital hits the ground. Whether these dynamics are analyzed with respect to the processes of differential inclusion at work in border politics or in relation to what Sassen (2014, 211) calls the "systemic edge" of capital's expansion—which involves tensions between "incorporation" and "expulsion" (for a discussion, see Mezzadra and Neilson 2015)—matters less, in our estimation, than its implications for an analysis of the contemporary state's role in the reproduction of labor power and the representation of aggregate capital. In chapter 3, we argued that the state's role in both of these respects has been fractured, and an analysis of the contemporary state needs to take into account how operations of capital today coalesce and interact with one another in ways that parallel, rival, and act in partnership with state powers. The rise of public-private partnerships as a governance model is one register of how this process is being actively reshaped. This is not the occasion to catalogue the myriad forms that such partnerships have assumed or the domains in which they have operated (from border control to the making of infrastructure and smart city initiatives). Nor do we seek empirical confirmation for the scandal that everyone knows to be true of these arrangements: that they allocate risk to the public and profit to the private. Rather, we are interested in public-private partnerships as indices of changes to the state form that reach well beyond questions of monetary flow and organizational structure.

Consider an example: the issuance by African states such as Nigeria, Kenya, and South Africa of electronic identity cards in partnership with Mastercard. Apart from serving for regular purposes of personal and official identification, these biometric cards enroll the body as a site of authentication for access to money and credit through Mastercard's payment systems. Such initiatives are thus celebrated as efforts of "financial inclusion," which incorporate subjects who are otherwise excluded from the global financial system into its circuits (see Cobbett 2015). Part of their purpose is to execute conditional cash transfers of the type discussed by Peck and Theodore (2015), but by outsourcing the management of public funds to a global financial services company, these states also create new relationships between the body of their populations and the operations of finance. Certainly, there are precedents in initiatives such as the establishment of privately administered biobanks for the storage of genetic information extracted from the populations of countries such as Estonia and Iceland (Gottweis and Petersen 2008). The use of biometric data to monitor and control electronic payments is also a technique employed by non-state agencies, as illustrated by the United Nations High Commissioner for Refugees' EyeCloud system, which facilitates direct cash payments to refugees (Lee 2016). But the partnership that merges the state identity card with the credit card poses a series of data-protection and sovereignty issues that involve a meshing of capital's financial and logistical operations. Where are the biometric data stored? How are they correlated with financial data generated by use of the card? In what territory are such financial data stored? What are the jurisdictional issues regarding protection of these data? Writing about the Nigerian case, Lukman Adebisi Abdulrauf (2014) worries that private organizations involved in this initiative collect personal information "without accountability" (181) and finds that the country's legal framework allows the transfer of "personhood to the control of others, usually governments and corporations" (188). More profoundly, the state's jurisdictional reach is challenged and paralleled by the nomos of the cloud, raising questions not only about the relation between sovereignty and law but also about the slippage between legal regimes of territoriality and state territorial control. This slippage can also take more "positive" and interesting forms—as, for instance, in the "constitutional dialogues" between South African and Indian courts to impose low-cost medicine against Big Pharma's claim to property rights and copyright (see Lollini 2009).

We have discussed how logistical spaces such as zones and corridors disarticulate the territory of the state and establish global connections that have political significance in their own right, establishing operative spaces of capital that intersect and articulate to processes of formal regional integration (such as the heterogeneous ones associated with the acronyms ASEAN, APEC, EU, and NAFTA) but also exceed them. The example of the Port of Piraeus in Greece, mentioned in chapter 2, is instructive in this regard, since the granting of a concession to operate the port to a subsidiary of the Chinese state-owned enterprise Cosco not only is mandated by the powers of the troika that exercises control over Greece's economic sovereignty but has also allowed the development of a strategic node in the Chinese program of global logistical and infrastructural expansion known as the Belt and Road Initiative (see Hatzopoulos et al. 2014). Whether one reads this China-led globalization as the party state's debt-funded response to economic crisis, the establishment of a new Bandung allowing coopera-

tion among states from the global South, or the extension of a new mercantilist ethos, it suggests a changing role for the state within processes
of regional integration, shifting patterns of trade, and strategic alignments
of economic and political power (Neilson et al. 2018; for the reference to
a "new Bandung" see, e.g., Paik 2016). At stake is nothing less than a reorientation of the Staatenwelt in relation to changes in the workings of
the world market. It would be possible to offer further examples of what
states are doing in this regard. The delegation of the state's monopoly on
violence to private military and security companies, for instance, provides
another mechanism by which state powers cede the possibility to control
or regulate the nexus of capital and politics. The existence of nonbinding
norms, such as the Montreux Document, which provides standards and best
practices for the activities of these companies (Cockayne 2008), testifies to
the presence of a layer of governance that seeks to step in or compensate
for the state's abdication of one of its characteristic modern powers. In this
instance, as in the others discussed earlier, it is important to affirm that
what is at play is not a waning of the state or its powers but a reorganization of the way in which states compose the world of politics in the face of
capital's operations.

What we witness is a melding, tension, and consonance between state
and capital that in many ways has historical precedents in the workings of
the chartered companies we examined in chapter 3. Reckoning with these
transformations means not only reassessing the state's ability to reproduce
labor power and represent aggregate capital but also assessing its capacity
to provide a front of resistance and regulation in struggles against capitalism. We do not disavow, as we further show later, the prospect that the
state can be "occupied" for a politics of transformation or that some of its
structures can be mobilized for anti-capitalist politics. It should be clear
that we do not offer a reactive state phobia or seek to romanticize the position of social movements that pit themselves, sometimes hopelessly and at
other times effectively, against both state and capital. Rather, in keeping
with our ambition to offer a realistic analysis of what states are doing today,
we extend a line of argument established in an earlier article: that "the
state is not powerful enough to confront contemporary capitalism; in order
to reopen politically a perspective of radical transformation, something
else, *a different source of power*, is absolutely necessary" (Mezzadra and
Neilson 2014, 787). In the next section, we explore the need for the making
of "a 'collective power' and 'institutions' outside (although not necessarily
against) the state as the condition even for a project of transformation that

aims at using the state" (Mezzadra and Neilson 2014, 787). We then close the book by asking how *a different source of power* for opposing capitalism might be conceived and practiced, a task that requires us to revisit the political meanings and potential of the concept of operations.

The State as a Field of Struggle

While an emphasis on its unity, as we have often remarked, has always characterized debates on the modern state, there is no shortage of arguments that point to the existence of more or less pronounced or even structural contradictions within its constitution. In a series of essays written before World War I, for instance, the German constitutional historian Otto Hintze ([1902] 1975; Schiera 1974) focused on multiple tensions and conflicts arising from the fact that the constitutional state combined its working as an apparatus of domination and command (*Herrschaft*) with the embodiment of a communitarian element (*Genossenschaft*). This very general conceptual framework has inspired important historical reconstructions, including the one by Gianfranco Poggi (1978) that we discussed in chapter 3 (see also Negri 1977). It also opens a productive angle of inquiry for the study of the multiple figures, crises, and transformations of the state in the twentieth century—for instance, in the case of the democratic welfare and social state that took shape in the West after World War II. From a theoretical point of view, a focus on contradictions, tensions, and conflicts within the state has characterized the work of a huge variety of thinkers and schools of thought. Take Pierre Bourdieu, to limit ourselves to just one important example. He understands the state as "the culmination of a process of concentration of different species of capital," ranging from "capital of physical force" to "economic capital, cultural . . . and symbolic capital," which leads to "the emergence of a specific, properly statist capital." This results in the "construction of a field of power, defined as the space of play within which the holders of capital (of different species) struggle in particular for power over the state" (Bourdieu 1994, 4–5).

In Marxist debates, the name Nicos Poulantzas is particularly redolent when it comes to the analysis of contradictions within the state (see, e.g., Aronowitz and Bratsis 2002; Jessop 1985). His work from the 1970s continues to inspire several scholarly and political debates, which affirm, for instance, his emphasis on the need to go beyond a unilateral focus on repression in the study of the state, a point that Poulantzas shares with Michel

Foucault, notwithstanding his bitter criticism of Foucault (see Hall 1980). Combining his reading of Antonio Gramsci and the notion of "ideological apparatuses" forged by Louis Althusser (2008), Poulantzas insists on the strategic relevance of hegemonic struggle (see, e.g., Poulantzas 2008, 182–85)—an argument that nowadays echoes across heterogeneous landscapes of political action and elaboration, from Latin America to Spain. More important for the analysis we pursue in this chapter is Poulantzas's emphasis on "the primacy of struggles over the state," since struggles (which means primarily but not exclusively class struggles) *constitute* the state while constantly going beyond its "apparatuses and institutions" (Poulantzas 1980, 45). Famously defined as "the material condensation" of a "relationship of forces" among "classes and class fractions" (Poulantzas 1980, 128), the state, in Poulantzas's view, is structurally traversed by "popular struggles," which bear on "its strategic field without necessarily being 'integrated' into the power of the dominant classes" (Poulantzas 1980, 151).

We are not interested here in rehearsing a criticism of Poulantzas's notion of the "relative autonomy" of the state and its political translation into a proposal for a "democratic road to socialism" in the 1970s (see Negri, in Hardt and Negri 1994, 148–50). Instead, we want to extrapolate from his writings the conceptual image of the state as a field of struggle, which also figures in the title of an important book published in 2010 by the Bolivian Comuna collective (see García Linera et al. 2010). Definitely one of the most important theoretical and political experiences in Latin America over recent years, Comuna has been very influential in Bolivian debates since the early 2000s, combining heterogeneous influences in an original way— from several strands of Latin American critical, Indigenous, and revolutionary thinking to the sociology of Pierre Bourdieu and autonomist Marxism (see Stefanoni 2015). Amazing reconstructions of recent Indigenous and social mobilizations and uprisings in Bolivia, such as the one provided by Raquel Gutiérrez Aguilar (2014), emerged against the background of this collective endeavor. The book *El estado: Campo de lucha* (The State: A Field of Struggle; García Linera et al. 2010) can be considered one of Comuna's final outcomes, as political developments in Bolivia (including such conflicts as the one surrounding road building in the Isiboro Sécure National Park and Indigenous Territory that we discussed in the previous chapter) successively led to the dissolution of the collective and to bitter polemics about the role of that country's Vice-President Álvaro García Linera, one of the founding members of Comuna. *El estado: Campo de lucha* can also be read for this reason as an important instance of the intense and theoretically sophisticated debates that shaped the long decade of so-called progressive governments in Latin America from the early 2000s. It is important to emphasize that within these heterogeneous and complex experiences (which include instances as diverse as Chavism in Venezuela, Lula's governments in Brazil, Kirchnerism in Argentina, and the Frente Amplio [Broad Front] in Uruguay), the state has *actually* been a field of struggle, with results that deserve much more detailed scrutiny than we can offer here.

García Linera squarely poses the issue at the center of his reflections as the question of "the state in times of transition" (García Linera et al. 2010, 7). By doing so he clearly harks back to older Marxist debates, but at the same time he addresses the main problem looming behind much more recent political developments and disputes about the state in Latin America and elsewhere. Just think of the Greek experience over the past few years (and particularly during the first government led by Syriza [the Coalition of the Radical Left], from January 2015 until the "deal" with the creditors on July 13 of the same year), or of the lively discussions that have surrounded the rise of the Podemos political party in Spain since 2013. With an abundance of references to Latin American experiences (above all in Spain, while in Greece Poulantzas's writings have often been invoked), these European instances have also raised vexed questions regarding the role of the state in processes of social, and even socialist, transformation under completely new conditions. Not surprisingly, the alternative between reform and revolution, which is strictly connected to Marxist discussions of the state, has also been rehearsed. We must confess that we do not find this alternative, with the reciprocal accusations of "betrayal" and "infantile disorder" it necessarily entails, particularly inspiring. We are more interested in analyses that stress, even within a theoretical framework very different from ours, the need to investigate the current predicament of socialist politics, connecting it to the crisis of the labor movement we discussed in chapter 5 (see, e.g., Honneth 2017, 40–41). There is a need to historicize the very juxtaposition between reform and revolution within the history of the international labor movement. We tend to agree with David Harvey, who recently advocated a reshuffling of the cards and the forging of an agenda of substantial radical reforms that "can become the cutting edge for revolutionary transformation" (Harvey 2014, 181). Interestingly, this position echoes the one articulated by Rosa Luxemburg in 1899, at the heyday of the historical debate on "revisionism" (see Luxemburg 2004, 129), as part of what she once called *revolutionäre Realpolitik*, or "revolutionary political realism" (Haug 2009).

Needless to say, this is just a hint at a political project and practice haunted by severe difficulties and pitfalls. Harvey himself speaks of the predicament of having to choose "between an impossible reform and an improbable revolution" (Harvey 2014, 130). The very notion of reform has been successfully appropriated by neoliberalism, as it is painfully clear in a country such as Greece. The various and politically heterogeneous attempts to reformulate a Keynesian framework for a consistent reformist politics (taking the notion of Keynesianism in a very wide and even loose sense to include the works of such diverse thinkers as Paul Krugman (2009), Thomas Piketty (2014), Joseph Stiglitz (2015), and Yanis Varoufakis (2016) face an economic, social, and political environment so radically transformed that old recipes need to be completely rethought, a task that actually may seem to verge on the impossible (see, e.g., De Nicola and Quattrocchi 2016; Marazzi 2010). "Taming" and "embedding" the extractive operations of capital, particularly as far as financial capital is concerned, requires a huge amount of political experimentation—and, above all, a huge number of struggles to make such experimentation effective and even possible. From this point of view, it is worth briefly coming back to Latin America. As in Greece and in Spain, in Latin America it was a formidable cycle of struggles—concatenating at the regional scale and often taking on an insurrectional character (e.g., in Ecuador following the Indigenous *levantamiento* [uprising] in 1990; in Bolivia, in 2000 and 2003; and in Argentina, in 2001)—that declared the end of the Washington Consensus and opened up the political space for the new progressive governments (see Mezzadra and Sztulwark 2015; on the uprising in Argentina specifically, see Colectivo Situaciones 2011). What resulted from this opening and "destitution" (or dismantling of existing political arrangements and depriving their foundations of power and legitimacy) were constituent processes, which in several cases (including Bolivia) led to innovative new constitutions (see, e.g., Clavero 2012; Gargarella 2015; Nolte and Schilling-Vacaflor 2012) but were concretely tangible even in countries such as Brazil and Argentina, where no new constitutions were issued. Powerful challenges to entrenched structures of racism and exclusion of the poor were raised both by the continued action of social movements and struggles and in many cases—although in different and often contradictory ways—by progressive governments.

Much discussion about the relations between social movements and the new governments in Latin America has revolved around a choice between confrontation and cooptation (Prevost et al. 2012). While this descriptively grasps some of the processes and stakes in Latin American politics of recent years, we do not find the confrontation-cooptation binary to be particularly politically enabling (Gago and Mezzadra 2017b; see also Brighenti and Mezzadra 2012). The autonomy of social movements has continued to express itself in many Latin American countries following the emergence of progressive governments, nurturing experiences that, at least in some cases, have taken the form of real counterpowers. The novelty of social policies, particularly in the first phase of many Latin American progressive governments, lay precisely in an attempt to root those policies within a field of tension between the action of the state and new forms of social mobilization and struggle. This is a very important question that, for us, displaces the simple binary of confrontation and cooptation. It also points to the need to reframe the whole question of the relations among governments, struggles, and movements, going beyond the prevailing model of a linear translation of movements' claims and demands into the construction of or actions by governments.

Such a crucial challenge certainly does not apply only to Latin American experiences, although these experiences enable us to materially instantiate and politically qualify the difficulties at hand. There are many factors behind the multiple crises and defeats of progressive governments in Latin America over the past few years, including the underestimation of the effects of the global economic crisis, which was initially perceived simply as an "opportunity" (see, e.g., Piqué 2008). It is no surprise, given the high degree of integration within the global market we mentioned in chapter 4 when discussing the critical notion of neo-extractivism (see also Cocco and Negri 2006), that the variegated mutations of the crisis eventually hit countries such as Argentina and Brazil. Moreover neo-developmentalism and the politics of social inclusion—the hallmarks of progressive governments— did not take into serious consideration the persistence and the constitutive role of processes of financialization (see Gago and Sztulwark 2016). Under these conditions, the weakening of efforts toward regional integration (which were particularly important in the 2000s) was a serious problem for national progressive governments. While processes of social transformation came increasingly to be centered on the state, the most original features of government action were also weakened, and the source of the state's power was steadily drained.

There is no need for us to discuss here the important work of Ernesto Laclau, which continues to be a significant reference in Latin American (as well as in Spanish) political debates (see Mezzadra and Neilson 2013a,

284–91). Nor can we dwell on other important aspects of the current crisis of progressive governments, which has led many commentators to speak of the end of their political cycle—including the role played by new forms of popular consumption and by the new middle classes that progressive policies of redistribution helped to create. Rather, it is important to note that Latin America in recent years has also witnessed processes of fracturing and disarticulation of the unity of the state (see Gago et al. 2014), which take extreme forms in the "dualization" of the state and in the emergence in many countries of a kind of "second state" connected to rentier dynamics; undeclared and illegal operations of capital; and old and new forms of patriarchy (Segato 2016). In her analysis of "femicides" in Ciudad Juárez, the anthropologist Rita Laura Segato undertakes a breathtaking investigation of the mutations of the structural nexus between sovereignty and violence in Mexico, where a "second," or "parallel" state (Segato 2013, 42–43) enters multiple relations with criminal actors to manage processes of securitization through the spread of fear. A specific form of "expressive violence" (which Segato [2013, 21–22] carefully distinguishes from "instrumental violence" because it aims to produce and express the effectiveness of implicit rules), inscribes itself onto women's bodies, reproducing and at the same time brutally altering the patriarchal norm historically connected with the state. If one thinks of the multiple roles played by this parallel state in the management of transit migration across what critical scholars and activists in Mexico call the "vertical border" (Aquino et al. 2012; Varela, forthcoming), it is possible to understand why a notion such as necropolitics (Mbembe 2003) continues to spark lively debates in that country (see, e.g., Fuentes Díaz 2012).

It is important to keep in mind such instances in which extreme violence is intertwined with state apparatuses. Far from being limited to Mexico, they multiply elsewhere in Latin America and the world, giving rise to new forms of social conflict and to peculiar and terrifying forms of private-public partnership. While such forms of governmental violence tend to produce their own territories and thus deserve careful investigation from the theoretical angle of the disarticulation of the state's unity, this disarticulation also takes on different and more promising shapes. Struggles for the right to the city, of which we gave some examples in chapter 5, are taking metropolitan territories in many parts of the world as a privileged scale of political action. While they confront the urban roots of the capitalist crisis, such struggles for urban commons often work within and against a set of processes that, as emphasized from the time of sociological debates on global cities in the early 1990s, tend to extrapolate metropolitan territories from national frameworks and to connect them into wider assemblages of power and production. Needless to say, this has completely different implications and potentialities in different cities. Nonetheless, "rebel cities" (Harvey 2012) proliferate across diverse geographical scales. Such a label circulates widely in Europe, where, particularly in the wake of the election of Ada Colau (a prominent figure within the Plataforma de Afectados por la Hipoteca, the transversal social union for housing rights we analyzed in the previous chapter) as mayor of Barcelona in May 2015, there is a lively debate on the prospects for a new municipalism. What is important to observe is that this debate (and the related political experiences, which are not limited to Barcelona but include other cities, from Madrid to Naples) registers a situation in which, within the framework of European crisis management over the past few years, cities have been steadily deprived of powers and budgetary autonomy (see Caccia 2016).

These debates and experiences are undoubtedly interesting and inspiring. Far from providing a model or pointing at an exclusive field of struggle and political experimentation, they are for us part of a more general and articulated collective effort to forge a politics of radical social transformation capable of effectively confronting the extractive operations of contemporary capital. We do not deny that the state can play a role, in specific and grounded situations, within this effort. Even a discredited concept such as planning deserves new consideration—for instance, in initiatives that strive to meet the challenges of the ecological crisis, as Naomi Klein (2014) contends. But the important experiences of Latin American progressive governments demonstrate the limits of the state—and particularly of a politics centered on the state as its privileged field and actor. We repeat once again what we wrote at the end of the previous section: it is a matter of political realism to acknowledge that, today, the state is not powerful enough to confront established and emergent formations of capitalism. From this perspective, the resurgence of "left nationalism" we are currently witnessing in many parts of the world, often connected with the invocation of some form of "left populism," appears as highly problematic. While there is no doubt that, in Spain, the use of populist rhetoric by part of Podemos initially contributed to opening new political space, taking populism as a strategic notion ends up nurturing a political imaginary that reproduces the trap of nationalism, overestimates the range of action of the state, and obscures behind the ghostly figure of a homogeneous people the powerful transformations that have reshaped the composition of living labor.

Moreover, as we suggested in chapter 2, there is a need to take stock of a long history of socialist, communist, and anticolonial politics within which the state has been conceived and practically constructed as the main actor of social transformation. Needless to say, this history is populated by a legion of "heresies"—from council communism to the multiple shades of autonomist Marxism, from the politics of autonomy within Indian anticolonialism to several instances of communal organizing in the Black Power Movement and Zapatismo, to mention just a few. These theoretical and political experiences provide a rich archive for contemporary efforts and struggles. But this does not mean that the mainstream of socialist, communist, and anticolonial politics can simply be obliterated, as is too often the case, for instance, within recent philosophical debates on communism (see Mezzadra and Neilson 2014). On the one hand, this is so because some of the problems that haunt that mainstream continue to be our problems, although under completely different conditions. On the other hand, the fact that socialism and communism were extreme instances of a politics centered on the state, with eventually questionable, if not disastrous results, in the twentieth century, and remain so in the popular imaginary in many parts of the world, requires a rigorous historical and political criticism. It is not by accident, for instance, as David Harvey (2014, 180) notes, that poll data in the United States show remarkable support for an egalitarian reform movement, "even as it demands that the state not be the vehicle to accomplish this." Combining this criticism of the legacy of past experiences and a realistic assessment of the role of the state within global capitalism, we understand the search for a communist politics today as part of a collective search for a politics of radical transformation not centered on the state (see also Gutiérrez Aguilar, in Brighenti 2013). We want to say once again that this does not mean discarding the persistence of the state and even the possibility to occupy and use it (or part of its apparatuses) for the sake of such a politics. But this can happen only within projects and practices that point at the establishment of a system of social counterpowers and, at the same time, are part and parcel of wider, transnational attempts to seize or create new political spaces.

Tintinnabulation

Do you remember those crazy days in September 2008 when the failure of Lehman Brothers spurred the collapse of Goldman Sachs and Morgan Stanley? Did you watch those ironic videos on YouTube showing bankers packing their stuff, going out to Main Street, and having to compete with Latino migrants offering their labor power to gang masters who contract daily workers for the construction sector? Did those videos offer you a kind of stamina and powerful antidote to the vexed question of "left melancholy" (Traverso 2017)? Well, they did for us. A bit of *Schadenfreude*—why not? But while this is a topic that, at least since Lucretius's *De rerum natura*, has attracted philosophical reflections, poetic and literary exercises, and, later, psychoanalytical ruminations, the tricky nature of Schadenfreude has also often been emphasized. In a book dedicated to the Lucretian founding figure of this motif, the spectator witnessing a shipwreck at sea, Hans Blumenberg (1996) has traced a line of thought—stretching from Pascal to Nietzsche—in which the security of the point of observation (i.e., the safe haven on dry land) is itself unmasked as a fraudulent illusion. We had no illusion, to be honest, in those September days. It should be clear from this book that we are quite skeptical regarding the identification and scapegoating of specific actors for the workings of capitalism and aggregate capital (although specific actors do have specific und often even lethal responsibilities and should be held accountable for them). Nevertheless, we were impressed by the way in which Goldman Sachs, clearly one of the main parties responsible for the mortgage crisis and excoriated in a famous *Rolling Stone* article as "a great vampire squid wrapped around the face of humanity" (Taibi 2010)—passed through investigations by the US Congress, Justice Department, and Securities and Exchange Commission eventually to emerge as one of the winners of the crisis. Hugely profiting from the loan facilities issued by the Federal Reserve in 2008, Goldman Sachs continues to rule the world, and its elite bankers continue to regard themselves as masters of the universe, as the saying goes.

To pick up a question we discussed in chapter 1, it is clear that in the wake of the crisis of 2007–2008, we have witnessed a further entrenchment of neoliberalism, and of the kind of extractive logics we analyzed as characteristic of contemporary operations of capital. Looking back at the past decade, one is reminded of Macbeth's words: "Tomorrow, and tomorrow, and tomorrow, / Creeps in this petty pace from day to day, / To the last syllable of recorded time" (Shakespeare [1623] 2015, 287). The entrenchment and even radicalization of neoliberalism has run parallel to its mutations and adaptations, including multiple combinations with nationalism and the politics of anxiety and fear nationalism has generated. These developments have spurred a global political cycle characterized by the rise of heterogeneous forces of the right, often verging on fascism—from Europe to Japan, from Latin America to India, from Turkey to Egypt and the United States. At the same time, the crisis continues to circulate through the conduits of the capitalist world system and has itself provided a peculiar and particularly harsh form of governmentality. In this frame, neoliberal language and policies have cast off their promissory and seductive tones, announcing a "new spirit of capitalism" (Boltanski and Chiapello 2006), and in full light have begun to deploy disciplinary and even punitive measures (see also Lazzarato 2012). In this regard, the invocation of a strong state is far from being merely rhetorical. So, to play with the title of a recent book by Pierre Dardot and Christian Laval (2016), we can ask: How do we put an end to this "nightmare that does not want to end"?

We have no plain answer to this question. But we agree with Dardot and Laval that it is misleading to reduce neoliberalism to a set of doctrines or even economic policies. Confronting neoliberalism means confronting the extractive logics of contemporary operations of capital that loom behind it. It also means taking seriously neoliberalism's rooting in the social fabric of life—as signaled by Verónica Gago's (2017) notion of "neoliberalism from below." Under these conditions, we have argued, a politics of radical transformation cannot be centered on the state. While there is a need to occupy, imagine, and invent new political spaces beyond the nation, it is also necessary to work toward the building of a system of counterpowers that can confront neoliberalism and operations of capital at the level of daily life. In the history of the communist movement, dualism of power has always been conceived of as a transitory situation, to be overcome through revolutionary rupture (Guastini 1978; Zavaleta Mercado 1974). In April 1917, in the peculiar Russian situation of war and revolution, Lenin spoke about a "dual power," referring to the existence, "alongside the Provisional government, the government of *bourgeoisie*," of "*another government*"—that of the "Soviets of Workers and Soldiers' Deputies" (Lenin [1917] 1999). His political wager, which was quite successful, at least at first, was to wait for the occasion to *overthrow* the provisional government and then to establish the dictatorship of the Soviets. Independently of how one retrospectively considers the history of the regime that emerged out of the October Revolution, what is needed today is something quite different: a rethinking of the problematic of dual power in terms of a stable political framework that is capable of articulating a political dynamics of struggle, transformation, and government through the establishment of a stable system of counterpowers.

This means reflecting on and reinventing the soviet, well beyond its instantiation in the October Revolution and its mutations in the following years in Russia, as an institution of self-organization and self-government while rethinking its relations with formal political institutions (see Hardt and Mezzadra 2017). The global history of social and political struggles in the twentieth century and up to the present provides a rich and heterogeneous archive of experiences analogous to the organization of soviets, most often without any reference to the October Revolution. From communal forms of peasant and Indigenous organization to workers' councils, from neighborhood assemblies in Argentina in the wake of the uprising of 2001 to the exercise of territorial counterpower by the Black Panthers in the United States or by the autonomous movement in Italy, we can see how the "spirit of the soviet" has remained alive and traveled across the globe in various mutations. Furthermore, the movements that seized and occupied the squares of major cities in several countries from 2011 to 2013 presented powerful though incipient instantiations of the soviet under contemporary conditions (see Hardt and Negri 2017). Many of these movements have now taken the form of metropolitan assemblies in which widely heterogeneous sets of social subjects gather to deliberate and forge institutions of self-government on the basis of social cooperation and struggle against dispossession and exploitation. Thus far, these assemblies have not risen to the level of dual power, as their critics and their participants will quickly affirm. Key, however, is the fact that these experiences have gone beyond the level of protest and resistance against the dominant power structure to create, even if only briefly, an autonomous counterpower. The potential articulation of such counterpowers alludes to the potential of a strategy of dual power.

This potential becomes apparent once the various axes of social struggle today and the problem of the temporal duration of their effects are considered from the angle of a theory of organization. A relatively stable political framework that articulates dynamics of struggle, transformation, and governance, establishing a lasting assemblage of counterpowers, may indeed be the most effective means of strengthening the existing movements. Moreover, a rethinking of dual power along the lines we are suggesting tackles the question of the state without ignoring the powerful transformations that have altered its structure and even challenged its institutional unity. The dualism of power that we have in mind thus requires a notion of governance that is rooted within a fabric of counterpowers from which it draws its force without putting into question their autonomy. It aims at politicizing social cooperation through institutions that are capable of organizing struggles, enabling their confluence and mutual empowerment, and foreshadowing different forms of life that combine social and economic emancipation with political liberation, as was originally the case for the institution of the soviet (see Negri 2017).

It should be clear that when we write about dual power, the two powers in question are not, and cannot be, homologous. Even when the state is seized by political forces engaged in a project of radical transformation, as we discussed in the case of Latin American progressive governments, the wide array of political forms and institutions that compose the "second" power must retain their autonomy and continue to work according to logics different from the ones permeating the ruling institutions—from representation to bureaucracy. This difference is key to the political productivity of the dualism of power, which allows it to be considered "a thoroughly expansive political form," to quote Marx's description of the Paris Commune, which, in his assessment, was different from "all the previous forms of government [that] had been emphatically repressive" (Marx 1988, 60). We think of the development, rooting, and entrenchment of a second power, instituted through struggles and social mobilization, as the crucial political element that can make a political form "expansive," holding in check the repressive aspects of established state institutions. But far from being limited to this control function, this second power plays a leading role in developing the strategy, as well as in prompting and deepening the process, of social transformation.

Such a political framework needs to come to grips with the continued presence of the state and the international system of states without conceiving this presence as the sole horizon of political struggle. Indeed, a dual-power approach allows for radical contestation of state institutions (and their entanglement with the operations of capital) even as it implies making demands of these same institutions or even redirecting their resources to oppositional ends. At the same time, it requires the building of self-organized or autonomous institutions and infrastructures outside and beyond the state from which the project of fabricating the common can begin. Such an approach, however, cannot constitute a retreat of struggles to the local—as much as strategies of occupation, encampment, social unionism, or even new municipalism can provide credible bases on which to build counterpower. It also requires grappling with the difficulties of building coalitional ties beyond national and local frames to reach, translate, and politically act across and against the variegated landscapes of contemporary capitalism. There should be no delusions as to the difficulty of this task, but such a strategy is the only one we see as viable in the face of competing proposals—for example, the "let it rip" attitude of acceleration-ism or the quietude of postcapitalist economic experiments, which labor under the hope of reaching an eventual tipping point where capital begins to crumble without ever having been subjected to a direct political chal-lenge. At stake for us is nothing less than a reframing of the political. This means not only reconceiving the political outside the frame of established or constituted power but also moving away from a viewpoint that automati-cally and unreflexively celebrates the resistance, the destitution of power—or, for that matter, the constituent power of insurrectionary movements. Believe us: we have experienced enough episodes of backbiting, trolling, baiting, accusation, and *ressentiment* in activist circles to know they are no more free of antipathy and protagonism than official state institutions. But our argument is not driven by such petty episodes. Rather, by rethinking the political in the conceptual and practical frame of operations, we seek to derive a politics capable of effectively opposing capital at a time that its operations tend to mask its unity and remove its aggregate effects from the institutional scaffolding of the state.

A politics of operations is necessarily involved in the world. When we write about the devastating effects of capital hitting the ground, we are conscious that the politics of capital's operations is necessarily messed up with dirt, extraction, and exploitation. A rethinking of politics with respect to operations cannot maintain the fantasy of "pure politics"—to recall a phrase introduced by Slavoj Žižek (2006, 55–56)—removed from the materiality of operations or enjoying the perch on the high moral ground. Politics in this regard cannot be separated from economy—or, for that matter, from culture and society. This is a perspective that makes sense once the material practices and struggles of those subjects who produce the world and its tissues of being are taken into account. As much as a politics of operations draws attention to the ways in which capital rearranges social relations on the ground, it also highlights how collective projects of libera-tion are played out on this same ground, where the world is fabricated and life is endured and enjoyed. The connection between operations and sub-jectivity emerges in this nexus.

In chapter 2, we briefly discussed the perspective that understands sub-jectivity as the "real abstraction" at the center of contemporary capitalist production. This viewpoint corresponds with an emphasis on the double genitive in the phrase "production of subjectivity," registering at once the "constitution of subjectivity" within and against capitalism and "the pro-ductive power of subjectivity, its capacity to produce wealth" (Read 2003,

102). The concept of operations allows us to add something more. For a start, it provides a way to chart the relations between subjectivity as produced with respect to the multiple operations that compose capitalism and the emergence of subjectivity in and through specific operations of capital. This gives us another axis along which to analyze the production of subjectivity, aside from the tug of subjection and subjectivation emphasized by Foucault (2014; for a useful collection of essays on this tension, see Cremonesi et al. 2016). In addition, it allows us to extend an analysis of a particular dimension of the production of subjectivity—that which Félix Guattari (1995, 2) identifies with "machinic productions of subjectivity." Although Guattari has in mind the production of subjectivity through computing, data banks, media, and other "non-human pre-personal" elements, he emphasizes how these transformations open possibilities of "heterogenesis" (9), which are "multi-componential" and have a "collective character" (24). Our analysis crosses this approach but adds caution around the way in which contemporary capitalism can make such heterogenesis into a device of extraction—for instance, through the action and work of subjects who recursively generate data sets through which they come to be known, governed, and exploited. This is one reason that we have reservations about a politics that seeks its subject in the citizen, as if the dynamics of differentiation, inclusion, and exclusion that shape this figure were sufficient to offset their own entanglement with the operations of capital. It is equally why we find the figure of the waged worker, whose contractual "freedom" is vouchsafed by a presumed coincidence between the unity of capital and the unity of the state, incapable of furnishing a subject who can politically contrast the differential workings and specific interventions of capital today. We continue to think that the debates around class and multitude offer a more fertile ground on which to discern and produce a political subject adequate to the times.

Our emphasis on operations flies in the face of a powerful and erudite line of analysis that finds political possibility in the deactivation of operative forms of power or an ontologically prior "inoperativity" (see, e.g., Agamben 2014). This is not the occasion to rehearse a full critique of this approach, its celebration of a potentiality that does not issue in action, or its theological derivation from the works of Paul of Tarsus (although see Neilson 2004). Suffice it to say that the concept of inoperativity, in its etymology but also in its philosophical elaboration, rests on the notion of operations. Not accidentally does Giorgio Agamben write that "inoperativity does not mean inertia, but names *an operation* that deactivates and renders works (of economy, of religion, of language, etc.) inoperative" (Agamben 2014, 69, emphasis added). The recognition that inoperativity can "be deployed only through a work," that it manifests itself as an "inoperative operation" (70), is surely sufficient to register the ontological relations at stake. The maneuvers Agamben makes to wrestle the priority of the inoperative from this paradoxical or chiasmatic arrangement are worthy of a circus contortionist. But whatever the virtuosity on display, his efforts "to define the truly human activity" (69) do not encompass a wide investigation of what operations can do (both within and beyond the realm of human action). This is surprising for a thinker who has engaged closely with the work of Hannah Arendt, who, in elaborating her famous distinction between work and labor, was well aware of the etymological nexus surrounding the Latin opus. It is worth probing the nuances and implications of this distinction further, since they have important consequences for our understanding of operations.

In *The Human Condition* (1998), Arendt relates labor to the life or biologically necessitated dimensions of human metabolism and reproduction. By contrast, "work" is inherently connected with the fabrication of an "'artificial' world of things" that endures beyond the act of creation (Arendt 1998, 7). While Arendt associates the rise of industrial modernity with the encroachment of labor on work and its consequent effects of alienation, we register the continuing role of the operation in the global present. For us, an operation is connected with the fabrication of an artificial world but does not necessarily produce a "work" or material "thing." In our understanding—and this is important when it comes to operations of capital—an operation produces a set of links or relations among things, or the framework or skeleton of a world. The term "operation," then, refers to the fabrication of the world; to the production of the connections, chains, and networks that materially envelop the planet, enabling and framing the labor and action of subjects well beyond those directly involved in the execution of the operation itself. What the operations of contemporary capital reveal is a blurring of the boundary between labor and work, which is to say that labor has become increasingly implicated in making the rules, parameters, protocols, standards, infrastructures, and codes that constitute the world. At the same time, we have to recognize that some of the key features of "action," the third concept discussed by Arendt, play an important role in the operations of capital, making them politically pregnant. In other words, these operations increasingly confront the elusiveness, plurality, and unpredictability of the "human condition," which for Arendt constituted the domain of action (see also Virno 2004, 49–71). It thus makes sense to speak of a politics of operations, taking into account both its structuring effect on relations among humans and the ways in which work, labor, and action are combined in the execution of specific tasks and in the social co-operation of different subjects that make operations possible.

The intertwining and blurring of boundaries among work, labor, and action is a distinguishing feature of what we might call the material constitution of contemporary operations of capital. Both in their workings and in the ways in which they hit the ground, these operations have powerful implications for the production of subjectivity, continually reframing and reinstating relations of exploitation and domination. They also work the boundary between the human and the nonhuman (the "machinic" no less than nature) in unprecedented ways. As we show in this book, these operations also challenge, limit, and incite transformations of the state, as well as a range of other political and social institutions. In the face of this material constitution of operations of capital, we must ask again the question regarding the kind of politics that can effectively confront them, opening up new prospects of liberation beyond capital's rule. Looking at contemporary theoretical debates on this question, we discern two prevailing approaches that seem to us at the same time challenging and limited. The first centers on the notion of *performativity*. Since the publication of *Gender Trouble* ([1990] 1999), Judith Butler has engaged in a rigorous and politically committed exploration of the potentialities of this concept for a radically democratic politics. As she explained in the preface to a new edition of the book in 1999, her first reference for "reading the performativity of gender" was Jacques Derrida's ([1987] 1992) work on Kafka's "Before the Law." She adds, "It is difficult to say what performativity is not only because my own views . . . have changed over time . . . but because so many others have taken it up and given it their own formulations" (Butler [1990] 1999, xiv).

Butler's *Notes toward a Performative Theory of Assembly* (2015) can be considered the provisional point of arrival of her theoretical elaborations on the topic of performativity within the framework of an engaged intervention into the debates surrounding social movements in many parts of the world since the occupation of squares in 2011. There are many points that we share and even admire in this book—for instance, Butler's take on precarity as the main motif running through a huge variety of movements (Butler 2015, 17). At the same time, we take a sympathetic distance from her claim of a primacy of ethics over politics (see, e.g., Butler 2015, 192, on non-violence). While we acknowledge the relevance of Butler's reflections on "the interdependency of living creatures," as well as on the ensuing "ethical and political obligations" (Butler 2015, 208), and recognize that the notion of performativity can definitely shed light on important political moments and dynamics, we think that it is unable to adequately grasp and effectively confront the radical challenges posed by contemporary operations of capital. This is so because the performative, by definition, is self-contained, even if its affective and embodied dimensions can trouble this containment. The performative is self-referring—which is to say that it constitutes that which it enunciates. The politics of performativity can thus be very effective in describing and theoretically understanding the dynamics at stake in processes of collective subject formation, as Butler shows in her discussion of "we the people" as "an assembly in the act of designating and forming itself" (Butler 2015, 179). But it remains silent about the ways in which this collective subject can confront its multiple outsides and others, which include both existing political institutions and what we might call, with an intentionally provocative Schmittian twist, its "enemy."

The language of enmity abundantly circulates, posing specific problems for the second approach to radical politics we want to discuss briefly here. This approach is centered on the notion of *event*. The most sophisticated philosophical version of this notion is found in the work of Alain Badiou, particularly in *Being and Event* (2005). Other important thinkers could be mentioned here, including, for instance, Jacques Rancière, who in *Disagreement* (1998) develops and invests hope in the political and the temporal primacy of the event. However, we want to focus here on a different instantiation of this primacy, which is manifest in the work of the Invisible Committee. Since the publication of *The Coming Insurrection* (2009), the Invisible Committee has combined a reading of Agamben's philosophy with heterogeneous theoretical influences, including the legacy of the Situationist International. In *To Our Friends* (Invisible Committee 2015), readers can find an attempt to take stock of the cycle of struggles and revolts since 2011 along with emphatic statements concerning the "global action of our party" (Invisible Committee 2015, 129)—although the committee is quick to add that "the only party to be built is the one that's already there" (16). There is no need to dwell critically here on the committee's political analysis of "what makes *irreversible*" the upheaval of Gezi Park in Istanbul (219) or of the "exemplary case" of Tahrir Square in Cairo (72), which looks quite questionable once the current situation in both countries is considered. Hazard is part of political theory and practice, and we have also paid a price for it in the past. What concerns us more is the politics of "*pure destitution*"

(74) articulated and proposed by the Invisible Committee. The moment of destitution, as well as other "negative" moments (negative in a descriptive sense) such as sabotage and blockade, which they emphasize in a conjuncture in which "power is logistic" (81), undoubtedly have important roles to play in specific struggles and movements. But to reduce radical and even revolutionary politics to the *event* of destitution nurtures an aesthetics— and eventually a nihilistic praise—of riots that confine the building and imagination of a different world to more or less small "communes," as well as to the multiplication of paths "leading to other communes" and connecting the "political territories" they create (229). Although the Invisible Committee is keen to stress that "the commune is not preoccupied with its self-definition," with its "identity" (204), the more general problems of "identity politics" haunt its emphasis on the meshing of the "physical" and "existential" meanings of territory of the commune (202). At the same time, the committee's celebration of riots, besides attracting the critique of "tailism" that we recalled in chapter 5, does not take into consideration the field of operations of an important fraction of contemporary aggregate capital—that is, insurance companies.

Taking a more theoretical angle, and going back to our notion of operations, we could say that the notions of performativity and event (even independently of the ways in which they are elaborated, related, stretched, used, and misused in contemporary critical and radical debates) can illuminate important aspects of the operation. "Performativity" can be taken as a good description of what we might call the operation's "trigger" and of its tendency to fabricate its own world, while "event" points at its creative capacities, at its "outcome." Without disregarding these moments, which need to be taken into account in radical political theory and practice, we stressed in chapter 2 the relevance of the uneven and broken pattering of opening and closure that is constitutive of the "interval" between the trigger and outcome of an operation. This is nothing more than an abstract, metaphorical, and heuristically useful point of view. But it allows us not only to elaborate a critique of contemporary capital's operations but also to gain a sense of the temporality, rhythm, and subjective composition of radical politics that is quite different from those projected by the notions of performativity and event. What we have in mind, and what we share with many scholars and activists in different parts of the world, is the theoretical search for and practical experimentation with a politics capable of confronting the operations of capital at the level of their encroachment on variegated fabrics of daily life. Such a politics must be effective at local sites of production, reproduction, and cooperation, opening up spaces liberated from exploitation at the same time that it builds connections, translations, and even institutions within wider geographies beyond the local and the national. It must also be capable of realistically confronting and negotiating the state's action, in its representative as well as postrepresentative logics, without ever giving up the unending task of a radical critique of representation and continuing to develop institutions of counterpower within a dual-power approach.

We want to repeat that we are aware of the difficulties and pitfalls of such a politics. But we also need to state once again that we are supported by the awareness that we are not alone in working along these lines. An extraordinary historical archive of revolutionary thought and practice, of struggles and uprisings, continues to be an essential source of inspiration. We thus close this book by conjuring subversive echoes and whispers from a distant past. In 1378 the Republic of Florence was swept by a huge proletarian revolt. The *ciompi* (cloth workers, and wool carders in particular), who were not part of the guild system and had therefore no voice in government, had been striking and demonstrating in May and June. They had shown and exercised their power on the streets of Florence. Some of the patrician palaces had gone up in flames. In July, the revolt took the form of a proper (and briefly successful) insurrection, which was bloodily repressed only at the end of August by the militias led by Michele di Lando, a former leader of the ciompi who turned against them. The insurrection thus was eventually defeated, but what is striking in a retrospective gaze is the amazing institutional creativity of the ciompi during the few months in which they actually ruled Florence. They did not limit themselves to taking control of existing institutions. They created new, autonomous ones—most notably, a self-governing organ located in the central district of Santa Maria Novella (see Lester 2015; Stella 1993).

In an article written in 1934, the young philosopher Simone Weil (who by that time had grown close to revolutionary syndicalist and Trotskyist circles) commented on the ciompi revolt. The proletariat, she noted, was not satisfied with the formal achievements it had been able to win; it continued to petition and, above all, gathered in Santa Maria Novella. "From that moment the city had two governments, one at the Palace, according to the new legality [which means the one established by the revolt], the other, not legal, in Santa Maria Novella," she wrote. "This extralegal government curiously resembles a soviet; and for some time we see the emergence, through the action of a newly formed proletariat, of the essential phenomenon of great workers' insurrections—dualism of power" (Weil [1934] 1960, 90–91; see also Lester 2015, 156–57). The ciompi revolt was not a marginal episode in the history of modern capitalism, since it happened at an important conjuncture of early financialization, characterized by pioneering technical innovations in the banking system (such as *contratti di cambio*; bills of exchange) that enabled the House of Medici to become "the leading organization in European high finance" (Arrighi 1994, 105). The revolt took place in the middle of this conjuncture, within which financialization meshed with massive investments of Florentine surplus capital to fund "warfare in the Italian inter-city-system and in the European world-economy at large" (Arrighi 1994, 105). The predicament and impoverishment of the ciompi that brought about the revolt was part of these powerful shifts within capitalism, which rapidly led to declining returns in the production of coarser cloth in which they were employed. As Giovanni Arrighi notes, this early episode in modern class struggle and the defeat of the ciompi point to a problem that would recur in the following centuries—that is, to "the fact that capital was endowed with a much greater flexibility and mobility than its opponents" (Arrighi 1994, 104). Taking note of this important observation, we also want to stress, in a more positive sense, the institutional creativity of the Florentine proletariat that led to the anticipation of "dualism of power" described by Weil.

Although in his *Istorie fiorentine* he celebrated the repression of the ciompi and the figure of Michele di Lando, we owe to Niccolò Machiavelli the realistic invention of a talk by one of the leaders of the ciompi, an extraordinary manifesto of proletarian class struggle at the dawn of capitalism. This speech has attracted the attention of several critical and radical thinkers, from Max Horkheimer (1930) to Michael Hardt and Antonio Negri (2009, 52). Machiavelli's anonymous rebel says, "Be not deceived about that antiquity of blood by which they [the noble and the rich] exalt themselves above us; for all men having had one common origin, are all equally ancient, and nature has made us all after one fashion. Strip us naked, and we shall all be found alike. Dress us in their clothing, and they in ours, we shall appear noble, they ignoble—for poverty and riches make all the difference" (Machiavelli 1988, 122–23). This powerful claim to a radical equality crosses the centuries and continues to echo in our present. It resonates wherever the poor, the exploited, and the dominated refuse subordination and stand up against oppression. As the story goes, on the night of August 31,

1378, the day the ciompi were defeated, the silence was broken by the bells of the Church of Sant'Ambrogio, one of the strongholds of the rebellion, ringing the tocsin. Since these church bells on the periphery of the city had been a tool for calling the poor to mobilization and insurgency over the preceding months, panic spread among Florence's ruling classes (Stella 1993, 69–73). The ciompi's counteroffensive did not happen that night. But those bells did not stop ringing.

References

Abdulrauf, Lukman Adebisi. 2014. "Do We Need to Bother about Protecting our Personal Data? Reflections on Neglecting Data Protection in Nigeria." *Yonsei Law Journal* 5(2): 163–91.

Agamben, Giorgio. 1998. *Homo Sacer: Sovereign Power and Bare Life*, trans. Daniel-Heller Roazen. Stanford, CA: Stanford University Press.

Agamben, Giorgio. 2005. *State of Exception*, trans. Kevin Attel. Chicago: Chicago University Press.

Agamben, Giorgio. 2014. "What Is a Destituent Power?" *Environment and Planning D, Society and Space* 32: 65–74.

Agnew, John. 1994. "The Territorial Trap: The Geographical Assumptions of International Relations Theory." *Review of International Political Economy* 1(1): 53–80.

Agnew, John. 2005. "Sovereignty Regimes: Territoriality and State Authority in Contemporary World Politics." *Annals of the Association of American Geographers* 95(2): 437–61.

Åhrén, Mattias. 2016. *Indigenous Peoples' Status in the International Legal System*. Oxford: Oxford University Press.

Aitken, Robert. 2017. "'All Data Is Credit Data': Constituting the Unbanked." *Competition and Change* 21(4): 274–300.

Akhter, Majed. 2015. "Infrastructures of Colonialism and Resistance." *Tanqueed*, no. 9 (August). Accessed January 31, 2017. http://www.tanqeed.org/2015/08/infrastructures-of-colonialism-and-resistance.

Albertazzi, Daniele, and Duncan McDonnell, eds. 2008. *Twenty-First Century Populism: The Spectre of Western European Democracy*. Houndmills, UK: Palgrave Macmillan.

Albert, Michel. 1993. *Capitalism against Capitalism*. London: Whurr.

Allen, Bruce W. 1997. "The Logistics Revolution and Transportation." *Annals of the American Academy of Political Science* 553: 106–16.

Allen, Theodore W. 1994. *The Invention of the White Race, Volume 1: Racial Oppression and Social Control*. London: Verso.

Allen, Theodore W. 1997. *The Invention of the White Race, Volume 2: The Origin of Racial Oppression in Anglo-America*. London: Verso.

AlShebabi, Omar. 2015. "Histories of Migration to the Gulf." In *Transit States: Labour, Migration and Citizenship in the Gulf*, ed. Abdullah Khalaf, Omar AlShebabi, and Adam Hanieh, 3–38. London: Pluto.

Altenried, Moritz. 2017. "Die Plattform als Fabrik. Crowdwork, Digitaler Taylorismus und die Vervielfältigung der Arbeit." PROKLA 187: 175–92.

Altenried, Moritz, Manuela Bojadžijev, Leif Jannis Höfler, Sandro Mezzadra, and Mira Wallis, eds. 2017. *Logistische Grenzlandschaften: Das Regime mobiler Arbeit nach dem "Sommer der Migration."* Münster: Unrast.

Althusser, Louis. 1971. "Ideology and Ideological State Apparatuses." In *Lenin and Philosophy and Other Essays*, trans. Ben Brewster, 121–76. New York: Monthly Review Press.

Althusser, Louis. 1999. *Machiavelli and Us*, trans. Gregory Elliott. London: Verso.

Althusser, Louis. 2008. *On Ideology*, trans. Ben Brewster. London: Verso.

Altvater, Elmar. 1980. "Il capitalismo si organizza: Il dibattito marxista dalla guerra mondiale alla crisi del '29." In *Storia del Marxismo*, vol. 3.1, 823–76. Turin: Einaudi.

Amendola, Giso. 2016. *Costituzioni precarie*. Rome: Manifestolibri.

Amoore, Louise. 2013. *The Politics of Possibility*. Durham, NC: Duke University Press.

Anderson, Perry. 1974. *Lineages of the Absolutist State*. London: Verso.

Anter, Andreas. 2014. *Max Weber's Theory of the Modern State*. London: Palgrave Macmillan.

Apicella, Sabrina. 2016. *Amazon in Leipzig: Von den Gründen (nicht) zu Streiken*. Berlin: Rosa-Luxemburg-Stiftung. Accessed October 27, 2016. https://www.rosalux.de/fileadmin/rls_uploads/pdfs/Studien/Studien_09–16_Amazon_Leipzig.pdf.

Appadurai, Arjun. 1996. *Modernity at Large*. Minneapolis: University of Minnesota Press.

Appadurai, Arjun. 2002. "Deep Democracy: Urban Governmentality and the Horizon of Politics." *Public Culture* 14(1): 21–47.

Aquino, Alejandra, Amarela Varela, and Frédéric Decossé, eds. 2012. *Desafiando fronteras: Control de movilidad y experiencias migratorias en contexto capitalista*. Oaxaca, Mexico: Frontera.

Ardant, Gabriel. 1975. "Financial Policy and the Economic Infrastructure of Modern States and Nations." In *The Formation of National States in Western Europe*, ed. Charles Tilly, 164–242. Princeton, NJ: Princeton University Press.

Arendt, Hannah. 1951. *The Origins of Totalitarianism*. New York: Harcourt, Brace.

Arendt, Hannah. 1998. *The Human Condition*. Chicago: University of Chicago Press.

Arias, Albert. 2015. "Tú a Boston y yo a Airbnb: Un análisis urbanístico de Barcelona." *La Trama Urbana*, January 22. Accessed December 19, 2016. https://

latramaurbana.net/2015/01/22/tu-a-boston-y-yo-a-airbnb-un-analisis-urbanistico
-de-barcelona.

Arndt, Heinz Wolfgang. [1944] 1963. *The Economic Lessons of the 1930s*. London:
Frank Cass.

Arndt, Heinz Wolfgang. 1981. "Economic Development: A Semantic History." *Economic Development and Cultural Change* 29 (3): 457–66.

Arnez, Marco, et al. 2013. TIPNIS: *Amazonia en resistencia contra el estado colonial en Bolivia*. Madrid: Otramérica.

Aronowitz, Stanley, and Peter Bratsis, eds. 2002. *Paradigm Lost: State Theory Reconsidered*. Minneapolis: University of Minnesota Press.

Arrighi, Giovanni. 1994. *The Long Twentieth Century: Money, Power, and the Origins of Our Times*. London: Verso.

Arrighi, Giovanni. 2007. *Adam Smith in Beijing*. London: Verso.

Arrighi, Giovanni. 2010. *The Long Twentieth Century: Money, Power, and the Origins of Our Times*. London: Verso.

Arrighi, Giovanni, and Beverly J. Silver. 2003. "Polanyi's 'Double Movement': The Belle Epoques of British and U.S. Hegemony Compared." *Politics and Society* 31(2): 325–55.

Assennato, Marco. 2016. "Voyage à travers la machine-temps du 37 mars." *Le Temps Modernes* 71(691): 79–92.

Augé, Marc. 1995. *Non-Places*. London: Verso.

Avis, James. 2012. "Global Reconstructions of Vocational Education and Training." *Globalisation, Societies and Education* 10(1): 1–11.

Badiou, Alain. 2005. *Being and Event*, trans. Oliver Feltham. London: Continuum.

Bairoch, Paul. 1993. *Economics and World History*. Chicago: University of Chicago Press.

Balibar, Étienne. 1990. "The Nation Form: History and Ideology." In Étienne Balibar and Immanuel Wallerstein, *Race, Nation, Class: Ambiguous Identities*, trans. Chris Turner, 86–106. London: Verso.

Balibar, Étienne. 1994. *Masses, Classes, Ideas: Studies on Politics and Philosophy before and after Marx*, trans. James Swenson. New York: Routledge.

Balibar, Étienne. 2012. "Exploitation." In *Political Concepts: A Critical Reader*. Accessed October 24, 2016. http://www.politicalconcepts.org/balibar-exploitation.

Balibar, Étienne. 2013. "Politics of the Debt." *Postmodern Culture* 23(3). Accessed June 7, 2018. https://muse.jhu.edu/article/554614.

Balibar, Étienne. 2016. *Europe, crise et fin?* Paris: Le Bord de l'Eau.

Banaji, Jairus. 2010. *Theory as History: Essays on Modes of Production and Exploitation*. Leiden: Brill Academic.

Barkan, Joshua. 2013. *Corporate Sovereignty*. Minneapolis: University of Minnesota Press.

Baucom, Ian. 2005. *Specters of the Atlantic: Finance Capital, Slavery, and the Philosophy of History*. Durham, NC: Duke University Press.

Behrends, Andrea. 2008. "Fighting for Oil When There Is No Oil Yet: The Darfur-Chad Border." *Focaal* 52: 39–56.

Benson, Koni. 2016. "Graphic Novel Histories: Women's Organized Resistance to Slum Clearance in Crossroads, South Africa, 1975–2015." *African Studies Review* 59(1): 199–214.

Benton, Lauren. 2010. *A Search for Sovereignty: Law and Geography in European Empires, 1400–1900*. Cambridge: Cambridge University Press.

Benton, Lauren, and Richard Jeffrey Ross. 2013. *Legal Pluralism and Empires, 1500–1850*. New York: New York University Press.

Benton, Lauren, and Benjamin Straumann. 2010. "Acquiring Empire by Law: From Roman Doctrine to Early Modern European Practice." *Law and History Review* 28(1): 1–38.

Berger, Johannes. 1994. "Ausbeutung." In *Historisch-Kritisches Wörterbuch des Marxismus*, vol. 1, ed. Wolfgang Fritz Haug, Frigga Haug, Peter Jehle and Wolfgang Küttler, 735–43. Hamburg: Berliner Institut fur Kritische Theorie.

Berti, Lapo, ed. 1978. *Moneta, crisi e stato capitalistico*. Milan: Feltrinelli.

Beveridge, William. [1942] 1969. *Social Insurance and Allied Services*. New York: Agathon Press.

Bhabha, Homi K. 1994. *The Location of Culture*. London: Routledge.

Biehl, Janet. 2016. "Revolution in Rojava: An Eyewitness Account." ROAR *Magazine*. October 20. Accessed October 24, 2016. https://roarmag.org/essays/revolution -rojava-pluto-book.

Bigo, Didier. 2001. "The Mobius Ribbon of Internal and External Security(ies)." In *Identity, Borders, Orders: Rethinking International Relations Theory*, ed. Mathias Albert, David Jacobson and Yosef Lapid, 91–166. Minneapolis: University of Minnesota Press.

Bigo, Didier. 2016. "Rethinking Security at the Crossroads of International Relations and Criminology." *British Journal of Criminology* 56(6): 1068–86.

Blackburn, Robin. 2006. "Finance's Fourth Dimension." *New Left Review* 39: 1–39.

Blackwell, Adrian, and Chris Lee. 2013. "Editorial Note." *Scapegoat: Architecture, Landscape, Political Economy* 4: iii–v.

Blanco, John D., and Yvonne del Valle. 2014. "Reorienting Schmitt's *Nomos*: Political Theology, and Colonial (and Other) Exceptions in the Creation of Modern and Global Worlds." *Política Común* 5. Accessed October 21, 2015. http://dx.doi.org /10.3998/pc.12322227.0005.001.

Block, Fred. 2008. "Swimming against the Current: The Rise of a Hidden Developmental State in the United States." *Politics and Society* 36(2): 169–206.

Blumenberg, Hans. 1996. *Shipwreck with Spectator: Paradigm of a Metaphor for Existence*, trans. Steven Rendall. Cambridge, MA: MIT Press.

Bobbio, Norberto. 1955. *Politica e cultura*. Turin: Einaudi.

Bojadžijev, Manuela. 2015. "Housing, Financialization, and Migration in the Current Global Crisis: An Ethnographically Informed View from Berlin." *South Atlantic Quarterly* 114(1): 29–45.

Bojadžijev, Manuela, and Sandro Mezzadra. 2015. "'Refugee Crisis' or Crisis of European Migration Policies?" In *Focaalblog*, November 12. Accessed October 27, 2016. http://www.focaalblog.com/2015/11/12/manuela-bojadzijev-and-sandro -mezzadra-refugee-crisis-or-crisis-of-european-migration-policies.

Bologna, Sergio. 2012. "Epica Los Angeles: Vince lo sciopero dei portuali." Accessed December 10, 2015. https://storify.com/furiacervelli/epico.

Bologna, Sergio. 2013. *Banche e crisi: Dal petrolio al container*. Rome: DeriveApprodi.

Boltanski, Luc, and Eve Chiapello. 2006. *The New Spirit of Capitalism*. London: Verso.

Bond, Patrick, Ana Garcia, Mariana Moreira, and Ruixue Bai. 2016. "Take the Ports! Contesting Power in Global South Export Hubs." Rosa-Luxemburg-Stiftung, New York Office, March. Accessed September 14, 2016. http://www.rosalux-nyc .org/ubernehmt-die-hafen.

Borghi, Vando, and Supriya Routh, eds. 2016. *Workers and the Global Informal Economy: Interdisciplinary Perspectives*. Abingdon, UK: Routledge.

Bourdieu, Pierre. 1994. "Rethinking the State: Genesis and Structure of the Bureaucratic Field." *Sociological Theory* 12(1): 1–18.

Bourdieu, Pierre. 1998. *What is Neoliberalism? A Programme for Destroying Collective Structures Which May Impede the Pure Market Logic: Utopia of Endless Exploitation*. Paris: Le Monde Diplomatique.

Bourdieu, Pierre. 2002. "Against the Policy of Depoliticization." *Studies in Political Economy: A Socialist Review* 69 (1): 31–41.

Bratton, Benjamin H. 2015. *The Stack: On Software and Sovereignty*. Cambridge, MA: MIT Press.

Braudel, Fernand. 1984. *The Perspective of the World*. New York: Harper and Row.

Bräutigam, Deborah, and Kevin P. Gallagher. 2014. "Bartering Globalization: China's Commodity-Backed Finance in Africa and Latin America." *Global Policy* 5(3): 346–52.

Braverman, Harry. 1998. *Labor and Monopoly Capital: The Degradation of Work in the Twentieth Century*. London: Monthly Review Press.

Brenner, Neil. 2004. *New State Spaces: Urban Governance and the Rescaling of Statehood*. Oxford: Oxford University Press.

Brenner, Neil, Jamie Peck, and Nick Theodore. 2010. "Variegated Neoliberalization: Geographies, Modalities, Pathways." *Global Networks* 10(2): 182–222.

Brighenti, Andrea Mubi. 2010. "On Territorology: Towards a General Science of Territory." *Theory, Culture and Society* 27(1): 52–72.

Brighenti, Maura. 2013. "Entrevista a Raquel Gutiérrez, Serie: Nuevo Conflicto Social: Extractivismo y Política de lo Común." *Lobo Suelto*, October 31. Accessed November 20, 2016. http://anarquiacoronada.blogspot.it/2013/10/serie-nuevo -conflicto-social.html.

Brighenti, Maura, and Sandro Mezzadra. 2012. "Il laboratorio politico latinoamericano: Crisi del neoliberalismo, movimenti sociali e nuove esperienze di governance." In *Populismo e democrazia radicale: In dialogo con Ernesto Laclau*, ed. Marco Baldassari and Diego Melegari, 299–319. Verona: Ombre Corte.

Brown, Wendy. 2015. *Undoing the Demos: Neoliberalism's Stealth Revolution*. Brooklyn, NY: Zone.

Bryan, Dick, and Michael Rafferty. 2006. *Capitalism with Derivatives*. Basingstoke, UK: Palgrave Macmillan.

Burawoy, Michael. 2003. "For a Sociological Marxism: The Complementary Convergence of Antonio Gramsci and Karl Polanyi." *Politics and Society* 31(2): 193–261.

Burnham, James. 1941. *The Managerial Revolution: What Is Happening in the World.* New York: John Day.

Butler, Judith. [1990] 1999. *Gender Trouble: Feminism and the Subversion of Identity.* New York: Routledge.

Butler, Judith. 2015. *Notes toward a Performative Theory of Assembly.* Cambridge, MA: Harvard University Press.

Byrd, Jodi A. 2011. *The Transit of Empire: Indigenous Critiques of Colonialism.* Minneapolis: University of Minnesota Press.

Cabral, Amilcar. 1973. *Return to the Source: Selected Speeches by Amilcar Cabral*, ed. African Information Service. New York: Monthly Review Press.

Caccia, Beppe. 2016. "Europa der Kommune: Wie wir zu einem neuen Munizipalismus Kommen." *Luxemburg—Gesellschaftsanalyse und Linke Praxis* 2: 68–73.

Cáceres, Daniel M. 2014. "Accumulation by Dispossession and Socio-Environmental Conflicts Caused by the Expansion of Agribusiness in Argentina." *Journal of Agrarian Change* 15(1): 116–47.

Call, Charles T. 2010. "Beyond the 'Failed State': Conceptual Alternatives." *European Journal of International Relations* 17(2): 303–26.

Callahan, William A. 2016. "China's 'Asian Dream': The Belt Road Initiative and the New Regional Order." *Asian Journal of Comparative Politics* 1(3): 226–43.

Carruth, Allison. 2014. "The Digital Cloud and the Micropolitics of Energy." *Public Culture* 26(73): 339–64.

Castel, Robert. 2003. *From Manual Workers to Wage Laborers.* New Brunswick, NJ: Transaction.

Castells, Manuel. 1996. *The Rise of the Network Society.* Cambridge: Blackwell.

Castells, Manuel. 1998. *End of Millennium.* Cambridge: Blackwell.

Cava, Bruno. 2014. "When Lulism Gets Out of Control." *South Atlantic Quarterly* 113(4): 846–55.

Cavanagh, Edward. 2011. "A Company with Sovereignty and Subjects of Its Own? The Case of the Hudson's Bay Company, 1670–1763." *Canadian Journal of Law and Society* 26(1): 25–50.

Caygill, Howard. 2013. *On Resistance: A Philosophy of Defiance.* London: Bloomsbury.

Center for Studies of the History of Modern Legal Thought. 2004–2005. "L'Europa e gli 'altri': Il diritto coloniale fra otto e novecento." *Quaderni Fiorentini* 33–34. Accessed June 9, 2018. http://www.centropgm.unifi.it/quaderni/33/index.htm.

Cerroni, Umberto, ed. 1964. *Teorie sovietiche del diritto.* Milan: Giuffrè.

Césaire, Aimé. 1955. *Discourse on Colonialism.* New York: Monthly Review Press.

Chakrabarty, Dipesh. 2000. *Provincializing Europe.* Princeton, NJ: Princeton University Press.

Chakrabarty, Dipesh. 2005. "Legacies of Bandung: Decolonisation and the Politics of Culture." *Economic and Political Weekly* (November 12): 4812–18.

Chakravartty, Paula, and Denise Ferreira da Silva. 2012. "Accumulation, Dispossession, and Debt: The Racial Logic of Global Capitalism—An Introduction." *American Quarterly* 64(3): 361–85.

Chalcraft, John T. 2005. "Pluralizing Capital, Challenging Eurocentrism: Toward Post-Marxist Historiography." *Radical History Review* 2005 (91): 13–39.

Chalfin, Brenda. 2010. *Neoliberal Frontiers: An Ethnography of Sovereignty in West Africa*. Chicago: University of Chicago Press.

Chalfin, Brenda. 2015. "Governing Offshore Oil: Mapping Maritime Political Space in Ghana and the Western Gulf of Guinea." *South Atlantic Quarterly* 114(1): 101–18.

Chance, Kerry Ryan. 2017. *Living Politics in South Africa's Urban Shacklands*. Chicago: Chicago University Press.

Chari, Sharad. 2015. "African Extraction, Indian Ocean Critique." *South Atlantic Quarterly* 114(1): 83–100.

Chase-Dunn, Christopher. 2010. "Adam Smith in Beijing: A World-Systems Perspective." *Historical Materialism* 18(1): 39–51.

Chatterjee, Partha. 1986. *Nationalist Thought and the Colonial World: A Derivative Discourse*. London: Zed.

Chatterjee, Partha. 2004. *Politics of the Governed: Reflections on Popular Politics in Most of the World*. New York: Columbia University Press.

Chen, Kuan-Hsing. 2010. *Asia as Method: Toward Deimperialization*. Durham, NC: Duke University Press.

Chibber, Vivek. 2013. *Postcolonial Theory and the Specter of Capital*. London: Verso.

Ciccarelli, Roberto. 2018. *Forza lavoro: Il lato oscuro della rivoluzione digitale*. Rome: DeriveApprodi.

Cizre, Ümit. 2016. "Turkey in a Tailspin: The Failed Coup Attempt of July 15." *Middle East Research and Information Project*, August 10. Accessed January 5, 2017. http://www.merip.org/mero/mero081016.

Clark, Gordon L., and Dariusz Wójcik. 2007. *The Geography of Finance*. Oxford: Oxford University Press.

Clausewitz, Carl von. [1832] 2007. *On War*, trans. Michael Howard and Peter Paret. Oxford: Oxford University Press.

Clavero, Bartolomé. 2012. "Tribunal Constitucional en Estado plurinacional: El reto constituyente de Bolivia." *Revista Española de Derecho Constitucional* 94: 29–60.

Clément, Carine. 2015. "Putin, Patriotism and Political Apathy." *Books and Ideas*, October 19. Accessed January 5, 2017. http://www.booksandideas.net/Putin-Patriotism-and-Political-Apathy.html.

Clover, Joshua. 2016. *Riot. Strike. Riot: The New Era of Uprisings*. London: Verso.

Coates, Ta-Nehisi. 2015. *Between the World and Me*. New York: Spiegel and Grau.

Cobbett, Elizabeth. 2015. "Biometric MasterCard." In *Making Things International I: Circuits and Motion*, ed. Mark B. Salter. 311–27. Minneapolis: University of Minnesota Press.

Cocco, Giuseppe. 2014. "June in Janeiro." *South Atlantic Quarterly* 113(4): 838–45.

Cocco, Giuseppe, and Antonio Negri. 2006. *Global: Biopoder y luchas en una América Latina globalizada*. Buenos Aires: Paidós.

Cockayne, James. 2008. "Regulating Private Military and Security Companies: The Content, Negotiation, Weaknesses and Promise of the Montreux Document." *Conflict Security Law* 13(3): 401–28.

Colectivo Ni Una Menos. 2017. "#DeseudendadasNosQueremos." *Página12*, June 2. https://www.pagina12.com.ar/41550-desendeudadas-nos-queremos.

Colectivo Situaciones. 2011. *19 & 20: Notes for a New Social Protagonism*. Brooklyn, NY: Autonomedia.

Colombo, Alessandro. 2014. *Tempi decisivi: Natura e retorica delle crisi internazionali*. Milan: Feltrinelli.

Comaroff, Jean, and John L. Comaroff. 2012. "Theory from the South: Or, How Euro-America Is Evolving toward Africa." *Anthropological Forum* 22(2): 113–31.

Commodity Futures Trading Commission and Securities and Exchange Commission. 2010. *Findings Regarding the Market Events of May 6*. Washington, DC: Commodity Futures Trading Commission and Securities and Exchange Commission.

Connell, Raewyn, and Nour Dados. 2014. "Where in the World Does Neoliberalism Come From?" *Theory and Society* 43(2): 117–38.

Connelly, Andrew. 2016. "The New Residents of the City Plaza Hotel in Downtown Athens Can Check Out Anytime They Like, but, for Now at Least, They Cannot Leave Greece." *IRIN*, May 6. Accessed October 24, 2016. http://www.irinnews .org/feature/2016/05/06/welcome-city-plaza-greece%E2%80%99s-refugee -hotel.

Cooper, Frederick. 2002. *Africa since 1940: The Past and the Present*. Cambridge: Cambridge University Press.

Cooper, Melinda. 2015. "Shadow Money and the Shadow Workforce: Rethinking Labor and Liquidity." *South Atlantic Quarterly* 114(2): 395–423.

Cooper, Melinda. 2017. *Family Values: Between Neoliberalism and the New Social Conservatism*. New York: Zone.

Cooper, Melinda, and Angela Mitropoulos. 2009. "In Praise of Usura." *Mute* 2(13). Accessed May 30, 2018. http://www.metamute.org/editorial/articles/praise-usura.

Cooper, Melinda, and Catherine Waldby. 2014. *Clinical Labor: Tissue Donors and Research Subjects in the Global Bioeconomy*. Durham, NC: Duke University Press.

Coraggio, José Luis, Alberto Acosta, and Esperanza Martínez. 2011. *Economía social y solidaria*. Quito, Ecuador: Abya-Yala.

Coulthard, Glenn. 2014. *Red Skin, White Masks: Rejecting the Colonial Politics of Recognition*. Minneapolis: University of Minnesota Press.

Coumans, Catherine, 2011. "Occupying Spaces Created by Conflict: Anthropologists, Development NGOs, Responsible Investment, and Mining." *Current Anthropology* 52(S3): 29–43.

Cowen, Deborah. 2010. "A Geography of Logistics: Market Authority and the Security of Supply Chains." *Annals of the Association of American Geographers* 100(3): 600–20.

Cowen, Deborah. 2014. *The Deadly Life of Logistics: Mapping Violence in Global Trade*. Minneapolis: University of Minnesota Press.

Cox, Robert W. 1987. *Production, Power, and World Order*. New York: Columbia University Press.

Crary, Jonathan. 2013. *24/7: Late Capitalism and the Ends of Sleep*. London: Verso.

Cremonesi, Laura, Orazio Ierra, Daniele Lorenzini, and Martina Tazzioli, eds. 2016. *Foucault and the Making of Subjects*. London: Rowman and Littlefield.

Crouch, Colin. 2004. *Post-Democracy*. Cambridge: Polity.

Crouch, Colin. 2005. *Capitalist Diversity and Change*. Oxford: Oxford University Press.

Crouch, Colin. 2009. "Privatised Keynesianism: An Unacknowledged Policy Regime." *British Journal of Politics and International Relations* 11(3): 382–99.

Crowley, Thomas. 2011. "The Battle for Indigenous Lands: Protesting Mining in Northeast India." *Dialogues, Proposals, Stories for Global Citizenship*, July. Accessed August 10, 2017. http://base.d-p-h.info/en/fiches/dph/fiche-dph-8889.html.

Crozier, Michel, Samuel P. Huntington, and Jōji Watanuki. 1975. *The Crisis of Democracy: Report on the Governability of Democracies to the Trilateral Commission.* New York: New York University Press.

Cuervo-Cazzura, Alvaro, and Ravi Ramamurti, eds. 2014. *Understanding Multinationals from Emerging Markets.* Cambridge: Cambridge University Press.

Cunow, Heinrich. 1921. *Die Marxsche Geschichts-, Gesellschafts- und Staatstheorie, Bd. 1: Grundzüge der Marxschen Soziologie.* Berlin: Buchhandlung Vorwärts.

Cuppini, Niccolò, Mattia Frapporti, and Maurilio Pirone. 2015. "Logistics Struggles in the Po Valley Region: Territorial Transformations and Processes of Antagonistic Subjectivation." *South Atlantic Quarterly* 114(1): 119–34.

Curato, Nicole. 2017. "Flirting with Authoritarian Fantasies: Rodrigo Duterte and the New Terms of Philippine Populism." *Journal of Contemporary Asia* 47(1): 142–53.

Dahrendorf, Ralf. 1959. *Class and Class Conflict in Industrial Society.* Stanford, CA: Stanford University Press.

Dal Maso, Giulia. 2015. "The Financialization Rush: Responding to Precarious Labor and Social Security by Investing in the Chinese Stock Market." *South Atlantic Quarterly* 114(1): 47–64.

Dardot, Pierre, and Christian Laval. 2014. *The New Way of the World.* London: Verso.

Dardot, Pierre, and Christian Laval. 2016. *Pour en finir avec ce cauchemar qui n'en finit pas: Comment le néolibéralisme défait la démocratie.* Paris: La Dècouverte.

Das, Raju J. 1996. "State Theories: A Critical Analysis." *Science and Society* 60(1): 27–57.

Dávalos, Pablo. 2010. *La democracia disciplinaria: El proyecto posneoliberal para América Latina.* Quito, Ecuador: Corporación para el Desarrollo de la Educación Universitaria.

Davis, Angela. 1983. *Women, Race and Class.* New York: Vintage.

Davis, Angela. 2017. "An Interview on the Future of Black Radicalism." In *Futures of Black Radicalism*, ed. Gaye Theresa Johnson and Alex Lubin, 241–48. London: Verso.

Dean, Jodi. 2012. *The Communist Horizon.* London: Verso.

Dean, Mitchell, and Kaspar Villadsen. 2016. *State Phobia and Civil Society: The Political Legacy of Michel Foucault.* Stanford, CA: Stanford University Press.

De Genova, Nicholas, ed. 2017. *The Borders of "Europe": Autonomy of Migration, Tactics of Bordering.* Durham, NC: Duke University Press.

De Genova, Nicholas, Sandro Mezzadra, and John Pickles, eds. 2015. "New Keywords: Migration and Borders." *Cultural Studies* 29(1): 1–33.

Deleuze, Gilles, and Félix Guattari. 1983. *Anti-Oedipus: Capitalism and Schizophrenia,* trans. Robert Hurley, Mark Seem, and Helen R. Lane. Minneapolis: University of Minnesota Press.

Deleuze, Gilles, and Félix Guattari. 1987. *A Thousand Plateaus: Capitalism and Schizophrenia,* trans. Brian Massumi. London: Athlone.

Del Lucchese, Filippo. 2014. "Machiavelli and Constituent Power: The Revolutionary Foundation of Modern Political Thought." *European Journal of Political Theory* 16(1): 3–23.

Demirović, Alex. 2008. "Zu welchem Zweck und auf welche Weise den Staat kritisieren?" In *Staatstheorien vor neuen Herausforderungen: Analyse und Kritik*, ed. Jens Wissel and Stefanie Wöhl, 24–47. Münster. Westfälisches Dampfboot.

Demirović, Alex. 2011. "Materialist State Theory and the Transnationalization of the Capitalist State." *Antipode* 43(1): 38–59.

De Nicola, Alberto, and Biagio Quattrocchi. 2016. *Sindacalismo sociale: Lotte e invenzioni istituzionali nella crisi Europea*. Rome: DeriveApprodi.

Denning, Michael. 2010. "Wageless Life." *New Left Review* 66: 79–97.

Derrida, Jacques. [1987] 1992. "Before the Law." In *Acts of Literature*, ed. Derek Attridge, 181–220. New York: Routledge.

Derrida, Jacques. 2005. *Rogues: Two Essays on Reason*. Stanford, CA: Stanford University Press.

Desai, Ashwin. 2002. *We Are the Poors: Community Struggles in Post-Apartheid South Africa*. New York: Monthly Review.

De Soto, Hernando. 1990. *The Other Path: The Invisible Revolution in the Third World*. New York: Harper and Row.

De Stefano, Valerio. 2016. "The Rise of the 'Just-In-Time Workforce': On-Demand Work, Crowd Work and Labour Protection in the 'Gig-Economy.'" *Comparative Labor Law and Policy* 37: 471–503.

Detrixhe, John, Nikolaj Gammeltoft, and Sam Mamudi. 2014. "High-Frequency Traders Chase Currencies." *Bloomberg.Com*. Accessed June 29, 2015. http://www.bloomberg.com/news/articles/2014-04-02/high-frequency-traders-chase-currencies-as-stock-volume-recedes.

Dey, Ishita, and Giorgio Grappi. 2015. "Beyond Zoning: India's Corridors of 'Development' and New Frontiers of Capital." *South Atlantic Quarterly* 1140(1): 153–70.

Dhillon, Jaskiran, and Nick Estes. 2016. "Introduction: Standing Rock, #NoDAPL, and Mni Wiconi." *Cultural Anthropology*, December 22. Accessed August 12, 2017. https://culanth.org/fieldsights/1007-introduction-standing-rock-nodapl-and-mni-wiconi.

Dirik, Dilar. 2016. "Building Democracy without the State." ROAR *Magazine* (Spring) (1). Accessed June 9, 2016. https://roarmag.org/magazine/building-democracy-without-a-state.

Dixon, Adam D. 2011. "Variegated Capitalism and the Geography of Finance: Towards a Common Agenda." *Progress in Human Geography* 35(2): 193–210.

Dixon, Jonathan. 2014. "From 'Pearls' to 'Arrows': Rethinking the 'String of Pearls' Theory of China's Naval Ambitions." *Comparative Strategy* 33(4): 389–400.

Dominijanni, Ida. 2001. "L'eccedenza della libertà femminile." In *Motivi della libertà*, ed. Ida Dominijanni, 47–87. Milan: FrancoAngeli.

Dörre, Klaus, Stephan Lessenich, and Hartmut Rosa. 2009. *Soziologie–Kritik–Kapitalismus*. Berlin: Suhrkamp.

Du Bois, W. E. B. 1945. *Color and Democracy: Colonies and Peace*. New York: Harcourt, Brace and Company.

Du Bois, W. E. B. 1946. *The World and Africa: An Inquiry into the Part which Africa has Played in World History*. New York: International Publishers.

Duménil, Gérard, and Dominique Lévy. 2004. *Capital Resurgent*. Cambridge, MA: Harvard University Press.

Durand, Cédric. 2017. *Fictitious Capital: How Finance Is Appropriating Our Future*, trans. David Broder. London: Verso.

Du Toit, Andries, and David Neves. 2007. "In Search of South Africa's Second Economy: Chronic Poverty, Economic Marginalisation and Adverse Incorporation in Mt. Frere and Khayelitsha." Working paper no. 1, Programme for Land and Agrarian Studies, University of the Western Cape, South Africa.

Dyer-Witheford, Nick. 2015. *Cyber-Proletariat: Global Labour in the Digital Vortex*. London: Pluto.

Dyer-Witheford, Nick, and Greig De Peuter. 2009. *Games of Empire*. Minneapolis: University of Minnesota Press.

Dymski, Gary A., and John E. Elliott. 1988. "Roemer versus Marx: Alternative Perspectives on Exploitation." *Review of Radical Political Economics* 20(2–3): 25–33.

Easterling, Keller. 2014. *Extrastatecraft: The Power of Infrastructure Space*. London: Verso.

Eckert, Amy. 2016. *Outsourcing War: The Just War Tradition in the Age of Military*. Ithaca, NY: Cornell University Press.

Eisenstein, Sergei. 1976. "Notes for a Film of 'Capital,'" trans. Maciej Sliwowski, Jay Leyda, and Annette Michelson. *October* (Summer): 3–26.

Eken, Bülent. 2014. "The Politics of the Gezi Park Resistance: Against Memory and Identity." *South Atlantic Quarterly* 113(2): 427–36.

Elden, Stuart. 2013. *The Birth of Territory*. Chicago: University of Chicago Press.

Elliott, William Yandell. [1928] 1968. *The Pragmatic Revolt in Politics: Syndicalism, Fascism, and the Constitutional State*. New York: Howard Fertig.

Engels, Friedrich. [1878] 1975. *Herrn Eugen Dührings Umwälzung der Wissenschaft (Anti-Dühring)*. In *Marx Engels Werke*, ed. Institut für Marxismus-Leninismus beim ZK der SED, vol. 20, 5–303. Berlin: Dietz.

Engels, Friedrich. [1845] 1887. *The Condition of the Working Class in England*. Stanford, CA: Stanford University Press.

Ericsson, Magnus. 2012. "Mining Industry Corporate Actors Analysis." Polinares Working Paper no. 16. March 12. Accessed December 22, 2015. http://www.eisource book.org/cms/Mining%20industry%20corporate%20actors%20analysis.pdf.

Escobar, Arturo. 2010. "Planning." In *The Development Dictionary: A Guide to Knowledge as Power*, ed. Wolfgang Sachs, 145–60. London: Zed Books.

Esposito, Roberto. 2012. *Living Thought: The Origins and Actuality of Italian Philosophy*, trans. Zakiya Hanafi. Stanford, CA: Stanford University Press.

Evans, Peter B., Dietrich Rueschemeyer, and Theda Skocpol. 1985. *Bringing the State Back In*. Cambridge: Cambridge University Press.

Ewald, François. 1986. *L' état providence*. Paris: B. Grasset.

Fanon, Frantz. 1963. *The Wretched of the Earth*, trans. Constance Farrington. New York: Grove Weidenfeld.

Fanon, Frantz. 1967. *Black Skin, White Masks*, trans. Charles Lam Markmann. New York: Grove.

Ferguson, James. 1990. *The Anti-Politics Machine: "Development," Depoliticization, and Bureaucratic Power in Lesotho*. Cambridge: Cambridge University Press.

Ferguson, James. 2006. *Global Shadows: Africa in the Neoliberal World Order*. Durham, NC: Duke University Press.

Ferguson, James. 2015. *Give a Man a Fish: Reflections on The New Politics of Distribution*. Durham, NC: Duke University Press.

Ferguson, James, and Akhil Gupta. 2002. "Spatializing States: Toward an Ethnography of Neoliberal Governmentality." *American Ethnologist* 29: 981–1002.

Ferrari, Bravo. 1972. "Il New Deal e il nuovo assetto delle istituzioni capitalistiche." In *Operai e stato: Lotte operaie e riforma dello Stato capitalistico tra rivoluzione d'ottobre e New Deal*, 101–34. Milan: Feltrinelli.

Figueroa Helland, Leonardo, and Stefan Borg. 2014. "The Lure of State Failure: A Critique of State Failure Discourse in World Politics." *Interventions* 16(6): 877–97.

Filippini, Michele. 2015. *Una politica di massa: Antonio Gramsci e la rivoluzione della società*. Rome: Carocci.

Fischer-Lescano, Andreas, and Gunther Teubner. 2004. "Regime-Collisions: The Vain Search for Legal Unity in the Fragmentation of Global Law." *Michigan Journal of International Law* 25(4): 999–1046.

Flohr, Mikkel, and Yannick Harrison. 2016. "Reading the Conjuncture: State, Austerity, and Social Movements. An Interview with Bob Jessop." *Rethinking Marxism* 28(2): 306–21.

Flora, Peter, and Arnold Joseph Heidenheimer. 1981. *The Development of Welfare States in Europe and America*. New Brunswick, NJ: Transaction.

Forcellini, Egidio. 1771. *Totius Latinitatis Lexicon*, 4 vols., ed. Jacobi Facciolati. Padua: Typis Seminarii.

Foucault, Michel. 1978. *The History of Sexuality*, vol. 1, trans. Robert Hurley. New York: Pantheon.

Foucault, Michel. 1982. "The Subject and Power." *Critical Inquiry* 8(4): 777–95.

Foucault, Michel. 2003. *Society Must Be Defended: Lectures at the Collège de France, 1975–76*, trans. David Macey. New York: Picador.

Foucault, Michel. 2007. *Security, Territory, Population: Lectures at the Collège de France, 1977–1978*, trans. Graham Burchell. Houndmills, UK: Palgrave Macmillan.

Foucault, Michel. 2008. *The Birth of Biopolitics: Lectures at the Collège de France, 1977–1978*, trans. Graham Burchell. Houndmills, UK: Palgrave Macmillan.

Foucault, Michel. 2014. *On the Government of Life: Lectures at the Collège de France, 1979–1980*, trans. Graham Burchell. Houndmills, UK: Palgrave Macmillan.

Fraser, Nancy. 2014. "Behind Marx's Hidden Abode." *New Left Review* 86: 55–72.

Fraser, Nancy. 2016. "Contradictions of Capital and Care." *New Left Review* 100: 99–117.

Friedman, Eli. 2014. *Insurgency Trap: Labor Politics in Postsocialist China*. Ithaca, NY: Cornell University Press.

Fröbel, Folker, Jürgen Heinrichs, and Otto Kreye. 1980. *The New International Division of Labor*. Cambridge: Cambridge University Press.

Fuentes Díaz, Antonio, ed. 2012. *Necropolítica: Violencia y excepción en América Latina*. Puebla, Mexico: Benemérita Universidad Autónoma de Puebla.

Fumagalli, Andrea, and Cristina Morini. 2010. "Life Put to Work: Towards a Life Theory of Value." *Ephemera: Theory and Politics in Organization* 10(3–4): 234–52.

Gago, Verónica. 2015. "Financialization of Popular Life and the Extractive Operations of Capital: A Perspective from Argentina." *South Atlantic Quarterly* 114(1): 11–28.

Gago, Verónica. 2017. *Neoliberalism from Below: Popular Pragmatics and Baroque Economies*, trans. Liz Mason-Deeze. Durham, NC: Duke University Press.

Gago, Verónica. 2018. "The Strategy of Flight: Problematizing the Figure of Trafficking." *South Atlantic Quarterly* 117(2): 333–56.

Gago, Verónica, and Sandro Mezzadra. 2017a. "A Critique of the Extractive Operations of Capital: Toward an Expanded Concept of Extractivism." *Rethinking Marxism* 29(4): 574–91.

Gago, Verónica, and Sandro Mezzadra. 2017b. "In the Wake of the Plebeian Revolt: Social Movements, 'Progressive' Governments, and the Politics of Autonomy in Latin America." *Anthropological Theory* 17(4): 474–96.

Gago, Verónica, Sandro Mezzadra, Sebastien Scolnik, and Diego Sztulwark. 2014. "Hay una nueva forma-estado? Apuntes Latino Americanos." *Utopía y Praxis Latinoamericana* 19(66): 177–83.

Gago, Verónica, and Diego Sztulwark. 2016. "The Temporality of Social Struggle at the End of the 'Progressive' Cycle in Latin America." *South Atlantic Quarterly* 115(3): 606–14.

Galli, Carlo. 2015. *Janus's Gaze: Essays on Carl Schmitt*. Durham, NC: Duke University Press.

Gallo Lassere, Davide. 2016. *Contre la loi travail et son monde: Argent, précarité et mouvements sociaux*. Paris: Eterotopia.

Gammeltoft-Hansen, Thomas, and Ninna Nyberg Sørensen. 2013. *The Migration Industry and the Commercialization of International Migration*. London: Routledge.

García Linera, Álvaro, Raúl Prada, Luis Tapia, and Oscar Vega Camacho. 2010. *El estado: Campo de lucha*. La Paz, Bolivia: Muela del Diablo.

García Linera, Álvaro. 2012. *Geopolítica de la Amazonía: Poder hacendal-patrimonial y acumulación capitalista*. La Paz, Bolivia: Vicepresidencia de la Nación.

Gargarella, Roberto. 2015. "El nuevo constitucionalismo Lationamericano." *Estudios Sociales* 48: 169–72.

Ghosh, Amitav. 2015. *Flood of Fire*. London: John Murray.

Gibson-Graham, J. K. 1996. *The End of Capitalism (As We Knew It)*. Minneapolis: University of Minnesota Press.

Gibson-Graham, J. K. 2006. *A Postcapitalist Politics*. Minneapolis: University of Minnesota Press.

Goldman, Michael. 2015. "With the Declining Significance of Labor, Who Is Producing Our Global Cities?" *International Labor and Working-Class History* 87: 137–64.

Goldstein, Alyosha. 2014. "Finance and Foreclosure in the Colonial Present." *Radical History Review* 118: 42–63.

Golub, Alex. 2014. *Leviathan at the Gold Mine: Creating Indigenous and Corporate Actors in Papua New Guinea*. Durham, NC: Duke University Press.

Golumbia, David. 2015. "The Amazonization of Everything." *Jacobin*, August 15. Accessed October 28, 2016. https://www.jacobinmag.com/2015/08/amazon-google -facebook-privacy-bezos.

Gottweis, Herbert, and Alan Petersen, eds. 2008. *Biobanks: Governance in Comparative Perspective*. London: Routledge.

Gough, Ian. 1979. *The Political Economy of the Welfare State*. London: Macmillan.

Graeber, David. 2011. *Debt: The First 5,000 Years*. Brooklyn, NY: Melville House.

Gramsci, Antonio. 1971. *Selections from the Prison Notebooks*, ed. and trans. Quintin Hoare and Geoffrey Nowell-Smith. New York: International Publishers.

Gramsci, Antonio. 2005. *The Southern Question*, trans. Pasquale Verdicchio. Montreal: Guernica.

Grappi, Giorgio. 2016. *Logistica*. Rome: Ediesse.

Gregson, Nicky, Mike Crang, and Constantinos N. Antonopoulos. 2017. "Holding Together Logistical Worlds: Friction, Seams and Circulation in the 'Global Warehouse.'" *Environment and Planning D: Society and Space* 35(3): 381–98.

Grindsted, Thomas Skou. 2016. "Geographies of High Frequency Trading: Algorithmic Capitalism and Its Contradictory Elements." *Geoforum* 68: 25–28.

Grossberg, Lawrence. 2010. "Modernity and Commensuration." *Cultural Studies* 24(3): 295–332.

Grossberg, Lawrence. 2015. *We All Want to Change the World: The Paradox of the U.S. Left. A Polemic*. London: Lawrence and Wishart.

Grossberg, Lawrence, Carolyn Hardin, and Michael Palm. 2014. "Contributions to a Conjunctural Theory of Valuation." *Rethinking Marxism* 26(3): 306–35.

Grugel, Jean, and Pía Riggirozzi. 2012. "Post-neoliberalism in Latin America: Rebuilding and Reclaiming the State after Crisis." *Development and Change* 43(1): 1–21.

Guastini, Riccardo. 1978. *I due poteri: Stato borghese e stato operaio nell' analisi marxista*. Bologna: Il Mulino.

Guattari, Félix. 1995. *Chaosmosis: An Ethico-Aesthetic Paradigm*, trans. Paul Bains and Julian Perfanis. Indianapolis: Indiana University Press.

Guha, Ranajit. 1997. *Dominance without Hegemony*. Cambridge, MA: Harvard University Press.

Gudynas, Eduardo. 2010. "The New Extractivism of the 21st Century: Ten Urgent Theses about Extractivism in Relation to Current South American Progressivism." Americas Program Report. Center for International Policy, Washington, DC.

Gupta, Akhil. 2012. *Red Tape: Bureaucracy, Structural Violence, and Poverty in India*. Durham, NC: Duke University Press.

Gutiérrez Aguilar, Raquel. 2014. *Rhythms of the Pachakuti: Indigenous Uprising and State Power in Bolivia*. Durham, NC: Duke University Press.

Habermas, Jürgen. 1975. *Legitimation Crisis*. Boston: Beacon.

Hall, Peter A., and David W. Soskice. 2001. *Varieties of Capitalism*. Oxford: Oxford University Press.

Hall, Stuart. 1980. "Introduction." In Nicos Poulantzas, *State, Power, Socialism*, trans. Patrick Camiller, vii–xviii. London: Verso.

Hall, Stuart, Doreen Massey, and Michael Rustin. 2015. "After Neoliberalism: Analysing the Present." In *After Neoliberalism?: The Kilburn Manifesto*, ed. Stuart Hall, Doreen Massey, and Michael Rustin, 3–19. London: Lawrence and Wishart.

Hao, Xiangchao. 2016. "The Magnet Effect of Market-Wide Circuit Breaker: Evidence from the Chinese Stock Market." *Social Science Research Network*, June 26. Accessed December 2, 2016. https://ssrn.com/abstract=2859540.

Hardt, Michael, and Sandro Mezzadra. 2017. "October! To Commemorate the Future." *South Atlantic Quarterly* 116(4): 649–68.

Hardt, Michael, and Antonio Negri. 1994. *Labor of Dionysus: A Critique of the State-Form*. Minneapolis: University of Minnesota Press.

Hardt, Michael, and Antonio Negri. 2000. *Empire*. Cambridge, MA: Harvard University Press.

Hardt, Michael, and Antonio Negri. 2009. *Commonwealth*. Cambridge, MA: Harvard University Press.

Hardt, Michael, and Antonio Negri. 2017. *Assembly*. Cambridge: Cambridge University Press.

Harney, Stefano. 2010. "The Real Knowledge Transfer." *Social Text Online*, August 26. Accessed January 7, 2016. http://socialtextjournal.org/periscope_topic/impact.

Harney, Stefano. 2015. "Jay-Walker. How Can It Be That Jay-Walking Has Become Punishable by Death?" *Transversal* (blog), September. Accessed September 16, 2016. http://transversal.at/blog/Jay-Walker.

Harney, Stefano, and Fred Moten. 2013. *The Undercommons: Fugitive Planning and Black Study*. Wivenhoe, UK: Minor Compositions.

Harney, Stefano, and Fred Moten. 2015. "Michael Brown." *Boundary 2* 42(4): 81–87.

Harney, Stefano, and Fred Moten. 2017. "Improvement and Perseveration: Or, Usufruct and Use." In *Futures of Black Radicalism*, ed. Gaye Theresa Johnson and Alex Lubin, 83–91. London: Verso.

Harootunian, Harry D. 2015. *Marx after Marx*. New York: Columbia University Press.

Harvey, David. 1989. *The Condition of Postmodernity*. Cambridge, MA: Blackwell.

Harvey, David. 2001a. "Globalization and the 'Spatial Fix.'" *geographische revue* 3(2): 23–30.

Harvey, David. 2001b. *Spaces of Capital*. New York: Routledge.

Harvey, David. 2003. *The New Imperialism*. Oxford: Oxford University Press.

Harvey, David. 2005. *A Brief History of Neoliberalism*. Oxford: Oxford University Press.

Harvey, David. 2011. *The Enigma of Capital*. Oxford: Oxford University Press.

Harvey, David. 2012. *Rebel Cities: From the Right to the City to the Urban Revolution*. London: Verso.

Harvey, David. 2014. *Seventeen Contradictions and the End of Capitalism*. New York: Oxford University Press.

Harvey, David. 2015. "Consolidating Power: Interview by the Activist Group AK Malabocas." *ROAR Magazine* (Winter): 270–82.

Hashmi, Zehra. 2015. "A Politics of Rage in Islamabad." *Tanqeed*, December. Accessed August 5, 2016. http://www.tanqeed.org/2015/12/a-politics-of-rage-in-islamabad.

Hatzopoulos, Pavlos, Nelli Kambouri, and Ursula Huws. 2014. "The Containment of Labour in Accelerated Global Supply Chains: The Case of Piraeus Port." *Work Organisation, Labour and Globalisation* 8(1): 5–21.

Haug, Frigga. 2009. "Revolutionäre Realpolitik—Die Vier-in-einem-Perspektive." In *Radikale Realpolitik: Plädoyer für eine andere Politik*, ed. Michael Brie, 11–25. Berlin: Karl Dietz.

Henely, Kalvin. 2012. "The Forgotten Space." *Slant Magazine*, February 12. Accessed January 8, 2016. http://www.slantmagazine.com/film/review/the-forgotten -space.

Hess, Sabine, Bernd Kasparek, Stefanie Kron, Mathias Rodatz, Maria Schwertl, and Simon Sontowski, eds. 2017. *Der lange Sommer der Migration: Grenzregime III*. Berlin: Assoziation A.

Hilferding Rudolf. [1910] 2006. *Finance Capital: A Study of the Latest Phase of Capitalist Development*. London: Routledge and Kegan Paul.

Hilger, Marie-Elisabeth, and Lucian Hölscher. 1982. "Kapital, Kapitalist, Kapitalismus." In *Geschichtliche Grundbegriffe*, 8 vols., ed. Otto Brunner, Werner Conze, and Reinhart Koselleck, 3:399–454. Stuttgart: Klett.

Hintze, Otto. [1902] 1975. "The Formation of States and Constitutional Development: A Study in History and Politics." In *The Historical Essays of Otto Hintze*, ed. Felix Gilbert and Robert M. Berdahl, 155–77. New York: Oxford University Press.

Hioe, Brian. 2017. "There's an Ongoing Indigenous Occupation in Taiwan." *Intercontinental Cry*, March 24. Accessed August 12, 2017. https://intercontinentalcry.org /theres-ongoing-indigenous-occupation-taiwan.

Hirsh, Max. 2016. *Airport Urbanism*. London: University of Minnesota Press.

Hobson, John A. [1902] 1965. *Imperialism: A Study*. Ann Arbor: University of Michigan Press.

Honneth, Axel. 2017. *The Idea of Socialism: Towards a Renewal*. Cambridge: Polity.

Horkheimer, Max. 1930. *Anfänge der Bürgerlichen Geschichtsphilosophie*. Stuttgart: Kohlhammer.

Horstmann, Alexander. 2007. "Violence, Subversion and Creativity in the Thai-Malaysian Borderland." In *Borderscapes: Hidden Geographies and Politics at Territory's Edge*, ed. Prem Kumar Rajaram and Carl Grundy-Warr, 137–60. Minneapolis: University of Minnesota Press.

Hudson, Michael. 2003. *Super Imperialism*. London: Pluto.

Invisible Committee. 2009. *The Coming Insurrection*. Los Angeles, CA: Semiotext(e).

Invisible Committee. 2015. *To Our Friends*. Los Angeles, CA: Semiotext(e).

Irani, Lilly C., and M. Six Silberman. 2016. "Stories We Tell about Labor: Turkopticon and the Trouble with 'Design.'" In *Proceedings of the SIGCHI Conference on Human Factors in Computing Systems*, 4573–86. New York: ACM.

Ives, Andrew. 2015. "Neoliberalism and the Concept of Governance: Renewing with an Older Liberal Tradition to Legitimate the Power of Capital." *Cahiers du MMMOC* 14(2). Accessed November 3, 2016. https://mimmoc.revues.org/2263.

Jameson, Fredric. 1991. *Postmodernism, or, The Cultural Logic of Late Capitalism*. Durham, NC: Duke University Press.

Jameson, Fredric. 2009. "Marx and Montage." *New Left Review* 58: 109–17.

Jameson, Fredric. 2015. "The Aesthetics of Singularity." *New Left Review* 92: 101–32.

Jameson, Fredric. 2016. *An American Utopia: Dual Power and the Universal Army*. London: Verso.

Jardim, Fabiana. 2013. "A Brief Genealogy of Governmentality Studies: The Foucault Effect and Its Developments. An Interview with Colin Gordon." *Educação e Pesquisa* 39(4): 1067–87.

Jellinek, Georg. [1914] 1990. *Allgemeine Staatslehre*. Berlin: O. Häring.

Jessop, Bob. 1985. *Nicos Poulantzas: Marxist Theory and Political Strategy*. London: Macmillan.

Jessop, Bob. 2012. "Rethinking the Diversity and Variability of Capitalism." In *Capitalist Diversity and Diversity within Capitalism*, ed. Christel Lane and Geoffrey Wood, 209–37. London: Routledge.

Johnson, Gaye Theresa, and Alex Lubin. 2017. "Introduction." In *Futures of Black Radicalism*, ed. Gaye Theresa Johnson and Alex Lubin, 9–18. London: Verso.

Johnson, Ron. 2017. "Nations Rising: Across North America Indigenous People Are Pushing for a Renewable Energy Future." *Utne Reader*, Spring. http://www.utne.com/environment/nations-rising-zmoz17szsel.

Jomini, Antoine Henri. [1838] 2008. *The Art of War*. Kingston, ON: Legacy.

Kaldas, Timothy E. 2016. "Tiran, Safir, and the Island of Executive Power in Egypt." Tahrir Institute for Middle East Policy, April 21. Accessed November 28, 2016. https://timep.org/commentary/tiran-sanafir-and-the-island-of-executive-power-in-egypt.

Kalecki, Michael. 1943. "Political Aspects of Full Employment." *Political Quarterly* 14(4): 322–30.

Kambouri, Nelli. 2014. "Dockworker Masculinities." *Logistical Worlds: Infrastructure, Software, Labour*, December 15. Accessed January 14, 2016. http://logisticalworlds.org/blogs/dockworker-masculinities#more-279.

Kang, Su-Dol. 2016. "South Korea as a Semi-Peripheral Workfare State." *Zapruder World* 3. Accessed December 15, 2016. http://www.zapruderworld.org/south-korea-semi-peripheral-workfare-state.

Karakayalí, Serhat, and Özge Yaka. 2014. "The Spirit of Gezi: The Recomposition of Political Subjectivities in Turkey." *New Formations* 83 (Winter): 117–38.

Karaman, Ozan. 2013a. "Defending Future Commons: The Gezi Experience." *Antipode Foundation*, August 27. Accessed October 3, 2016. https://antipodefoundation.org/2013/08/27/intervention-defending-future-commons-the-gezi-experience-by-ozan-karaman-2.

Karaman, Ozan. 2013b. "Urban Neoliberalism with Islamic Characteristics." *Urban Studies* 50(16): 3412–27.

Kasparek, Bernd, and Mark Speer. 2015. "Of Hope: Hungary and the Long Summer of Migration." *Bordermonitoring*, September 9. Accessed October 10, 2016. http://bordermonitoring.eu/ungarn/2015/09/of-hope-en.

Kelley, Robin D. G. 2017. "The Rest of Us: Rethinking Settler and Native." *American Quarterly* 69(2): 267–76.

Kern, Stephen. 1983. *The Culture of Time and Space, 1880–1918*. Cambridge, MA: Harvard University Press.

Keynes, John Maynard. [1916] 2013. *The Collected Works of John Maynard Keynes, Volume 7: The General Theory of Employment, Interest and Money*, ed. Elizabeth Johnson and David Moggridge. Cambridge: Cambridge University Press.

Klein, Lawrence R. 1947. *The Keynesian Revolution.* New York: Macmillan.

Klein, Naomi. 2007. *The Shock Doctrine.* New York: Henry Holt.

Klein, Naomi. 2014. *This Changes Everything: Capitalism versus the Climate.* New York: Simon and Schuster.

Klooster, Wim. 2009. *Revolutions in the Atlantic World: A Comparative History.* New York: New York University Press.

Knapp, Michael, Anja Flach, and Ercan Ayboğa. 2016. *Revolution in Rojava: Democratic Autonomy and Women's Liberation in the Syrian Kurdistan*, trans. Janet Biehl. London: Pluto.

Kocka, Jürgen. 1974. "Organisierter Kapitalismus oder Staatsmonopolistischer Kapitalismus? Begriffliche Vorbemerkungen." In *Organisierter Kapitalismus. Voraussetzungen und Anfänge*, ed. Heinrich August Winkler, 19–35. Göttingen: Vandenhoeck and Ruprecht.

Kocka, Jürgen. 2016. *Capitalism: A Short History*, trans. Jeremiah Rimmer. Princeton, NJ: Princeton University Press.

Kolstø, Pål. 2006. "The Sustainability and Future of Unrecognized Quasi-States." *Journal of Peace Research* 43(6): 723–40.

Korzybski, Alfred. [1933] 1994. *Science and Sanity*, 5th ed. Englewood, NJ: Institute for General Semantics.

Krippner, Greta R. 2011. *Capitalizing on Crisis.* Cambridge, MA: Harvard University Press.

Krugman, Paul. 2009. *The Return of Depression Economics and the Crisis of 2008.* New York: W. W. Norton.

Küçük, Bülent, and Ceren Özselçuk. 2016. "The Rojava Experience: Possibilities and Challenges of Building a Democratic Life." *South Atlantic Quarterly* 115(1): 184–96.

Laclau, Ernesto. 2005. *On Populist Reason.* London: Verso.

Laing, Anna F. Forthcoming. "Subaltern Geographies in the Plurinational State of Bolivia: The TIPNIS Conflict." In *Subaltern Geographies: Subaltern Studies, Space and the Geographical Imagination*, ed. Tariq Jazeel and Stephen Legg. Athens: University of Georgia Press.

Larkin, Brian. 2013. "The Politics and Poetics of Infrastructure." *Annual Review of Anthropology* 42(1): 327–43.

Latouche, Serge. 1993. *In the Wake of the Affluent Society: An Exploration into Postdevelopment.* London: Zed Books.

Latour, Bruno. 2014. "On Some of the Affects of Capitalism." Lecture presented at the Royal Academy, Copenhagen, February 26. Accessed March 10, 2015. http://www.bruno-latour.fr/sites/default/files/136-AFFECTS-OF-K-COPENHAGUE.pdf.

Lavinas, Lena. 2013. "21st Century Welfare." *New Left Review* 84: 5–40.

Lazzarato, Maurizio. 2012. *The Making of the Indebted Man: An Essay on the Neoliberal Condition*, trans. Joshua David Jordan. Los Angeles, CA: Semiotext(e).

Le Cour Grandmaison, Olivier. 2010. *De l'indigénat: Anatomie du'un "monstre" juridique: Le droit colonial en Algérie et dans l'empire français.* Paris: La Découverte.

Le Pichon, Alain. 2006. *China Trade and Empire.* Oxford: Oxford University Press.

LeCavalier, Jesse. 2016. *The Rule of Logistics: Walmart and the Architecture of Fulfillment*. Minneapolis: University of Minnesota Press.

Lederer, Emil. 1918–19. "Die Ökonomische Umschichtung im Kriege." *Archiv für Sozialwissenschaft und Sozialpolitik* 45: 1–39, 430–63.

Lee, Justin. 2016. "UNHCR, IrisGuard Launch EyeCloud to Assist Refugees with Biometric Banking." *Biometric Update*, January 20. Accessed December 11, 2016. http://www.biometricupdate.com/201601/unhcr-irisguard-launch-eyecloud-to -assist-refugees-with-biometric-banking.

Lees, Loretta, Hyun Bang Shin, and Ernesto López Morales. 2016. *Planetary Gentrification*. Cambridge: Polity.

Lefebvre, Henri. 1968. *Le droit à la ville*. Paris: Anthropos.

Lefebvre, Henri. 2009. *State, Space, World: Selected Essays*, ed. Neil Brenner and Stuart Elden, trans. Neil Brenner, Stuart Elden, and Gerald Moore. Minneapolis: University of Minnesota Press.

Leguizamón, Amalia. 2016. "Disappearing Nature? Agribusiness, Biotechnology and Distance in Argentine Soybean Production." *Journal of Peasant Studies* 43(2): 313–30.

Lenin, Vladimir I. [1902] 1978. *What Is to Be Done? Burning Questions of Our Movement*, trans. Joe Fineberg and George Hanna. New York: International Publishers.

Lenin, Vladimir I. [1917] 1975. *Imperialism, the Highest Stage of Capitalism: A Popular Outline*. Beijing: Foreign Language Press.

Lenin, Vladimir I. [1917] 1999. "The Dual Power." *Pravda*, April 9. Accessed December 20, 2016. https://www.marxists.org/archive/lenin/works/1917/apr/09.htm.

Leong, Nancy. 2013. "Racial Capitalism." *Harvard Law Review* 126(8): 2151–2226.

Lester, Jeremy. 2015. *Spogliateci tutti ignudi: I quaranta giorni che sconvolsero Firenze, e perciò il mondo, nel 1378*. Bologna: Pendragon.

Levinson, Mark. 2006. *The Box: How the Shipping Container Made the World Smaller and the World Economy Bigger*. Princeton, NJ: Princeton University Press.

Lewis, Michael. 2014. *Flash Boys*. London: Allen Lane.

Liberti, Stefano. 2016. *I signori del cibo*. Rome: Minimum Fax.

Lim, Kean Fan. 2010. "On China's Growing Geo-economic Influence and the Evolution of Variegated Capitalism." *Geoforum* 41(5): 677–88.

Lindahl, Hans. 2013. *Fault Lines of Globalization: Legal Order and the Politics of A-legality*. Oxford: Oxford University Press.

Lindquist, Johan, and Biao Xiang. 2014. "Migration Infrastructure." *International Migration Review* 48(1): 122–48.

Lipsitz, George. 2015. "From Plessy to Ferguson." *Cultural Critique* 90: 119–39.

LiPuma, Edward, and Benjamin Lee. 2004. *Financial Derivatives and the Globalization of Risk*. Durham, NC: Duke University Press.

Lollini, Andrea. 2009. "Proprietà intellettuale, bilanciamento degli interessi e farmaci 'low cost'. I casi di India e Sudafrica." *Rivista Trimestrale di Diritto Pubblico* 58(1): 115–54.

Lowe, Lisa. 2015. *The Intimacies of Four Continents*. Durham, NC: Duke University Press.

Lucarelli, Stefano, and Carlo Vercellone. 2013. "The Thesis of Cognitive Capitalism: New Research Perspectives. An Introduction." *Knowledge Cultures* 1(4): 1–15.

Luhmann, Niklas. 1997. "Globalization or World Society: How to Conceive of Modern Society?" *International Review of Sociology* 7(1): 67–79.

Luisetti, Federico, John Pickles, and Wilson Kaiser. 2015. *The Anomie of the Earth: Philosophy, Politics, and Autonomy in Europe and the Americas.* Durham, NC: Duke University Press.

Lukács, Georg. [1923] 1971. *History and Class Consciousness*, trans. Rodney Livingstone. Cambridge, MA: MIT Press.

Lukács, Georg. 2002. *A Defence of History and Class Consciousness: Tailism and the Dialectic*, trans. Esther Leslie. London: Verso.

Luxemburg, Rosa. [1913] 2003. *The Accumulation of Capital*, trans. Agnes Schwarzschild. New York: Routledge.

Luxemburg, Rosa. 2004. *The Rosa Luxemburg Reader*, ed. Peter Hudis and Kevin B. Anderson. New York: New York University Press.

Lyotard, Jean-François. 1984. *The Postmodern Condition*. Minneapolis: University of Minnesota Press.

Macherey, Pierre. 2014. *Le sujet des normes*. Paris: Éditions Amsterdam.

Machiavelli, Niccolò. 1988. *Florentine Histories*, trans. Laura Banfield and Harvey Mansfield Jr. Princeton, NJ: Princeton University Press.

MacKenzie, Donald. 2014. "A Sociology of Algorithms: High-Frequency Trading and the Shaping of Markets." University of Edinburgh, June. Accessed June 5, 2015. http://www.sps.ed.ac.uk/__data/assets/pdf_file/0004/156298/Algorithms25.pdf.

MacLeavy, Julie, and Columba Peoples. 2010. "War on Terror, Work in Progress: Security, Surveillance, and the Configuration of the U.S. Workfare State." *GeoJournal* 75: 339–46.

Malfliet, Katlijin. 1987. "The Economic Function and Purpose of Personal Property and Its Legal Implementation." In *Soviet Law and Economy*, ed. Olimpiad S. Iofee and Mark W. Janis, 79–101. Dordrecht: Martin Nijhoff.

Malvaldi, Marco, and Dino Leporini. 2014. *Capra e calcoli*. Rome: Laterza.

Mamdani, Mahmood. 1996. *Citizen and Subject*. Princeton, NJ: Princeton University Press.

Mann, Michael. 1984. "The Autonomous Power of the State: Its Origins, Mechanisms and Results." *European Journal of Sociology* 25(2): 185–213.

Marazzi, Christian. 2010. *The Violence of Financial Capitalism*, trans. Kristina Lebedeva. Los Angeles, CA: Semiotext(e).

Marazzi, Christian. 2015. "Money and Financial Capital." *Theory, Culture and Society*, 32(7–8): 39–50.

Marcuse, Herbert. 2002. *One-Dimensional Man: Studies in the Ideology of Advanced Industrial Society*. London: Routledge.

Mariátegui, José Carlos. [1928] 1988. *Seven Interpretive Essays on Peruvian Reality*. Austin: University of Texas Press.

Marshall, Thomas Humphrey. 1950. *Citizenship and Social Class*. Cambridge: Cambridge University Press.

Martin, Craig. 2016. *Shipping Container*. London: Bloomsbury Academic.

Martin, Randy. 2002. *Financialization of Daily Life*. Philadelphia: Temple University Press.

Martin, Randy. 2013. "After Economy? Social Logics of the Derivative." *Social Text* 31(1): 83–106.

Martinez, Miguel. 2017. *The Right to Squat the City: Squatters, Housing Struggles and Urban Politics*. London: Routledge.

Martínez, Paola. 2013. *Bolivia frente a la IIRSA-COSIPLAN: Entre el extractivismo y la integración?* Buenos Aires: Clacso.

Martínez Moreno, Rubén. 2016. "El capitalismo colaborativo tiene un plan." *Ctxt*, April 20. Accessed December 19, 2016. http://ctxt.es/es/20160420/Politica/5502/economia-colaborativa-redistribucion-renta-economia-social-airbnb.htm.

Marx, Karl. 1937. *The Poverty of Philosophy*. London: Martin Lawrence Limited.

Marx, Karl. 1971. *Theories of Surplus Value*, vol. 3. Moscow: Progress.

Marx, Karl. 1973. *Grundrisse: Foundations of the Critique of Political Economy*, trans. Martin Nicolaus. Harmondsworth, UK: Penguin.

Marx, Karl. 1977. *Capital*, vol.1, trans. Ben Fowkes. New York: Vintage.

Marx, Karl. 1978. *Capital*, vol. 2, trans. David Fernbach. London: Penguin.

Marx, Karl. 1981. *Capital*, vol. 3, trans. David Fernbach. London: Penguin.

Marx, Karl. 1988. *Civil War in France*. 2nd ed. New York: International Publishers.

Marx, Karl, and Friedrich Engels. 2008. *The Communist Manifesto*, ed. David Harvey. London: Pluto.

Mason, Paul. 2015. *Postcapitalism: A Guide to Our Future*. New York: Straus and Giroux.

Mattei, Ugo, and Laura Nader. 2008. *Plunder: When the Rule of Law Is Illegal*. Oxford: Wiley-Blackwell.

Maurer, Bill, Taylor C. Nelms, and Lana Swartz. 2013. "'When Perhaps the Real Problem Is Money Itself!': The Practical Materiality of Bitcoin." *Social Semiotics* 23(2): 261–77.

Mazzucato, Mariana. 2013. *The Entrepreneurial State: Debunking Public versus Private Sector Myths*. New York: Anthem.

Mbembe, Achille. 2003. "Necropolitics." *Public Culture* 15(1): 11–40.

Mbembe, Achille. 2013. *Critique de la raison nègre*. Paris: La Découverte.

McNeill, Donald. 2015. "Global Firms and Smart Technologies: IBM and the Reduction of Cities." *Transactions of the Institute of British Geographers* 40(4): 562–74.

McNeish, John-Andrew. 2013. "Extraction, Protest and Indigeneity in Bolivia: The TIPNIS Effect." *Latin American and Caribbean Ethnic Studies* 8(2): 221–42.

Medico International. 2016. "Nach Putschversuch: Illiberale Demokratie oder Faschismus in der Türkei?" August 10. Accessed October 24, 2016. https://www.medico.de/illiberale-demokratie-oder-faschismus-in-der-tuerkei-16512.

Medina, Eden. 2011. *Cybernetic Revolutionaries: Technology and Politics in Allende's Chile*. Cambridge, MA: MIT Press.

Melamed, Jodi. 2015. "Racial Capitalism." *Critical Ethnic Studies* 1(1): 76–85.

Mendes, Alexandre F. 2014. "Between Shocks and Finance: Pacification and the Integration of the Favela into the City in Rio de Janeiro." *South Atlantic Quarterly* 113(4): 866–73.

Meng, Guang-Wen. 2005. "Evolutionary Model of Free Economic Zones." *Chinese Geographical Science* 15(2): 103–12.

Menga, Ferdinando. 2014. "A-legality: Journey to the Borders of Law. In Dialogue with Hans Lindahl." *Etica e Politica/Ethics and Politics* 17(2): 919–39.

Mezzadra, Sandro. 2018. *In the Marxian Workshops: Producing Subjects*, trans. Yari Lanci. London: Roman and Littlefield.

Mezzadra, Sandro, and Brett Neilson. 2012. "Borderscapes of Differential Inclusion: Subjectivity and Struggles on the Threshold of Justice's Excess." In *The Borders of Justice*, ed. Étienne Balibar, Sandro Mezzadra, and Ranabir Samaddar, 181–203. Philadelphia: Temple University Press.

Mezzadra, Sandro, and Brett Neilson. 2013a. *Border as Method, or, The Multiplication of Labor*. Durham, NC: Duke University Press.

Mezzadra, Sandro, and Brett Neilson. 2013b. "Extraction, Logistics, Finance." *Radical Philosophy* 178: 8–18.

Mezzadra, Sandro, and Brett Neilson. 2014. "The Materiality of Communism: Politics beyond Representation and the State." *South Atlantic Quarterly* 113(4): 777–90.

Mezzadra, Sandro, and Brett Neilson. 2015. "Operations of Capital." *South Atlantic Quarterly* 114(1): 1–9.

Mezzadra, Sandro, and Brett Neilson. 2017. "On the Multiple Frontiers of Extraction: Excavating Contemporary Capitalism." *Cultural Studies* 31(2–3): 185–204.

Mezzadra, Sandro, and Diego Sztulwark. 2015. "Political Anatomy of the South American Conjuncture: Images of Development and New Social Conflict in the Present Period." *Viewpoint Magazine*, August 6. Accessed October 27, 2016. https://viewpointmag.com/2015/08/06/political-anatomy-of-the-south-american -conjuncture-images-of-development-and-new-social-conflict-in-the-present -period.

Mignolo, Walter D. 2000. "La colonialidad a lo largo y a lo ancho: El hemisferio occidental en el horizonte colonial de la modernidad." In *La colonialidad del saber: Eurocentrismo y ciencias sociales*, ed. Edgardo Lander, 55–85. Buenos Aires: Clacso.

Miguez, Pablo, and Juan Santarcángelo. 2015. "El rol del estado en el desarrollo económico." Unpublished paper. Accessed October 12, 2016. https:// www.academia.edu/8268666/El_rol_del_Estado_en_el_desarrollo _econ%C3%B3mico.

Mirowski, Philip. 2002. *Machine Dreams*. Cambridge: Cambridge University Press.

Mirowski, Philip. 2013. *Never Let a Serious Crisis Go to Waste*. London: Verso.

Mirowski, Philip, and Dieter Plehwe. 2009. *The Road from Mont Pèlerin*. Cambridge, MA: Harvard University Press.

Mitchell, Don. 2012. *The Right to the City: Social Justice and the Fight for Public Space*. New York: Guilford.

Mitra, Iman Kumar, Ranabir Samaddar, and Samita Sen, ed. 2017. *Accumulation in Post-Colonial Capitalism*. New York: Springer.

Mitropoulos, Angela, and Brett Neilson. 2006. "Cutting Democracy's Knot." *Culture Machine* 8. Accessed December 15, 2016. https://www.culturemachine.net/index.php/cm/article/view/40/48.

Moore, Jason W. 2015. *Capitalism in the Web of Life: Ecology and the Accumulation of Capital*. London: Verso.

Mosco, Vincent. 2014. *To the Cloud: Big Data in a Turbulent World*. Boulder, CO: Paradigm.

Mouffe, Chantal. 2005. *The Return of the Political*. London: Verso.

Moulier Boutang, Yann. 2012. *Cognitive Capitalism*. Cambridge: Polity.

Murch, Donna. 2015. "Historicizing Ferguson." *New Politics* 15-3(59). Accessed August 20, 2016. http://newpol.org/content/historicizing-ferguson.

Nancy, Jean-Luc. 1991. *The Inoperative Community*, trans. Peter Conner and Lisa Garbus. Minneapolis: University of Minnesota Press.

Nápoli, Bruno, Celeste Perosino, and Walter Bosisio. 2014. *La dictadura del capital financiero. El golpe militar corporativo y la trama bursátil*. Buenos Aires: Ediciones Continente.

Natali, Denise. 2010. *The Kurdish Quasi-State: Development and Dependency in Post-War Gulf Iraq*. Syracuse, NY: Syracuse University Press.

Negri, Antonio. 1974. *Crisi dello stato piano: Comunismo e organizzazione rivoluzionaria*. Milan: Feltrinelli.

Negri, Antonio. 1977. *La forma stato: Per la critica dell'economia politica della costituzione*. Milan: Feltrinelli.

Negri, Antonio. 1999. *Insurgencies, Constituent Power and the Modern State*. Minneapolis: University of Minnesota Press.

Negri, Antonio. 2014. *Factory of Strategy: Thirty-Three Lessons on Lenin*, trans. Arianna Bove. New York: Columbia University Press.

Negri, Antonio. 2016a. "Chi ha paura di Virginia Woolf?" *Euronomade*, October 21. Accessed November 12, 2016. http://www.euronomade.info/?p=8183.

Negri, Antonio. 2016b. "Ripensando all'arma dello sciopero." In *Sindacalismo sociale: Lotte e invenzioni istituzionali nella crisi europea*, ed. Alberto De Nicola and Biagio Quattrocchi, 69–76. Rome: DeriveApprodi.

Negri, Antonio. 2017. "Soviet: Within and Beyond the 'Short Century,'" trans. Arianna Bove. *South Atlantic Quarterly* 116(4): 835–49.

Neilson, Brett. 2004. "*Potenza Nuda*? Sovereignty, Biopolitics, Capitalism." *Contretemps* 5(December): 63–78.

Neilson, Brett. 2010. "Politics without Action, Economy without Labor." *Theory and Event* 13(1). Accessed June 8, 2018. https://muse.jhu.edu/article/377390.

Neilson, Brett. 2012. "Fracking." In *Depletion Design: A Glossary of Network Ecologies*, ed. Carolin Wiedemann and Soenke Zehle, 83–86. Amsterdam: Institute of Network Cultures.

Neilson, Brett. 2014. "Zones: Beyond the Logic of Exception." *Concentric: Literary and Cultural Studies* 40(2): 11–28.

Neilson, Brett. 2015. "A City that Exports Air: Containers, Traffic and Logistics in Sydney's Intermodal Network and Beyond." In *Cargomobilities: Moving Materials in a Global Age*, ed. Thomas Birtchnell, Satya Savistsky, and John Urry, 48–64. London: Routledge.

Neilson, Brett, Ned Rossiter, and Ranabir Samaddar, eds. 2018. *Logistical Asia: The Labour of Making a World Region*. Singapore: Palgrave.

Neocleous, Mark. 2006. "From Social to National Security: On the Fabrication of Economic Order." *Security Dialogue* 37(3): 363–84.

Ness, Immanuel. 2016. *Southern Insurgency: The Coming of the Global Working Class*. London: Pluto.

Nichols, Robert. 2017. "Theft Is Property! The Recursive Logic of Dispossession." *Political Theory* (April 2): 1–26.

Nigam, Aditya. 2016. "Afro-Asian Solidarity and the 'Capital' Question: Looking beyond the Last Frontier." *Inter-Asia Cultural Studies* 17(1): 33–51.

Nolte, Detlef, and Almut Schilling-Vacaflor, eds. 2012. *New Constitutionalism in Latin America. Promises and Practice*. Aldershot, UK: Ashgate.

Nunes, Rodrigo. 2013. "Building on Destruction." *South Atlantic Quarterly* 112(3): 568–76.

Öcalan, Abdullah. 2015. *Manifesto for a Democratic Civilization*, vol. 1. Porsgrunn, Norway: New Compass.

O'Connor, James. 1973. *The Fiscal Crisis of the State*. New York: St. Martin's.

O'Connor, Sarah. 2016. "When Your Boss Is an Algorithm." *Financial Times*, September 8. Accessed September 30, 2016. https://www.ft.com/content/88fdc58e-754f-11e6-b60a-de4532d5ea35.

Offe, Claus. 1984. *Contradictions of the Welfare State*. Cambridge, MA: MIT Press.

Ong, Aihwa. 2000. "Graduated Sovereignty in South-East Asia." *Theory, Culture and Society* 17(4): 55–75.

Ong, Aihwa. 2006. *Neoliberalism as Exception*. Durham, NC: Duke University Press.

Ongün, Emre. 2016. "Turkey's Authoritarian Turn." *Jacobin*, May 24. Accessed August 12, 2016. https://www.jacobinmag.com/2016/05/turkey-erdogan-pkk-hdp-ocalan-suruc-rojava-syria.

Orléan, André. 1999. *Le pouvoir de la finance*. Paris: Odile Jacob.

Osborne, Peter. 2013. *Anywhere or Not at All*. London: Verso.

Oudenampsen, Merijn. 2010. "Political Populism: Speaking to the Imagination." *Open* 20: 6–20.

Ouma, Stefan. 2016. "From Financialization to Operations of Capital: Historicizing and Disentangling the Finance–Farmland-Nexus." *Geoforum* 72: 82–93.

Paik, Wondam. 2016. "The 60th Anniversary of the Bandung Conference and Asia." *Inter-Asia Cultural Studies* 17(1): 148–57.

Panitch, Leo. 2010. "Giovanni Arrighi in Beijing: An Alternative to Capitalism?" *Historical Materialism* 18(1): 74–87.

Panzieri, Raniero. 1973. *La ripresa del marxismo-leninismo in Italia*. Milan: Sapere.

Parikka, Jussi. 2015. *A Geology of Media*. Minneapolis: University of Minnesota Press.

"The Party We Need." 2016. *Jacobin*, no. 23 (Fall), special issue.

Pasquinelli, Matteo, ed. 2014. *Gli algoritmi del capitale: Accelerazionismo, macchine della conoscenza e autonomía del comune*. Verona: Ombre Corte.

Peano, Irene. 2017. "Global Care-Commodity Chains: Labour Re/Production and Agribusiness in the District of Foggia, Southeastern Italy." *Sociologia del lavoro* 146: 24–39.

Peck, Jamie. 2013. "Explaining (with) Neoliberalism." *Territory, Politics, Governance* 1(2): 132–57.

Peck, Jamie, and Nick Theodore. 2007. "Variegated Capitalism." *Progress in Human Geography* 31(6): 731–72.

Peck, Jamie, and Nick Theodore. 2015. *Fast Policy: Experimental Statecraft at the Thresholds of Neoliberalism*. Minneapolis: University of Minnesota Press.

Pelinka, Anton. 2011. "The European Union as an Alternative to the Nation-State." *International Journal of Politics, Culture, and Society* 24(1): 21–30.

Perrotta, Domenico. 2017. "Processing Tomatoes in the Era of the Retailing Revolution: Mechanization and Migrant Labour in Northern and Southern Italy." In *Migration and Agriculture: Migration and Change in the Mediterranean Area*, ed. Alessandra Corrado, Carlos de Castro and Domenico Perrotta, 58–75. London: Routledge.

Perulli, Paolo. 2014. *Terra mobile: Atlante della società globale*. Turin: Einaudi.

Peters, John Durham. 2015. *The Marvelous Clouds: Toward a Philosophy of Elemental Media*. Chicago: University of Chicago Press.

Peterson, Kristin. 2014. *Speculative Markets: Drug Circuits and Derivative Life in Nigeria*. Durham, NC: Duke University Press.

Petram, Lodewijk Otto. 2011. "The World's First Stock Exchange: How the Amsterdam Market for Dutch East India Company Shares Became a Modern Securities Market, 1602–1700." Academisch Proefschrift, University of Amsterdam.

Piketty, Thomas. 2014. *Capital in the 21st Century*. Cambridge, MA: Harvard University Press.

Piqué, Martín. 2008. "Hay que apostar al Mercado Regional: Entrevista con Marco Aurelio Garcia." *Página 12*, October 5. Accessed November 17, 2016. https://www.pagina12.com.ar/diario/elmundo/4–112803–2008–10–05.html.

Pirie, Iain. 2013. "Globalization and the Decline of the Developmental State." In *Beyond the Developmental State: Industrial Policy into the Twenty-first Century*, ed. Ben Fine, Jyoti Saraswati, and Daniela Tavasci, 146–68. London: Pluto.

Pirita Tenhunen, Lotta, and Raúl Sáncez Cedillo. 2016. "Il sindacalismo sociale della PAH e il problema della verticalizzazione delle lotte." In *Sindacalismo sociale: Lotte e invenzioni istituzionali nella crisi Europea*, ed. Alberto De Nicola and Biagio Quattrocchi, 112–27. Rome: DeriveApprodi.

Pirone, Maurilio. 2016. "Le nuove frontiere della valorizzazione: Logistica, piattaforme web e Taylorismo digitale." *Euronomade*, October 21. Accessed October 27, 2016. http://www.euronomade.info/?p=8175.

Piven, Frances Fox, and Richard A. Cloward. 1998. *The Breaking of the American Social Compact*. New York: New Press.

Poggi, Gianfranco. 1978. *The Development of the Modern State*. Stanford, CA: Stanford University Press.

Polanyi, Karl. [1944] 2001. *The Great Transformation: The Political and Economic Origins of Our Time*. Boston: Beacon.

Porter, Michael E. 1985. *Competitive Advantage*. New York: Free Press.

Porter, Michael E. 1987. "From Competitive Advantage to Corporate Strategy." *Harvard Business Review* 59: 43–59.

Poulantzas, Nicos. 1980. *State, Power, Socialism*, trans. Patrick Camiller. London: Verso.

Poulantzas, Nicos. 2008. "The Problem of the Capitalist State." In *The Poulantzas Reader*, ed. James Martin. 172–85. London: Verso.

Poulantzas, Nicos, and Ralph Miliband. 1972. "The Problem of the Capitalist State." In *Ideology in Social Science: Readings in Critical Social Theory*, ed. Robin Blackburn, 238–62. New York: Vintage.

Preobrazhensky, Yevgeni. 1965. *The New Economics*. Oxford: Clarendon.

Prevost, Gary, Carlos Oliva Campos and Harry E. Vanden, eds. 2012. *Social Movements and Leftist Governments in Latin America: Confrontation or Co-optation?* London: Zed.

Procacci, Giovanna. 1993. *Gouverner la misère : La question sociale en France 1789–1848*. Paris: Seuil.

Proença, Domício, and E. E. Duarte. 2005. "The Concept of Logistics Derived from Clausewitz: All That Is Required So That the Fighting Force Can Be Taken as a Given." *Journal of Strategic Studies* 28(4): 645–77.

Puhle, Hans-Jürgen. 1984. "Historische Konzepte des Entwickelten Industriekapitalismus: 'Organisierter Kapitalismus' und 'Korporatismus.'" *Geschichte und Gesellschaft* 10(2): 165–84.

Quijano, Aníbal. 1979. "Prólogo. José Carlos Mariátegui: Reencuentro y debate." In José Carlos Mariátegui, *Siete ensayos de interpretación de la realidad peruana*, ix–cxii. Caracas: Biblioteca Ayacucho.

Rancière, Jacques. 1998. *Disagreement: Politics and Philosophy*, trans. Julie Rose. Minneapolis: University of Minnesota Press.

"Rank and File." 2016. *Jacobin*, no. 22 (Summer), special issue.

Rankin, Katharine N. 2013. "A Critical Geography of Poverty Finance." *Third World Quarterly* 34(4): 547–68.

Rao, Anupama. 2009. *The Caste Question: Dalits and the Politics of Modern India*. Berkeley: University of California Press.

Read, Jason. 2003. *The Micro-Politics of Capital: Marx and the Prehistory of the Present*. Albany: State University of New York Press.

Read, Jason. 2014. "Abstract Materialism: Sohn-Rethel and the Task of a Materialist Philosophy Today." *Unemployed Negativity*, April 13. Accessed November 23, 2016. http://www.unemployednegativity.com/2014/04/abstract-materialism-sohn-rethel-and.html.

Reno, William. 1998. *Warlord Politics and African States*. Boulder, CO: Lynne Rienner.

Ricardo, David. [1817] 1821. *On the Principles of Political Economy and Taxation*. London: John Murray.

Ricciardi, Maurizio. 2013. "Dallo stato moderno allo stato globale: Storia e trasformazione di un concetto." *Scienza e Politica* 25(48): 75–93.

Rivera Cusicanqui, Silvia. 2015. "Strategic Ethnicity, Nation, and (Neo)colonialism in Latin America." *Alternautas* 2(2): 81–107.

Robert, Rudolph. 1969. *Chartered Companies and Their Role in the Development of Overseas Trade*. London: Bell.

Robinson, Cedric. 2000. *Black Marxism: The Making of the Black Radical Tradition*. Chapel Hill: University of North Carolina Press.

Robinson, William I. 2007. "Beyond the Theory of Imperialism: Global Capitalism and the Transnational State." *Societies Without Borders* 2: 5–26.

Rodney, Walter. 1972. *How Europe Underdeveloped Africa*. London: Bogle-L'Ouverture.

Roediger, David. 1991. *The Wages of Whiteness: Race and the Making of American Working Class*. London: Verso.

Roediger, David. 2017. *Race, Class and Marxism*. London: Verso.

Roemer, John. 1982. *A General Theory of Exploitation and Class*. Cambridge, MA: Harvard University Press.

Roemer, John. 1984. "Exploitation, Class and Property Relations." In *After Marx*, ed. Terence Ball and James Farr, 184–211. Cambridge: Cambridge University Press.

Romano, Santi. [1918] 1969. *Corso di diritto coloniale*. Rome: Athenaeum.

Rosanvallon, Pierre. 2008. *Counter-Democracy: Politics in an Age of Distrust*, trans. Arthur Goldhammer. Cambridge: Cambridge University Press.

Ross, Andrew. 2014. *Creditocracy and the Case for Debt Refusal*. New York: OR Books.

Rossiter, Ned. 2016. *Logistical Nightmares: Infrastructure, Software, Labour*. London: Routledge.

Rostow, Walt Whitman. 1960. *The Stages of Economic Growth: A Non-Communist Manifesto*. Cambridge: Cambridge University Press.

Roy, Ananya. 2010. *Poverty Capital*. New York: Routledge.

Ruccio, David. 2011. "Cooperatives, Surplus, and the Social." *Rethinking Marxism* 23(3): 334–40.

Ruparelia, Sanjay. 2015. "'Minimum Government, Maximum Governance': The Restructuring of Power in Modi's India." *South Asia* 38(4): 755–75.

Rushdie, Salman. 1988. *The Satanic Verses*. New York: Viking Penguin.

Sablowski, Thomas. 2008. "Kapitalfraktionen." In *Historisch-kritisches Wörterbuch des Marxismus*, vol. 7, ed. Wolfgang Fritz Haug, 203–20. Berlin: Argument.

Sacchetto, Devi, and Rutvica Andrijasevic. 2015. "Beyond China: Foxconn's Assembly Plants in Europe." *South Atlantic Quarterly* 114(1): 215–24.

Sack, Robert David. 1986. *Human Territoriality*. Cambridge: Cambridge University Press.

Sadowski, Jathan, and Karen Gregory. 2015. "Is Uber's Ultimate Goal the Privatization of City Governance?" *The Guardian*, September 15. Accessed December 22, 2015. https://www.theguardian.com/technology/2015/sep/15/is-ubers-ultimate-goal-the-privatisation-of-city-governance.

Samaddar, Ranabir. 2007. *The Materiality of Politics*, 2 vols. London: Anthem.

Samaddar, Ranabir. 2016. *A Post-colonial Enquiry into Europe's Debt and Migration Crisis*. Singapore: Springer.

Santos, Fabiano, and Fernando Guarnieri. 2016. "From Protest to Parliamentary Coup: An Overview of Brazil's Recent History." *Journal of Latin American Cultural Studies* 25(4): 485–94.

Sanyal, Kalyan K. 2007. *Rethinking Capitalist Development*. London: Routledge.

Sassen, Saskia. 1990. *The Global City*. Princeton, NJ: Princeton University Press.

Sassen, Saskia. 2006. *Territory, Authority, Rights*. Princeton, NJ: Princeton University Press.

Sassen, Saskia. 2007. *A Sociology of Globalization*. New York: W. W. Norton.

Sassen, Saskia. 2010. "A Savage Sorting of Winners and Losers: Contemporary Versions of Primitive Accumulation." *Globalizations* 7(1–2): 23–50.

Sassen, Saskia. 2013. "When Territory Deborders Territoriality." *Territory, Politics, Governance* 1(1): 21–45.

Sassen, Saskia. 2014. *Expulsions: Brutality and Complexity in the Global Economy*. Cambridge, MA: Harvard University Press.

Schiera, Pierangelo. 1974. *Otto Hintze*. Naples: Guida.

Schiera, Pierangelo. 2004. *Lo stato moderno: Origini e degenerazioni*. Bologna: Clueb.

Schmidt, Ingo. 2012. "Rosa Luxemburg's Accumulation of Capital: A Centennial Update with Additions from Long Wave Theory and Karl Polanyi's Great Transformation." *Critique* 40(3): 337–56.

Schmitt, Carl. 1935. "Die Rechtswissenschaft im Führerstaat." *Zeitschrift der Akademie für Deutsches Recht* 2: 435–40.

Schmitt, Carl. [1936] 1988. "Vergleichender Überblick über die neueste Entwicklung des Problems der gesetzgeberischen Ermächtigungen: 'Legislative Delegationen.'" In Carl Schmitt, *Positionen und Begriffe im Kampf mit Weimar–Genf–Versailles*, 214–29. Berlin: Duncker und Humblot.

Schmitt, Carl. 1988. *The Crisis of Parliamentary Democracy*. Cambridge, MA: MIT Press.

Schmitt, Carl. [1950] 2003. *The Nomos of the Earth in the International Law of the Jus Publicum Europaeum*. New York: Telos.

Schmitt, Carl. 2015. *Stato, grande spazio, nomos*, ed. and trans. Giovanni Gurisatti. Milan: Adelphi.

Schmitter, Philippe C. 1974. "Still the Century of Corporatism?" *Review of Politics* 36(1): 85–131.

Scholz, Trebor. 2016. "Platform Cooperativism: Challenging the Corporate Sharing Economy." Rosa Luxemburg Stiftung, New York Office, January. Accessed May 30, 2016. http://www.rosalux-nyc.org/publications/#pdf_modal_7.

Seeley, John Robert. 1883. *The Expansion of England*. London: Macmillan.

Segato, Rita Laura. 2013. *La escritura en el cuerpo de las mujeres asesinadas en Ciudad Juárez*. Buenos Aires: Tinta Limón.

Segato, Rita Laura. 2016. "Patriarchy from Margin to Center: Discipline, Territoriality, and Cruelty in the Apocalyptic Phase of Capital." *South Atlantic Quarterly* 115(3): 615–24.

Selwyn, Benjamin, and Satoshi Miyamura. 2014. "Class Struggle or Embedded Markets? Marx, Polanyi and the Meanings and Possibilities of Social Transformation." *New Political Economy* 19(5): 639–61.

Sen, Arup Kumar. 2014. "The Struggle for Independent Unions in India's Industrial Belts: Domination, Resistance, and the Maruti Suzuki Autoworkers." In *New Forms of Worker Organization: The Syndicalist and Autonomist Restoration of Class-Struggle Unionism*, ed. Immanuel Ness. 84–96. Oakland, CA: PM Press.

Sexton, Jared. 2015. "Unbearable Blackness." *Cultural Critique* 90: 159–78.

Shakespeare, William. [1623] 2015. *Macbeth*, ed. Sandra Clark and Pamela Mason. The Arden Shakespeare. London: Bloomsbury.

Sidaway, James D. 2007. "Spaces of Postdevelopment." *Progress in Human Geography* 31(3): 345–61.

Silver, Beverly J. 2003. *Forces of Labor*. Cambridge: Cambridge University Press.

Simmel, Georg. 1968. *The Conflict in Modern Culture and Other Essays*, trans. K. Peter Etzkorn. New York: Teachers College Press.

Simone, Abdou Maliq. 2004. "People as Infrastructure: Intersecting Fragments in Johannesburg." *Public Culture* 16(3): 407–29.

Simpson, Audra. 2014. *Mohawk Interruptus: Political Life across the Borders of Settler States*. Durham, NC: Duke University Press.

Singh, Nikhil Pal. 2017. "On Race, Violence, and 'So-Called Primitive Accumulation.'" In *Futures of Black Radicalism*, ed. Gaye Theresa Johnson and Alex Lubin, 39–58. London: Verso.

Slobodian, Quinn. 2014. "The World Economy and the Color Line: Wilhelm Röpke, Apartheid, and the White Atlantic." *German Historical Institute Bulletin Supplement* 10: 61–87.

Slobodian, Quinn. 2018. *Globalists: The End of Empire and the Birth of Neoliberalism*. Cambridge, MA: Harvard University Press.

Smith, Adam. [1776] 1904. *An Inquiry into the Nature and Causes of the Wealth of Nations*, vol. 2. London: Methuen.

Smith, Linda Tuhiwai. 1999. *Decolonizing Methodologies: Research and Indigenous Peoples*. London: Zed Books.

Smith, Neil. 1996. *The New Urban Frontier: Gentrification and the Revanchist City*. London: Routledge.

Sohn-Rethel, Alfred. 1978. *Intellectual and Manual Labour: A Critique of Epistemology*. London: Macmillan.

Souza, Jessé. 2012. *Os Batalhadores Brasileiros: Nova classe nédia ou nova classe trabalhadora?* Belo Horizonte, Brazil: Universidade Federal de Minas Gerais.

Spivak, Gayatri Chakravorty. 1985. "Subaltern Studies: Deconstructing Historiography." In *Subaltern Studies: Writings on South Asian History and Society*, ed. Ranajir Guha, 330–63. New Delhi: Oxford University Press.

Spivak, Gayatri Chakravorty. 1999. *A Critique of Postcolonial Reason*. Cambridge, MA: Harvard University Press.

Sprenger, Florian. 2015. *The Politics of Micro-Decisions: Edward Snowden, Net Neutrality, and the Architectures of the Internet*, trans. Valentine A. Pakis. Lüneburg, Germany: Meson.

Srnicek, Nick. 2017. *Platform Capitalism*. Cambridge: Polity.

Srnicek, Nick, and Alex Williams. 2015. *Inventing the Future: Postcapitalism and a World without Work*. London: Verso.

Standing, Guy. 2011. *The Precariat: The New Dangerous Class*. London: Bloomsbury Academic.

Stefanoni, Pablo. 2015. "Los intelectuales y las tensiones de la revolución." *Brecha*, May 28. Accessed November 15, 2016. http://brecha.com.uy/los-intelectuales-y -las-tensiones-de-la-revolucion.

Stella, Alessandro. 1993. *La révolte des ciompi: Les hommes, les lieux, le travail*. Paris: Éditions de l'Ecole des Hautes Études en Sciences Sociales.

Stephens, Robert. 2014. "In Defense of the Ferguson Riots." *Jacobin*, August 14. Accessed June 10, 2016. https://www.jacobinmag.com/2014/08/in-defense-of-the -ferguson-riots.

Stern, Philip J. 2011. *The Company-State: Corporate Sovereignty and the Early Modern Foundations of the British Empire in India*. New York: Oxford University Press.

Stiglitz, Joseph. 2015. *The Great Divide*. London: Penguin.

Streeck, Wolfgang. 2009. *Re-forming Capitalism*. Oxford: Oxford University Press.

Streeck, Wolfgang. 2014. *Buying Time*. London: Verso.

Summers, Lawrence. 2013. "Why Stagnation Might Prove to be the New Normal." *Financial Times*, December 15. Accessed May 28, 2018. https://www.ft.com /content/87cb15ea-5d1a-11e3-a558-00144feabdc0.

Summers, Lawrence. 2016. "The Age of Secular Stagnation: What It Is and What to Do About It." *Foreign Affairs* 95(2): 2–9.

Sunder Rajan, Kaushik. 2006. *Biocapital: The Constitution of Postgenomic Life*. Durham, NC: Duke University Press.

Sunder Rajan, Kaushik. 2012. "Pharmaceutical Crises and Questions of Value: Terrains and Logics of Global Therapeutic Politics." *South Atlantic Quarterly* 111(2): 321–46.

Supiot, Alain. 2013. *Grandeur et misère de l'état social*. Paris: Fayard.

Svampa, Maristella. 2015. "Commodities Consensus: Neoextractivism and Enclosure of the Commons in Latin America." *South Atlantic Quarterly* 114(1): 65–82.

Svampa, Maristella, and Enrique Viale. 2014. *Maldesarollo: La Argentina del extractivismo y el despojo*. Buenos Aires: Katz.

Swinton, John. 1880. "Interview with Karl Marx." *The Sun*, September 6. Accessed August 10, 2016. http://www.hartford-hwp.com/archives/26/021.html.

Swyngedouw, Erik. 2016. *La naturaleza no existe: La sostenibilidad como síntoma de una planificacíon despolitizada*. Buenos Aires: Puentoaéro.

Taibi, Matt. 2010. "The Great American Bubble Machine." *Rolling Stone*. April 5. Accessed June 8, 2018. https://www.rollingstone.com/politics/news/the-great -american-bubble-machine-20100405.

Tándeter, Enrique. 1993. *Coercion and Market: Silver Mining in Colonial Potosí, 1692–1826*. Albuquerque, NM: New Mexico University Press.

Taussig, Michael T. 1980. *The Devil and Commodity Fetishism in South America*. Chapel Hill: University of North Carolina Press.

Taussig, Michael T. 1984. "Culture of Terror—Space of Death. Roger Casement's Putumayo Report and the Explanation of Torture." *Comparative Studies in Society and History* 26(3): 467–97.

Taylor, Keeanga-Yamhatta. 2016. *From #Blacklivesmatter to Black Liberation*. Chicago: Haymarket.

Teubner, Gunther. 2012. *Verfassungsfragmente: Gesellschaftlicher Konstitutionalismus in der Globalisierung*. Berlin: Suhrkamp.

Théorie Communiste. 2011. "Communization in the Present Tense." In *Communization and Its Discontents: Contestation, Critique, and Contemporary Struggles*, ed. Benjamin Noys, 41–60. Wivenhoe, UK: Minor Compositions.

Therborn, Göran. 2012. "Class in the 21st Century." *New Left Review* 78: 5–29.

Thieme, Tatiana A. 2013. "The 'Hustle' amongst Youth Entrepreneurs in Mathare's Informal Waste Economy." *Journal of Eastern African Studies* 7(3): 389–412.

Tible, Jean. 2016. "Golpe á la brasilera. Crisis política y económica, impedimentos, y luchas democráticas." *Revista Politica Latinoamericana* 2: 1–22.

Tiessen, Matthew. 2012. "High-Frequency Trading and the Nodes of Profit." *Volume/Archis* 32: 108–11.

Tilly, Charles. 1975. "Reflections on the History of European State-Making." In *The Formation of National States in Western Europe*, ed. Charles Tilly, 3–83. Princeton, NJ: Princeton University Press.

Toscano, Alberto. 2013. "Gaming the Plumbing: High-Frequency Trading and the Spaces of Capital." *Mute Magazine*, January 16. Accessed April 10, 2015. http://www.metamute.org/editorial/articles/gaming-plumbing-high-frequency-trading-and-spaces-capital.

Toscano, Alberto. 2014. "Lineaments of the Logistical State." *Viewpoint Magazine* 4. Accessed November 7, 2016. https://viewpointmag.com/2014/09/28/lineaments-of-the-logistical-state.

Toscano, Alberto, and Jeff Kinkle. 2015. *Cartographies of the Absolute*. Winchester, UK: Zero.

Tóth, Csaba. 2014. "Full Text of Viktor Orbán's Speech at Băile Tușnad (Tusnádfürdő) of 26 July 2014." *Budapest Beacon*, July 29. Accessed November 28, 2016. http://budapestbeacon.com/public-policy/full-text-of-viktor-orbans-speech-at-baile-tusnad-tusnadfurdo-of-26-july-2014/10592.

Traverso, Enzo. 2002. *Totalitarismo: storia di un dibattito*. Milan: Mondadori.

Traverso, Enzo. 2017. *Left-Wing Melancholia: Marxism, History, and Memory*. New York: Columbia University Press.

Tsing, Anna. 2005. *Friction: An Ethnography of Global Connection*. Princeton, NJ: Princeton University Press.

Tsing, Anna. 2009. "Supply Chains and the Human Condition." *Rethinking Marxism* 21(2): 148–76.

Tsing, Anna. 2012. "On Nonscalability: The Living World Is Not Amenable to Precision-Nested Scales." *Common Knowledge* 18(3): 505–24.

Tsing, Anna. 2015. "What Is Emerging? Supply Chains and the Remaking of Asia." *Professional Geographer* 68(2): 330–37.

Tully, John A. 2011. *The Devil's Milk: A Social History of Rubber*. New York: Monthly Review.

Urry, John. 2007. *Mobilities*. Cambridge: Polity.

Van Creveld, Martin. 1977. *Supplying War: Logistics from Wallenstein to Patton*. Cambridge: Cambridge University Press.

Varela, Amarela. Forthcoming. "Capitalismo caníbal: Migraciones, violencia y necropolítica en Mesoamérica." In *América Latina en movimiento. Autonomía de la migración, fronteras y nuevas geografías de lucha*, ed. Blanca Cordero, Sandro Mezzadra, and Amarela Varela. Madrid: Traficantes de sueños.

Varoufakis, Yanis. 2011. *The Global Minotaur: America, the True Origins of the Financial Crisis and the Future of the World Economy*. London: Zed.

Varoufakis, Yanis. 2015. "The Economic Case for Authentic Democracy." December 9. Accessed December 17, 2016. https://yanisvaroufakis.eu/2015/12/09/the
-economic-case-for-authentic-democracy-ted-global-geneva-8th-december-2015.

Varoufakis, Yanis. 2016. *And the Weak Suffer What They Must? Europe's Crisis and America's Economic Future*. New York: Nation.

Vatikiotis, Leonidas. 2013. "In Piraeus, Chinese Investment Brings Chinese Labour Standards." June 3. Accessed November 10, 2016. http://leonidasvatikiotis
.wordpress.com/2013/06/03/in-piraeus-chinese-investment-brings-chinese
-labour-standards-ex-employee-reveals-harrowing-conditions-at-cosco-container
-terminal-in-greece-prin-newspaper.

Venediktov, Anatolii Vasilevich. [1948] 1953. *La proprietà socialista dello stato*. Turin: Einaudi.

Veracini, Lorenzo. 2010. *Settler Colonialism: A Theoretical Overview*. Houndmills, UK: Palgrave Macmillan.

Vercellone, Carlo, 2013. "The Becoming Rent of Profit? The New Articulation of Wage, Rent and Profit." *Knowledge Cultures* 1(2): 194–207.

Vergès, Françoise. 2017. "Racial Capitalocene." In *Futures of Black Radicalism*, ed. Gaye Theresa Johnson and Alex Lubin, 72–82. London: Verso.

Virno, Paolo. 1999. *Il ricordo del presente*. Turin: Bollati Boringhieri.

Virno, Paolo. 2003. *A Grammar of the Multitude: For an Analysis of Contemporary Forms of Life*, trans. Isabella Bertoletti, James Cascaito, and Andrea Casson. Cambridge, MA: Semiotext(e).

Virno, Paolo. 2004. *The Grammar of the Multitude: For an Analysis of Contemporary Forms of Life*, trans. Isabella Bertoletti, James Casciato, and Andrea Casson. Los Angeles, CA: Semiotext(e).

Virno, Paolo. 2008. *Multitude between Innovation and Negation*, trans. Isabella Bertoletti, James Cascaito, and Andrea Casson. Los Angeles, CA: Semiotext(e).

Virilio, Paul. [1977] 2006. *Speed and Politics*. Los Angeles, CA: Semiotext(e).

Vora, Kalindi. 2015. *Life Support: Biocapital and the New History of Outsourced Labor*. Minneapolis: Minnesota University Press.

Walker, Gavin. 2016a. "The 'Ideal Total Capitalist': On the State-Form in the Critique of Political Economy." *Crisis and Critique* 3(3): 435–54.

Walker, Gavin. 2016b. *The Sublime Perversion of Capital: Marxist Theory and the Politics of History in Modern Japan*. Durham, NC: Duke University Press.

Walker, Richard. 2010. "Karl Marx between Two Worlds: The Antinomies of Giovanni Arrighi's Adam Smith in Beijing." *Historical Materialism* 18(1): 52–73.

Walker, Rob. B. J. 1993. *Inside/Outside: International Relations as Political Theory*. New York: Cambridge University Press.

Wallerstein, Immanuel. 1974. *The Modern World-System*. New York: Academic.

Wallerstein, Immanuel. 1985. *Il capitalismo storico*, trans. Carmine Donzelli. Turin: Einaudi.

Walters, William. 2012. *Governmentality: Critical Encounters*. London: Routledge.

Wang, Hui. 2003. *China's New Order*. Cambridge, MA: Harvard University Press.

Wang, Hui. 2009. *The End of the Revolution*. London: Verso.

Wang, Hui. 2016. *China's Twentieth Century*, trans. Saul Thomas. London: Verso.

Warner, Michael, ed. 1993. *Fear of a Queer Planet: Queer Politics and Social Theory.* Minneapolis: University of Minnesota Press.

Watson, Irene. 2015. *Aboriginal People, Colonialism and International Law: Raw Law.* Abingdon, UK: Routledge.

Watson, Irene, Fiona Allon, Fiona Nicholl, and Brett Neilson. 2002. "Introduction: On What Grounds? Sovereignties, Territorialities and Indigenous Rights." *Borderlands E-Journal* 1(2). Accessed August 15, 2017. http://www.borderlands.net .au/vol1no2_2002/editors_intro.html.

Weber, Max. 1992. *The Protestant Ethic and the Spirit of Capitalism.* London: Routledge.

Weber, Max. [1919] 2008. "Politics as a Vocation." In *Max Weber's Complete Writings on Academic and Political Vocations*, ed. John Dreijmanis, 155–208. New York: Algora.

Weeks, Kathi. 2011. *The Problem with Work: Feminism, Marxism, Antiwork Politics, and Postwork Imaginaries.* Durham, NC: Duke University Press.

Wei, Ruan. 2012. "Two Concepts of Civilization." *Comparative Civilizations Review* 67: 16–26.

Weil, Simone. (1934) 1960. "Un soulèvement proletarian à Florence au XIVe siècle." In *Écrites historiques et politiques*, 85–101. Paris: Gallimard.

Welker, Marina. 2014. *Enacting the Corporation: An American Mining Firm in Post-authoritarian Indonesia.* Berkeley: University of California Press.

Westkämpfer, Engelbert. 2007. "Digital Manufacturing in the Global Era." In *Digital Enterprise Technology*, ed. Pedro Filipe Cunha and Paul G. Maropoulos, 3–14. New York: Springer.

Williams, Eric. 1944. *Capitalism and Slavery.* Chapel Hill: University of North Carolina Press.

Williams, Raymond. 1960. *Border Country.* London: Chatto and Windus.

Winichakul, Thongchai. 1994. *Siam Mapped.* Honolulu: University of Hawaii Press.

Wolfe, Patrick. 1999. *Settler Colonialism and the Transformation of Anthropology: The Politics and Poetics of an Ethnographic Event.* London: Cassell.

Wolfe, Patrick. 2016. *Traces of History: Elementary Structures of Race.* London: Verso.

Wood, Ellen Meiksins. 2003. *Empire of Capital.* London: Verso.

Wood, Ellen Meiksins. 2012. *The Ellen Meiksins Wood Reader*, ed. Larry Patriquin. Leiden: Brill.

Xulin, Dong. 2011. "World Crisis, Currency War, and the End of US/Dollar Hegemony: A Conversation with Michael Hudson." *International Critical Thought* 1(1): 92–107.

Yap, Chuin-Wei. 2016. "China's New Security Challenge: Angry Mom-and-Pop Investors." *Wall Street Journal*, April 12. Accessed August 6, 2016. http://www .wsj.com/articles/chinas-new-security-challenge-angry-mom-and-pop-investors-1460473432.

Zavaleta Mercado, René. 1974. *El poder dual en América Latina.* Mexico City: Siglo Veintiuno.

Zechner, Manuela, and Bue Rübner Hansen. 2015. "Building Power in a Crisis of Social Reproduction." *ROAR Magazine* (Winter): 132–51.

Zhang, Weiwei. 2012. *The China Wave: Rise of a Civilizational State*. Singapore: World Scientific.

Ziegelmayer, Eric. 2014. "Capitalist Impact on Krill in Area 48 (Antarctica)." *Capitalism Nature Socialism* 25(4): 36–53.

Žižek, Slavoj. 2006. *The Parallax View*. Cambridge, MA: MIT Press.

Žižek, Slavoj. 2013. "The Simple Courage of a Decision: A Leftist Tribute to Thatcher." *New Statesman*, April 17. Accessed December 18, 2016. http://www.newstatesman.com/politics/politics/2013/04/simple-courage-decision-leftist-tribute-thatcher.

Index

dal Maso, Giulia, 45
Dardot, Pierre, 46, 241
dark pools, 28
data mining, 2, 38, 44, 72, 144–46. *See also* algorithms
Dávila, Juan Pablo, 155
Davis, Angela, 42
Dean, Jodi, 10
debt, 9, 29, 44, 137, 161, 215
decolonization, 115, 116–17, 131, 223
de facto states/para-states/pseudo-states, 223
degradation, cultural, 179–80
deindustrialization, 190–91, 199
Deleuze, Gilles, 36–37
Delhi-Mumbai Industrial Corridor, 152–53, 197
Deliveroo, 81–82, 198
demand, effective, 62
democracy, 10–12; conflictual, 12; crisis of, 97; deep, 182; New Deal, 61, 97, 118; popular, 121; "post-democratic" forms of governance, 11, 222; radical, 11, 12, 187; representative, 11; social, 95
democratic corporatism, 62
Democratic Party of the People, Turkey, 171
democratic social state, 14, 119–21
denationalization, 218–19
dependency theory, 63, 122–23
depoliticization, 217–18
deregulation, 157–58
derivative life, 200–201
derivatives, 92, 110, 136, 159, 201
Derrida, Jacques, 221, 247
desarrollismo (developmentalism), 123, 125–26
de Soto, Hernando, 126
De Souza, Amarildo, 168–69
destitution, politics of, 235, 244, 248–49
development, 63, 78, 88, 97, 113
developmentalism (desarrollismo), 123, 125–26
developmental state, 14, 63, 122–30, 119221
Dey, Ishita, 152–53, 196

difference, 13, 32–38, 45, 113, 116; capitalist variegation, 36–37; Port of Piraeus example, 34, 71–72; production of, 36–37, 43; racial and sexual, 37; varieties of capitalism, 35
differential accumulation, 128, 130
differential inclusion, 9, 138, 167, 224, 229
digitalization, 68, 83
di Lando, Michele, 250, 251
Disagreement (Rancière), 248
Discourse on Colonialism (Césaire), 115
dispossession, 1–2, 39–40, 78, 88, 167–69; accumulation by, 9, 127; accumulation without, 127; exploitation and, 203, 205; India, 126, 196. *See also* expulsion
dissensual conviviality, 8–9
Dixon, Adam, 36
dollar, 30, 55, 98, 157
domination, 23, 34, 42, 95, 105; of capital, 58, 66, 76, 179, 190, 203–4; by state, 115–17, 232; struggle and, 188–89
Don Mueang Airport, 17–18, 19, 20–21, 24
Dörre, Klaus, 88
Drucker, Peter, 68
dual power, 11–12, 241–43, 250–51
Du Bois, W. E. B., 115, 116–17
Dumbarton Oaks conference, 116–17
Durand, Cédric, 160
Dutch East India Company, 110–11
Duterte, Rodrigo, 225
Dyer-Witheford, Nick, 175, 206

Easterling, Keller, 135, 213
Eastern Europe, 98, 121–22
Economic Commission for Latin America of the United Nations (CEPAL), 123, 125–26
Economic Lessons of the 1930s, The (Arndt), 118–19
economic sphere: cybernetics, 68–69, 125; governance models, 29–30; politics and, 91–93, 100
effective demand, 62
efficiency, 149–50
Egypt, 225; Tahrir Square, 170, 248

international division of labor, 23, 61, 193
international law, 39, 99–100, 105–7.
   See also global capitalism
International Monetary Fund, 71, 124
International Organization for Standard-
   ization, 149
investment, 45, 49, 62, 156–60
Invisible Committee, 248–49
"iron cage," 75
Isiboro Sécure National Park and Indig-
   enous Territory (TIPNIS, Bolivia), 40,
   192–96, 233
isomorphy, 36–37
Israel, 173
Istanbul, Turkey, 168–70
Istorie fiorentine (Machiavelli), 251
Italy, 98, 128

Jameson, Fredric, 32, 55, 146, 158
Jellinek, Georg, 116
Jessop, Bob, 35, 226
Johnson, Gaye Theresa, 43
joint stock companies, 26, 59, 60, 110
Jomini, Antoine-Henri, 147–48
Joyce, James, 57
jurisdiction, 24, 26, 28, 107, 109, 111, 113,
   230
jus publicum Europaeum, 104–5
Justice and Development Party (Turkey),
   169, 171
justi hostes (just enemies), 104

Kalecki, Michael, 63
Kambouri, Nelli, 72
Kang, Su-Dol, 184
Kelley, Robin D. G., 41
Keynes, John Maynard, 62
Keynesian revolution, 120, 235
Kinkle, Jeff, 64
Klein, Naomi, 46, 183, 238
knowledge production, 18, 87, 137, 141
Kondratieff, Nikolai, 155–57
Korzybski, Alfred, 27
Krippner, Greta, 157–58
Küçük, Bülent, 172
Kurdish struggle, 171–72
Kurdistan Workers' Party (PKK), 172

labor: abstract, 81–85; compulsion to
   work, 161, 178–79; debt and, 161;
   forced, 99, 141–42; "free" wage, 14,
   58, 124, 129, 159, 182, 183, 203–4; gig
   economy, 81–86, 92, 146; labor power,
   58–59; logistical, 153; as opposed to
   work, 4–5, 246–46; reproduction of,
   62; social, 84–85; social cooperation
   and, 176–84; socialization of, 61, 93,
   96–98, 157; as source of property, 121,
   124; subsumption of, 77; surplus, 81;
   surplus populations, 8, 14, 124, 175,
   197–200; working day, 59, 80–84;
   work-on-demand applications, 81–82
labor, living, 65, 86; African peoples, 41;
   as capital's "other," 6–7; extraction and,
   166–67; gap with social cooperation,
   83, 176, 179–80, 185, 188, 192, 205,
   208; gendered and raced qualities,
   72; heterogeneity of, 7; independent
   contractors, 81–82; individual worker,
   177–79; informal workers, 153, 184,
   196–97; international division of labor,
   23; precarious, 71–72; protests and,
   176–77; social cooperation and, 8, 9,
   14, 83; subjects of struggle, 184–92.
   See also multiplication of labor
labor contract, 58–59
labor movements, crisis of, 180–82
Lagos pharmaceutical market, 200–201
Landnahme, 88, 92
latifundia, 129
Latin America: developmental state,
   122–25; feminist thought, 45; neo-
   extractivism debates, 9, 38–39, 134–35;
   popular economies, 44–45, 79, 160,
   200, 208; progressive governments, 14,
   38–39, 53, 134, 193–94, 211, 236, 238,
   243; social and solidarity economy, 183;
   struggles, 234–36; women, violence
   against, 45, 237
Laval, Christian, 46, 241
law: class struggle and, 121; global, 213;
   Indigenous, 195; legal pluralism,
   106–7, 213; legal spaces of globalization, 213–14; *lex mercatoria,* 213, 214; of
   nations, 99

metropolis-colony relation, 116, 169

metropolitan assemblies, 242–43

Mexico, debt crisis of 1982, 157

micro-credit, 160

middle class, 169, 237

Middle East, Greater, 99

migration, 12, 171, 210; crisis rhetoric, 50; forced, 28; industry, 227–28; "new workers," 181; retailer-driven production chains, 45

Miliband, Ralph, 97

militarization of society, 148

military dictatorships, 125

military theory, 147–48

Mill, John Stuart, 112, 116

mining, language of, 38, 142, 144

Mirowski, Philip, 46, 69

mixed constitution, 64, 101

mobilities paradigm, 20

mobility: of Earth, 28, 28

modes of production, 75, 78, 97

Modi, Narendra, 225

money, as abstract, 84–85; shadow, 158–59

money market, 158–59

monopoly, 60, 96, 97, 112

Monsanto, 1–2

Montreux Document, 231

Moore, Jason W., 38, 198

Morales, Evo, 193–94

mortgage foreclosures, 29, 240; Plataforma de Afectados por la Hipoteca, 170–71

most favored nation clauses, 109

Moten, Fred, 135, 153–54, 174

Mouffe, Chantal, 187

Movimento Passe Livre (Free Fare Movement), 168–69

multinational corporations, 34, 214–15

municipalism, 238, 243

Muslim Brotherhood, 225

mutual funds, 158–59

mutualism, 183, 207

Nancy, Jean-Luc, 5

nationalism, 13, 50–51, 103, 131, 238; neoliberalism and, 240–41

National Recovery Act (United States), 118

National Union of Mineworkers (NUM, South Africa), 185

nation-states, 6, 11, 27–28, 50, 130, 151–52, 220–22; borders, 22; international order and, 100–102, 108; struggle and, 179, 187; varieties of capitalism literature, 35

NAVIS-SPARCS N4 system, 72

need economy, 78

Negri, Antonio, 12, 100–101, 173

neo-developmentalism, 131

neo-extractivism, 9, 38–39, 126, 134–35, 164, 192–93

neo-institutionalist thinkers, 34–35

neoliberalism, 46–47, 125–27; confronting, 11; as "development strategy," 130; industrialization, 125–26, 130–31; Latin American experiments, 125; nationalism and, 13, 50–51, 103, 240–41; origins, 14; regional and spatial variegation, 46; reorganization of capitalism, 56; state intervention and, 49; subjectivity, production of, 91–93; and Turkey, 169

Neoliberalism as Exception (Ong), 47

Ness, Immanuel, 175, 184, 189–91

new capitalism, 60, 62, 114, 180

New Deal, 61, 97, 118, 119–20, 159

New York City, 1975 default, 97

New York Stock Exchange, 48

Nichols, Robert, 40, 195

Nigeria, 200–201

Nomos of the Earth in the International Law of the Jus Publicum Europaeum, The (Schmitt), 104–6, 115, 198

nonaligned countries, 123

non-capital, 65, 76, 79, 164

non-human nature, 66

non-places, 20

non-state law, 106–7

non-West, as sites of resistance, 34

norm, meaning of, 213

nostalgia, 179–80

Notes toward a Performative Theory of Assembly (Butler), 247

Nunes, Rodrigo, 174–75

Greenwich Mean Time, 19; logistics and, 150–51; operations of capital and, 70; turnover time, 149–51. *See also* space/spatiality

To Our Friends (Invisible Committee), 248–49

Toscano, Alberto, 31, 64

total capital, 6, 32, 37, 59, 63

totalization/totality, 32–33; dialectical concept of, 64–65

Traces of History (Wolfe), 41

trading, 31, 69, 136

trading curb, 48

trading posts, 108–9

transition, 9–10, 156; politics of, 48–54

transport, 21, 45, 73, 134, 141, 148–50; airports, 17–20; container shipping, 71–72, 149–50; slow steaming, 150–51

Treaty of Nanking, 109

Trilateral Commission, 97

Trump, Donald, 226

Tsing, Anna, 45–46, 141, 149

Turing machine, 69

Turkey, 225; Erdoğan regime, 172–73; Gezi Park movement, 168–71, 248; Rojava canton, 171–73

Two Days, One Night (film), 57

Uber, 146

Ulysses (Joyce), 57

Undoing the Demos (Brown), 46

Unidade de Policia Pacificadora (Brazil), 168–69

unions: All-China Federation of Trade Unions, 185, 207; crisis of, 180–81; global South, 184–85; Greece, 72; India, 184; United States, 119

United Kingdom, 223

United Nations, 117

United Nations High Commissioner for Refugees' EyeCloud system, 230

United States, 60; 9/11 attacks, 99; deregulation, 157–58; dominance without hegemony, 23; Federal Reserve, 157, 240; New Deal, 61, 97, 118, 159; New York City, 1975 default, 97; police violence, 173–74; post-

World War II social compact, 119; racial capitalism, 41; as "rogue state," 221; subprime crisis, 28–29, 43–44; symbiotic economic relationship with China, 29–30; unions, 119

urban environments, 145–46, 197, 237–38; global cities, 29, 31, 197, 238; "rebel cities," 238; struggles in, 170, 182

value chains, 68

van Creveld, Martin, 147

variegated capitalism, 36–37, 46, 52, 166, 226; indirect exploitation, 92; subsumption of labor, 77–78

varieties of capitalism, 35, 128

Varieties of Capitalism (edited by Hall and Soskice), 35

Varoufakis, Yanis, 30

Venediktov, A. V., 121

"vertical border," 237

Vietnam War, 24, 123, 149

violence, 99; Black struggles against police violence, 43; of dispossession, 88; expressive and instrumental, 237; of extraction, 39, 99, 134, 137–38, 140–45, 202; of financialization, 160; "hitting the ground," 2–3, 13, 22, 70; of logistics, 147–48; police, 43, 168–69, 173–74, 192, 193; state monopoly on, 103; structural, 174; struggle as, 186–87; against women, in Latin America, 45, 237

Virilio, Paul, 150

Virno, Paolo, 87

Volcker shock, 1979, 158–59

von Stroheim, Erich, 56–57

Vora, Kalindi, 145

Vyshinsky, Andrey, 121

wageless labor/life, 182, 197

Walker, Gavin, 37, 70

Walker, Rob, 219

Wallerstein, Immanuel, 22–23

Wall Street (film), 56

Walmart, 45

Wang, Hui, 47, 131, 181, 189, 222–23

war, 51, 104, 131, 221